SHORTCAKE CAKE

STORY AND ART BY
suu Morishita

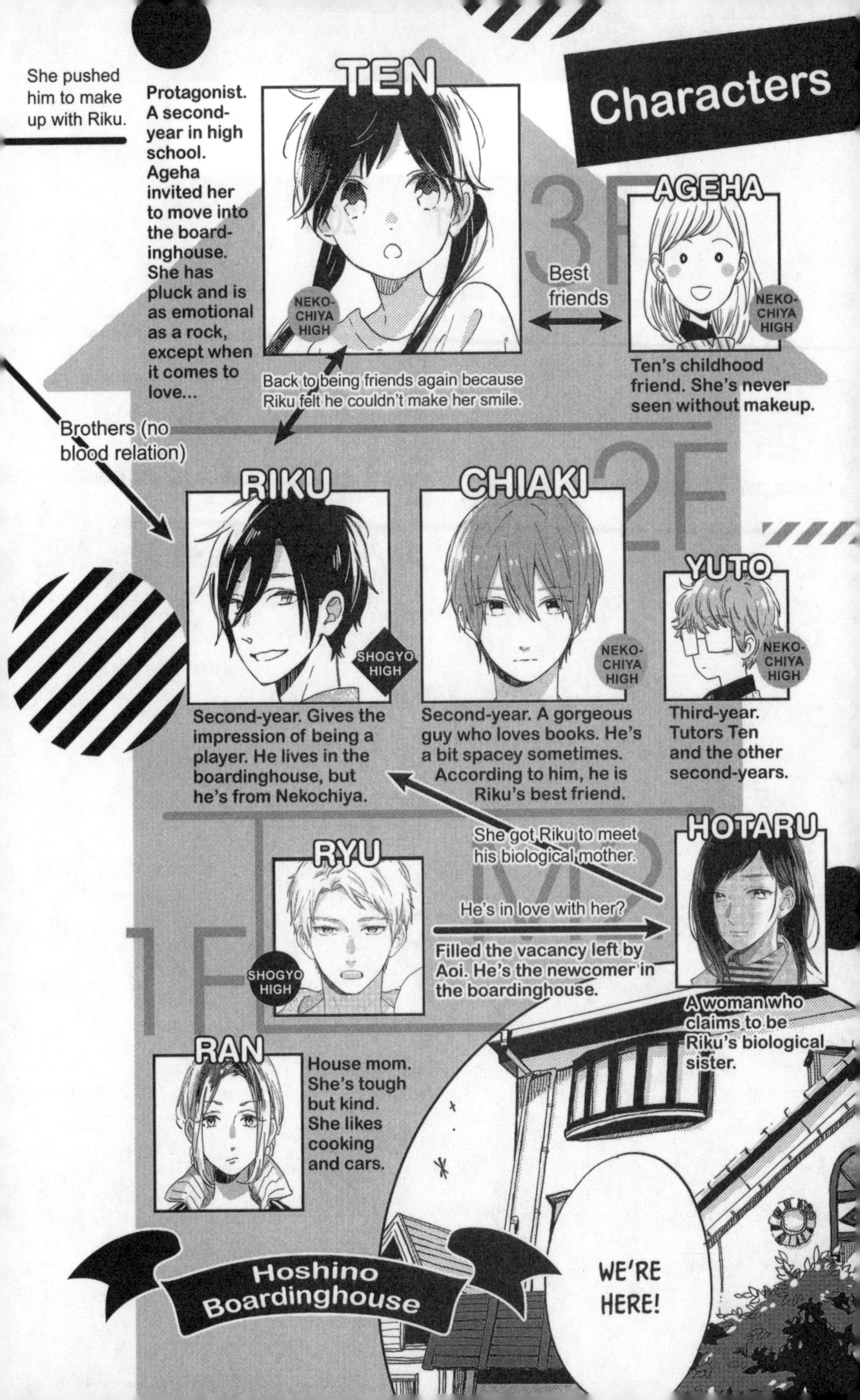
Characters
TEN
Protagonist. A second-year in high school. Ageha invited her to move into the boardinghouse. She has pluck and is as emotional as a rock, except when it comes to love...
She pushed him to make up with Riku.
NEKO-CHIYA HIGH
Best friends
AGEHA
NEKO-CHIYA HIGH
Ten's childhood friend. She's never seen without makeup.
3F
Back to being friends again because Riku felt he couldn't make her smile.
Brothers (no blood relation)
2F
RIKU
SHOGYO HIGH
Second-year. Gives the impression of being a player. He lives in the boardinghouse, but he's from Nekochiya.
CHIAKI
NEKO-CHIYA HIGH
Second-year. A gorgeous guy who loves books. He's a bit spacey sometimes. According to him, he is Riku's best friend.
YUTO
NEKO-CHIYA HIGH
Third-year. Tutors Ten and the other second-years.
She got Riku to meet his biological mother.
HOTARU
A woman who claims to be Riku's biological sister.
M2
RYU
SHOGYO HIGH
He's in love with her?
Filled the vacancy left by Aoi. He's the newcomer in the boardinghouse.
1F
RAN
House mom. She's tough but kind. She likes cooking and cars.
Hoshino Boardinghouse
WE'RE HERE!

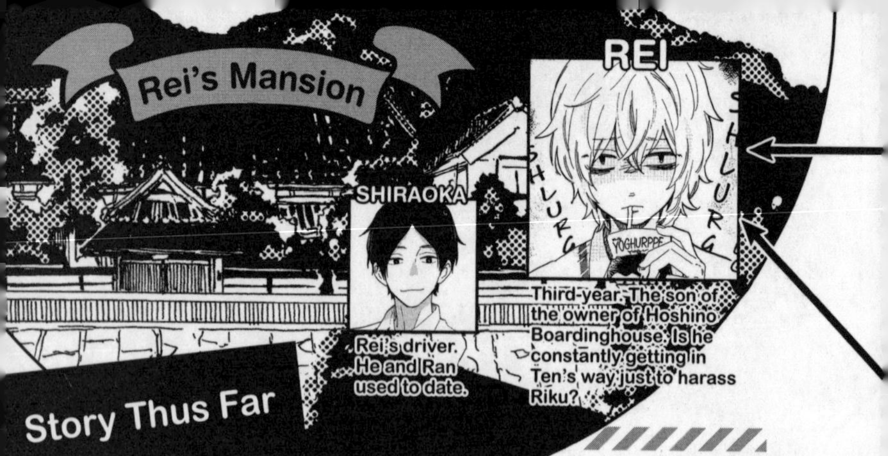
Rei's Mansion
REI
SHLURG SHLURG
YOGHURPPE
SHIRAOKA
Third-year. The son of the owner of Hoshino Boardinghouse. Is he constantly getting in Ten's way just to harass Riku?
Rei's driver. He and Ran used to date.

Story Thus Far

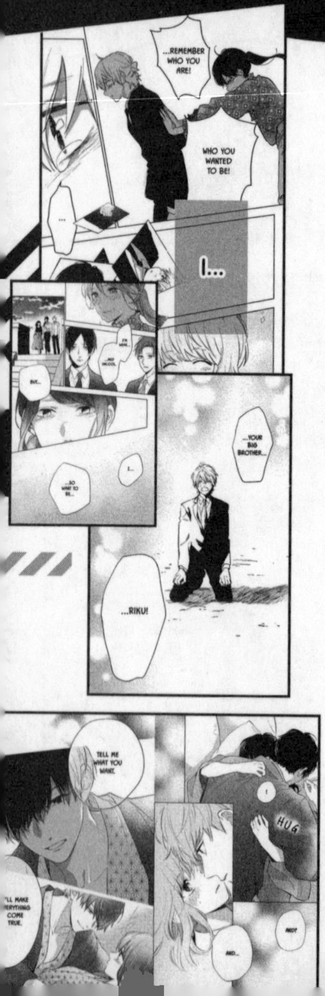
...REMEMBER WHO YOU ARE!
WHO YOU WANTED TO BE!
...
I...
...YOUR BIG BROTHER...
I...
...RIKU!
TELL ME WHAT YOU WANT.
!
HUG
AND...

Ten commuted two hours to school by bus, until her friend Ageha invited her to move into the Hoshino Boardinghouse. The place is full of characters, and it's there that she meets Riku and Chiaki, and soon starts going out with Riku.

Ten is determined to learn more about the past that Riku refuses to talk about. She and Chiaki reach out to Shiraoka to find out more.

They learn that Riku never knew his biological parents, and that he was raised by Rei's parents. Riku was eventually kicked out of the Mizuhara household after their parents died. Shiraoka's story is crushing.

Ten wants to help Riku, but when he finds out that she knows about his past, he pushes her further away and wants to go back to being just friends. Ten tells Riku that she won't just wait for him and heads straight to see his brother, Rei.

The day comes when Riku and his biological mother meet. Ten manages to convince Rei to come, so he shows up as well. When his mother asks Riku to live with her, he replies that his real mother is Mahoro—Rei's mother and the woman who raised him. After witnessing Riku's response, and with a little more encouragement from Ten, Rei is finally able to say the words he couldn't before. He wants to be Riku's big brother again. The two embrace and put an end to their long feud.

After moving back into the Mizuhara house, Riku invites the gang from the boardinghouse to a hot springs resort. Late at night at the resort, Riku beckons Ten into a private room...

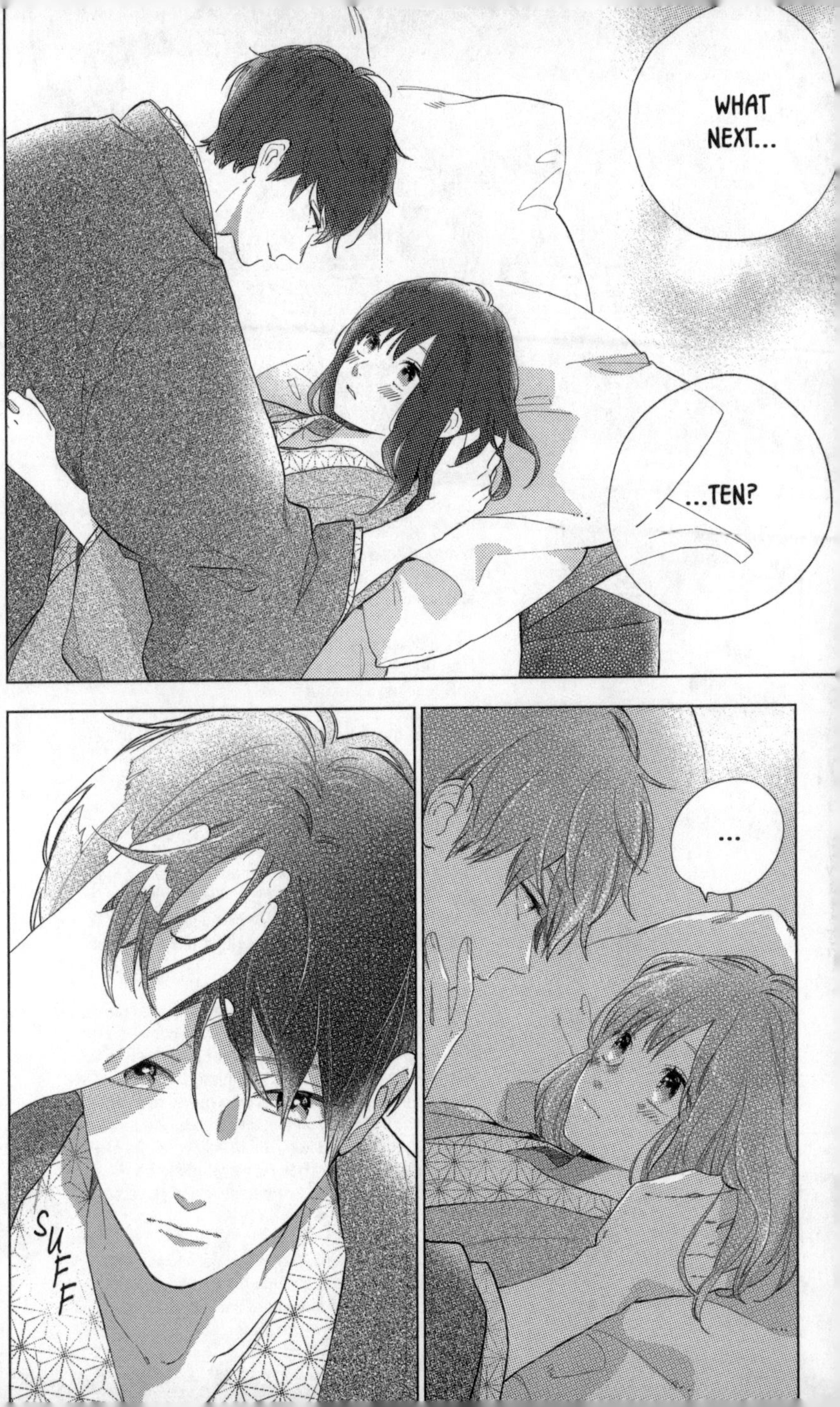
WHAT NEXT...
...TEN?
...
SUFF

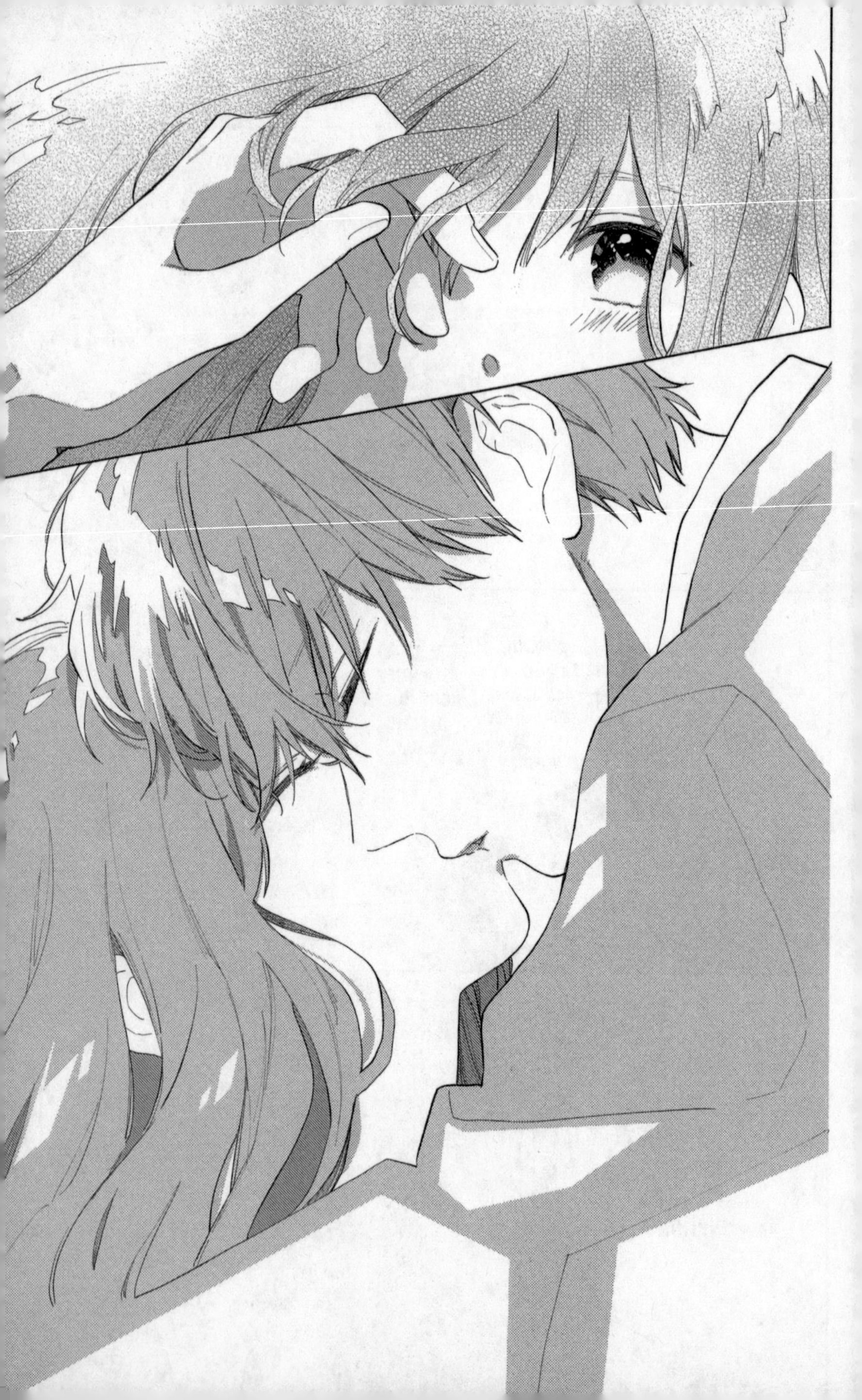

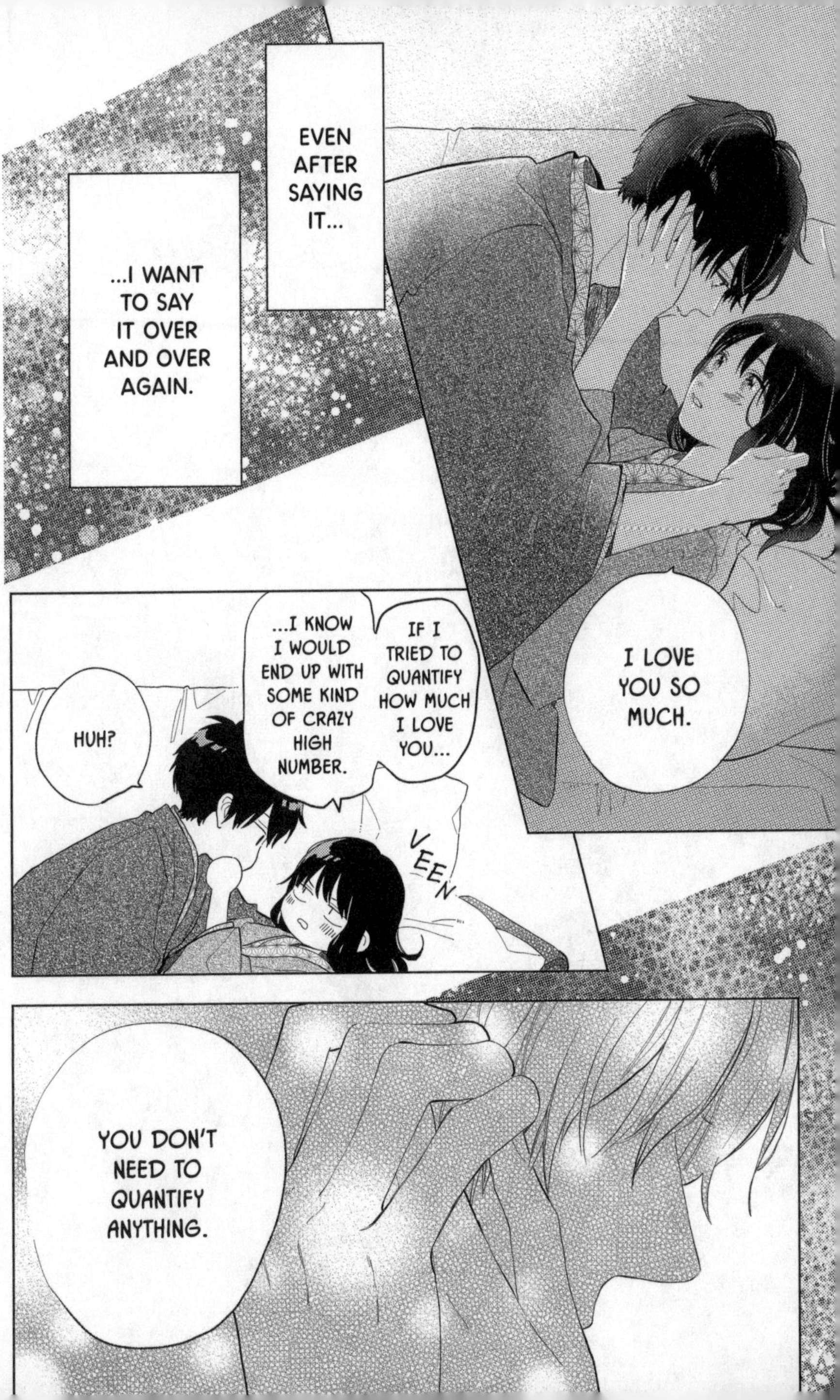
EVEN AFTER SAYING IT...
...I WANT TO SAY IT OVER AND OVER AGAIN.
I LOVE YOU SO MUCH.
IF I TRIED TO QUANTIFY HOW MUCH I LOVE YOU...
...I KNOW I WOULD END UP WITH SOME KIND OF CRAZY HIGH NUMBER.
VEEN
HUH?
YOU DON'T NEED TO QUANTIFY ANYTHING.

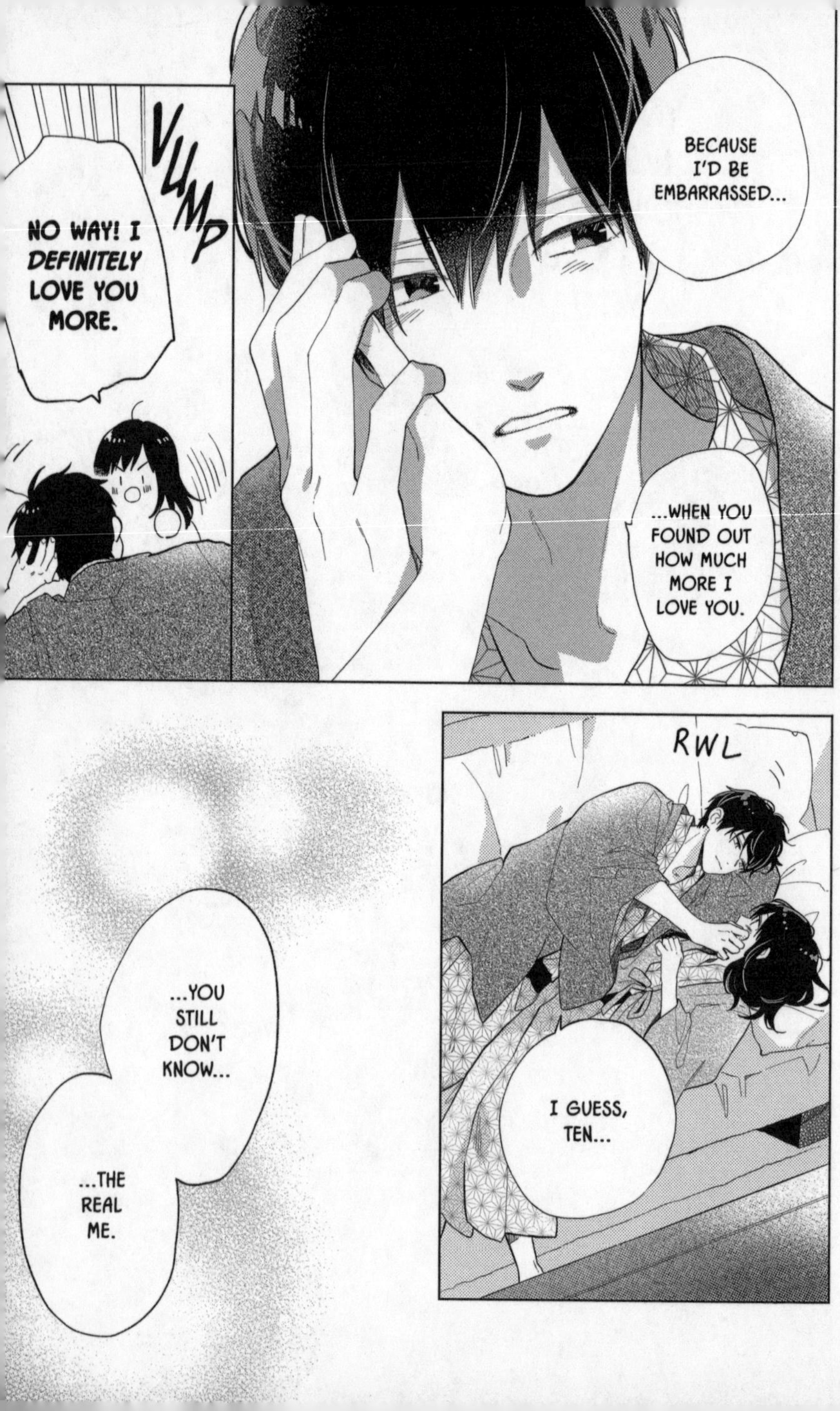
BECAUSE I'D BE EMBARRASSED...
...WHEN YOU FOUND OUT HOW MUCH MORE I LOVE YOU.
VUMP
NO WAY! I *DEFINITELY* LOVE YOU MORE.
RWL
I GUESS, TEN...
...YOU STILL DON'T KNOW...
...THE REAL ME.

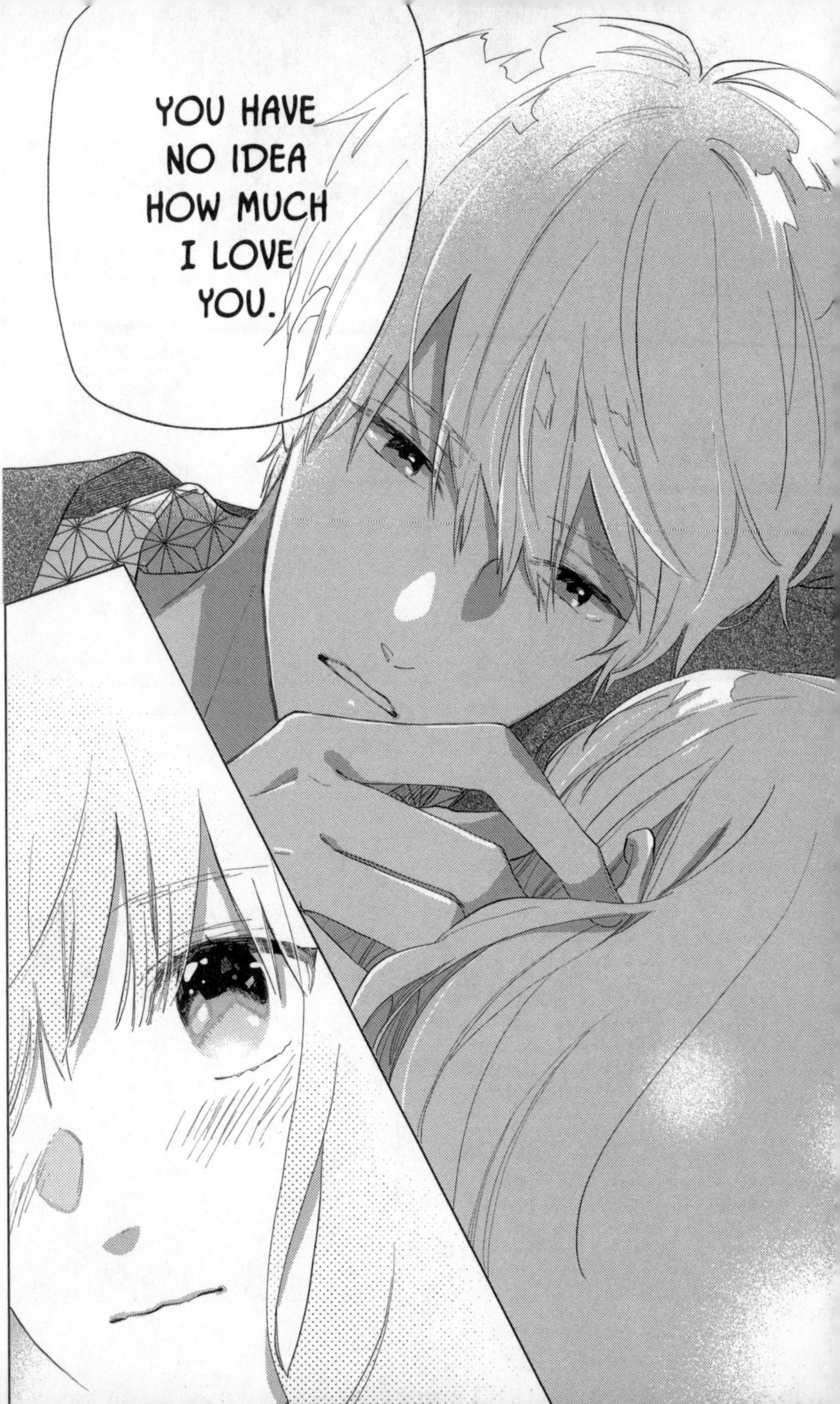
YOU HAVE NO IDEA HOW MUCH I LOVE YOU.

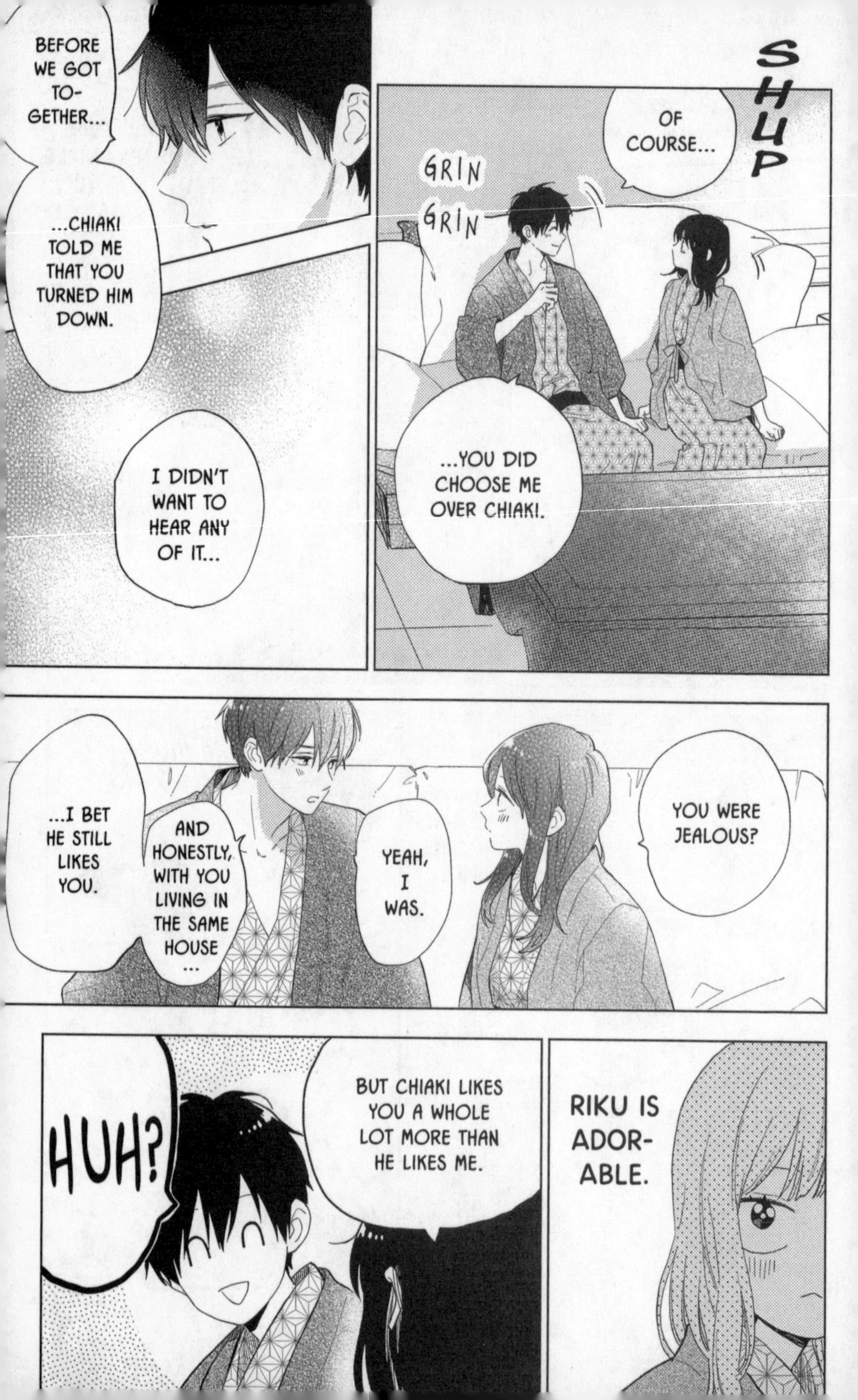
SHUP
OF COURSE...
GRIN GRIN
...YOU DID CHOOSE ME OVER CHIAKI.
BEFORE WE GOT TO-GETHER...
...CHIAKI TOLD ME THAT YOU TURNED HIM DOWN.
I DIDN'T WANT TO HEAR ANY OF IT...
YOU WERE JEALOUS?
YEAH, I WAS.
AND HONESTLY, WITH YOU LIVING IN THE SAME HOUSE...
...I BET HE STILL LIKES YOU.
RIKU IS ADOR-ABLE.
BUT CHIAKI LIKES YOU A WHOLE LOT MORE THAN HE LIKES ME.
HUH?

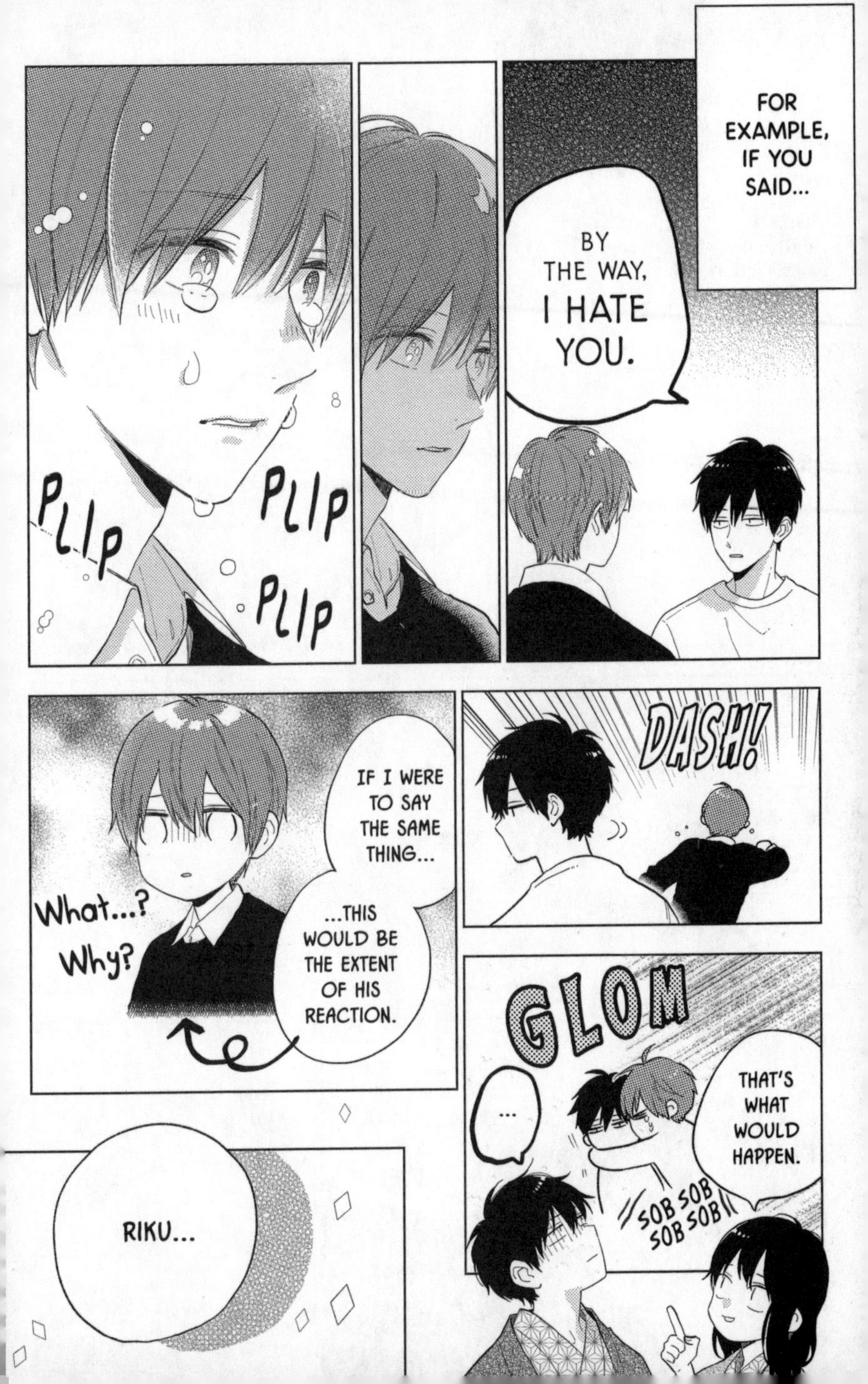
FOR EXAMPLE, IF YOU SAID...
BY THE WAY, I HATE YOU.
PLIP
PLIP
PLIP
DASH!
IF I WERE TO SAY THE SAME THING...
...THIS WOULD BE THE EXTENT OF HIS REACTION.
What...?
Why?
GLOM
...
THAT'S WHAT WOULD HAPPEN.
SOB SOB SOB SOB
RIKU...

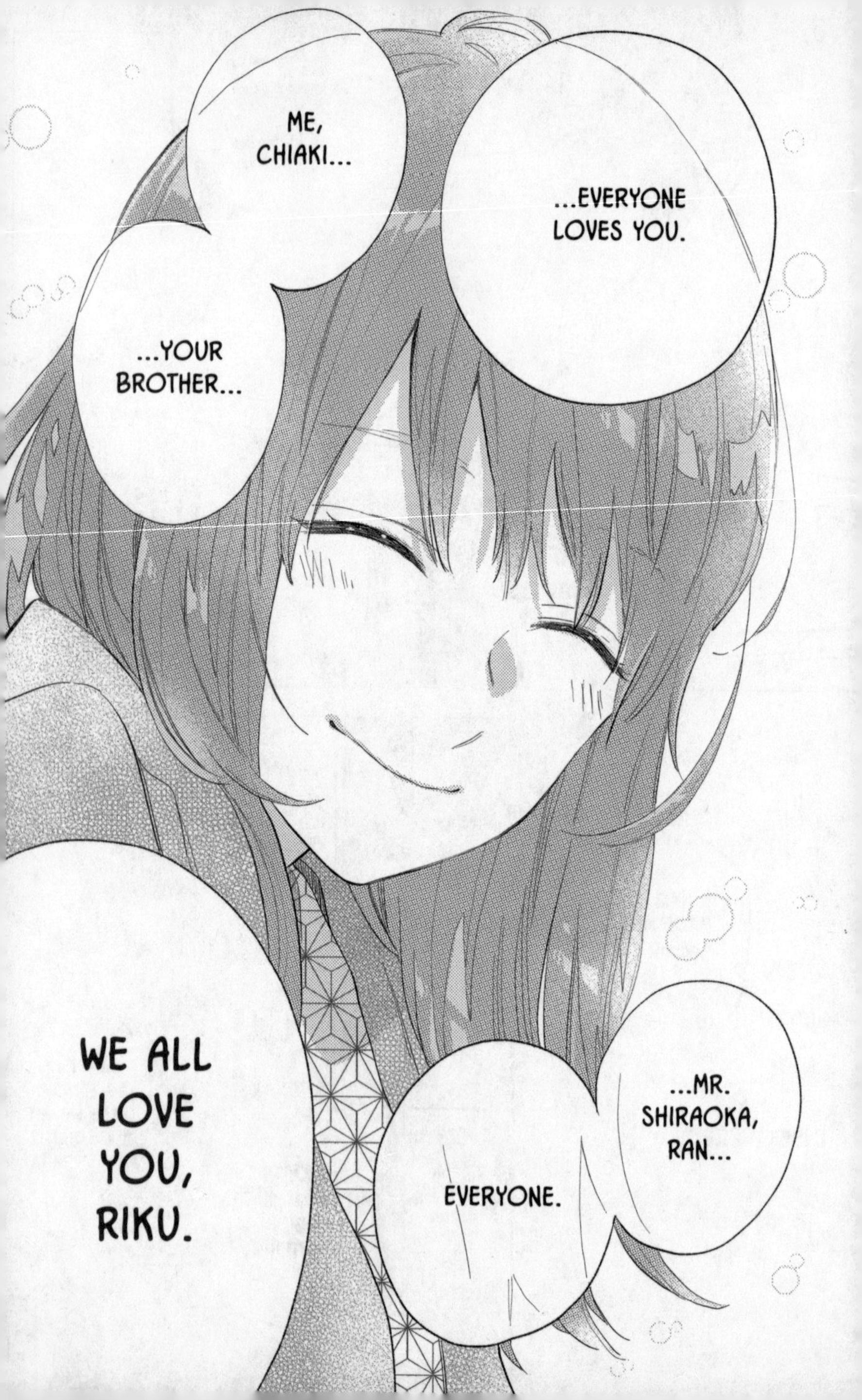
ME, CHIAKI...
...EVERYONE LOVES YOU.
...YOUR BROTHER...
...MR. SHIRAOKA, RAN...
EVERYONE.
WE ALL LOVE YOU, RIKU.

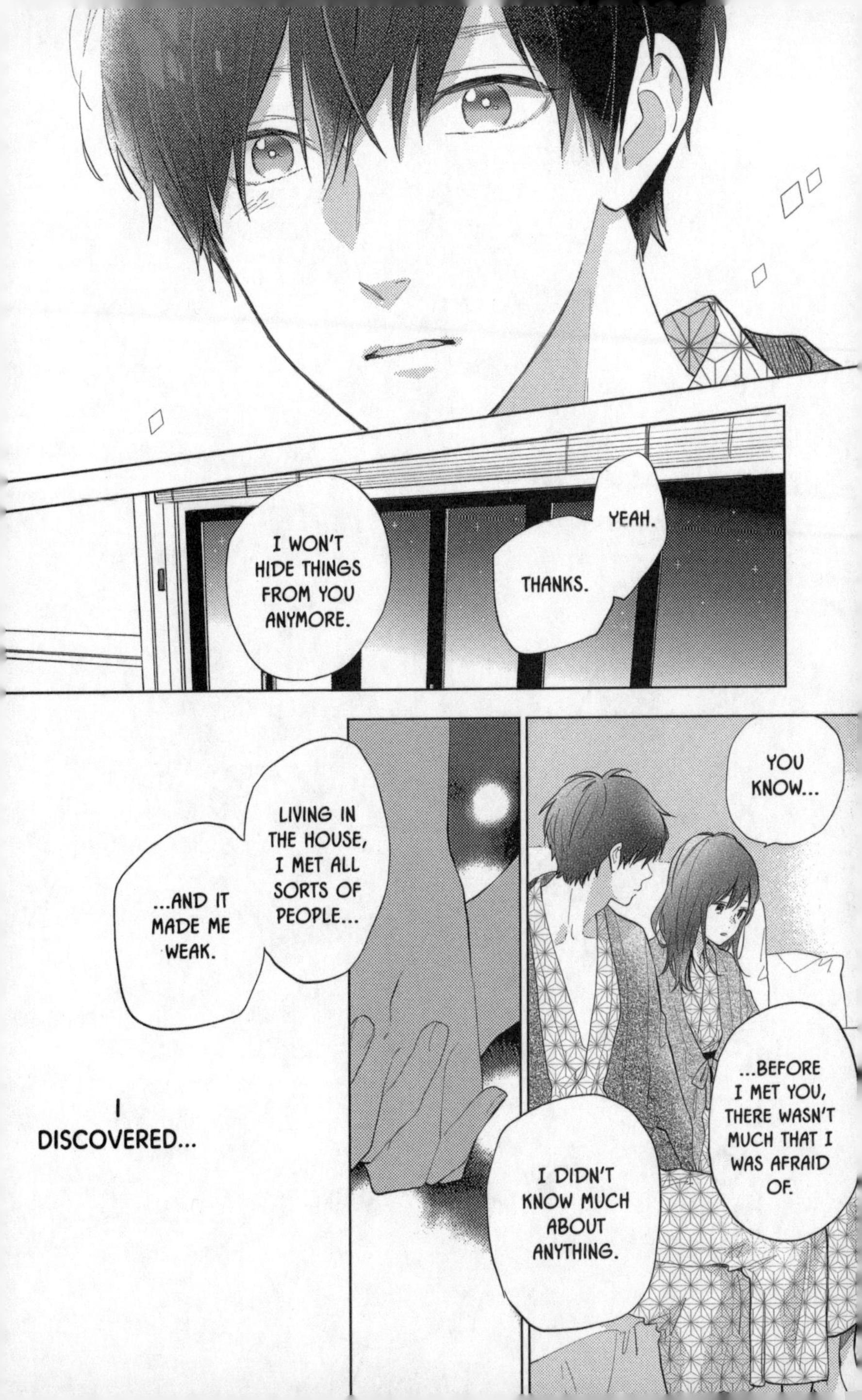
YEAH.
THANKS.
I WON'T HIDE THINGS FROM YOU ANYMORE.
YOU KNOW...
...BEFORE I MET YOU, THERE WASN'T MUCH THAT I WAS AFRAID OF.
I DIDN'T KNOW MUCH ABOUT ANYTHING.
LIVING IN THE HOUSE, I MET ALL SORTS OF PEOPLE...
...AND IT MADE ME WEAK.
I DISCOVERED...

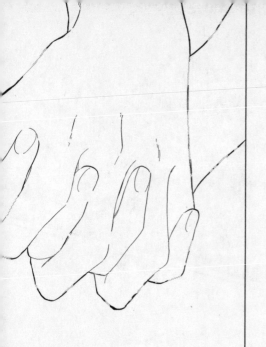

...THAT
PEOPLE...

...ARE
TRULY...

I NEED YOU
MORE THAN
ANYTHING...

...FRAGILE.

...RIKU.

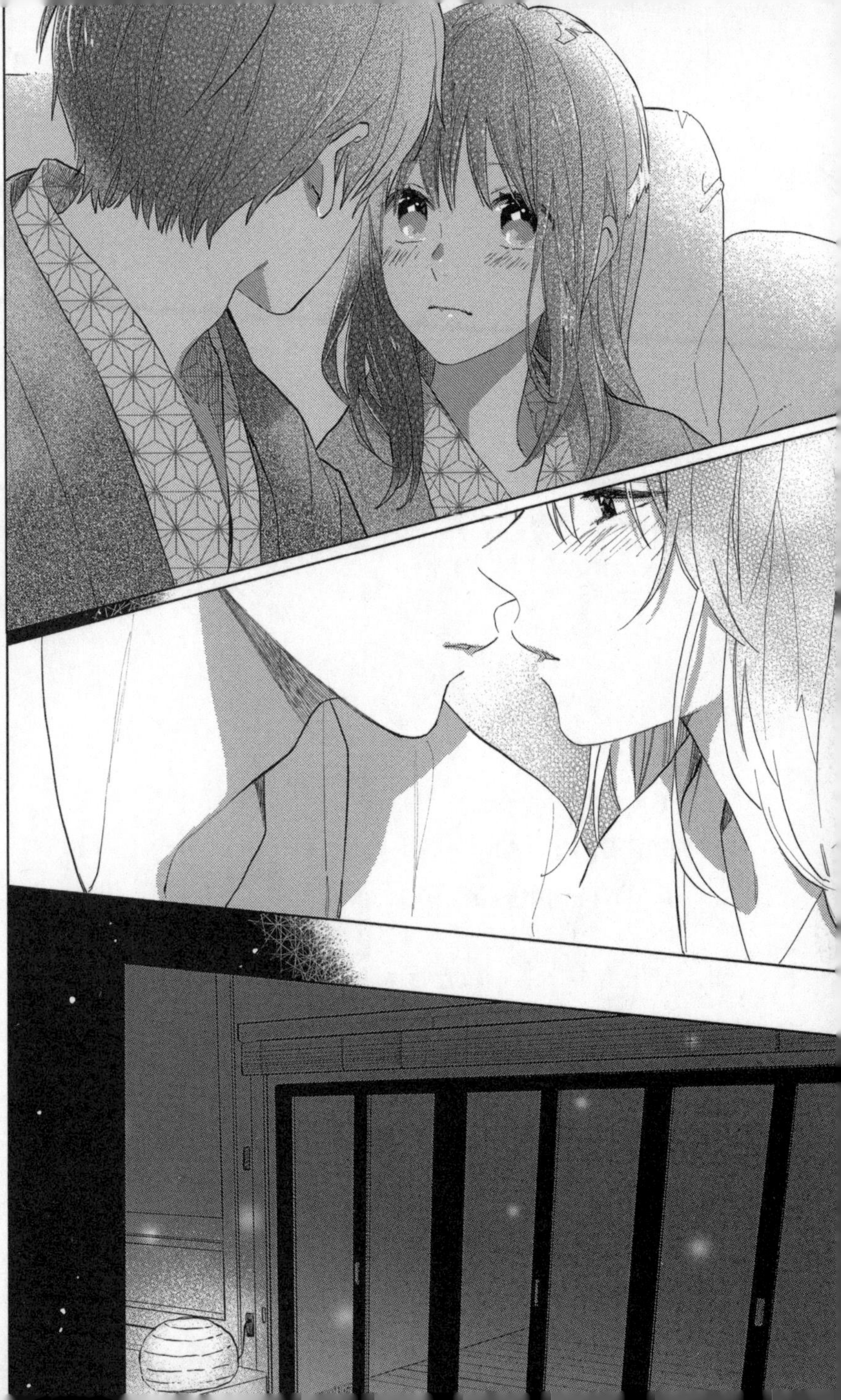

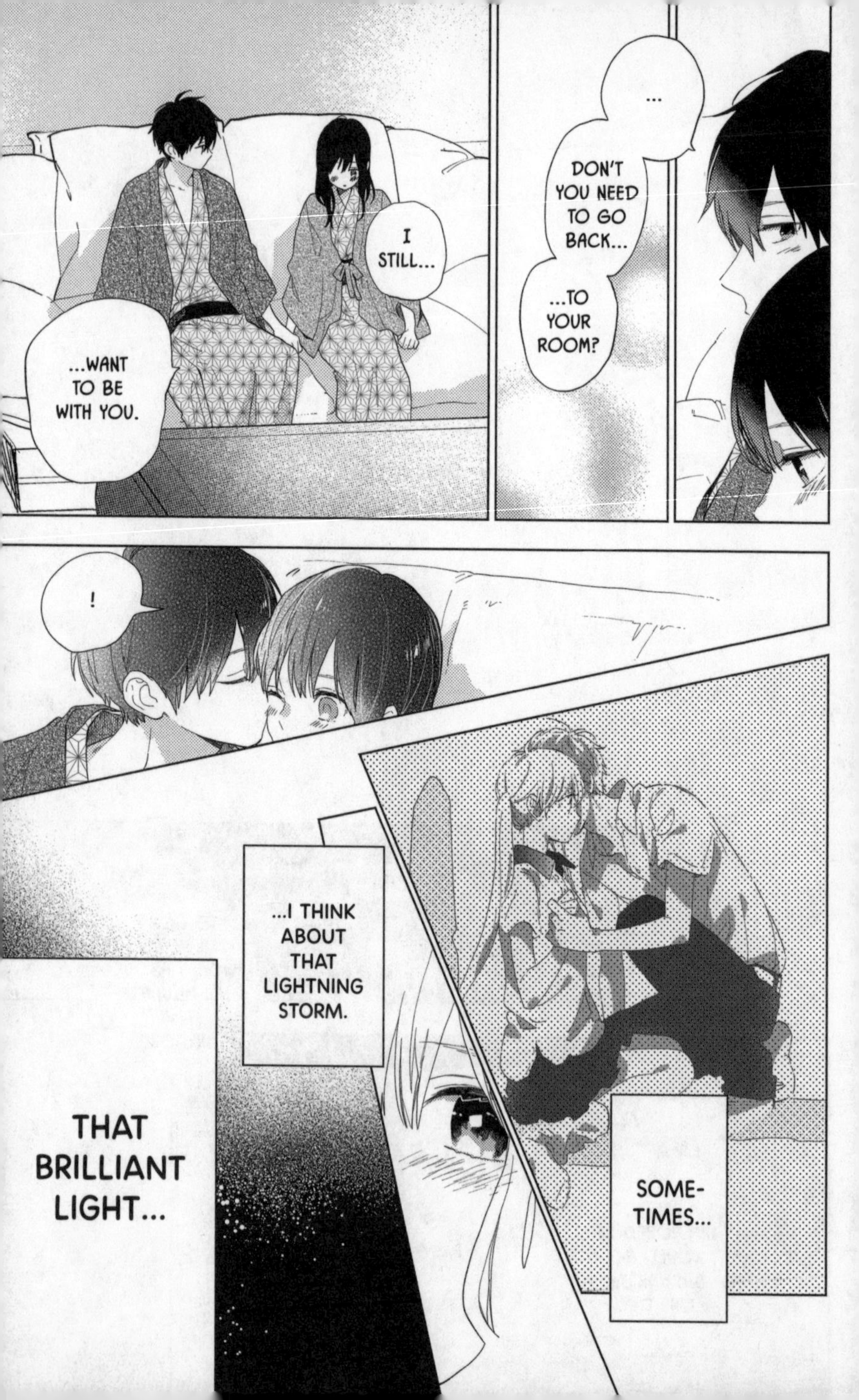
...
DON'T YOU NEED TO GO BACK...
...TO YOUR ROOM?
I STILL...
...WANT TO BE WITH YOU.
!
SOME-TIMES...
...I THINK ABOUT THAT LIGHTNING STORM.
THAT BRILLIANT LIGHT...

...MIGHT HAVE BEEN YOU.

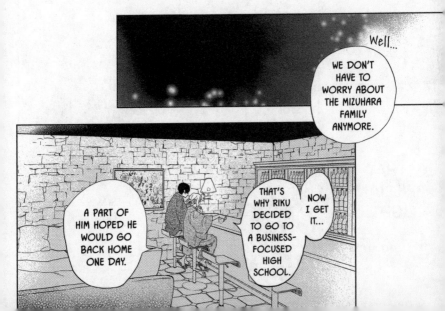

Well...
WE DON'T HAVE TO WORRY ABOUT THE MIZUHARA FAMILY ANYMORE.
NOW I GET IT...
THAT'S WHY RIKU DECIDED TO GO TO A BUSINESS-FOCUSED HIGH SCHOOL.
A PART OF HIM HOPED HE WOULD GO BACK HOME ONE DAY.

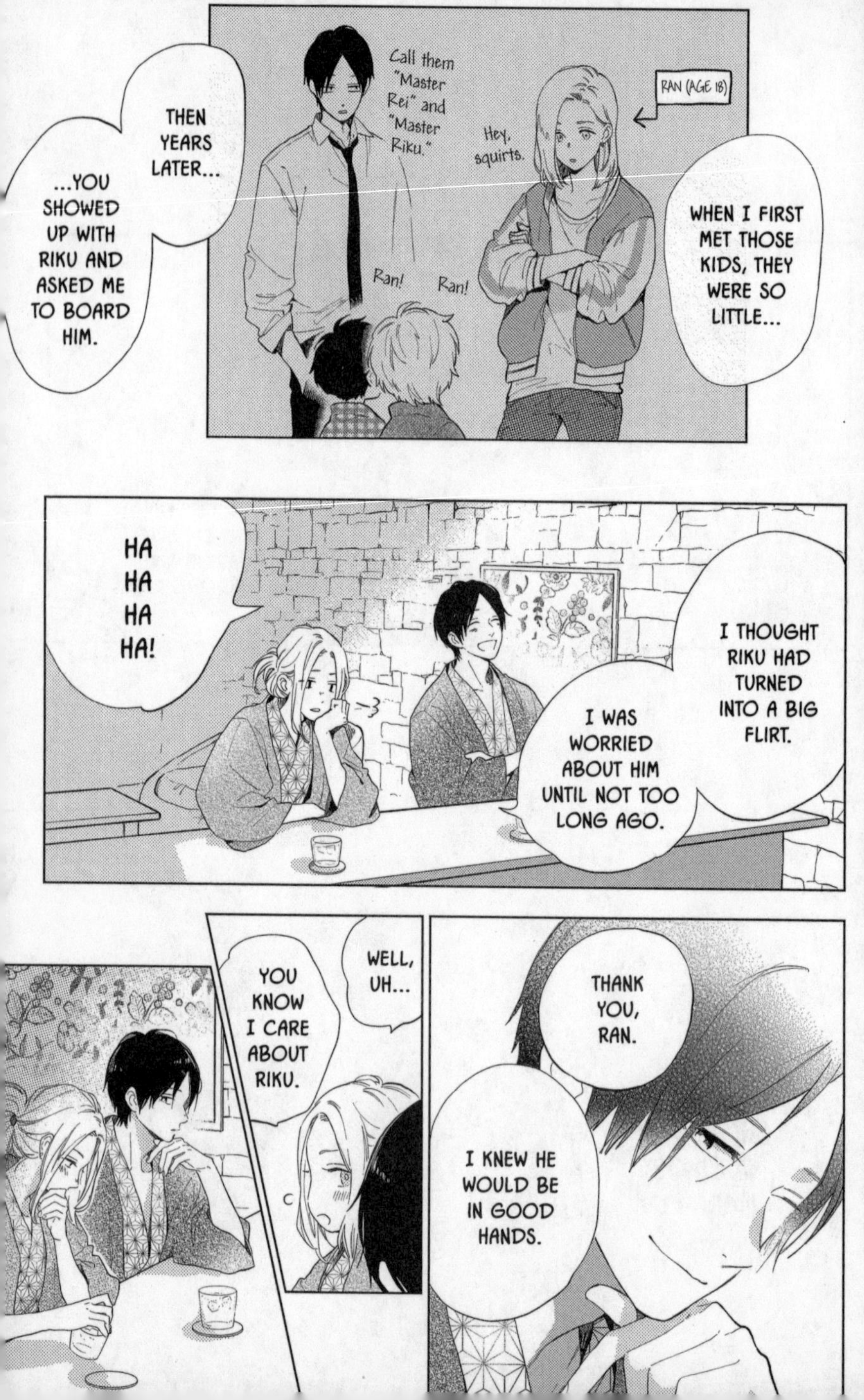
RAN (AGE 18)
WHEN I FIRST MET THOSE KIDS, THEY WERE SO LITTLE...
Hey, squirts.
Call them "Master Rei" and "Master Riku."
Ran!
Ran!
THEN YEARS LATER...
...YOU SHOWED UP WITH RIKU AND ASKED ME TO BOARD HIM.
I THOUGHT RIKU HAD TURNED INTO A BIG FLIRT.
I WAS WORRIED ABOUT HIM UNTIL NOT TOO LONG AGO.
HA HA HA HA!
THANK YOU, RAN.
I KNEW HE WOULD BE IN GOOD HANDS.
WELL, UH...
YOU KNOW I CARE ABOUT RIKU.

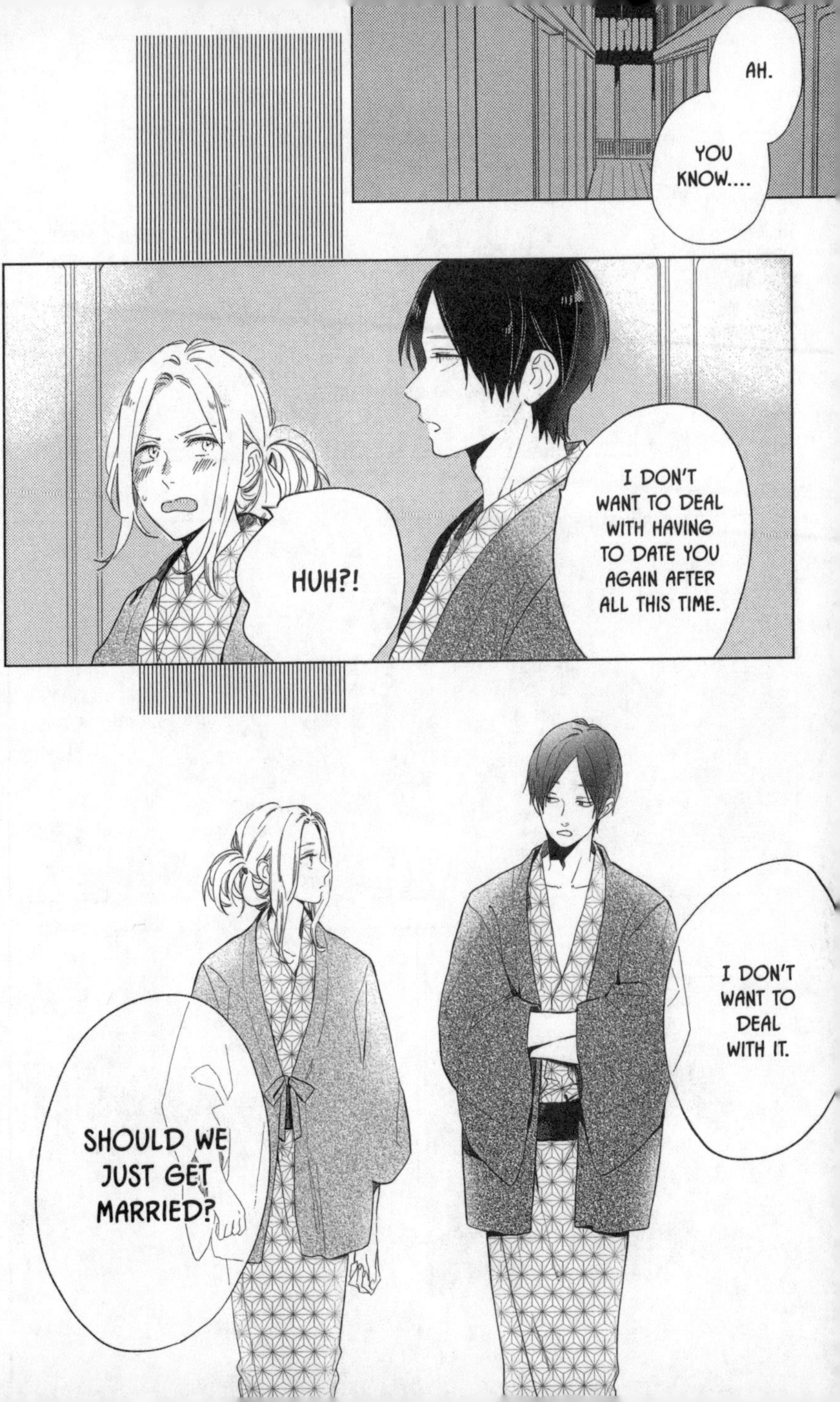
AH.
YOU KNOW....
I DON'T WANT TO DEAL WITH HAVING TO DATE YOU AGAIN AFTER ALL THIS TIME.
HUH?!
I DON'T WANT TO DEAL WITH IT.
SHOULD WE JUST GET MARRIED?

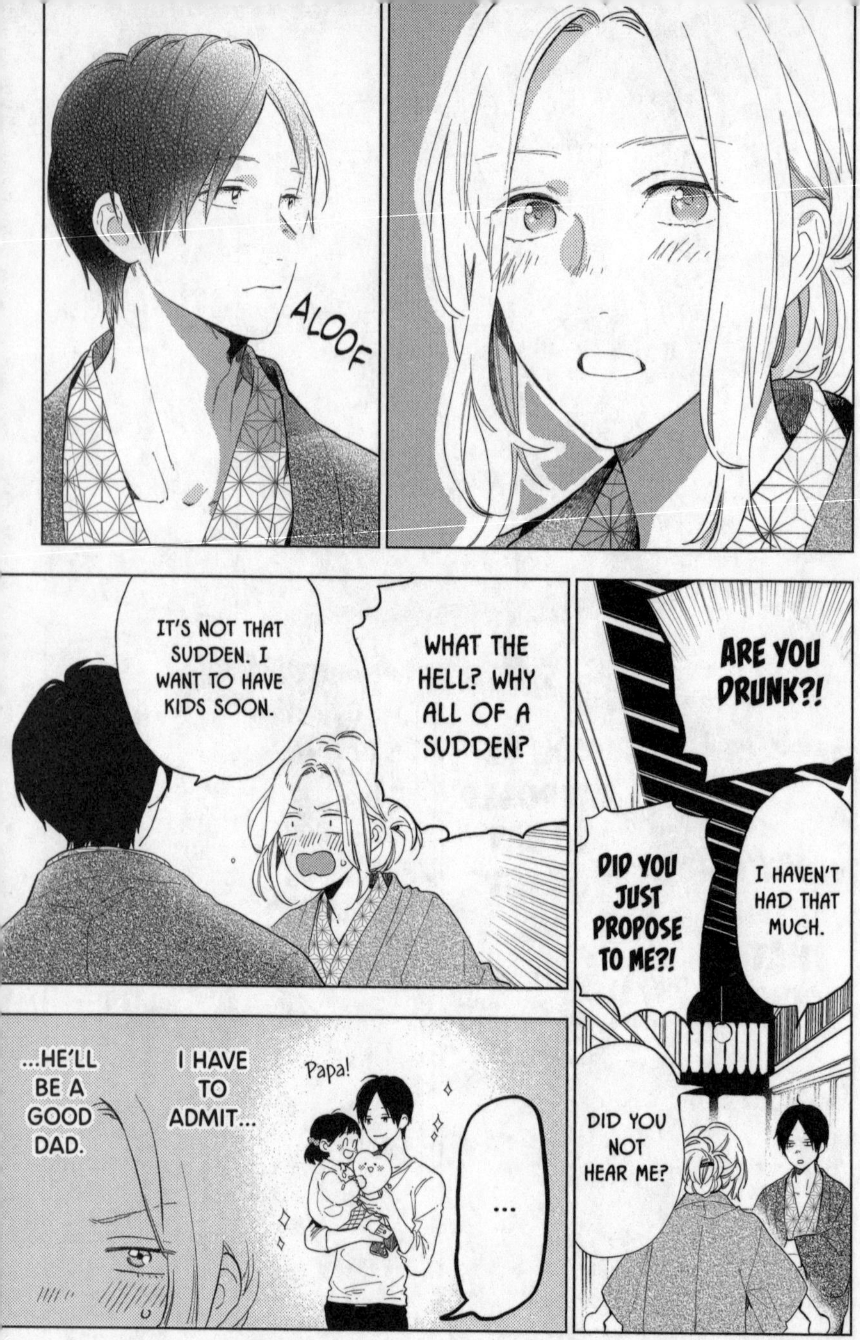
ALOOF
ARE YOU DRUNK?!
I HAVEN'T HAD THAT MUCH.
DID YOU JUST PROPOSE TO ME?!
DID YOU NOT HEAR ME?
WHAT THE HELL? WHY ALL OF A SUDDEN?
IT'S NOT THAT SUDDEN. I WANT TO HAVE KIDS SOON.
...
Papa!
I HAVE TO ADMIT...
...HE'LL BE A GOOD DAD.

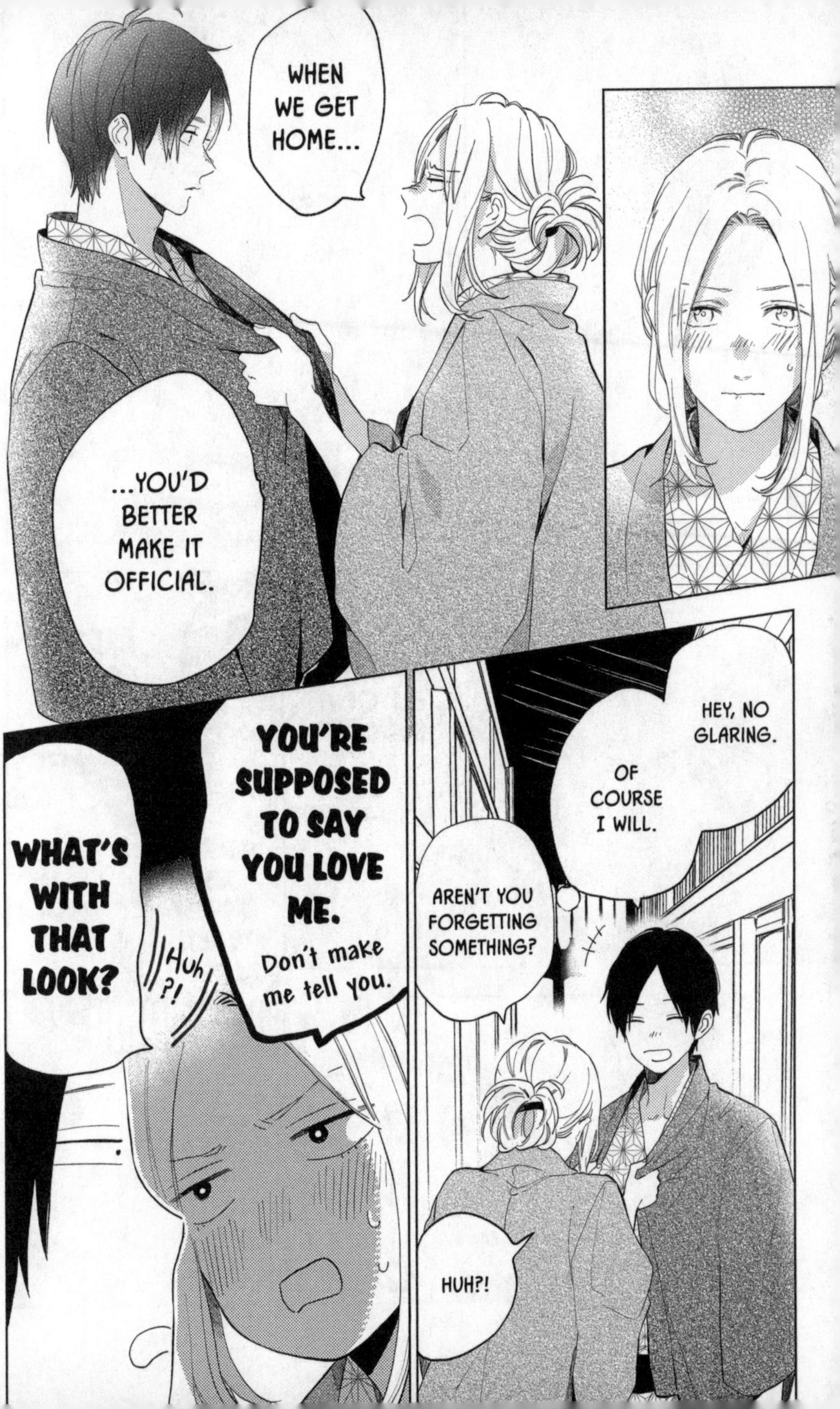
WHEN WE GET HOME...
...YOU'D BETTER MAKE IT OFFICIAL.
HEY, NO GLARING.
OF COURSE I WILL.
AREN'T YOU FORGETTING SOMETHING?
HUH?!
YOU'RE SUPPOSED TO SAY YOU LOVE ME.
Don't make me tell you.
Huh ?!
WHAT'S WITH THAT LOOK?

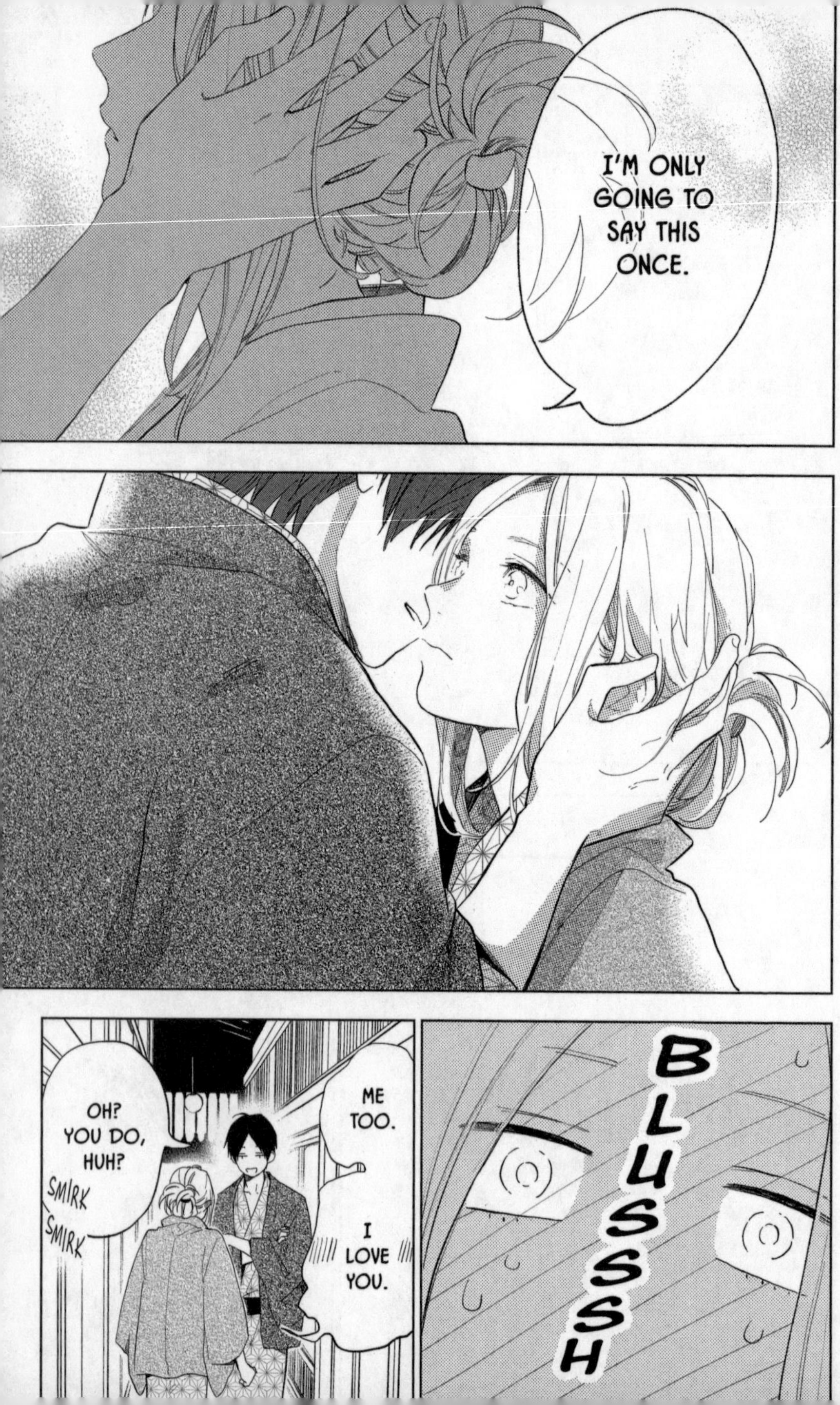
I'M ONLY GOING TO SAY THIS ONCE.
BLUSSSH
ME TOO.
I LOVE YOU.
OH? YOU DO, HUH?
SMIRK SMIRK

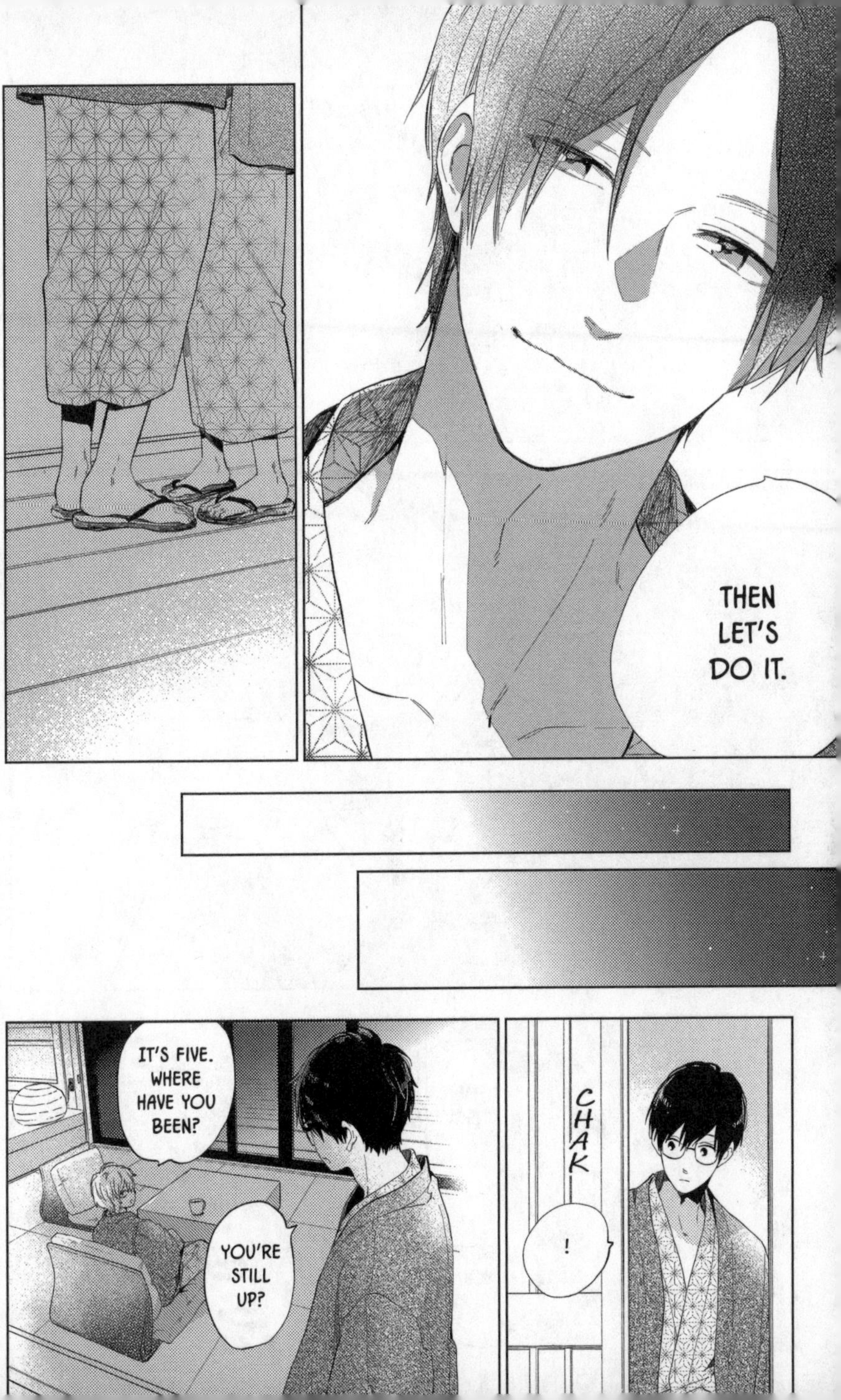
THEN LET'S DO IT.
CHAK
!
IT'S FIVE. WHERE HAVE YOU BEEN?
YOU'RE STILL UP?

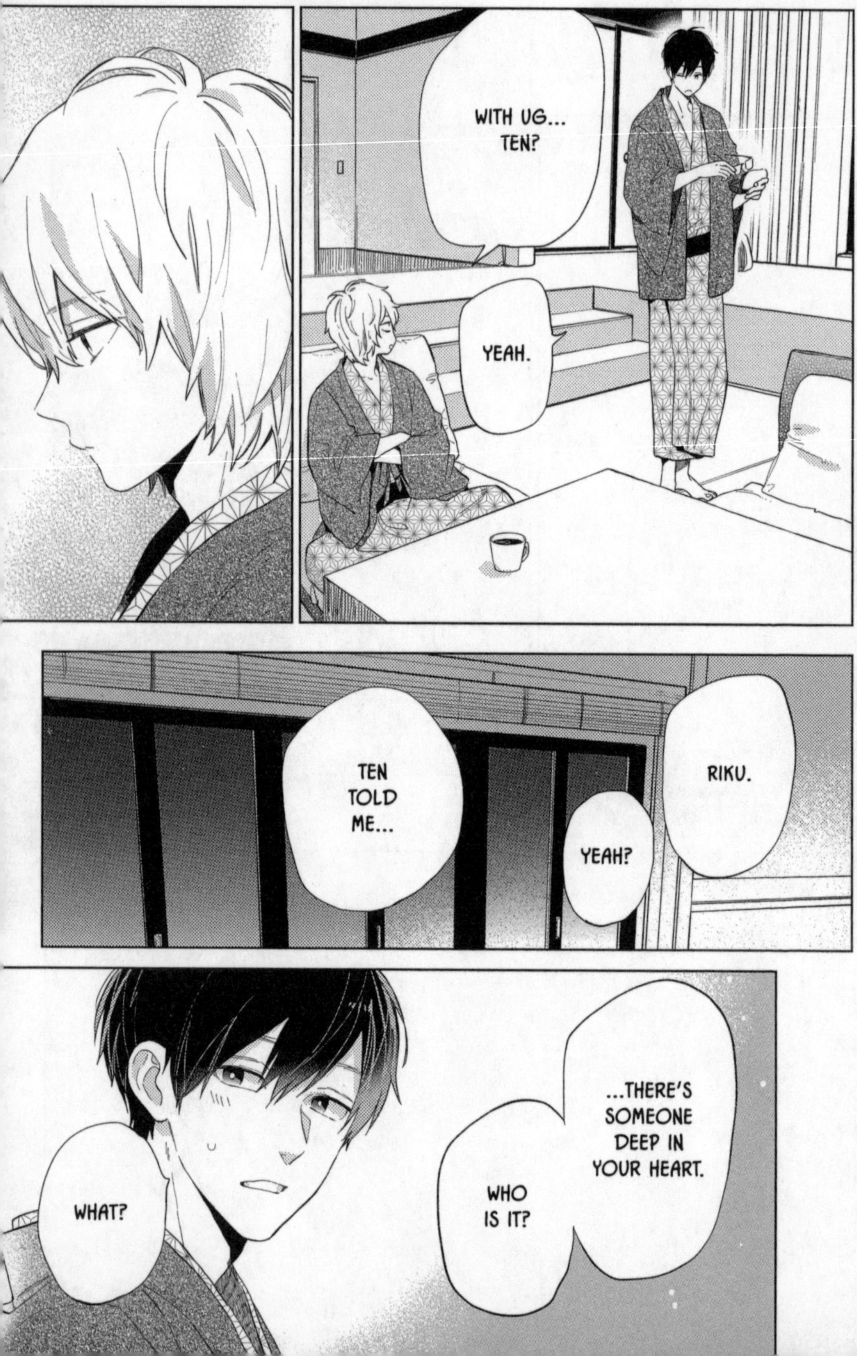
WITH US... TEN?
YEAH.
RIKU.
YEAH?
TEN TOLD ME...
...THERE'S SOMEONE DEEP IN YOUR HEART.
WHO IS IT?
WHAT?

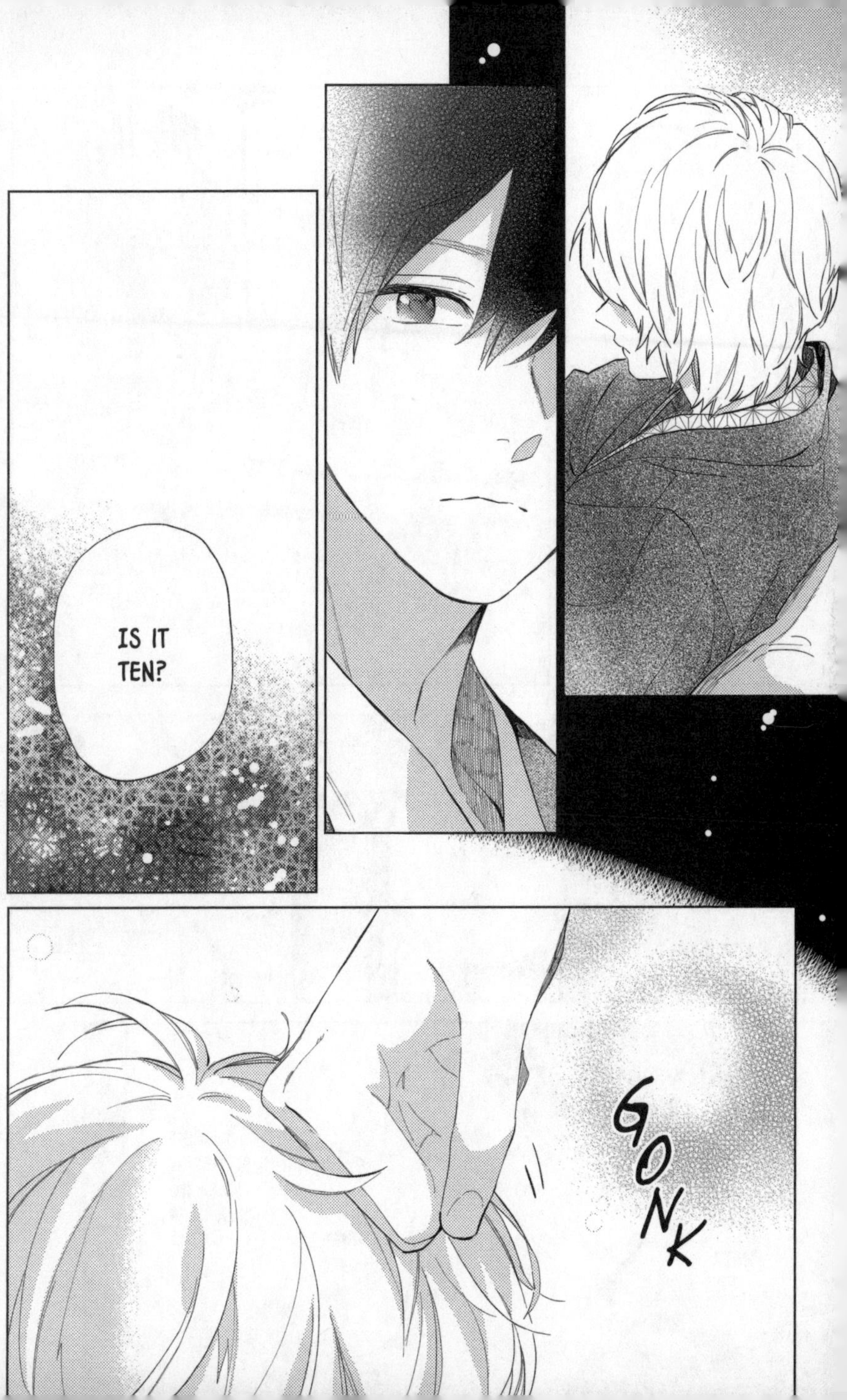
IS IT TEN?
GONK

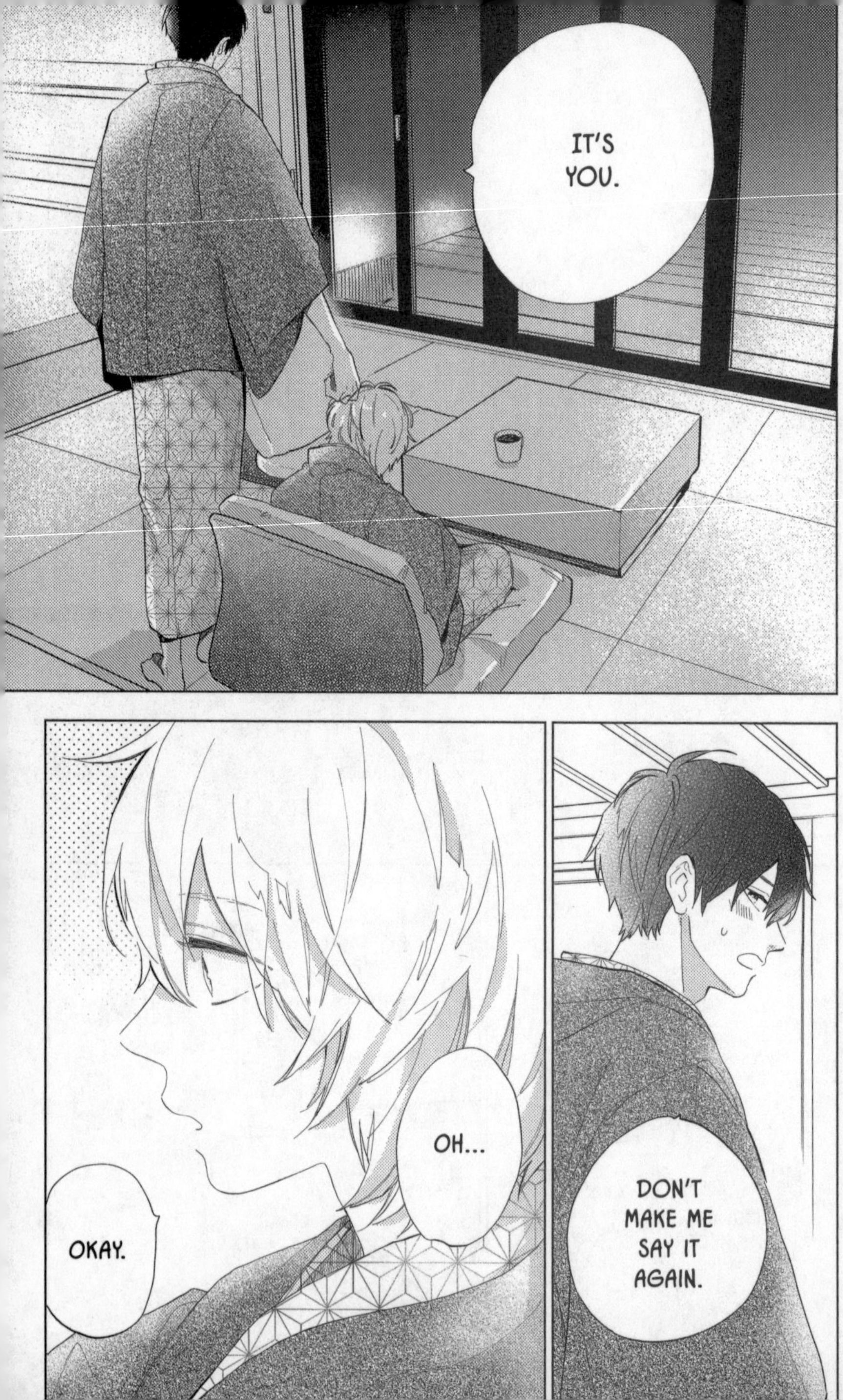
IT'S YOU.
DON'T MAKE ME SAY IT AGAIN.
OH...
OKAY.

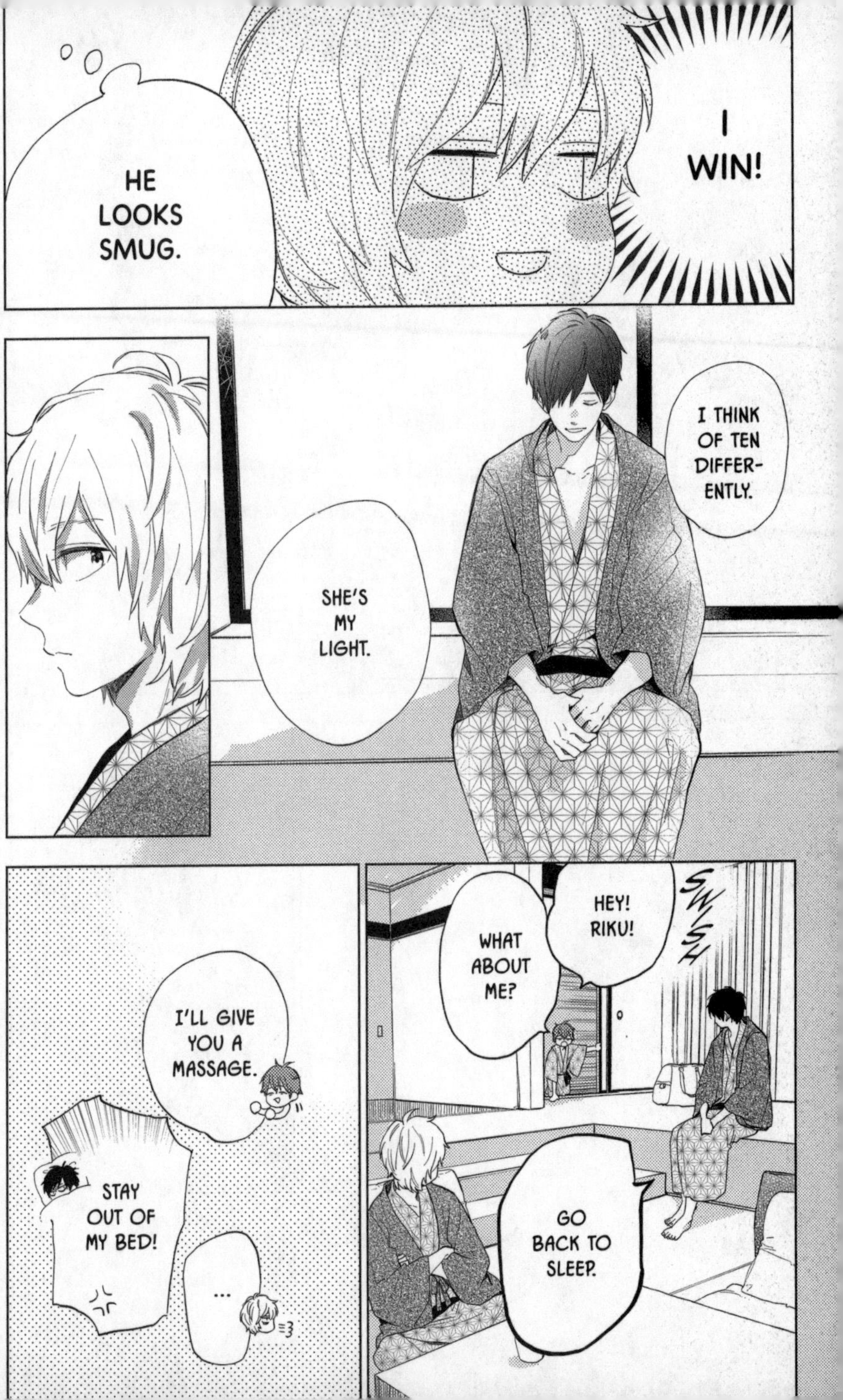
I WIN!
HE LOOKS SMUG.
I THINK OF TEN DIFFERENTLY.
SHE'S MY LIGHT.
SWISH
HEY! RIKU!
WHAT ABOUT ME?
GO BACK TO SLEEP.
I'LL GIVE YOU A MASSAGE.
STAY OUT OF MY BED!
...

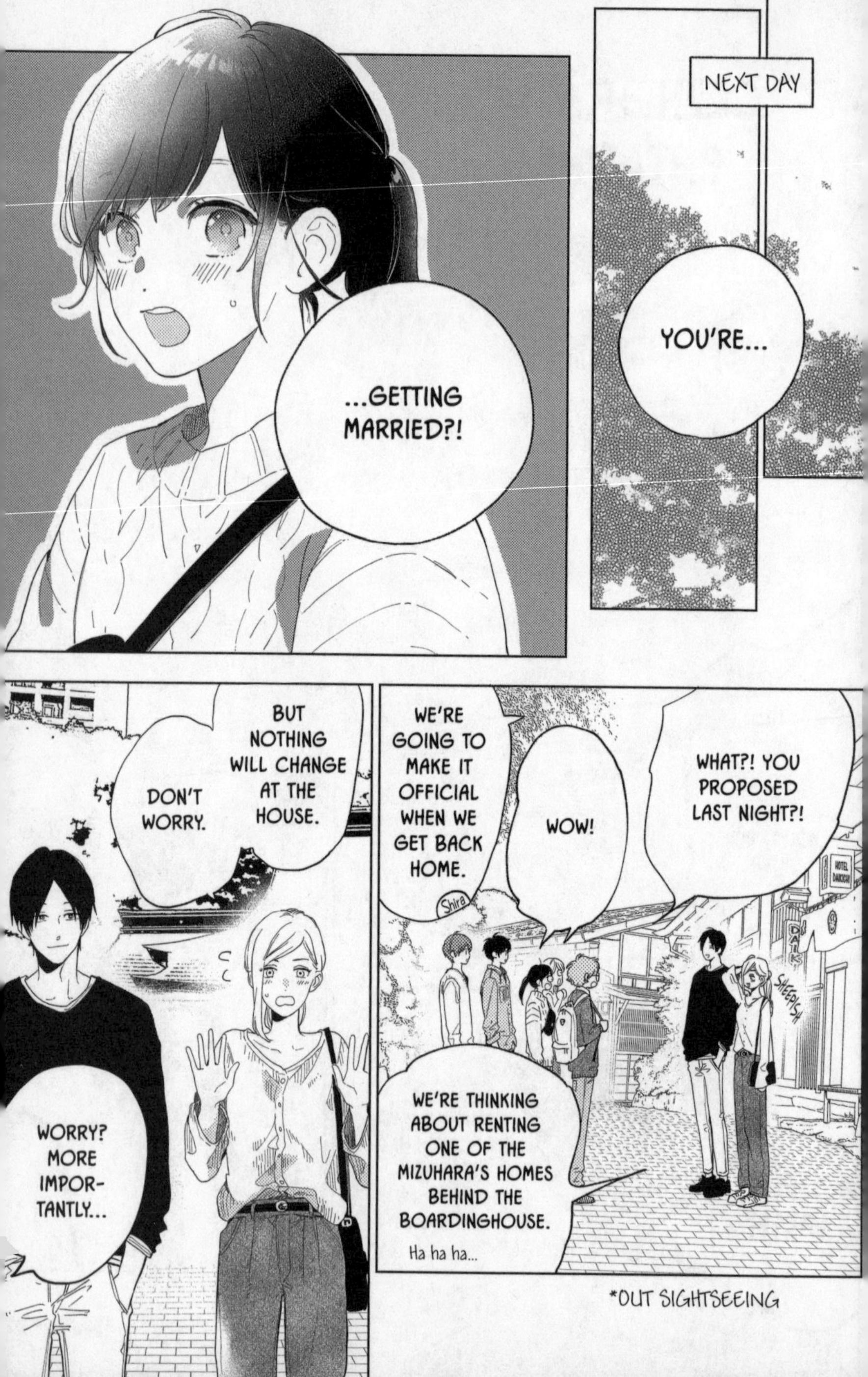
NEXT DAY
YOU'RE...
...GETTING MARRIED?!
WHAT?! YOU PROPOSED LAST NIGHT?!
WOW!
WE'RE GOING TO MAKE IT OFFICIAL WHEN WE GET BACK HOME.
Shira
SHEEPISH
WE'RE THINKING ABOUT RENTING ONE OF THE MIZUHARA'S HOMES BEHIND THE BOARDINGHOUSE.
Ha ha ha...
BUT NOTHING WILL CHANGE AT THE HOUSE.
DON'T WORRY.
WORRY? MORE IMPOR-TANTLY...

*OUT SIGHTSEEING

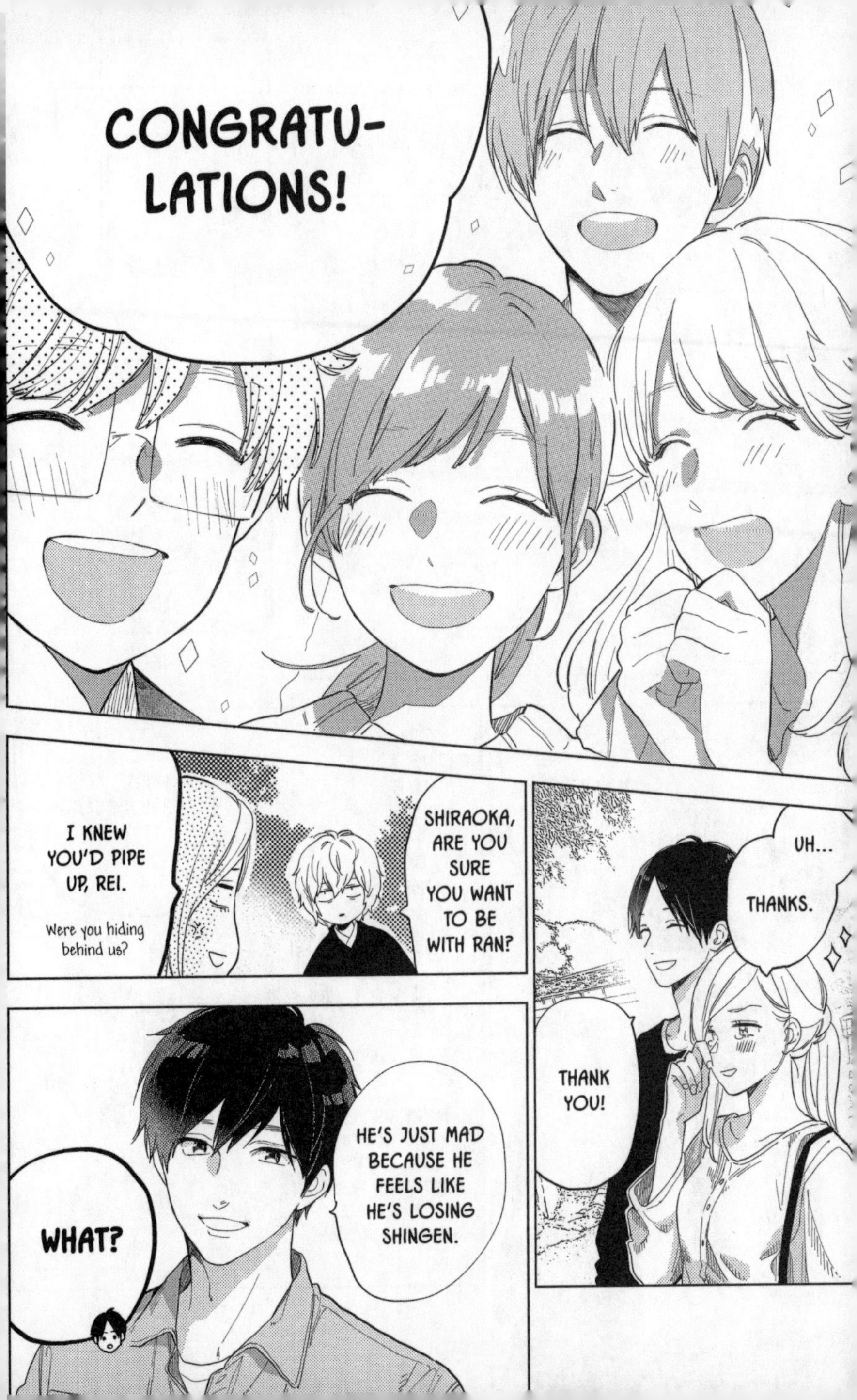
CONGRATU-LATIONS!
UH... THANKS.
THANK YOU!
SHIRAOKA, ARE YOU SURE YOU WANT TO BE WITH RAN?
I KNEW YOU'D PIPE UP, REI.
Were you hiding behind us?
HE'S JUST MAD BECAUSE HE FEELS LIKE HE'S LOSING SHINGEN.
WHAT?

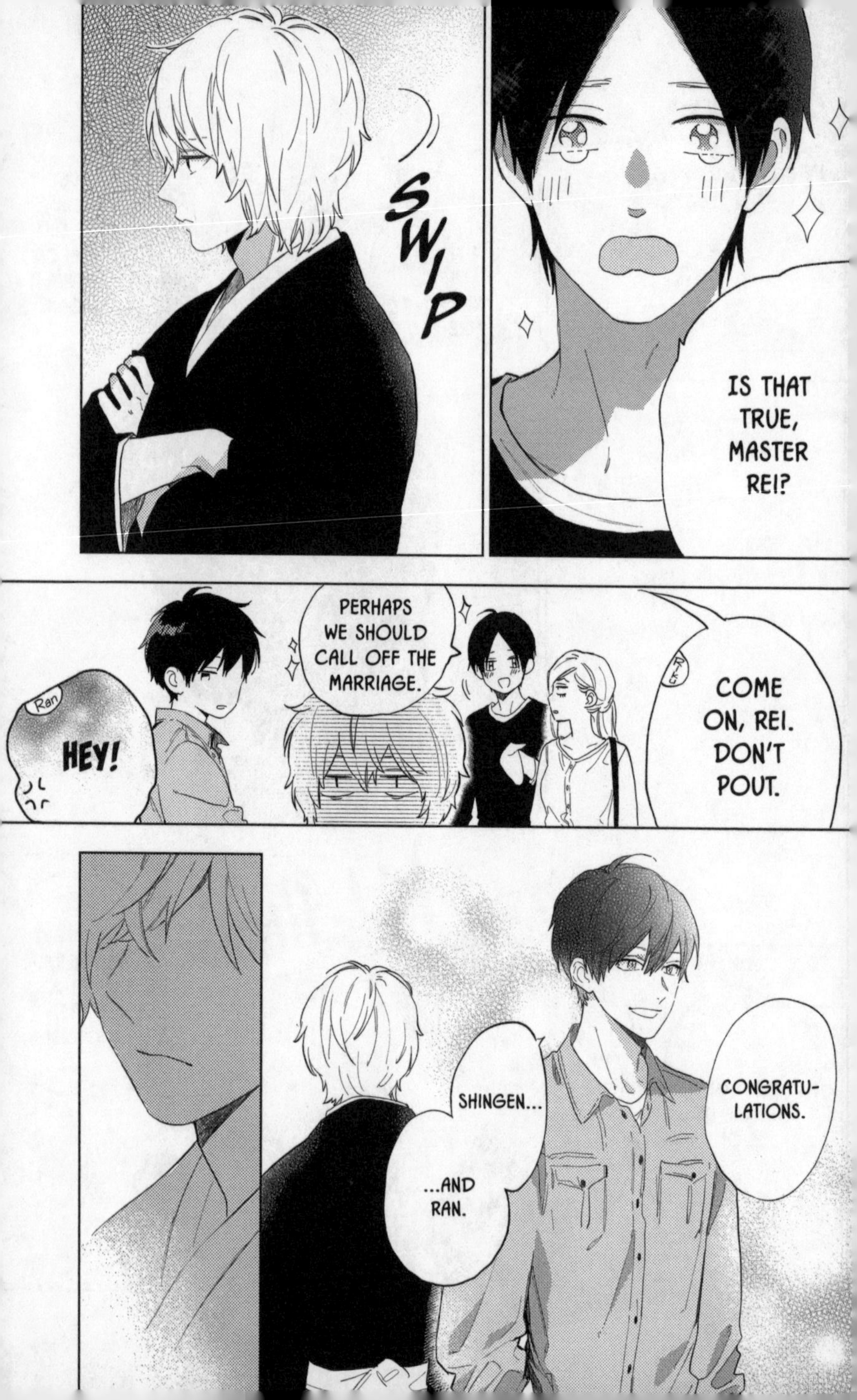
IS THAT TRUE, MASTER REI?
SWIP
COME ON, REI. DON'T POUT.
PERHAPS WE SHOULD CALL OFF THE MARRIAGE.
Ran
HEY!
CONGRATU-LATIONS.
SHINGEN...
...AND RAN.

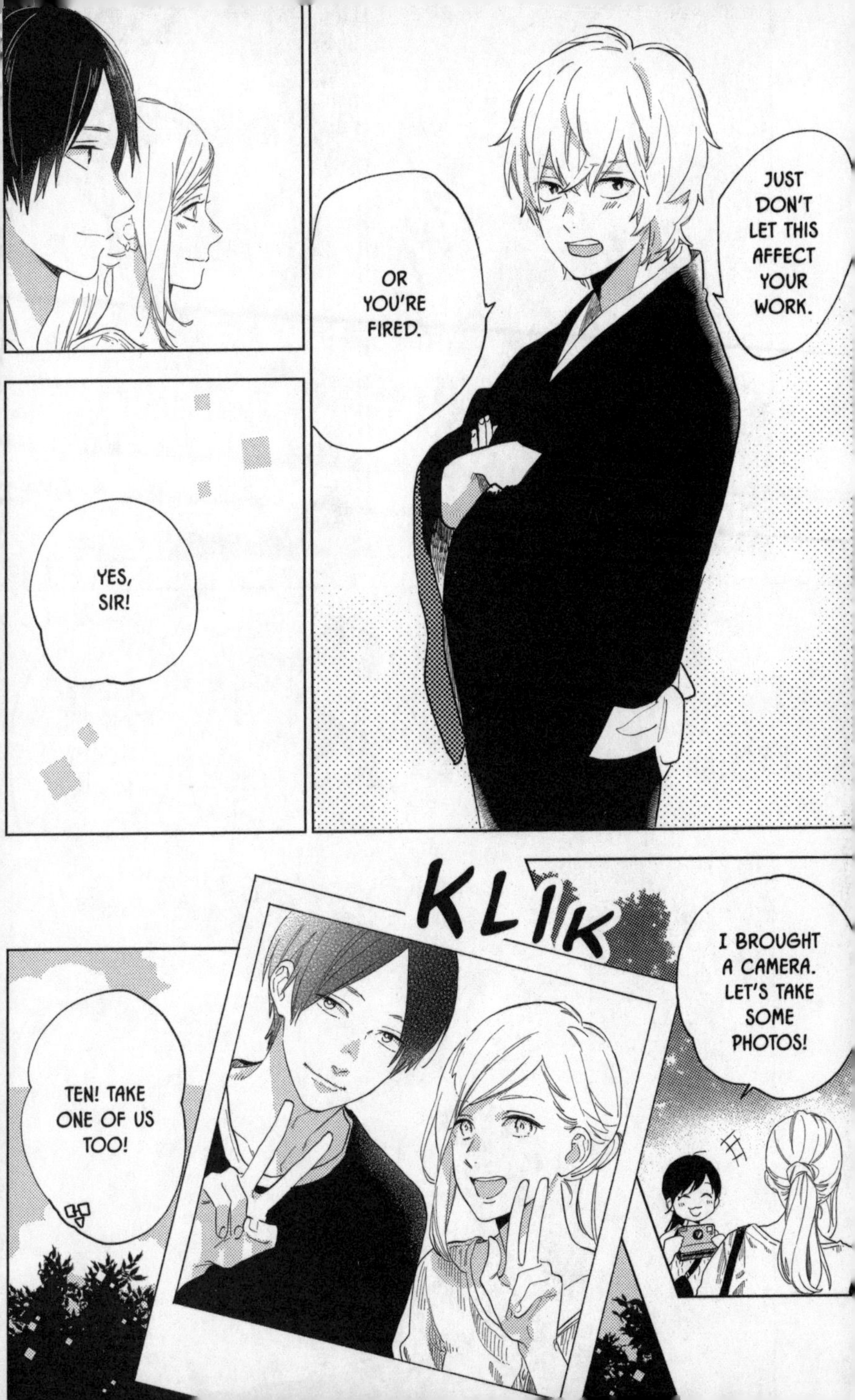
JUST DON'T LET THIS AFFECT YOUR WORK.
OR YOU'RE FIRED.
YES, SIR!
I BROUGHT A CAMERA. LET'S TAKE SOME PHOTOS!
KLIK
TEN! TAKE ONE OF US TOO!

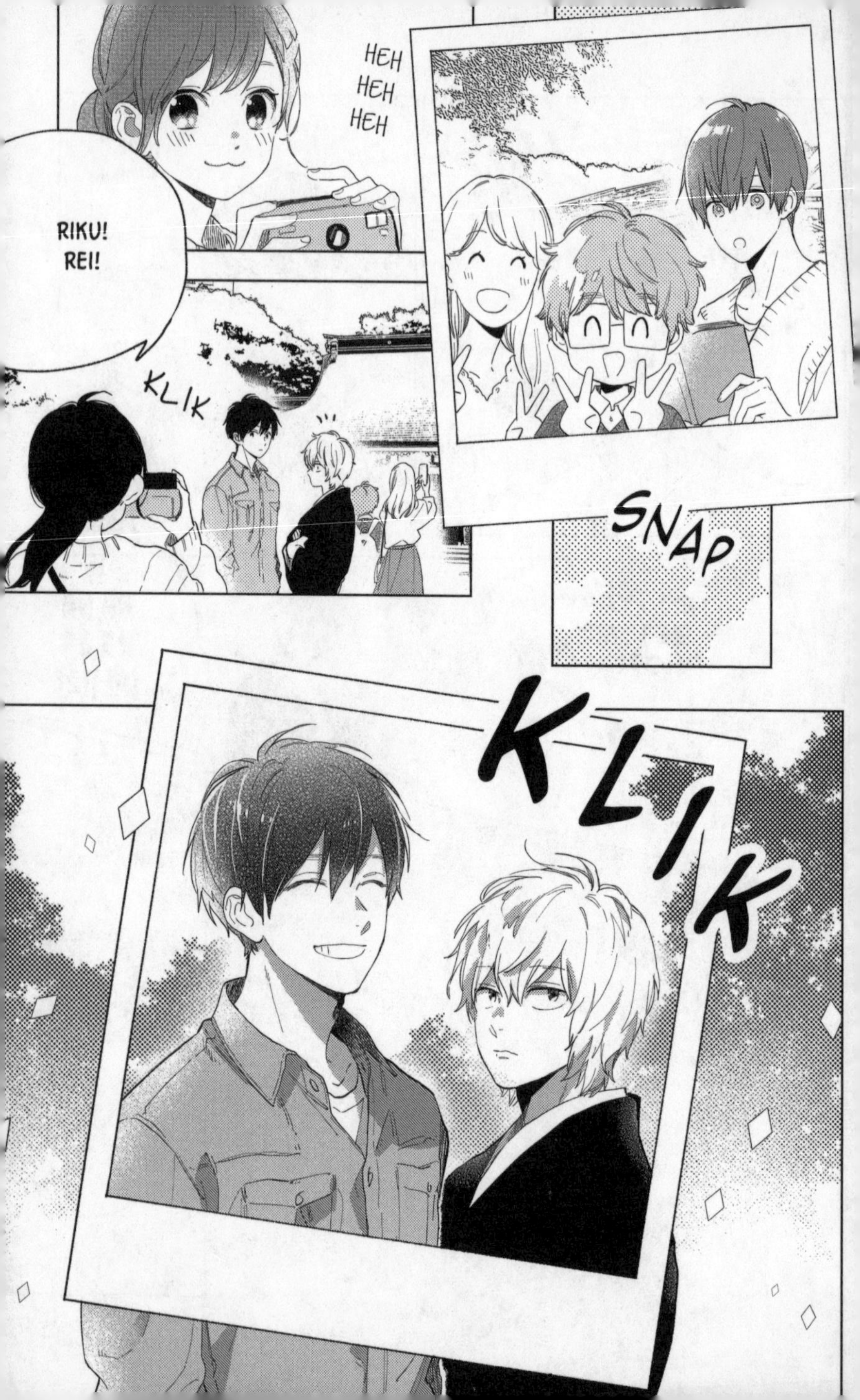
SNAP
HEH HEH HEH
RIKU! REI!
KLIK
KLIK

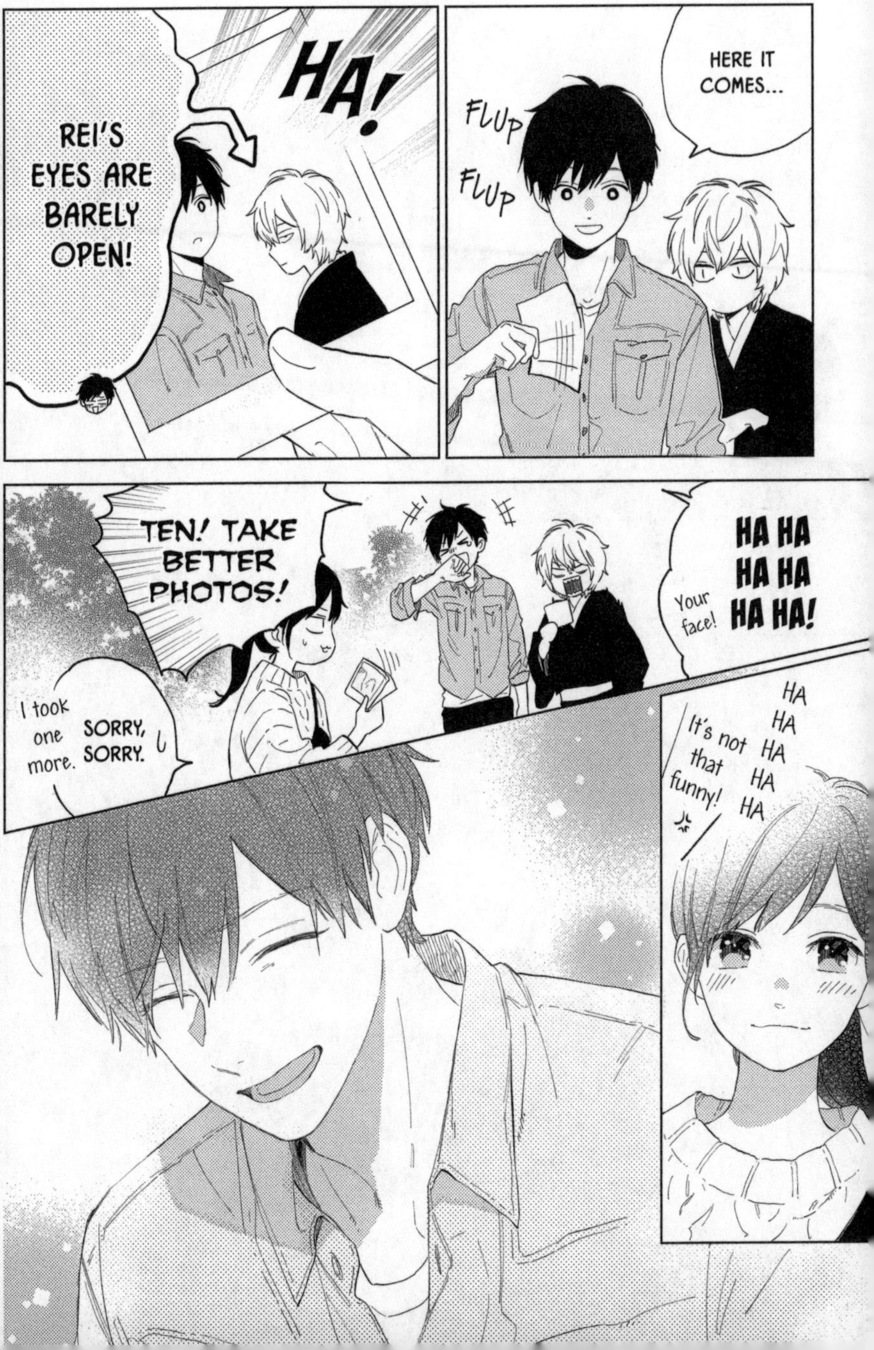
HERE IT COMES...
FLUP
FLUP
HA!
REI'S EYES ARE BARELY OPEN!
HA HA HA HA HA HA!
Your face!
TEN! TAKE BETTER PHOTOS!
SORRY, SORRY.
I took one more.
HA HA HA HA HA
It's not that funny!

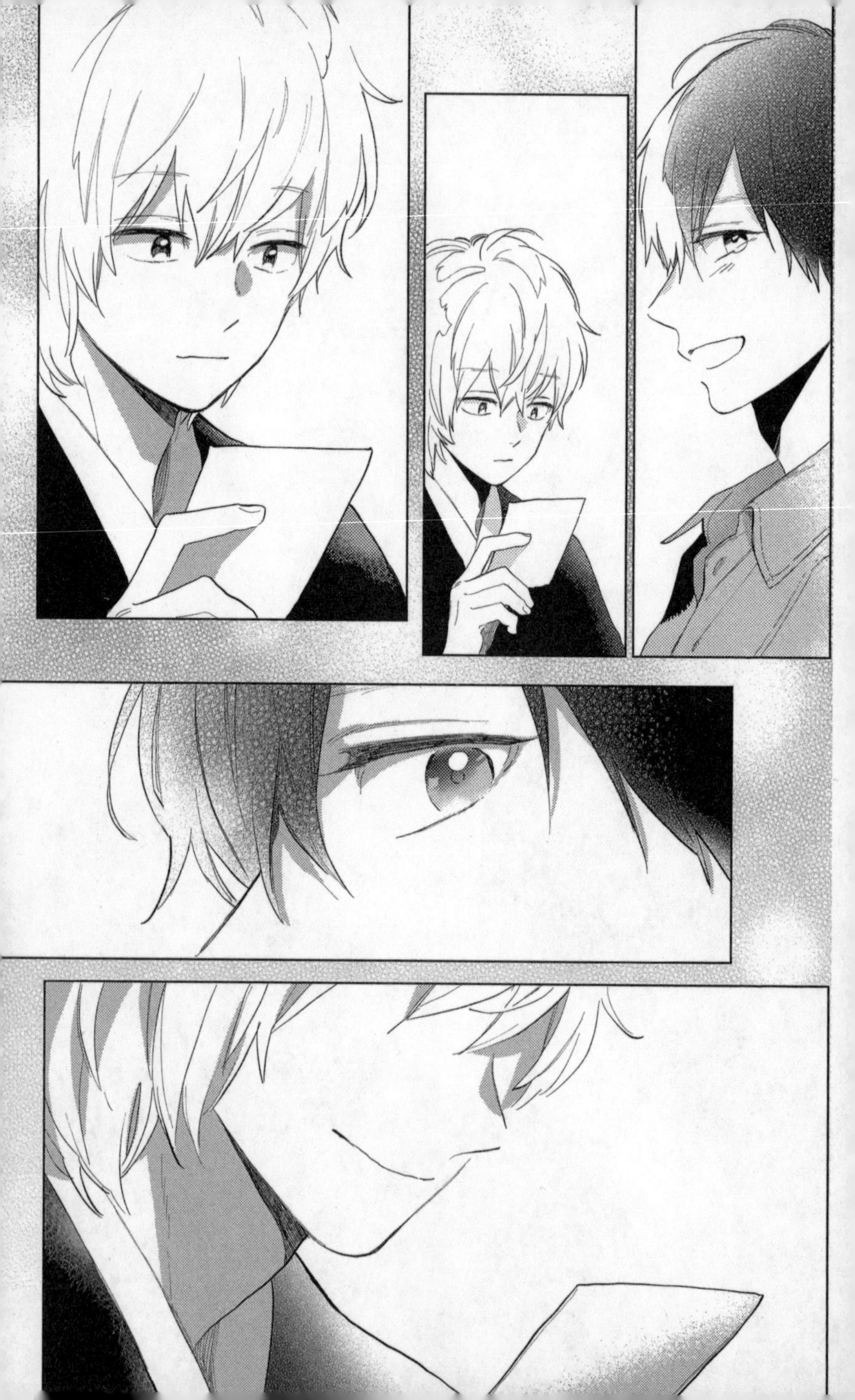

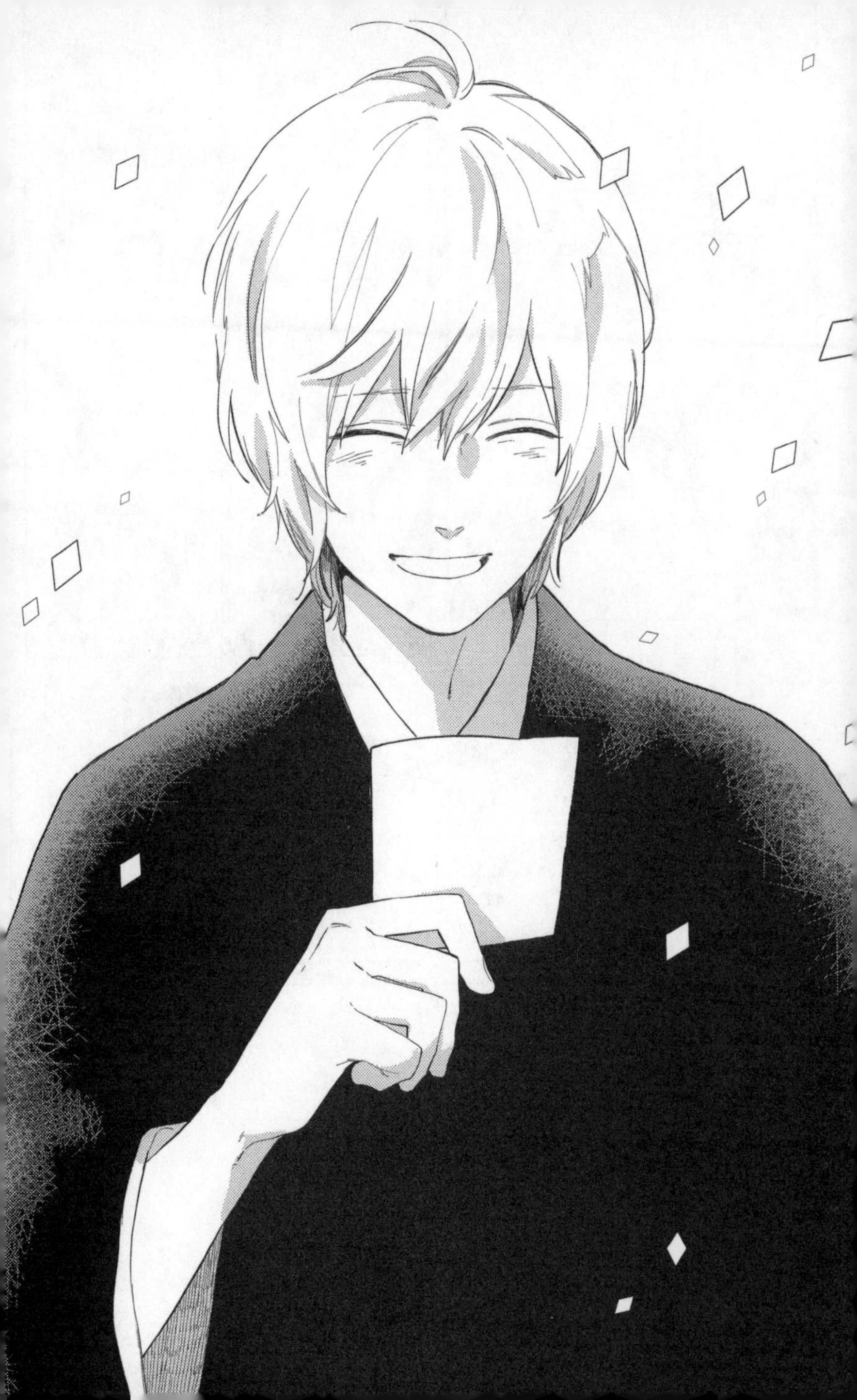

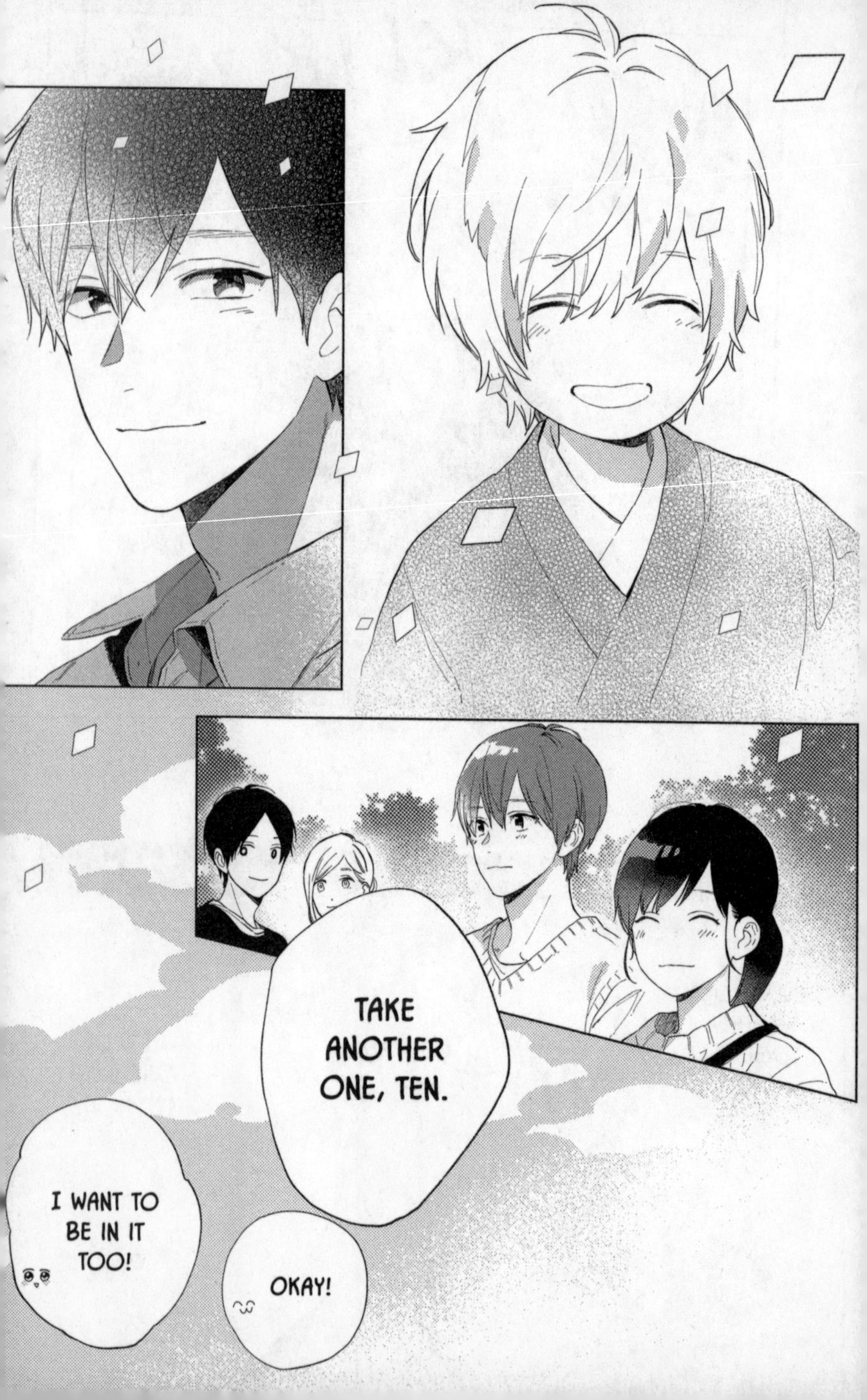
TAKE ANOTHER ONE, TEN.
I WANT TO BE IN IT TOO!
OKAY!

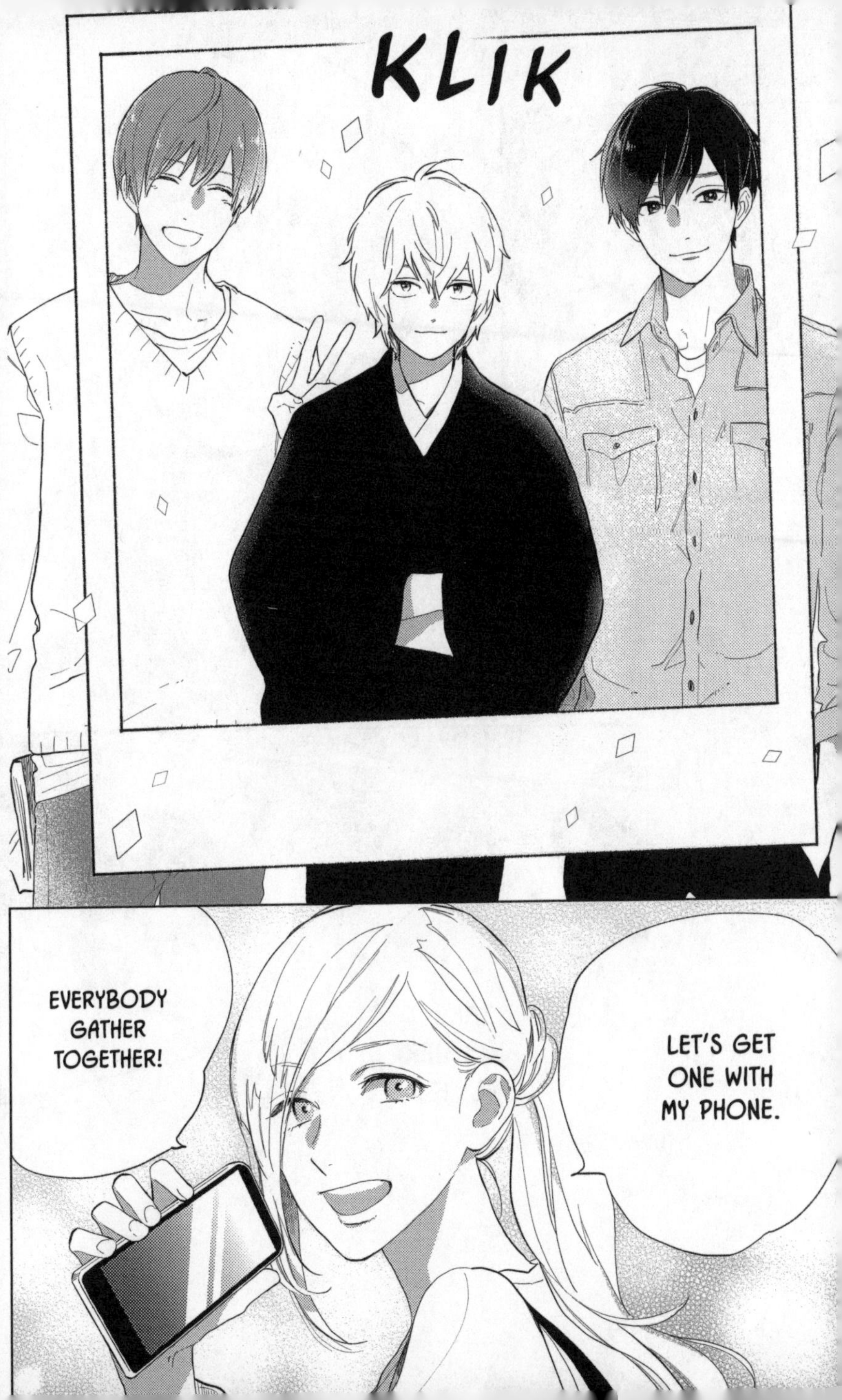
KLIK
LET'S GET ONE WITH MY PHONE.
EVERYBODY GATHER TOGETHER!

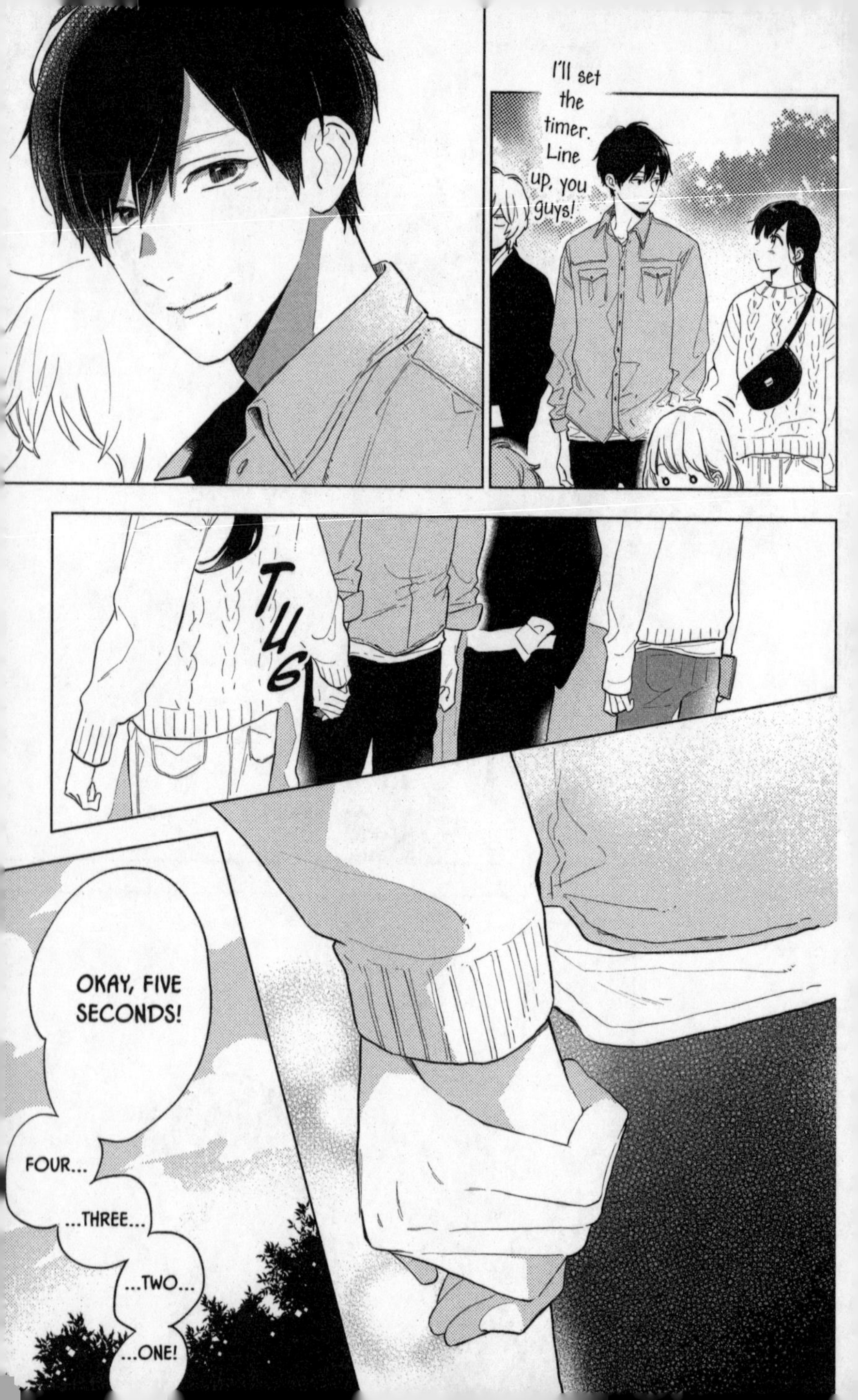
I'll set the timer. Line up, you guys!
TUG
OKAY, FIVE SECONDS!
FOUR...
...THREE...
...TWO...
...ONE!

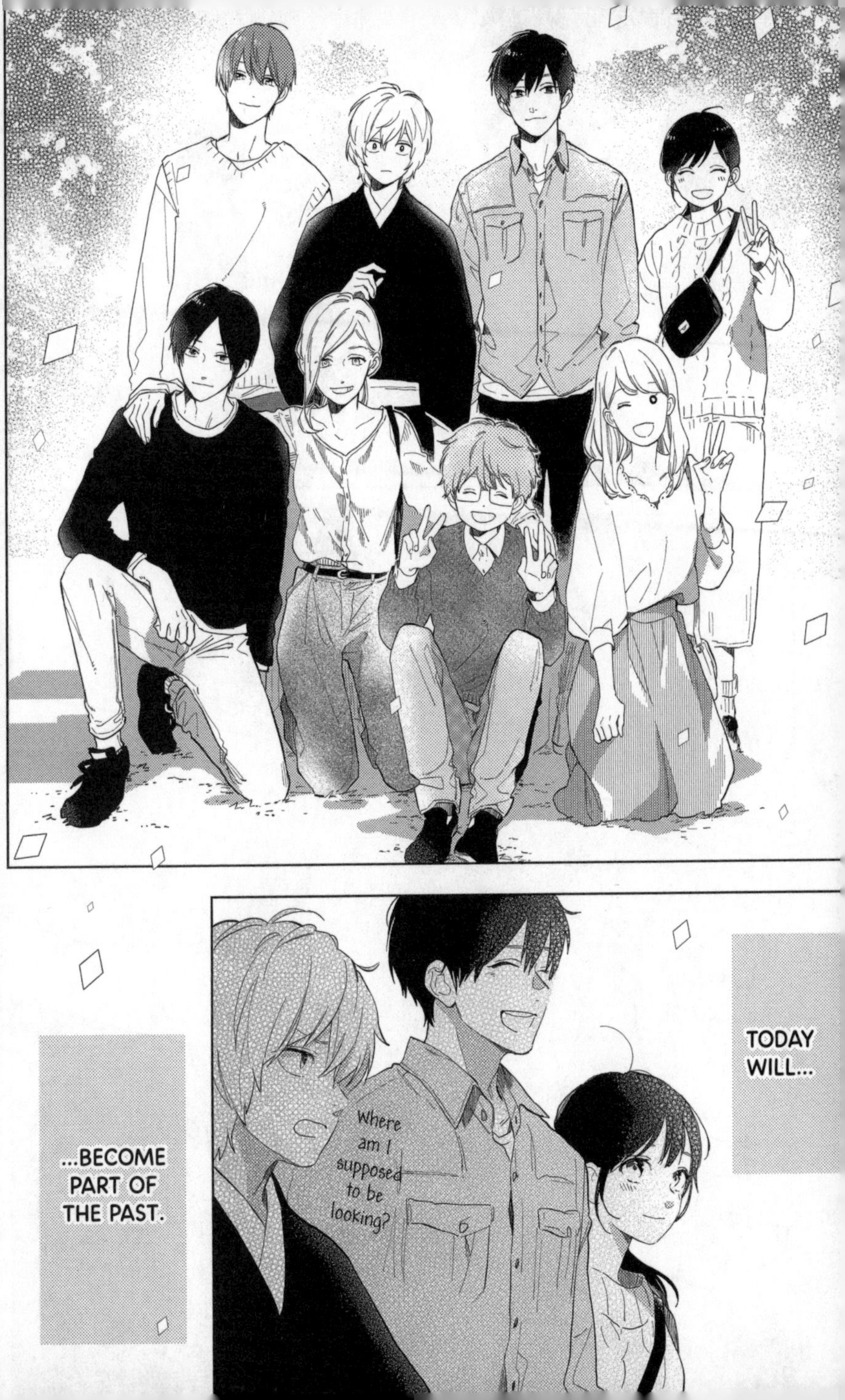
TODAY WILL...
Where am I supposed to be looking?
...BECOME PART OF THE PAST.

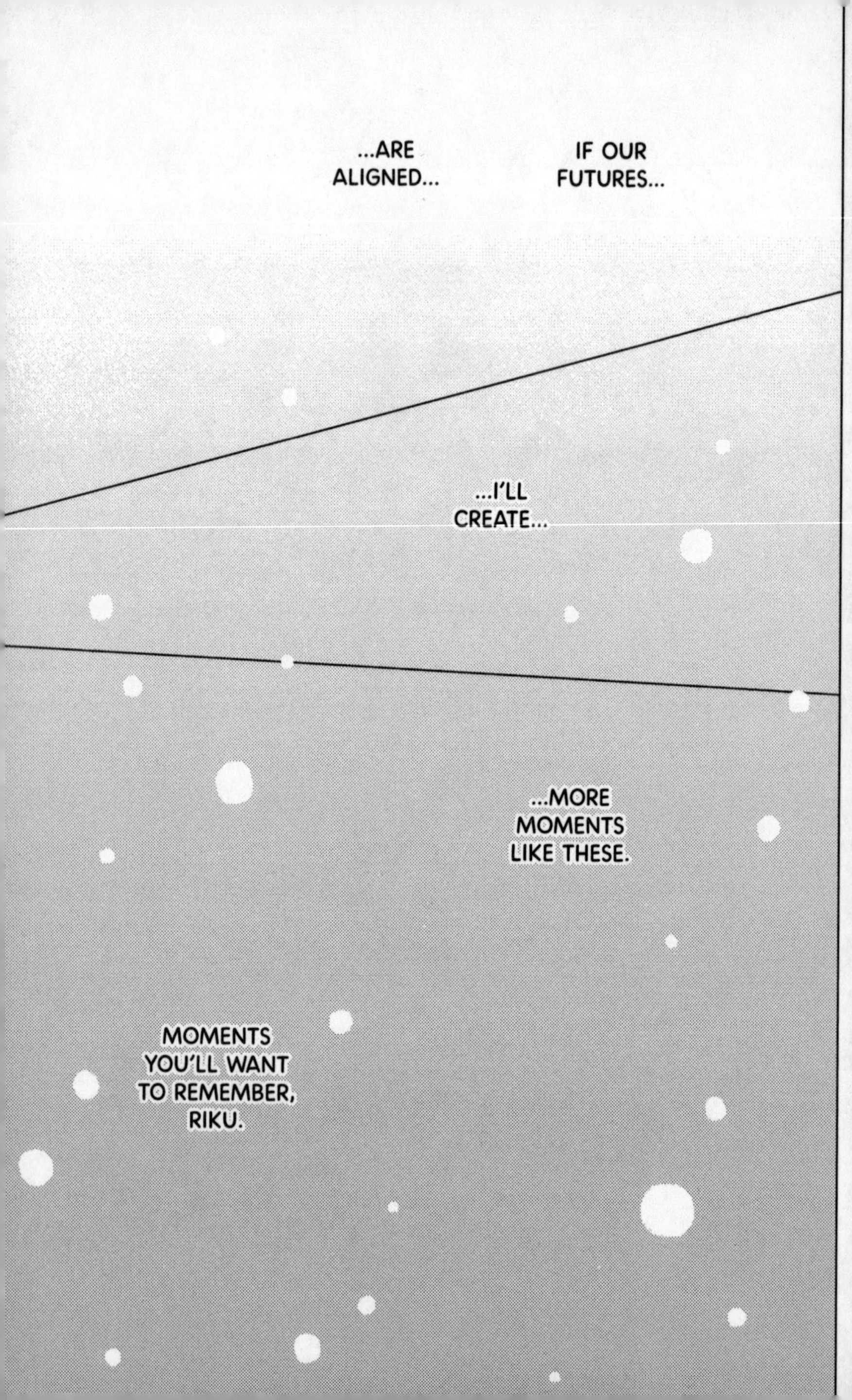
IF OUR FUTURES...
...ARE ALIGNED...
...I'LL CREATE...
...MORE MOMENTS LIKE THESE.
MOMENTS YOU'LL WANT TO REMEMBER, RIKU.

SHORTCAKE CAKE

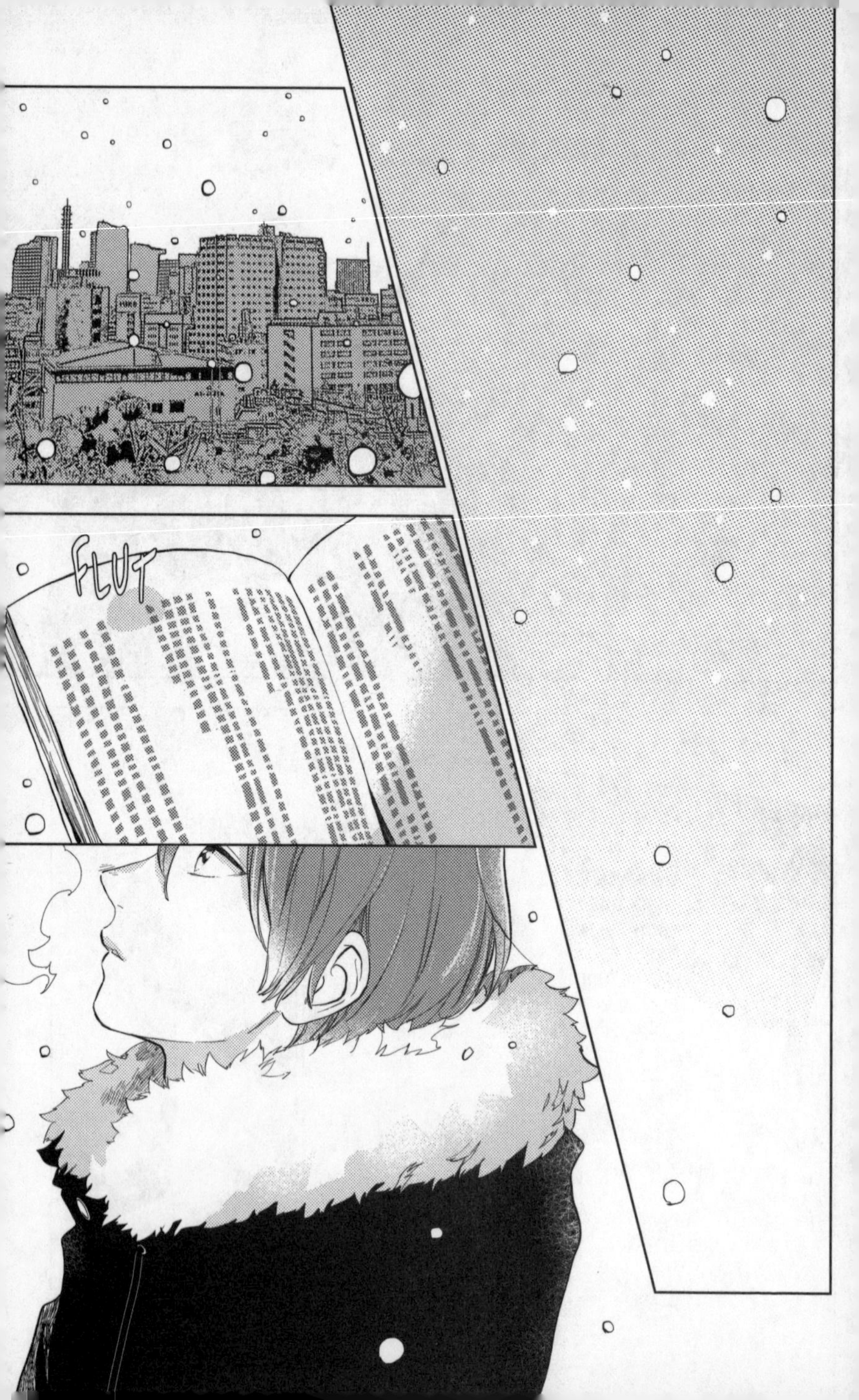
FLUT

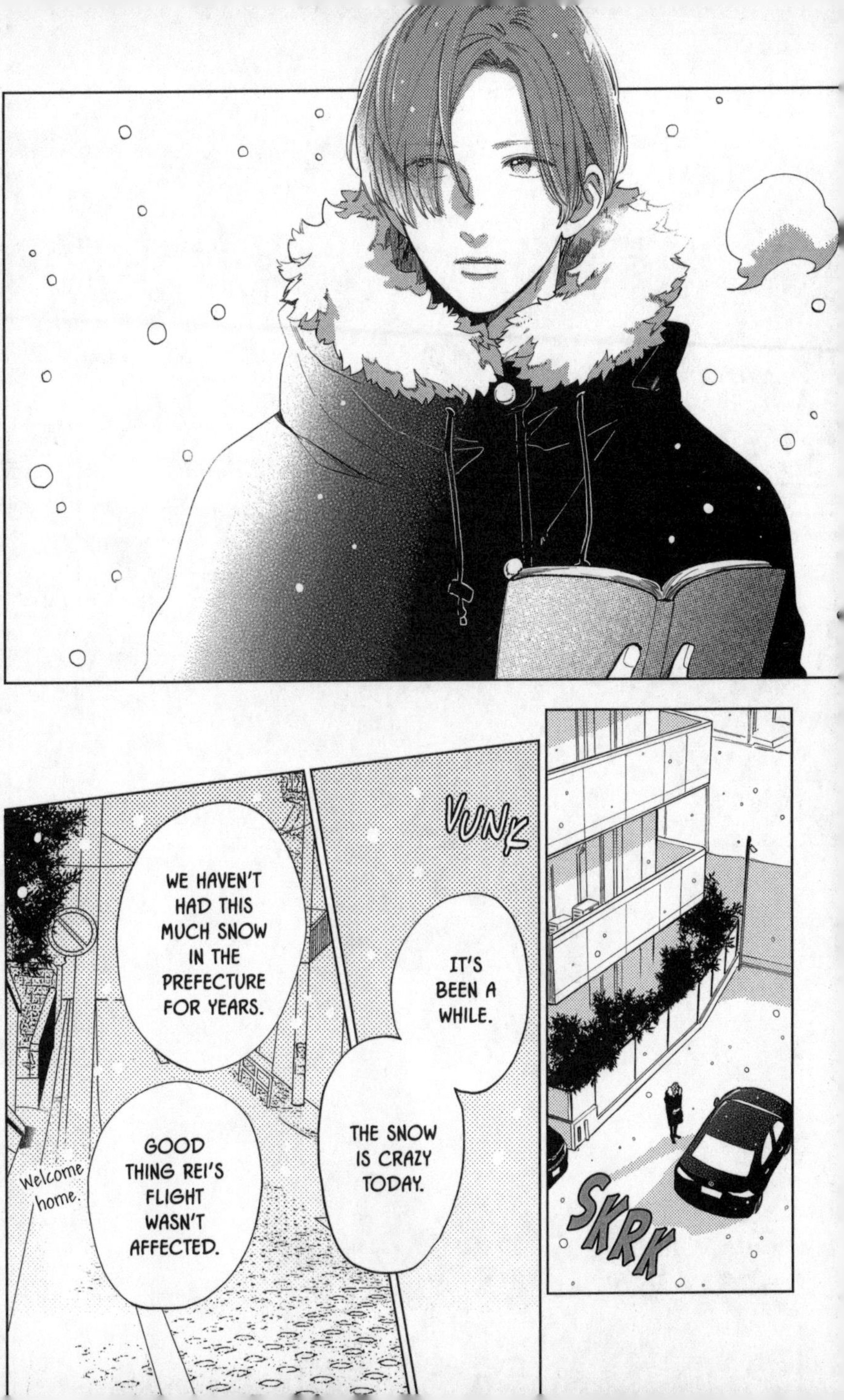
SKRK
VUNK
IT'S BEEN A WHILE.
THE SNOW IS CRAZY TODAY.
WE HAVEN'T HAD THIS MUCH SNOW IN THE PREFECTURE FOR YEARS.
GOOD THING REI'S FLIGHT WASN'T AFFECTED.
Welcome home.

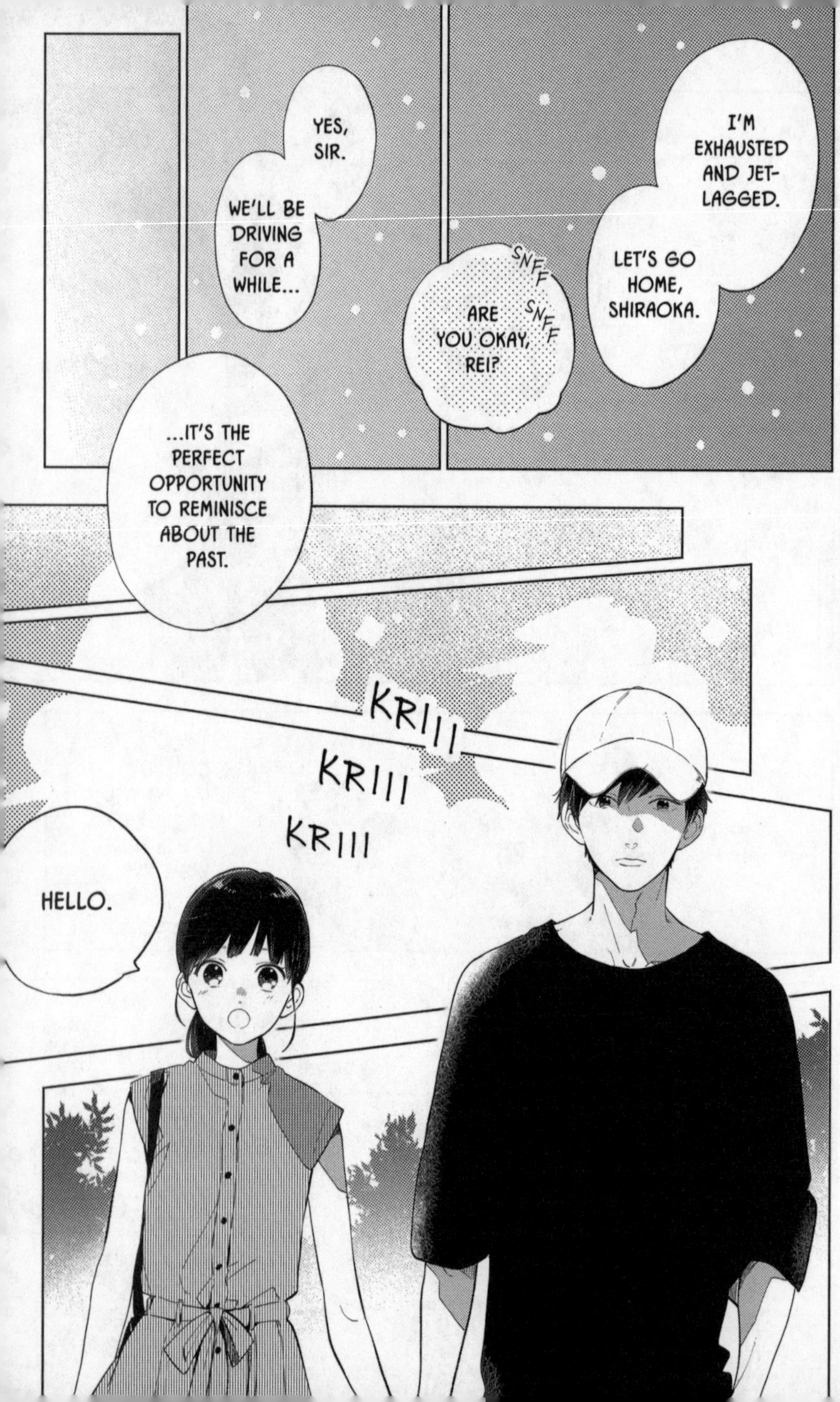
I'M EXHAUSTED AND JET-LAGGED.
LET'S GO HOME, SHIRAOKA.
SNFF SNFF
ARE YOU OKAY, REI?
YES, SIR.
WE'LL BE DRIVING FOR A WHILE...
...IT'S THE PERFECT OPPORTUNITY TO REMINISCE ABOUT THE PAST.
KRIII KRIII KRIII
HELLO.

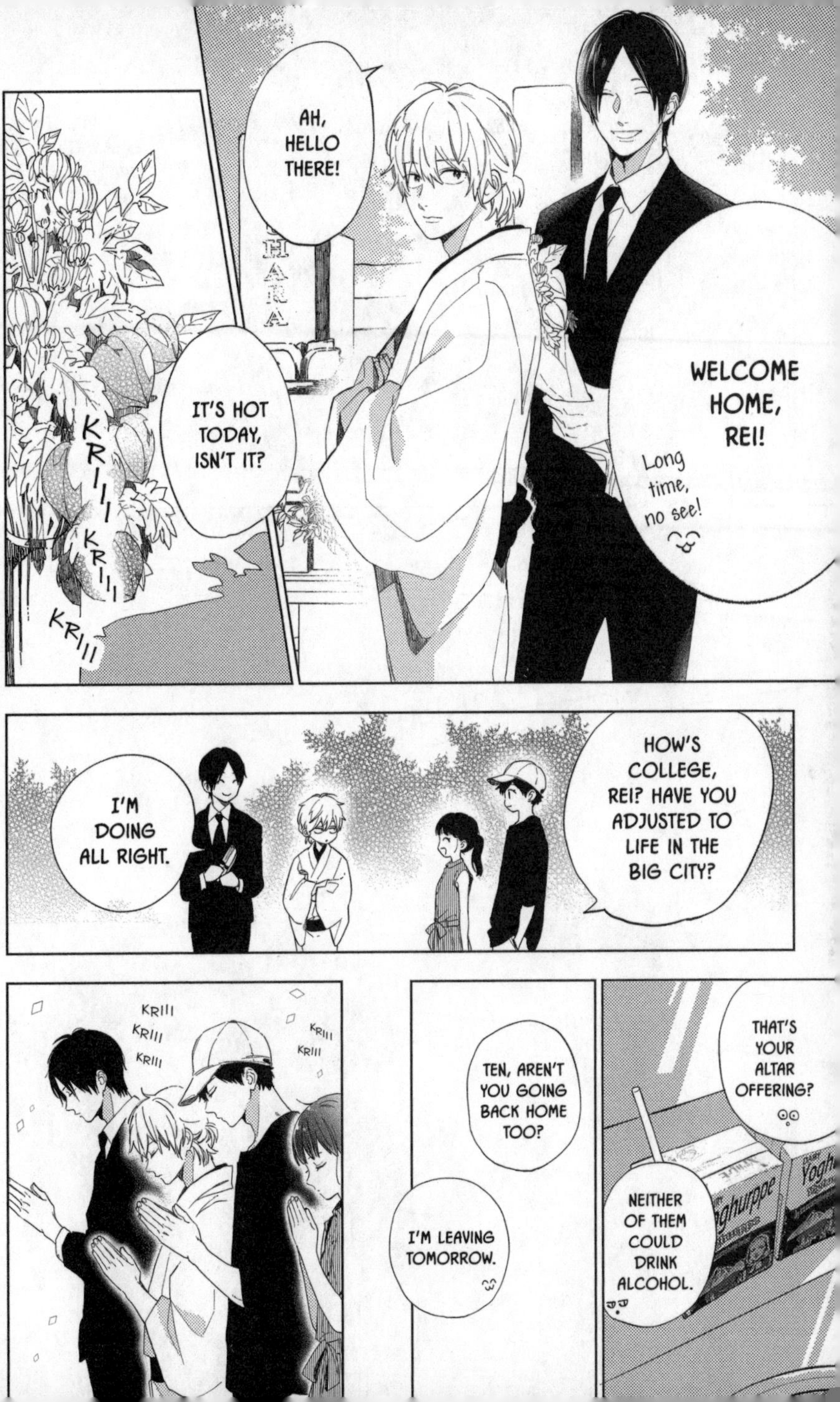
WELCOME HOME, REI!
Long time, no see!
AH, HELLO THERE!
HARA
IT'S HOT TODAY, ISN'T IT?
KRIII
KRIII
KRIII
HOW'S COLLEGE, REI? HAVE YOU ADJUSTED TO LIFE IN THE BIG CITY?
I'M DOING ALL RIGHT.
THAT'S YOUR ALTAR OFFERING?
Yoghurppe
NEITHER OF THEM COULD DRINK ALCOHOL.
TEN, AREN'T YOU GOING BACK HOME TOO?
I'M LEAVING TOMORROW.
KRIII
KRIII
KRIII
KRIII
KRIII

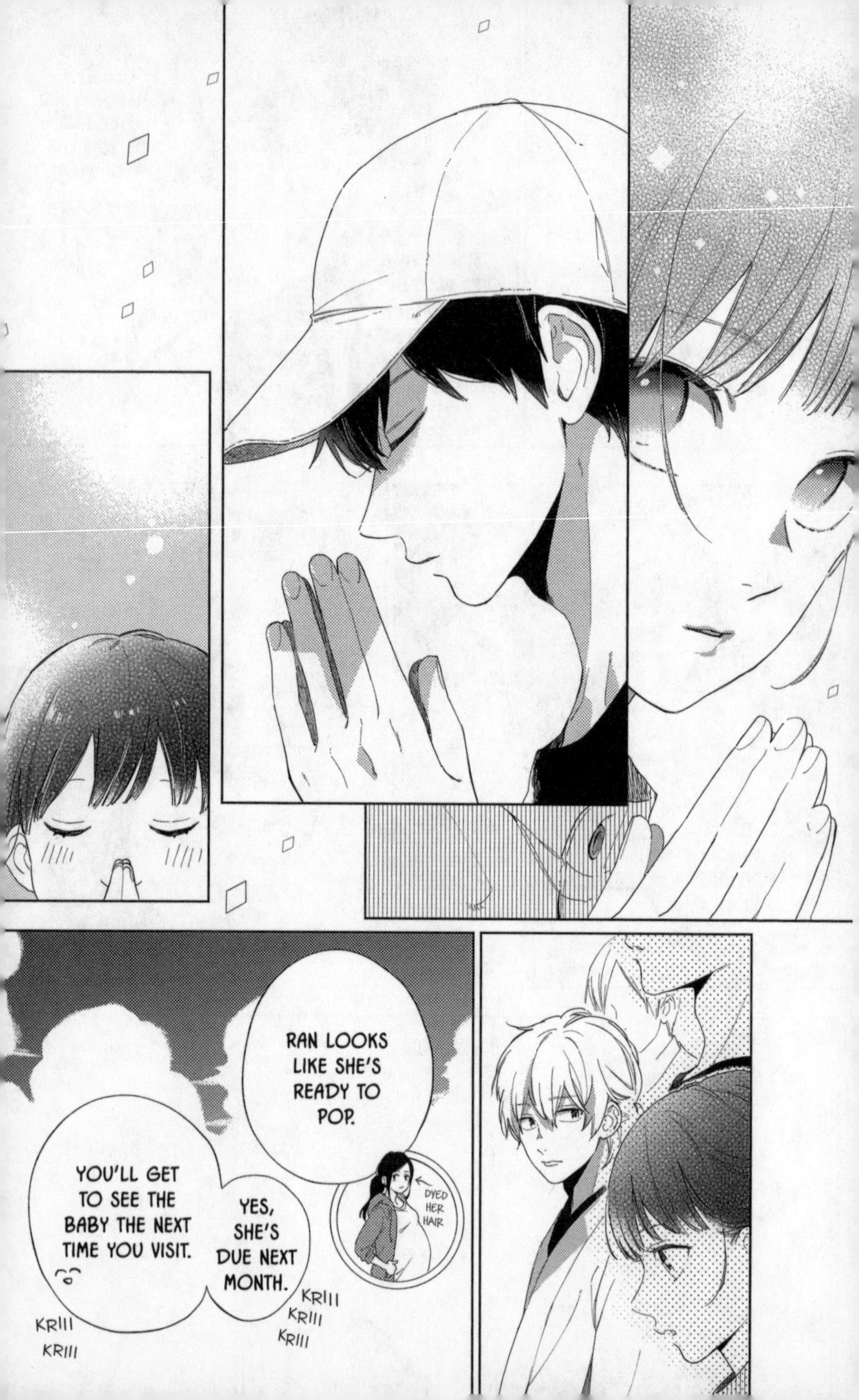
RAN LOOKS LIKE SHE'S READY TO POP.
DYED HER HAIR
YES, SHE'S DUE NEXT MONTH.
KRIII KRIII KRIII
YOU'LL GET TO SEE THE BABY THE NEXT TIME YOU VISIT.
KRIII KRIII

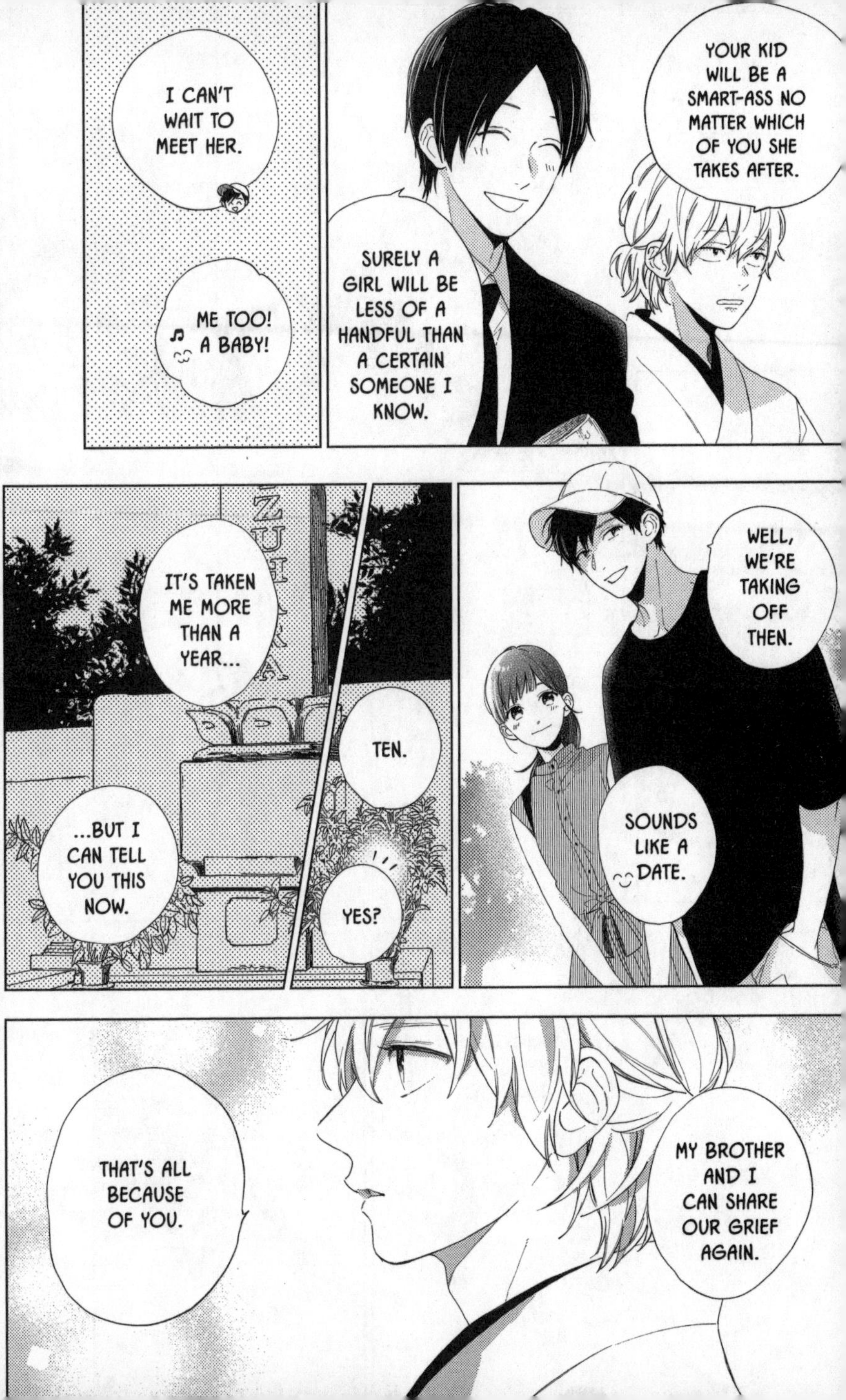
YOUR KID WILL BE A SMART-ASS NO MATTER WHICH OF YOU SHE TAKES AFTER.
SURELY A GIRL WILL BE LESS OF A HANDFUL THAN A CERTAIN SOMEONE I KNOW.
I CAN'T WAIT TO MEET HER.
ME TOO! A BABY!
WELL, WE'RE TAKING OFF THEN.
SOUNDS LIKE A DATE.
TEN.
YES?
IT'S TAKEN ME MORE THAN A YEAR...
...BUT I CAN TELL YOU THIS NOW.
MY BROTHER AND I CAN SHARE OUR GRIEF AGAIN.
THAT'S ALL BECAUSE OF YOU.

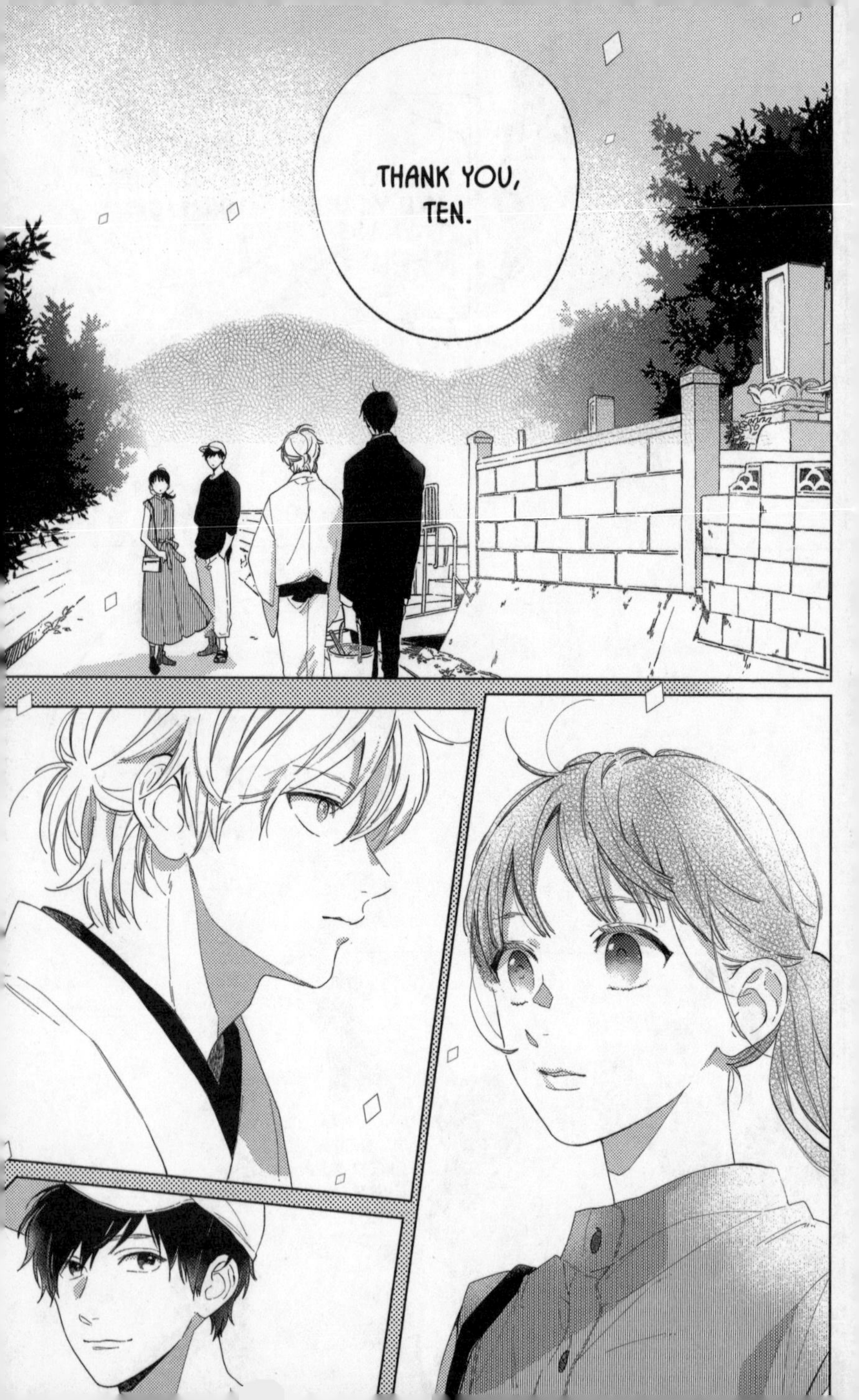
THANK YOU, TEN.

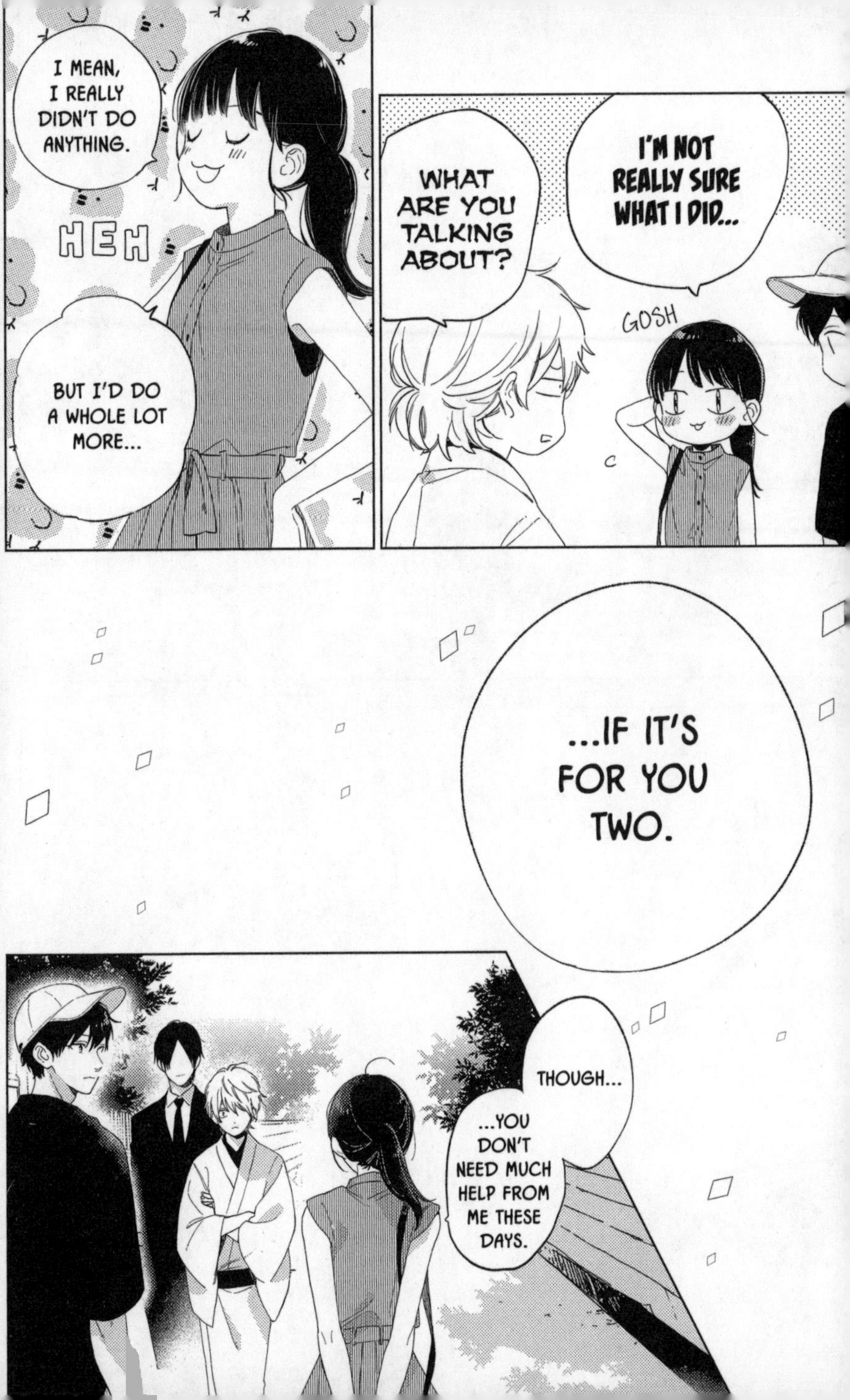
I'M NOT REALLY SURE WHAT I DID...
WHAT ARE YOU TALKING ABOUT?
GOSH
I MEAN, I REALLY DIDN'T DO ANYTHING.
HEH
BUT I'D DO A WHOLE LOT MORE...
...IF IT'S FOR YOU TWO.
THOUGH...
...YOU DON'T NEED MUCH HELP FROM ME THESE DAYS.

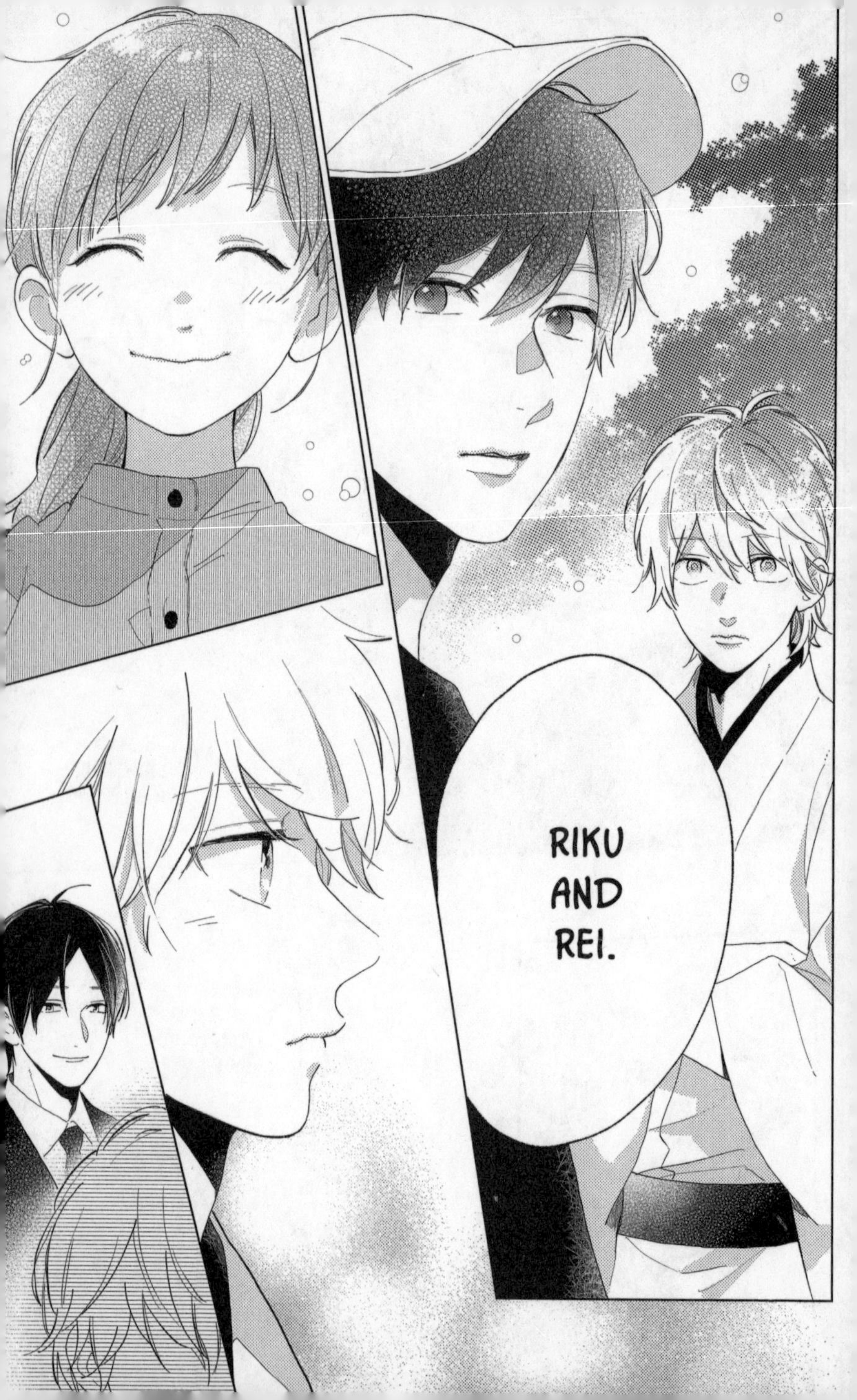
RIKU AND REI.

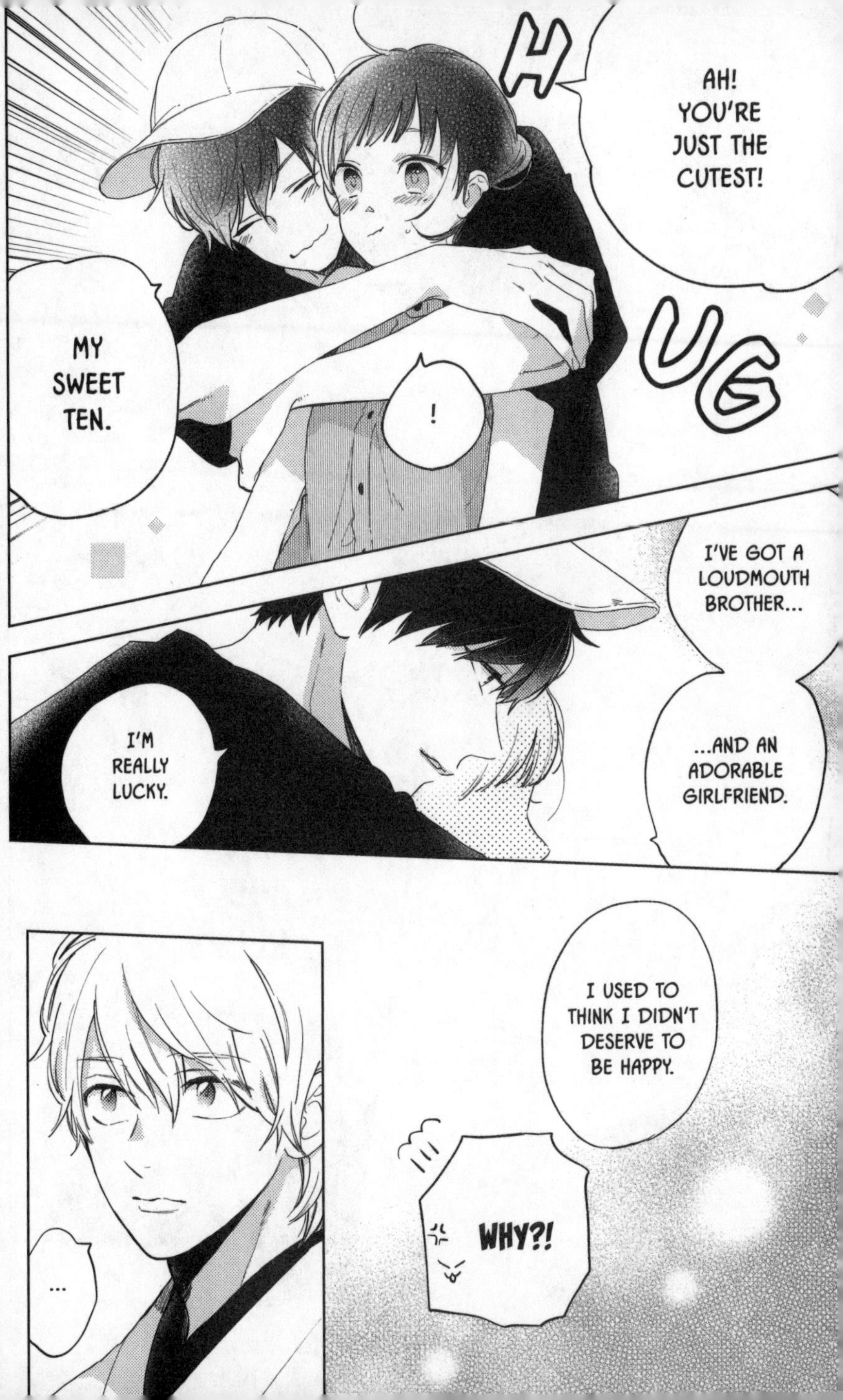
AH! YOU'RE JUST THE CUTEST!
HUG
!
MY SWEET TEN.
I'VE GOT A LOUDMOUTH BROTHER...
...AND AN ADORABLE GIRLFRIEND.
I'M REALLY LUCKY.
I USED TO THINK I DIDN'T DESERVE TO BE HAPPY.
WHY?!
...

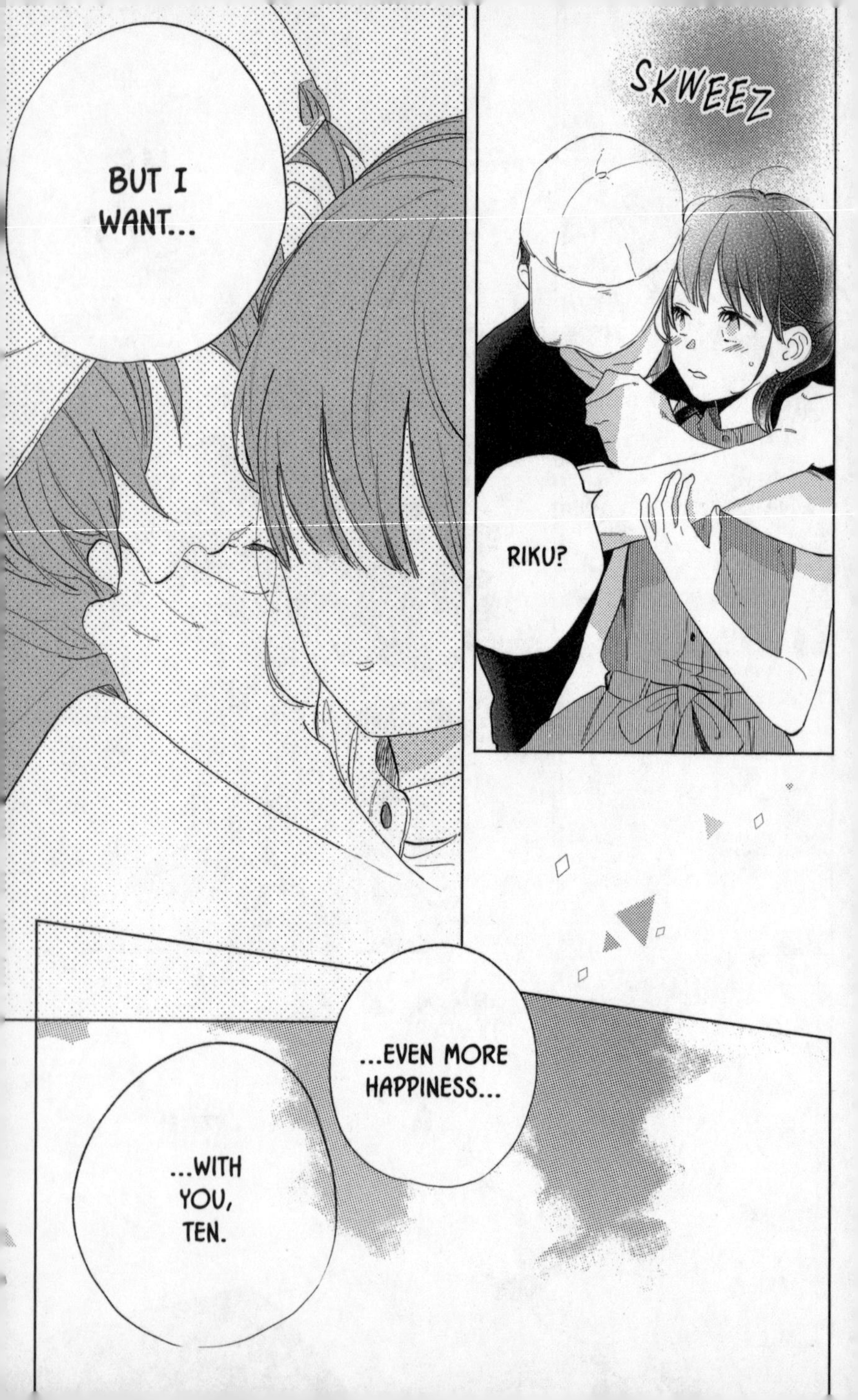
SKWEEZ
RIKU?
BUT I WANT...
...EVEN MORE HAPPINESS...
...WITH YOU, TEN.

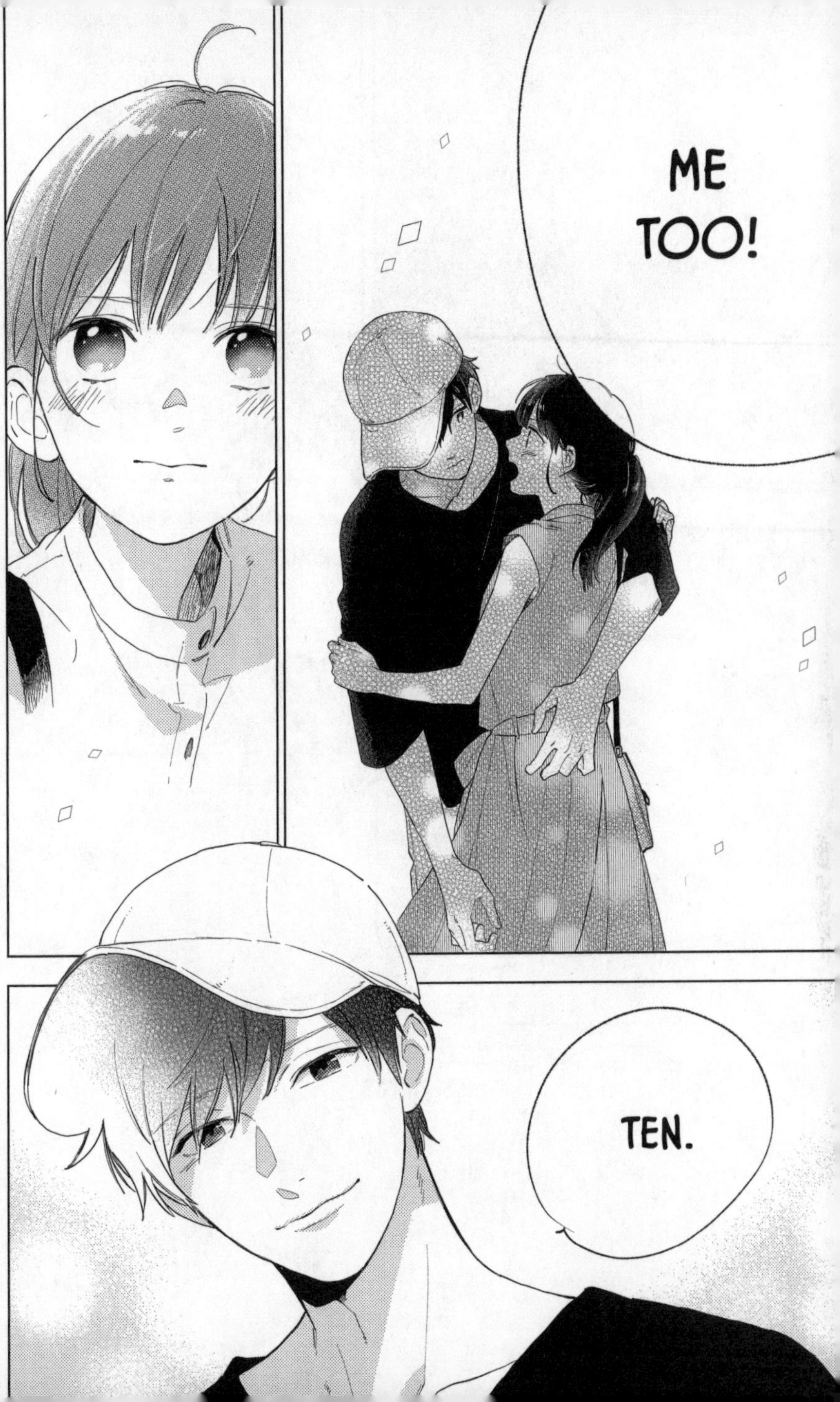
ME TOO!
TEN.

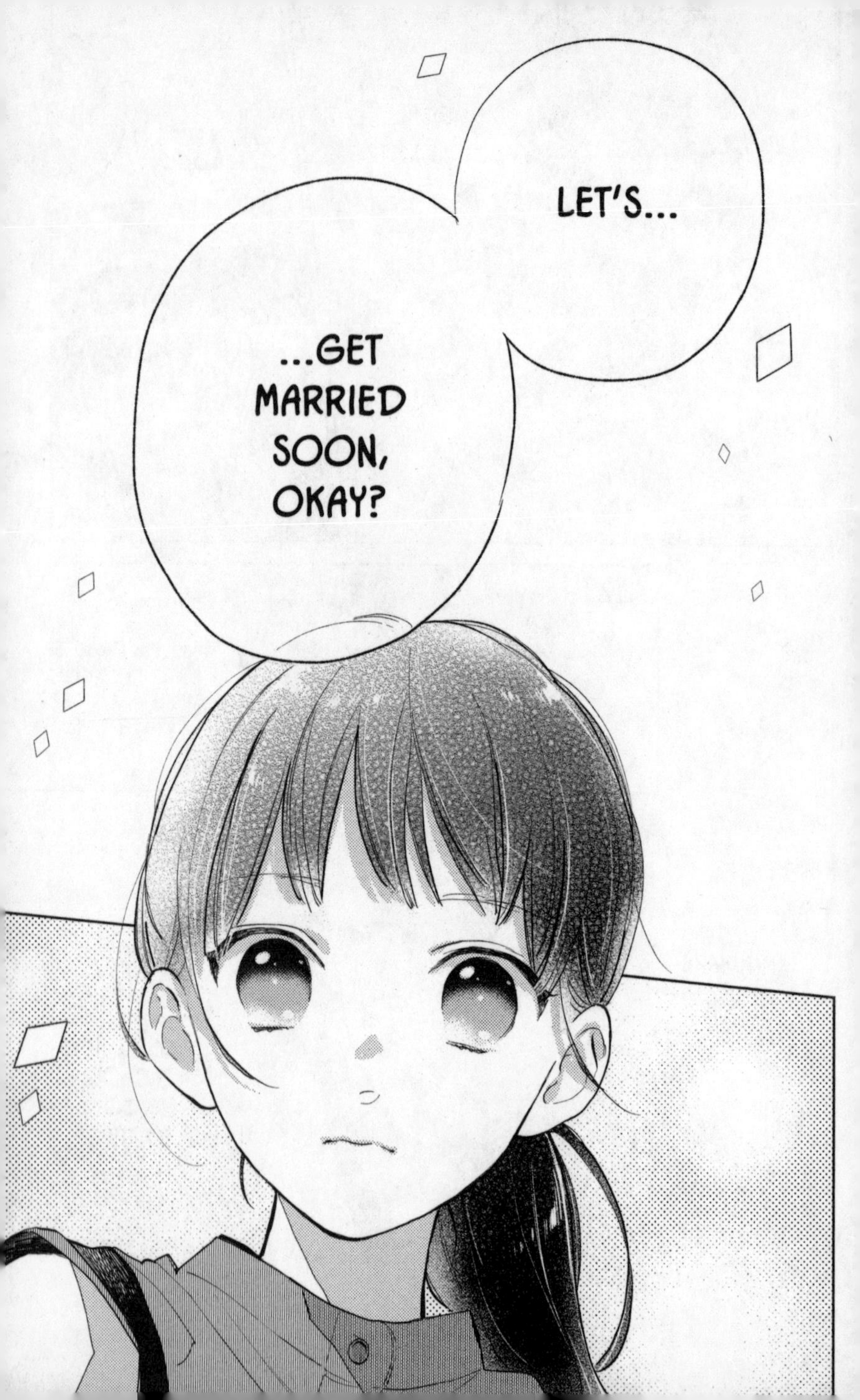
LET'S...
...GET MARRIED SOON, OKAY?

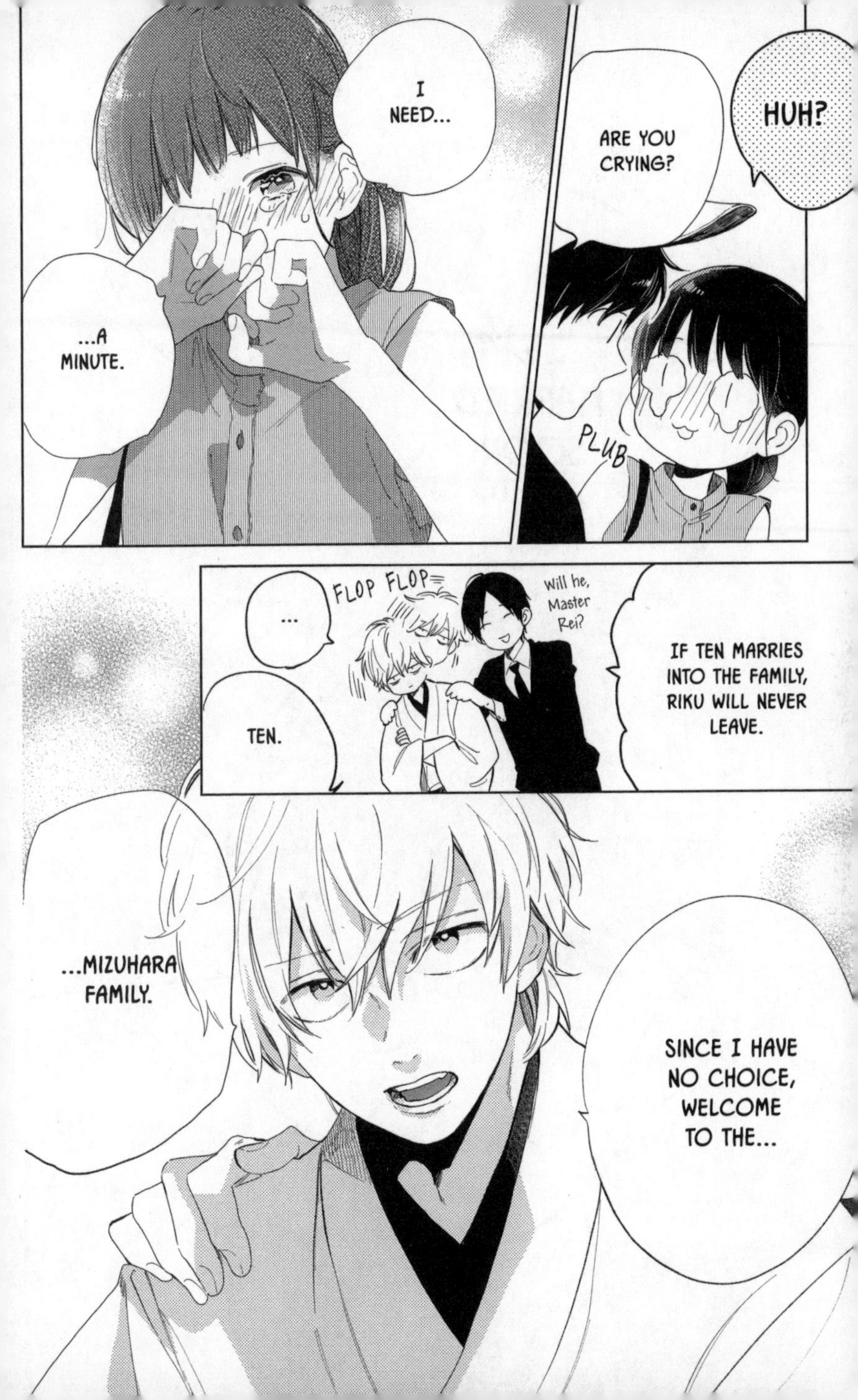
HUH?
ARE YOU CRYING?
PLUB
I NEED...
...A MINUTE.
IF TEN MARRIES INTO THE FAMILY, RIKU WILL NEVER LEAVE.
Will he, Master Rei?
FLOP FLOP
...
TEN.
SINCE I HAVE NO CHOICE, WELCOME TO THE...
...MIZUHARA FAMILY.

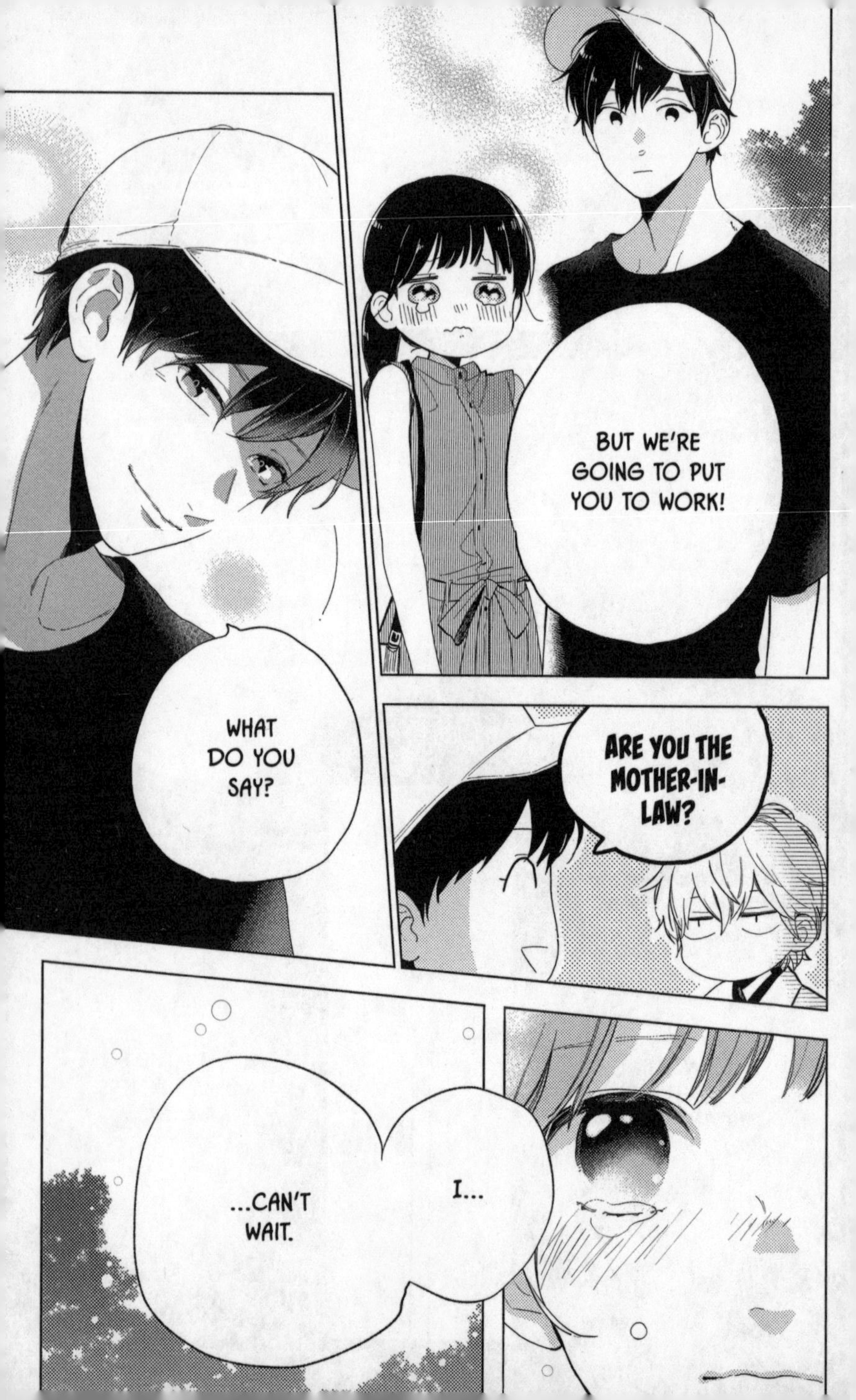
BUT WE'RE GOING TO PUT YOU TO WORK!
WHAT DO YOU SAY?
ARE YOU THE MOTHER-IN-LAW?
I...
...CAN'T WAIT.

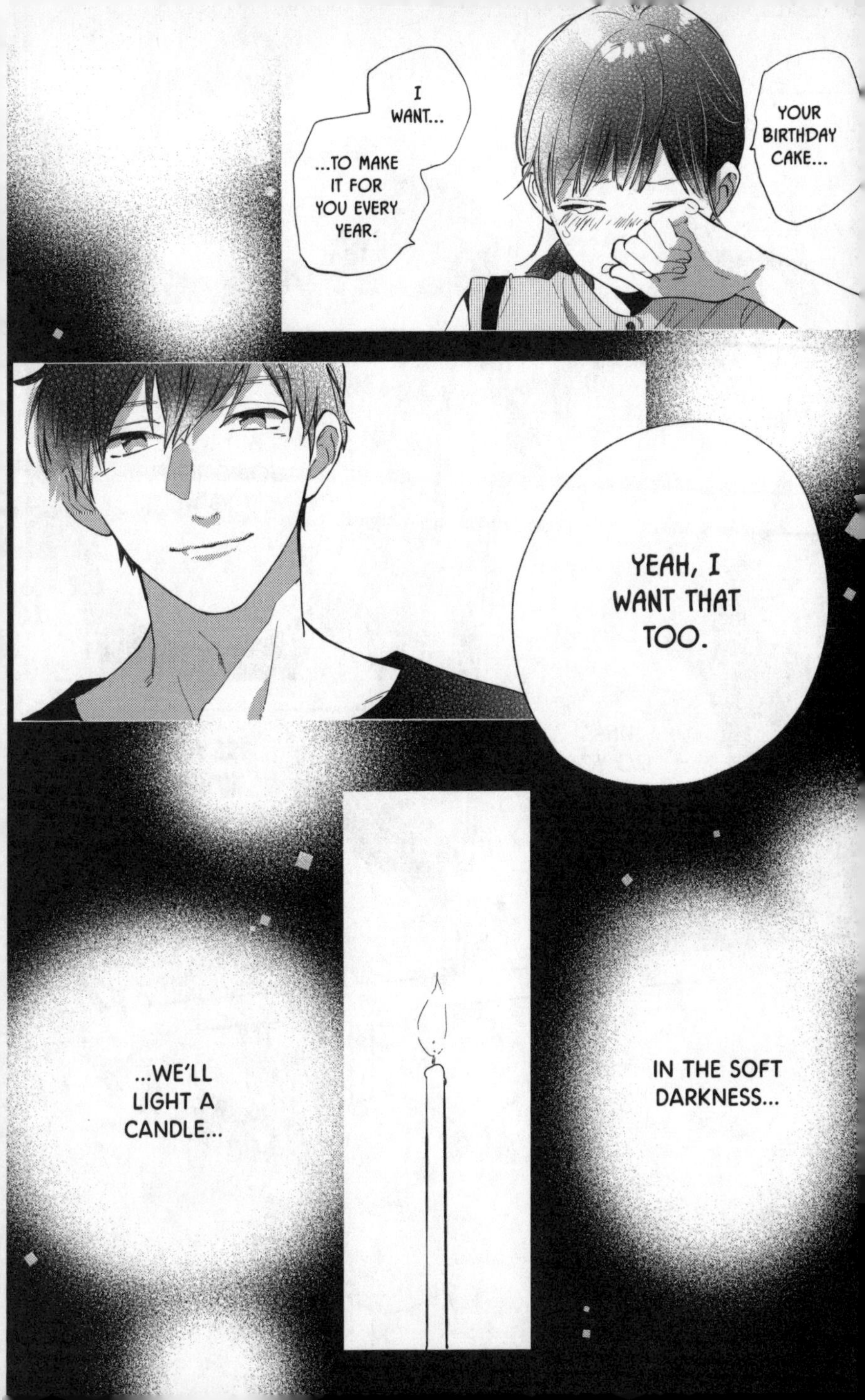
YOUR BIRTHDAY CAKE...
I WANT...
...TO MAKE IT FOR YOU EVERY YEAR.
YEAH, I WANT THAT TOO.
IN THE SOFT DARKNESS...
...WE'LL LIGHT A CANDLE...

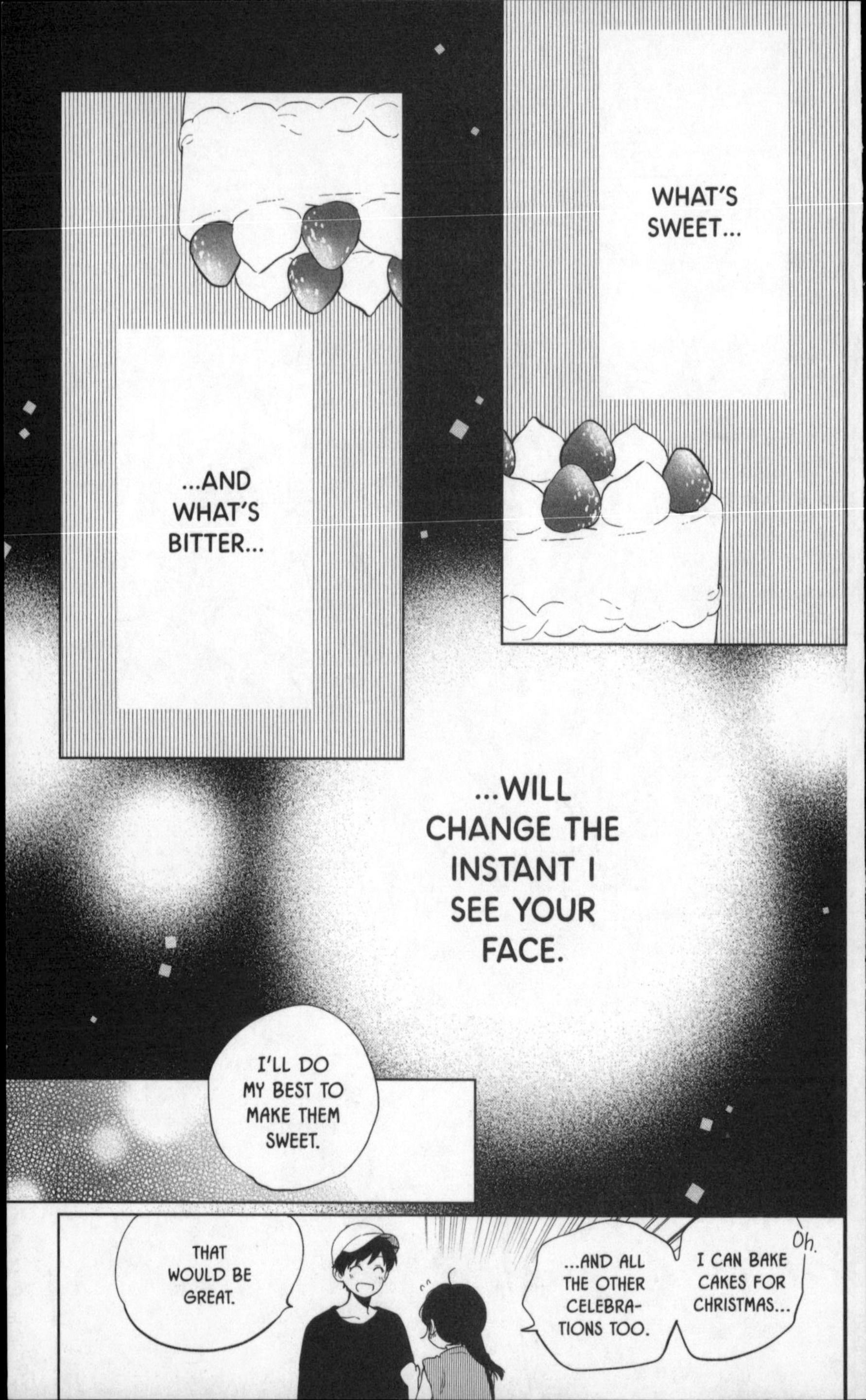
WHAT'S SWEET...
...AND WHAT'S BITTER...
...WILL CHANGE THE INSTANT I SEE YOUR FACE.
I'LL DO MY BEST TO MAKE THEM SWEET.
Oh.
I CAN BAKE CAKES FOR CHRISTMAS...
...AND ALL THE OTHER CELEBRA-TIONS TOO.
THAT WOULD BE GREAT.

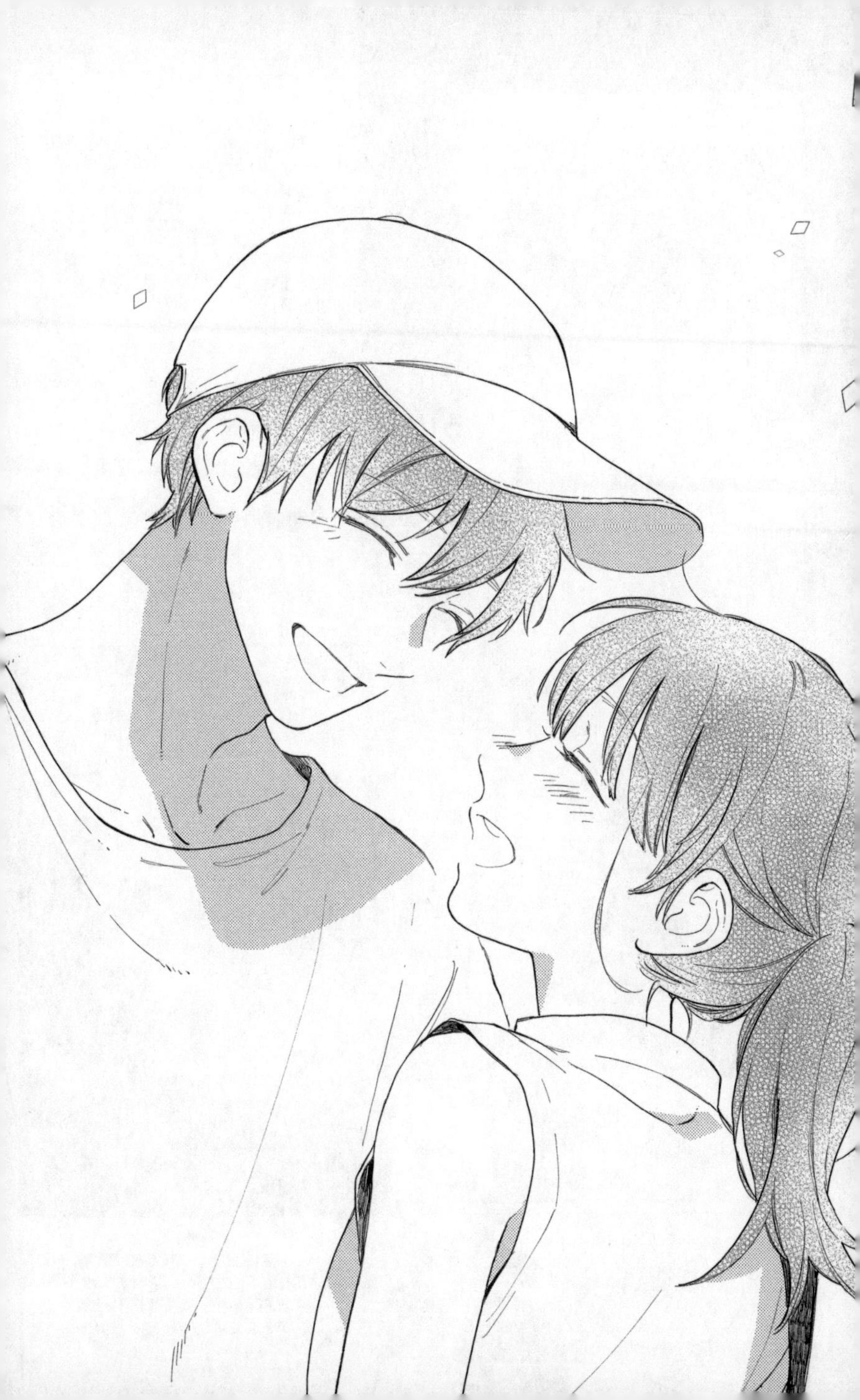

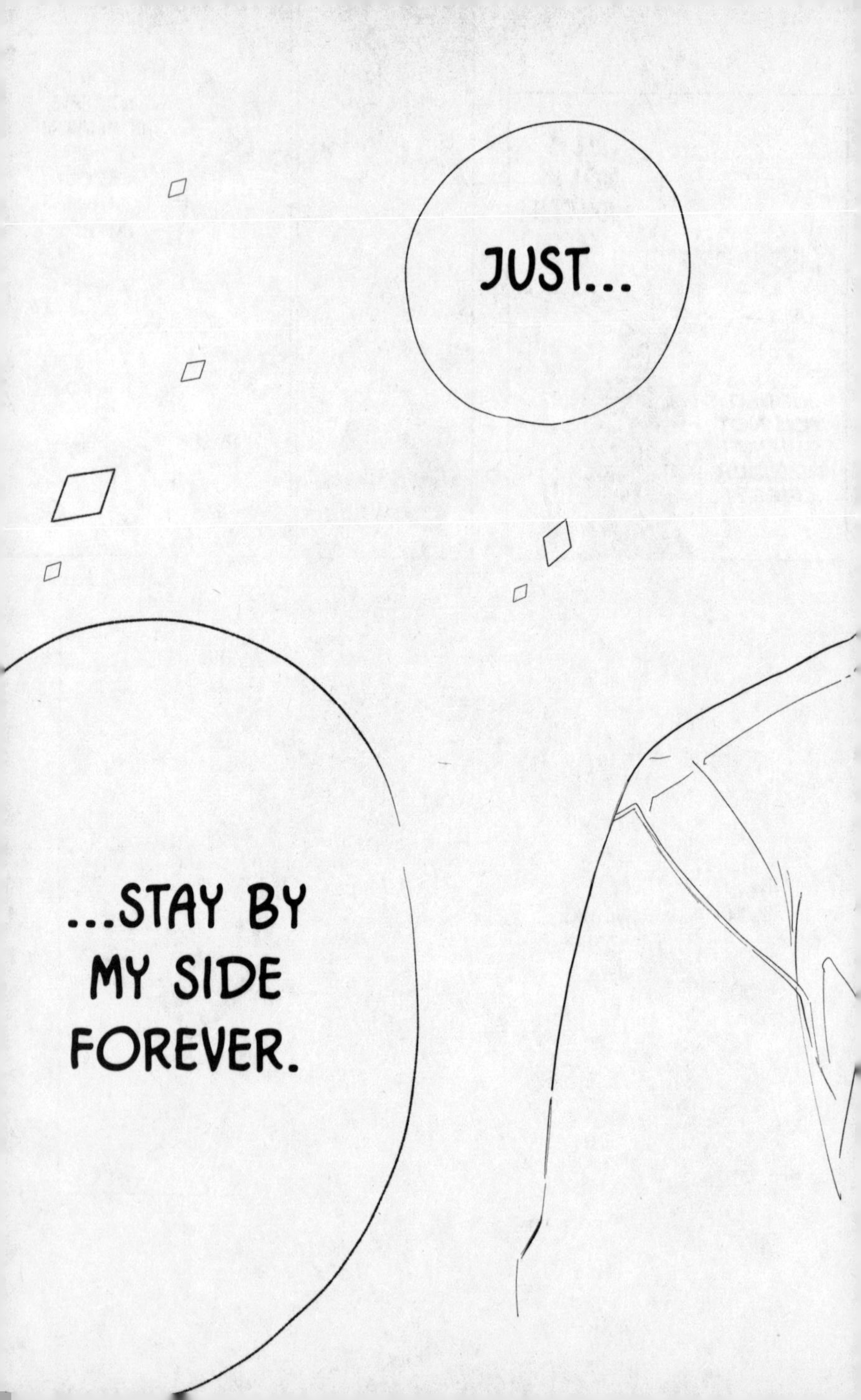
JUST...
...STAY BY MY SIDE FOREVER.

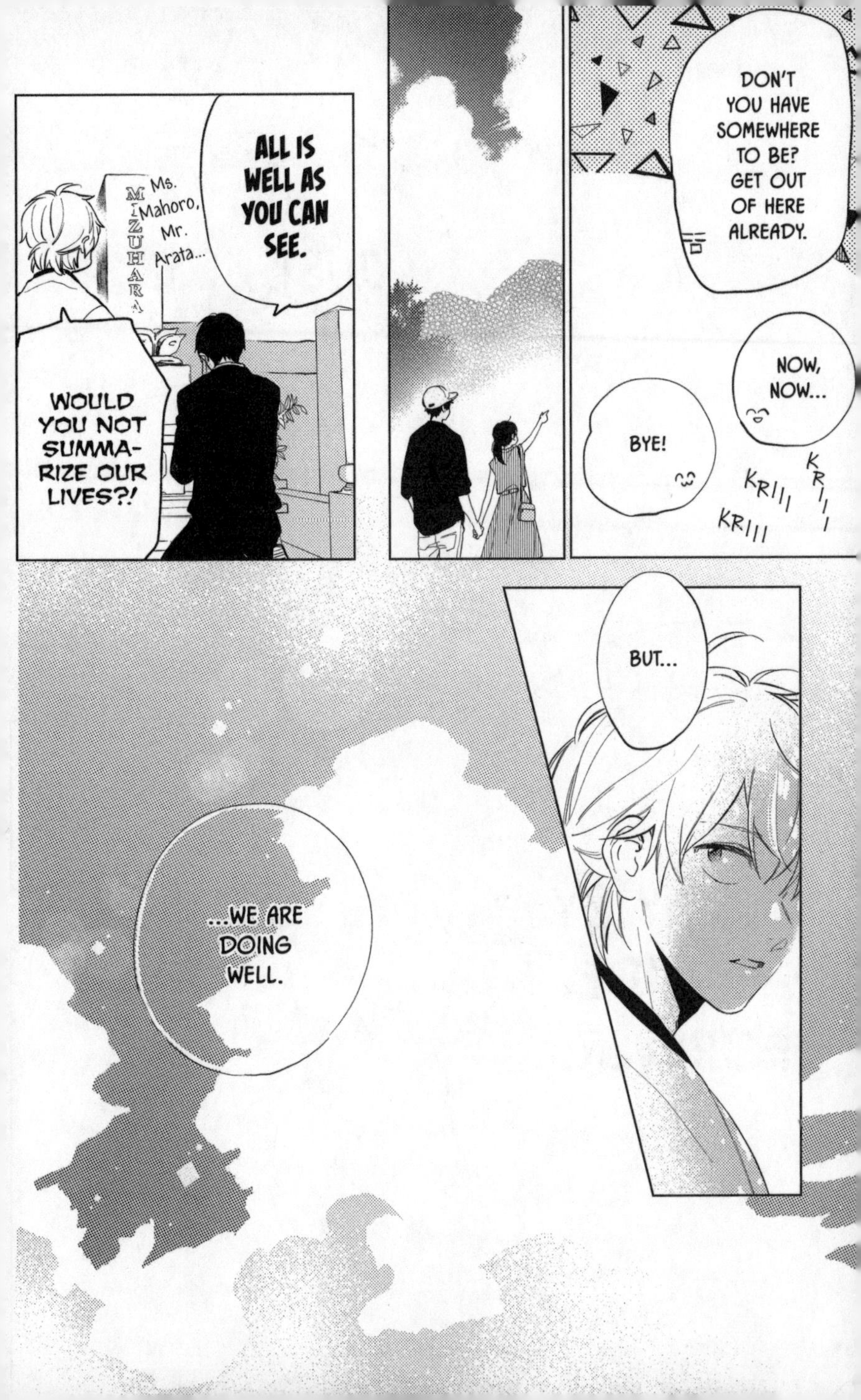
DON'T YOU HAVE SOMEWHERE TO BE? GET OUT OF HERE ALREADY.
NOW, NOW...
BYE!
KRIII
KRIII
KRIII
ALL IS WELL AS YOU CAN SEE.
Ms. Mahoro, Mr. Arata...
MIZUHARA
WOULD YOU NOT SUMMA-RIZE OUR LIVES?!
BUT...
...WE ARE DOING WELL.

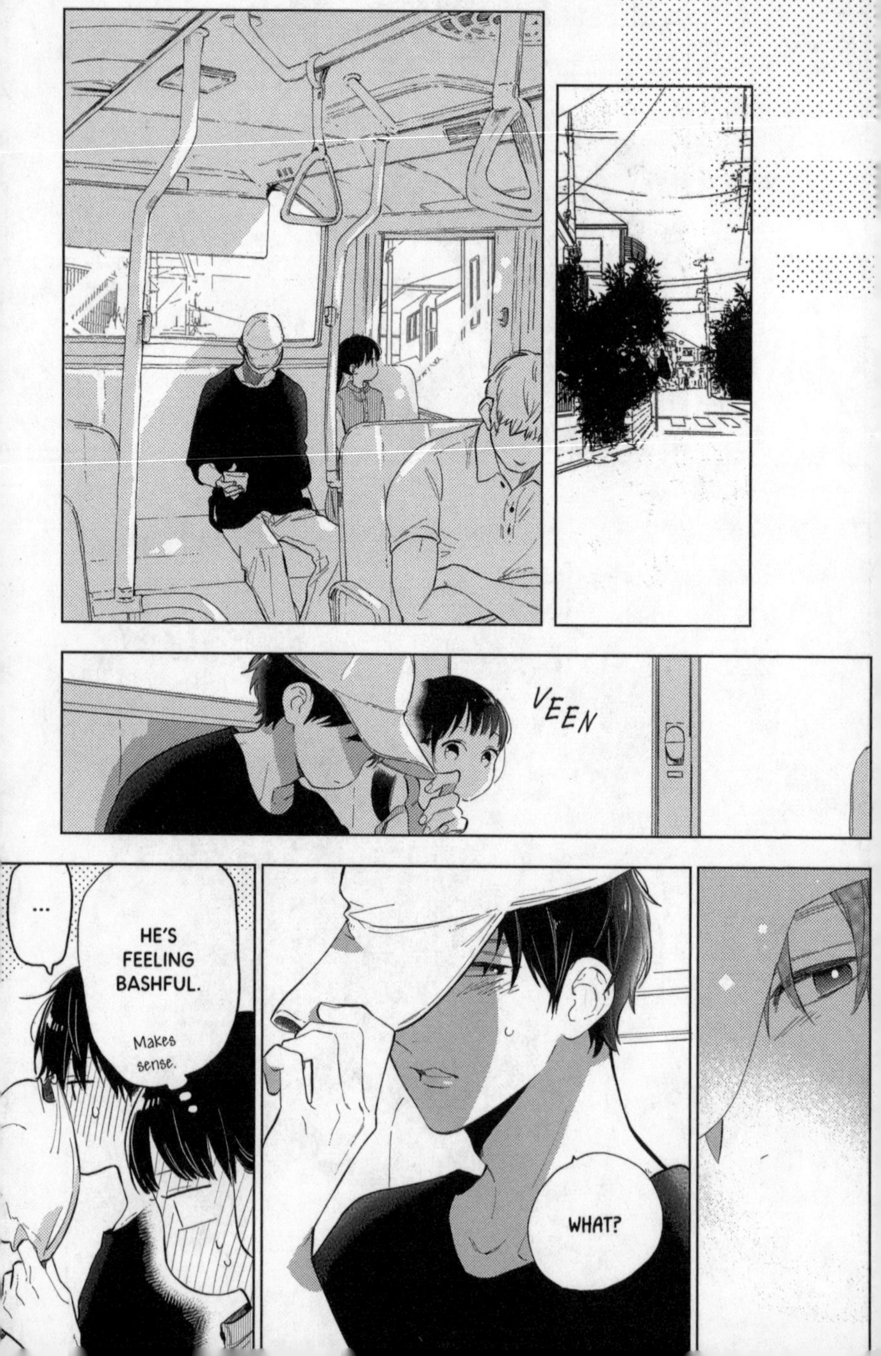
VEEN
WHAT?
...
HE'S FEELING BASHFUL.
Makes sense.

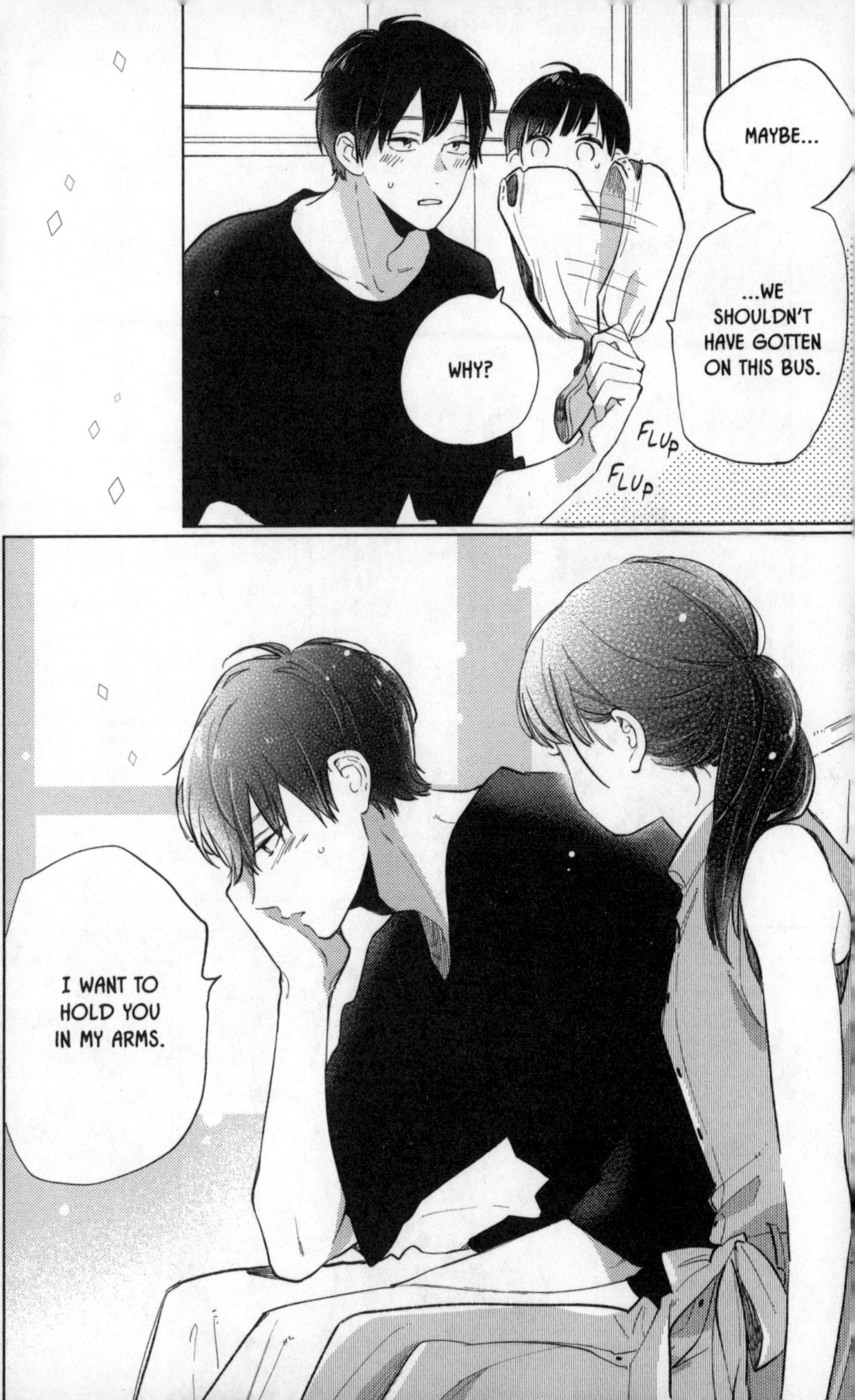
MAYBE...
...WE SHOULDN'T HAVE GOTTEN ON THIS BUS.
FLUP
FLUP
WHY?
I WANT TO HOLD YOU IN MY ARMS.

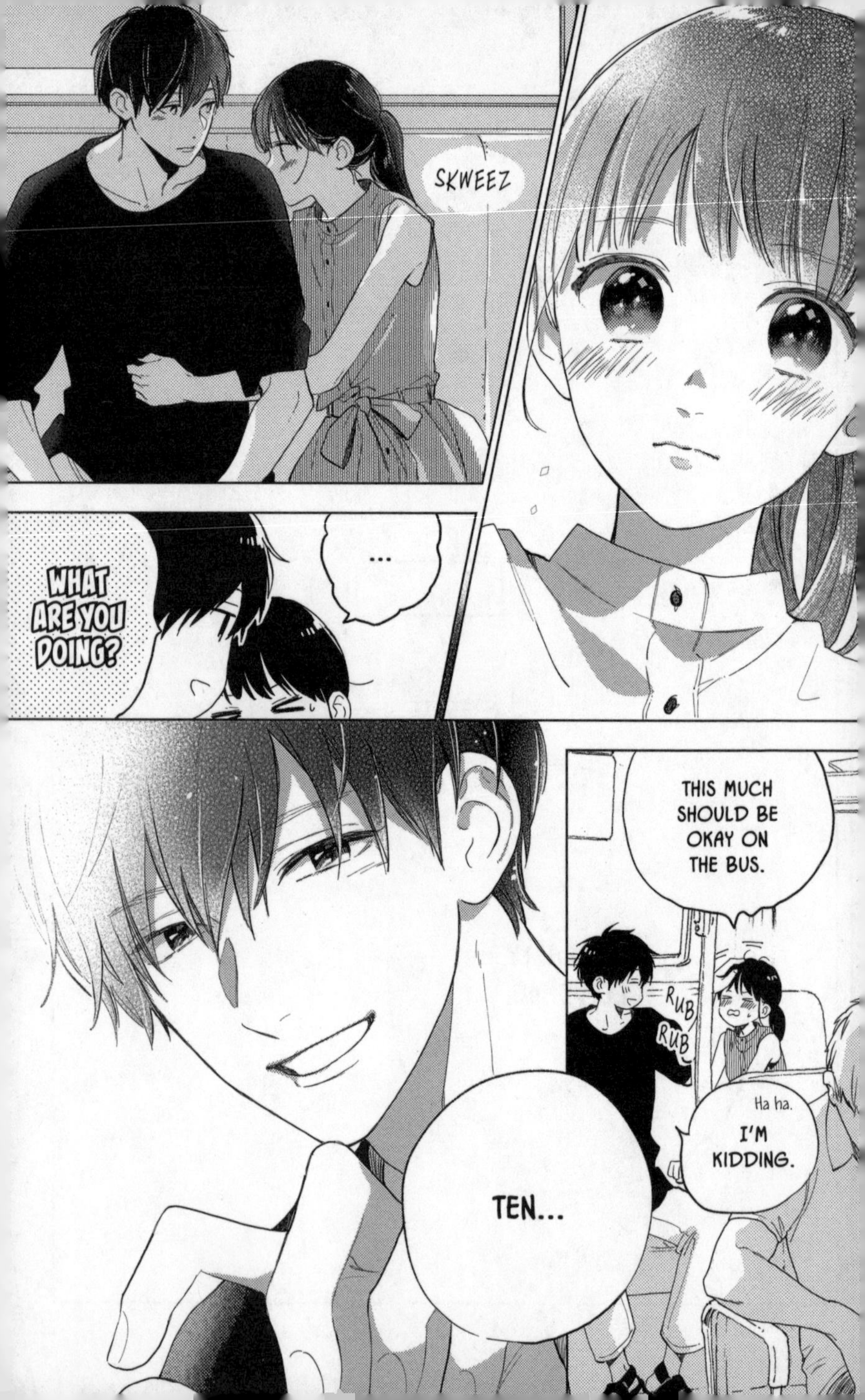
SKWEEZ
...
WHAT ARE YOU DOING?
THIS MUCH SHOULD BE OKAY ON THE BUS.
RUB RUB
Ha ha. I'M KIDDING.
TEN...

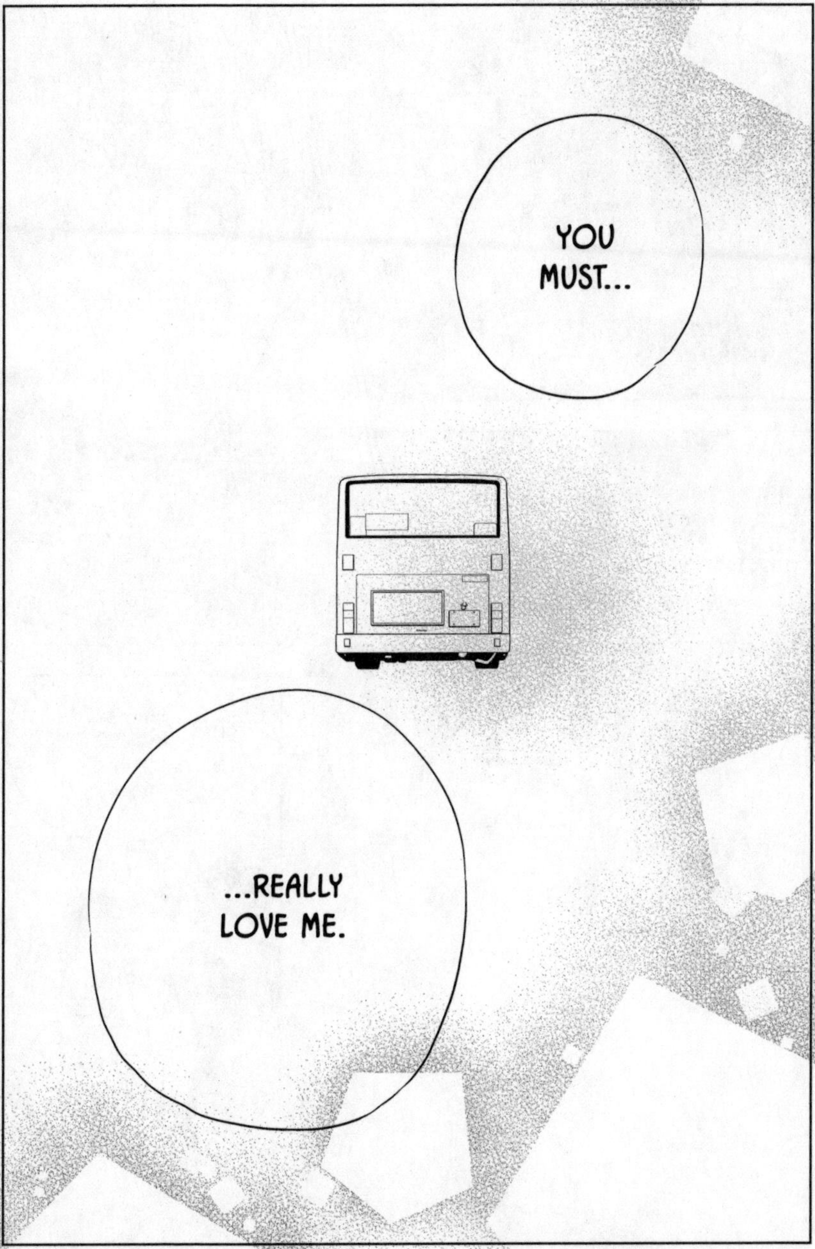
YOU MUST...
...REALLY LOVE ME.

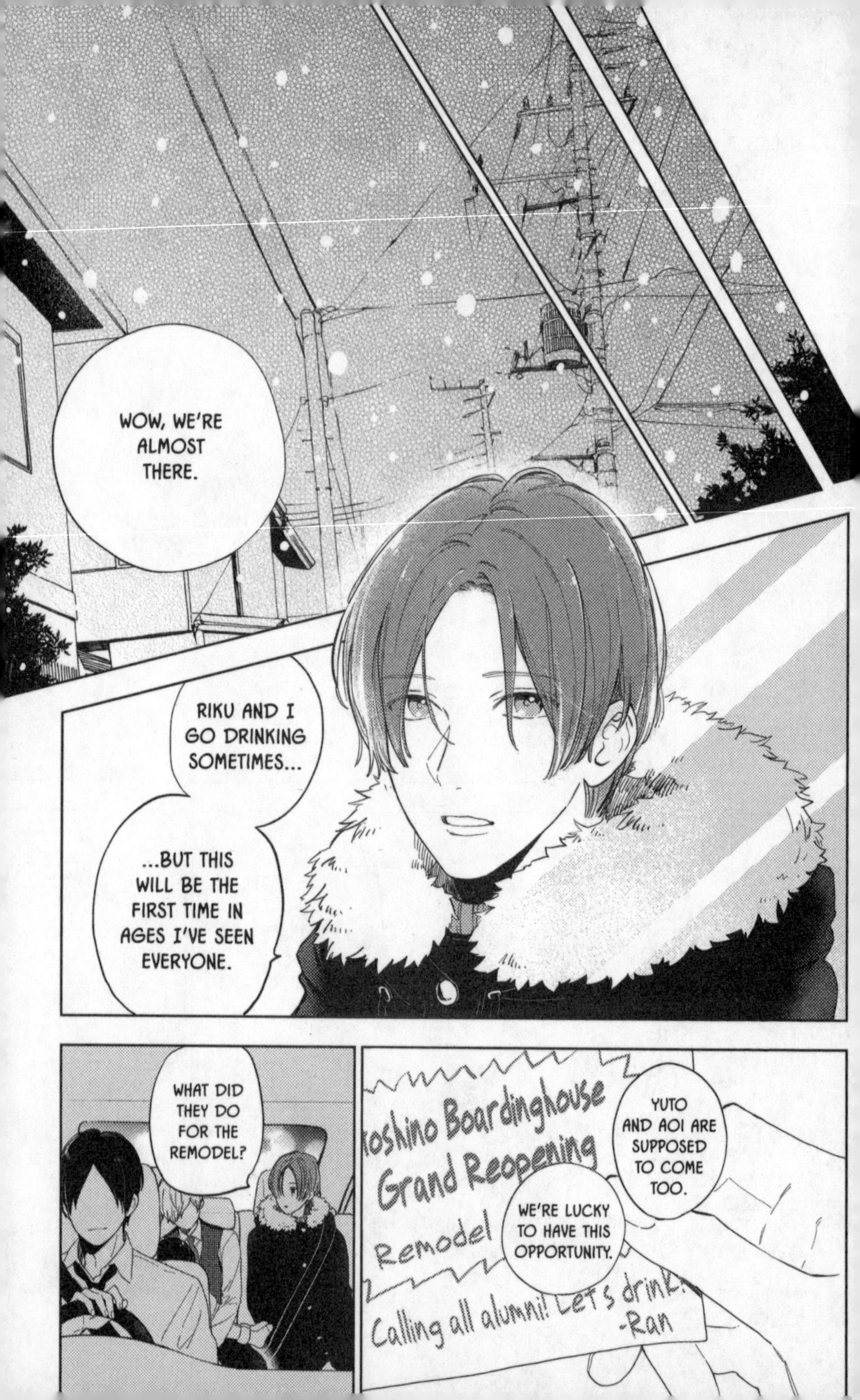
WOW, WE'RE ALMOST THERE.
RIKU AND I GO DRINKING SOMETIMES...
...BUT THIS WILL BE THE FIRST TIME IN AGES I'VE SEEN EVERYONE.
YUTO AND AOI ARE SUPPOSED TO COME TOO.
WE'RE LUCKY TO HAVE THIS OPPORTUNITY.
oshino Boardinghouse
Grand Reopening
Remodel
Calling all alumni! Let's drink!
-Ran
WHAT DID THEY DO FOR THE REMODEL?

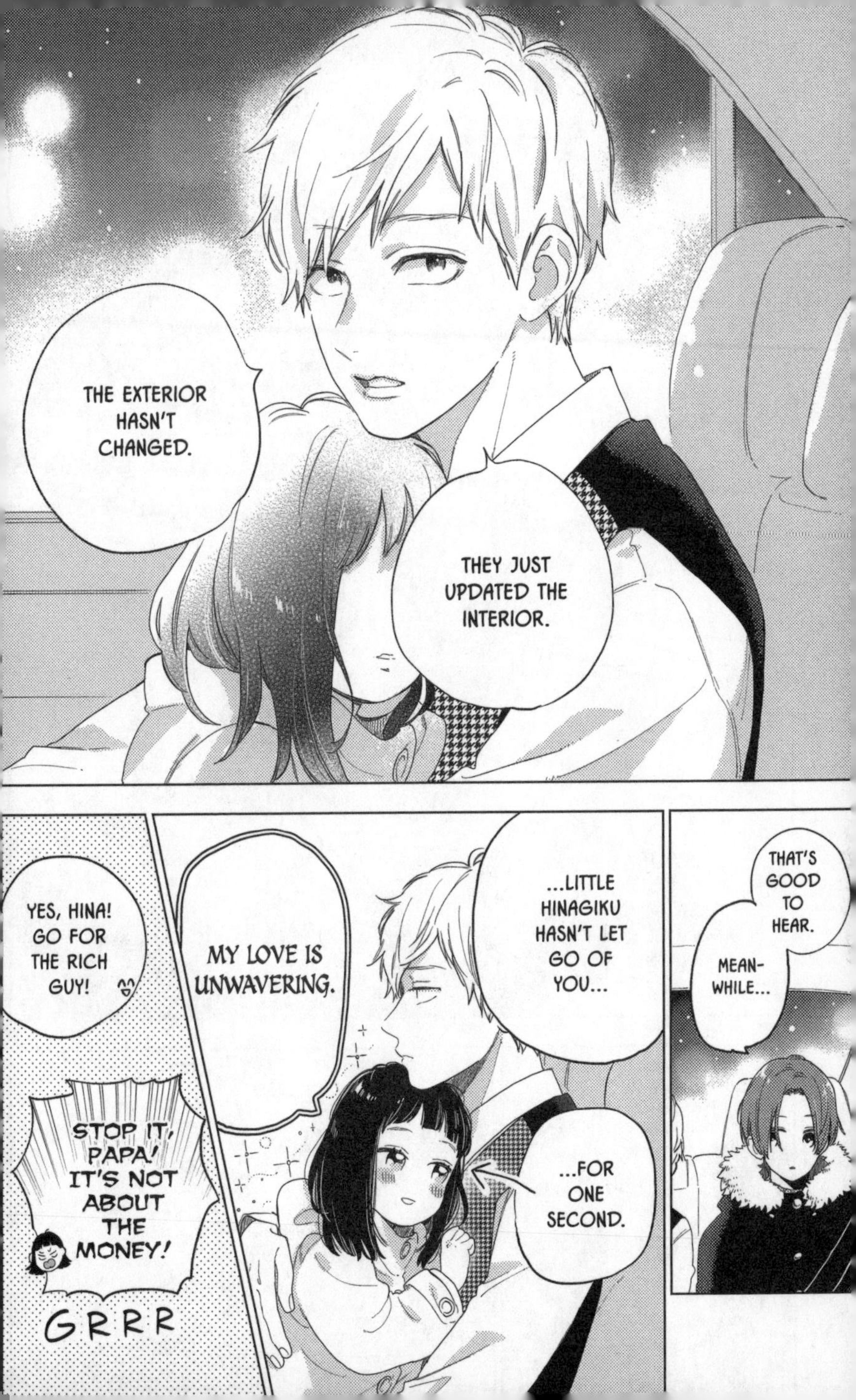
THE EXTERIOR HASN'T CHANGED.
THEY JUST UPDATED THE INTERIOR.
THAT'S GOOD TO HEAR.
MEAN-WHILE...
...LITTLE HINAGIKU HASN'T LET GO OF YOU...
...FOR ONE SECOND.
MY LOVE IS UNWAVERING.
YES, HINA! GO FOR THE RICH GUY!
STOP IT, PAPA! IT'S NOT ABOUT THE MONEY!
GRRR

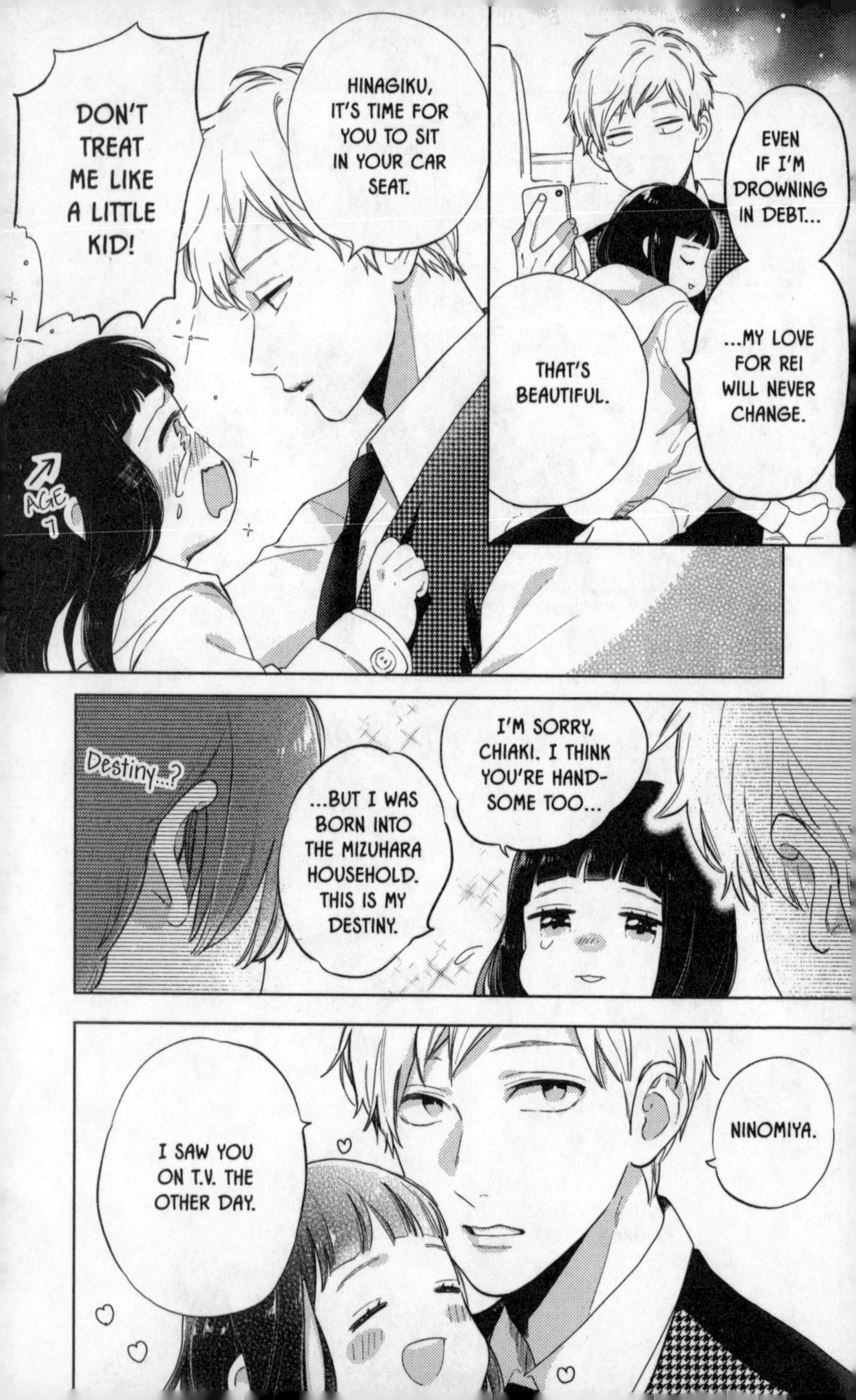
EVEN IF I'M DROWNING IN DEBT...
...MY LOVE FOR REI WILL NEVER CHANGE.
THAT'S BEAUTIFUL.
HINAGIKU, IT'S TIME FOR YOU TO SIT IN YOUR CAR SEAT.
DON'T TREAT ME LIKE A LITTLE KID!
AGE 7
I'M SORRY, CHIAKI. I THINK YOU'RE HAND-SOME TOO...
...BUT I WAS BORN INTO THE MIZUHARA HOUSEHOLD. THIS IS MY DESTINY.
Destiny...?
NINOMIYA.
I SAW YOU ON T.V. THE OTHER DAY.

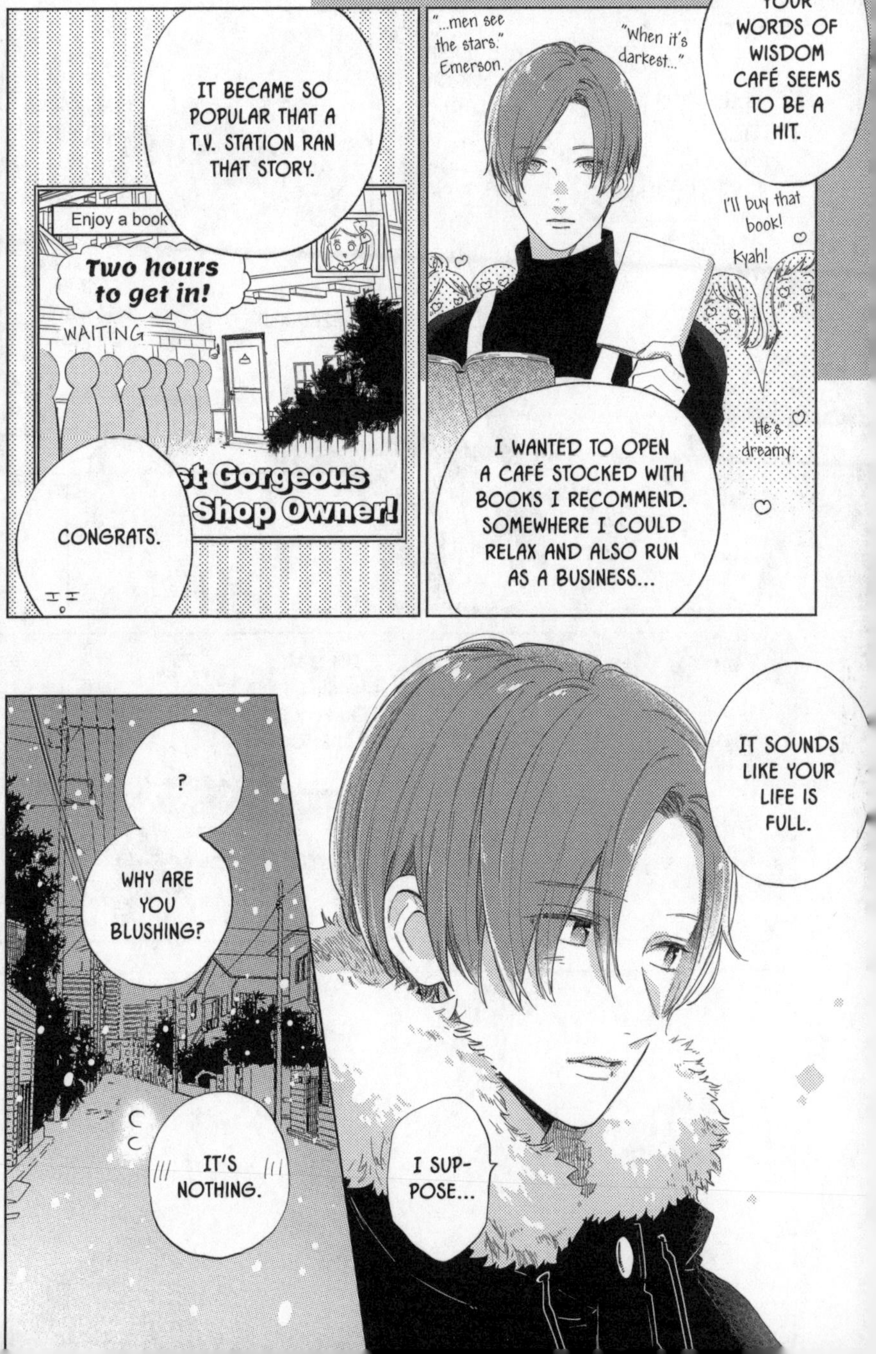
YOUR WORDS OF WISDOM CAFÉ SEEMS TO BE A HIT.
"When it's darkest..."
"...men see the stars." Emerson.
I'll buy that book!
Kyah!
He's dreamy.
I WANTED TO OPEN A CAFÉ STOCKED WITH BOOKS I RECOMMEND. SOMEWHERE I COULD RELAX AND ALSO RUN AS A BUSINESS...
IT BECAME SO POPULAR THAT A T.V. STATION RAN THAT STORY.
Enjoy a book
Two hours to get in!
WAITING
st Gorgeous Shop Owner!
CONGRATS.
IT SOUNDS LIKE YOUR LIFE IS FULL.
I SUP-POSE...
?
WHY ARE YOU BLUSHING?
IT'S NOTHING.

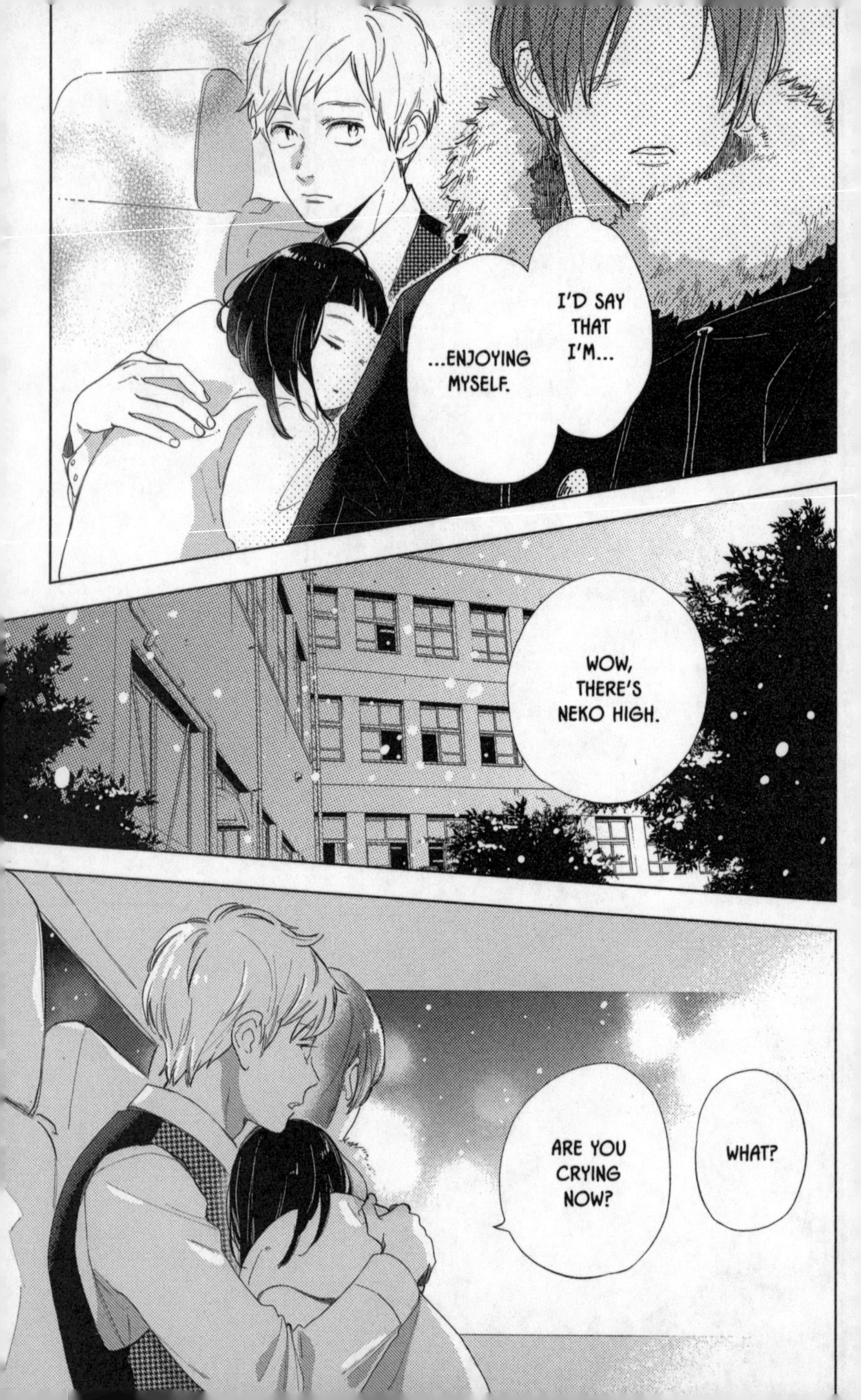
I'D SAY THAT I'M...
...ENJOYING MYSELF.
WOW, THERE'S NEKO HIGH.
WHAT?
ARE YOU CRYING NOW?

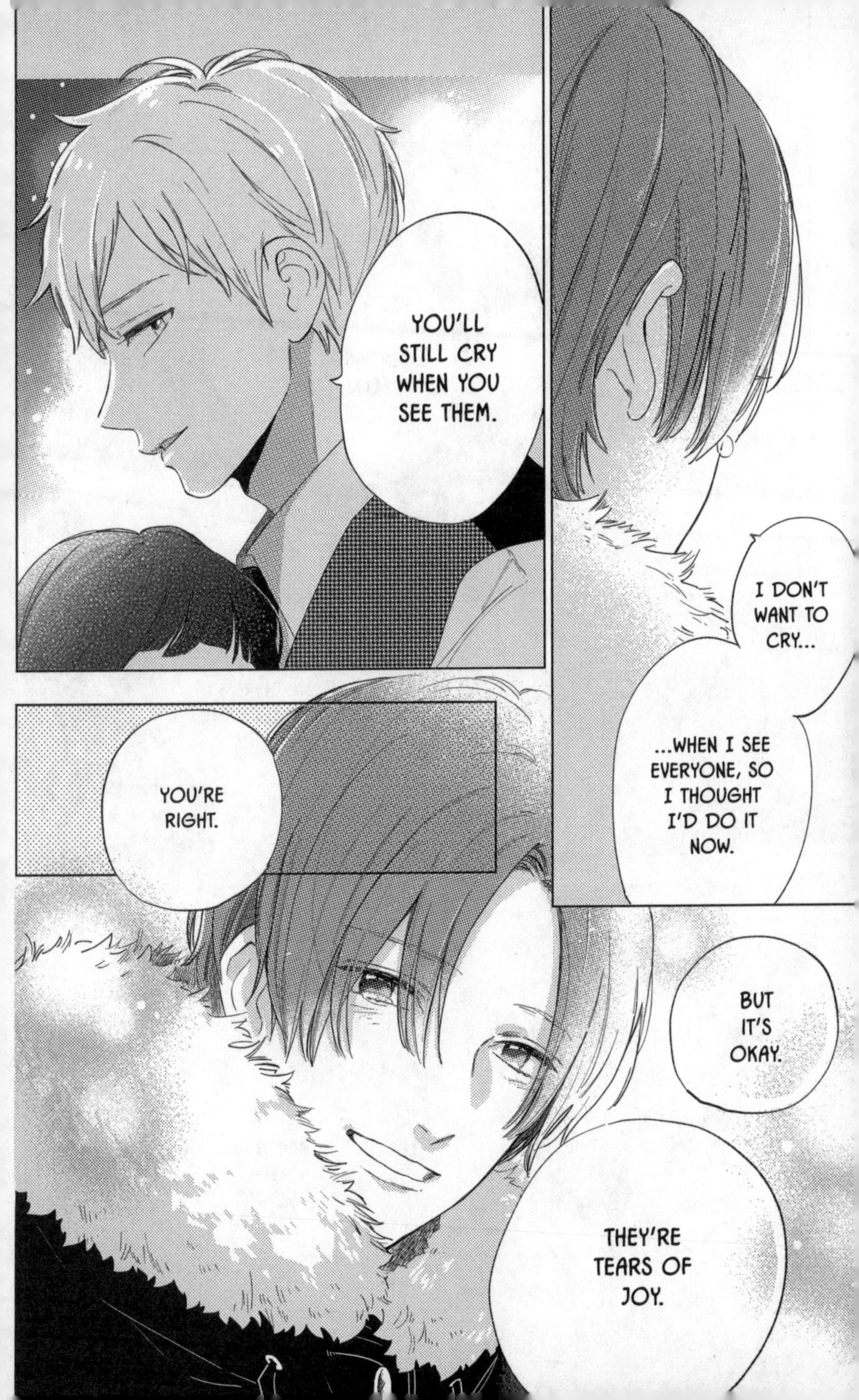
I DON'T WANT TO CRY...
...WHEN I SEE EVERYONE, SO I THOUGHT I'D DO IT NOW.
YOU'LL STILL CRY WHEN YOU SEE THEM.
YOU'RE RIGHT.
BUT IT'S OKAY.
THEY'RE TEARS OF JOY.

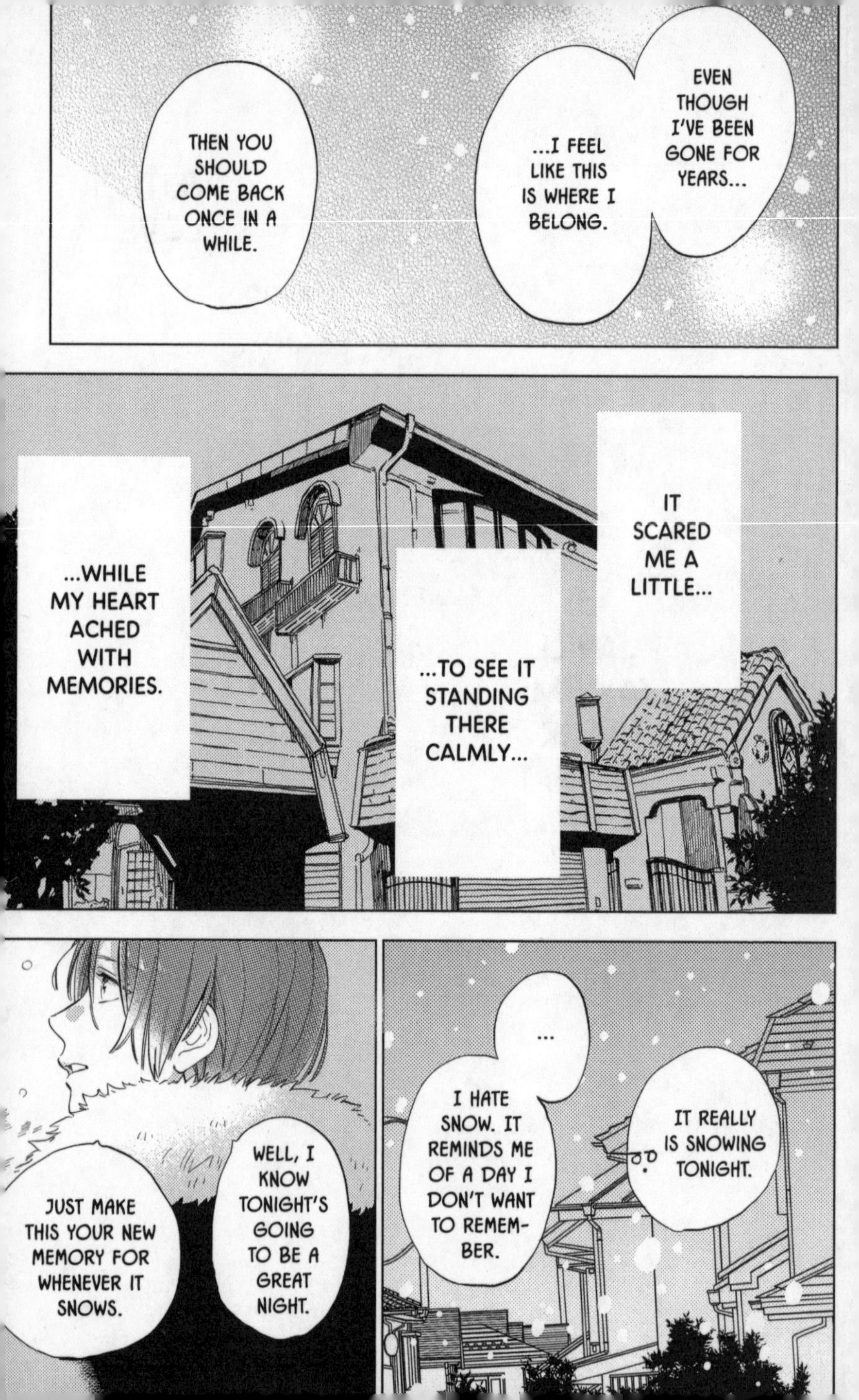
EVEN THOUGH I'VE BEEN GONE FOR YEARS...
...I FEEL LIKE THIS IS WHERE I BELONG.
THEN YOU SHOULD COME BACK ONCE IN A WHILE.
IT SCARED ME A LITTLE...
...TO SEE IT STANDING THERE CALMLY...
...WHILE MY HEART ACHED WITH MEMORIES.
IT REALLY IS SNOWING TONIGHT.
...
I HATE SNOW. IT REMINDS ME OF A DAY I DON'T WANT TO REMEMBER.
WELL, I KNOW TONIGHT'S GOING TO BE A GREAT NIGHT.
JUST MAKE THIS YOUR NEW MEMORY FOR WHENEVER IT SNOWS.

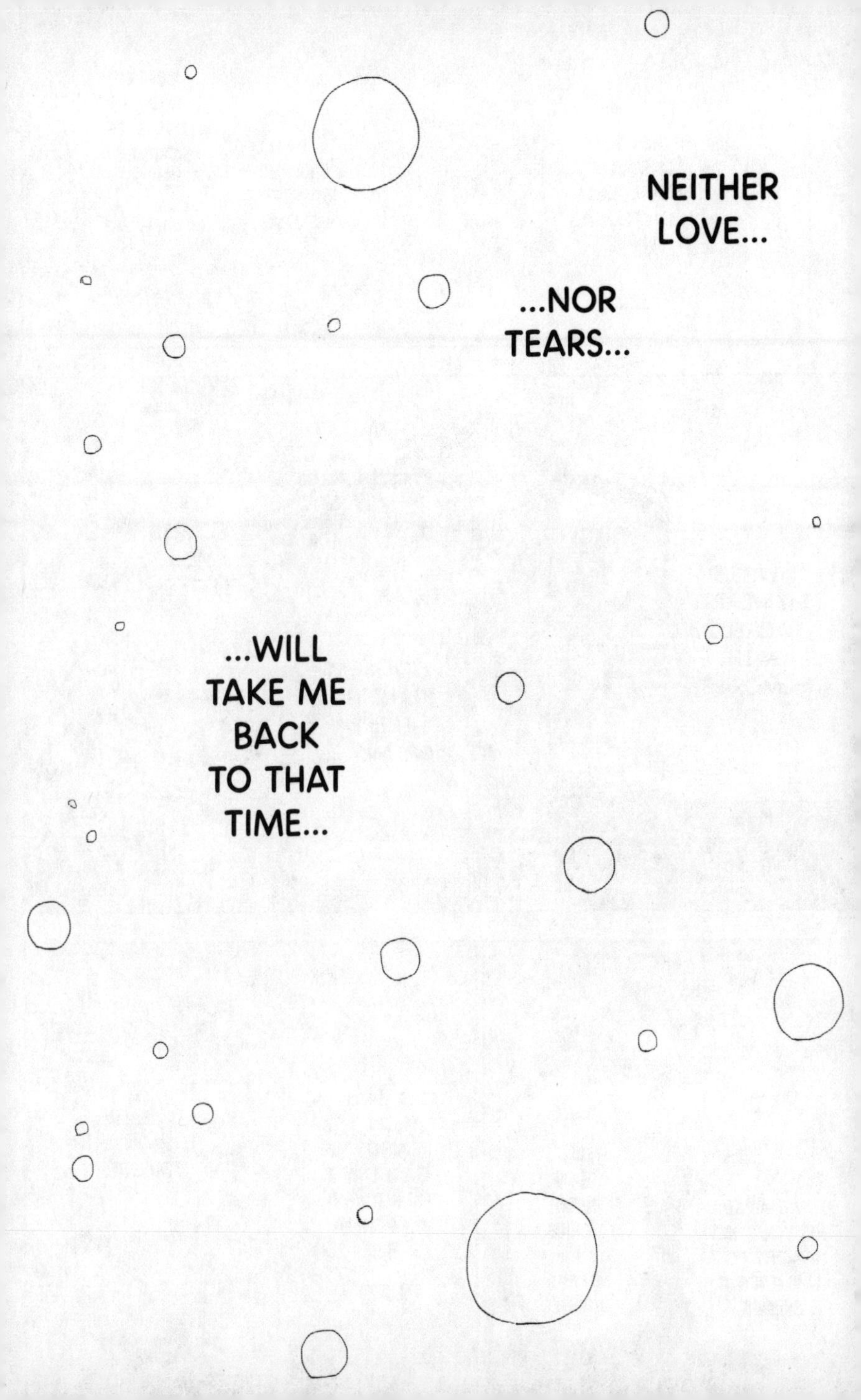
NEITHER LOVE...
...NOR TEARS...
...WILL TAKE ME BACK TO THAT TIME...

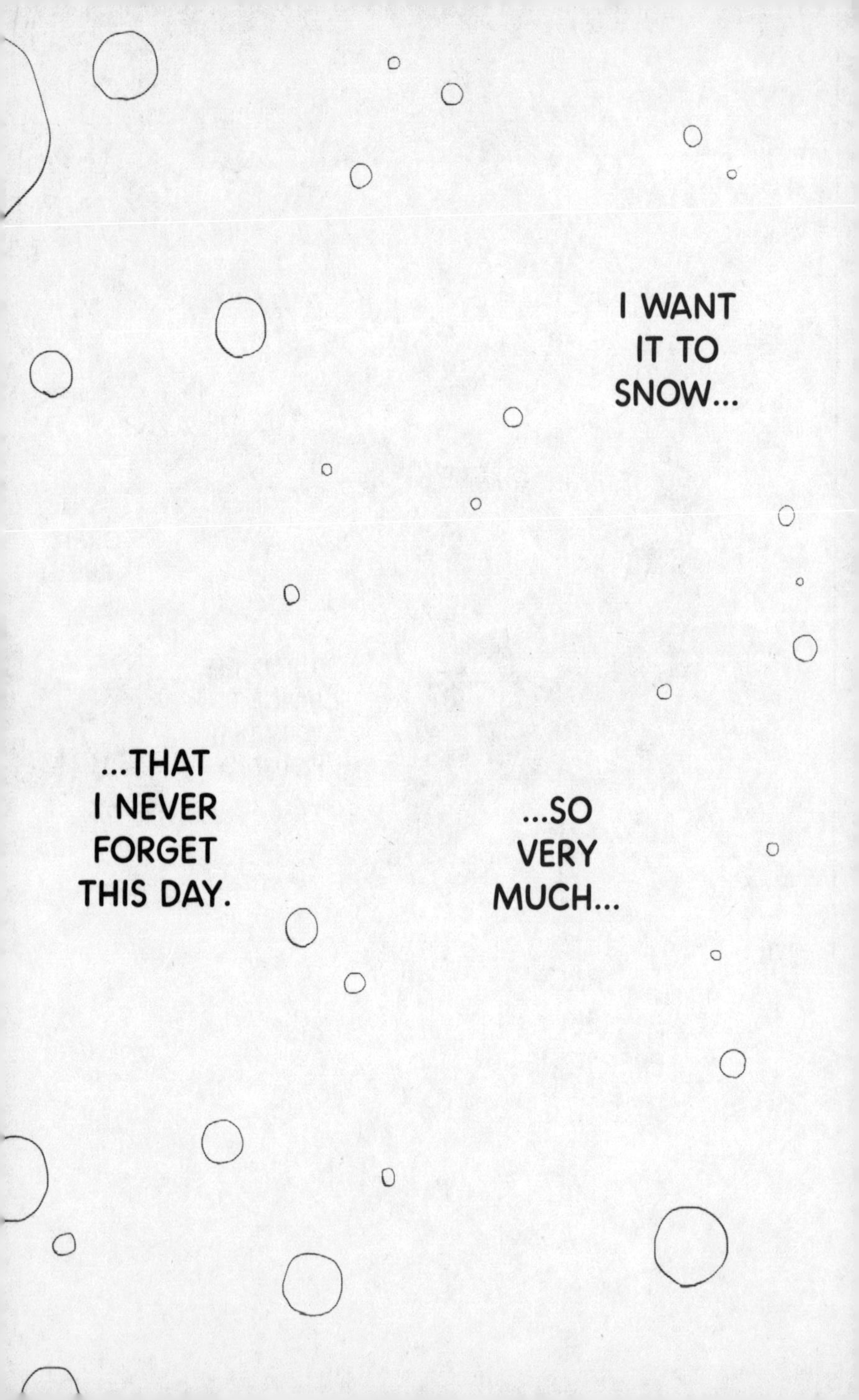
I WANT IT TO SNOW...
...SO VERY MUCH...
...THAT I NEVER FORGET THIS DAY.

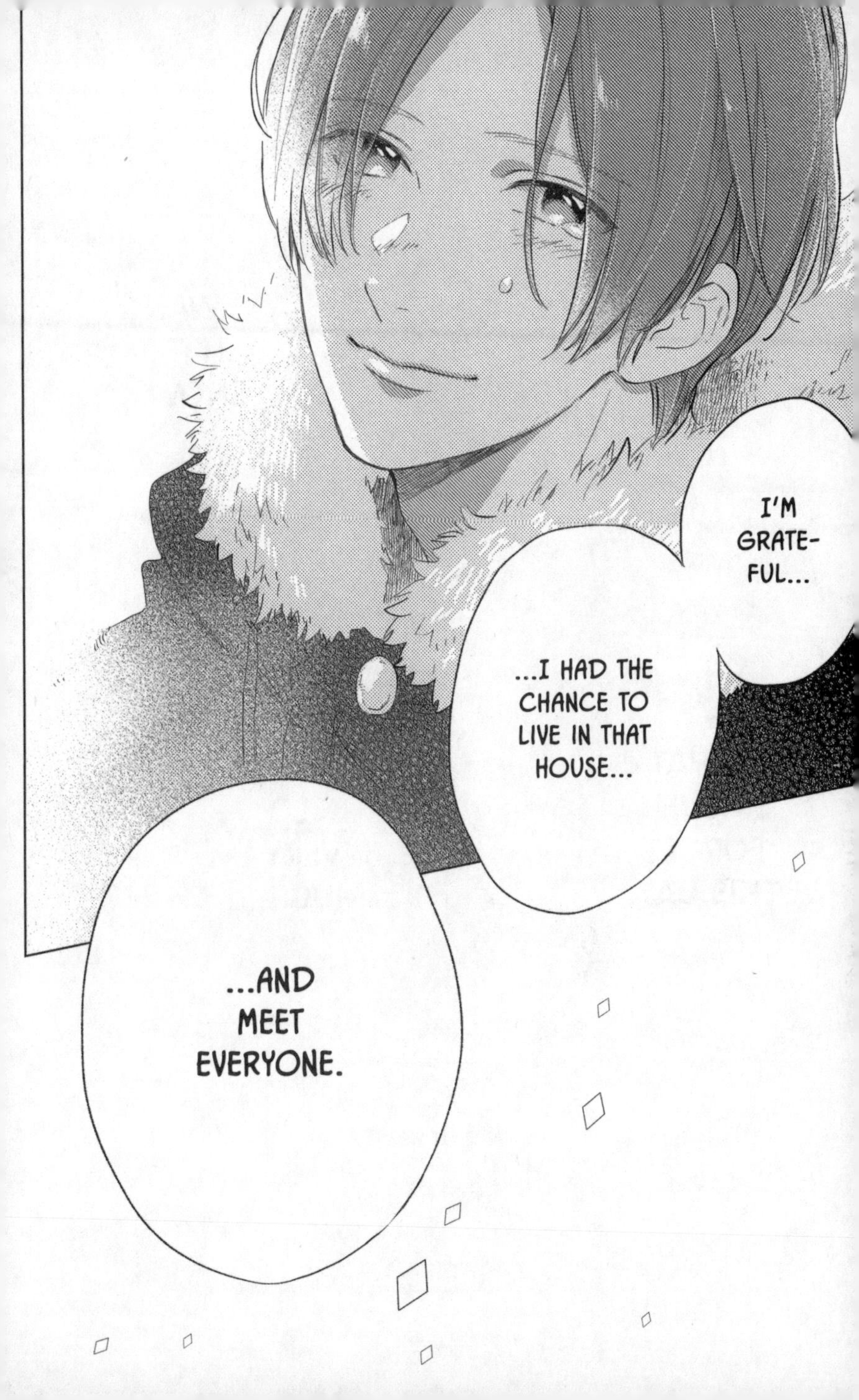
I'M GRATE-FUL...
...I HAD THE CHANCE TO LIVE IN THAT HOUSE...
...AND MEET EVERYONE.

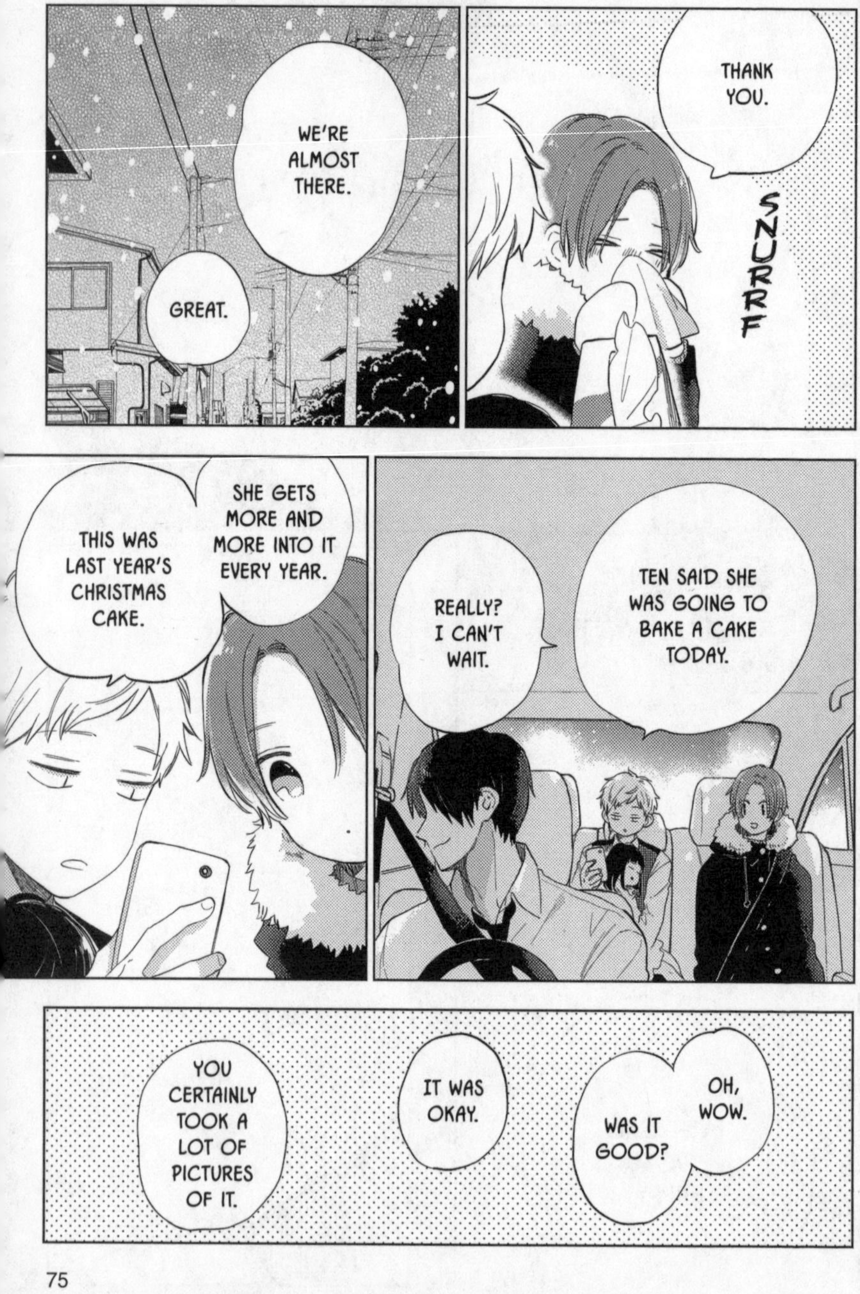
THANK YOU.
SNURRF
WE'RE ALMOST THERE.
GREAT.
TEN SAID SHE WAS GOING TO BAKE A CAKE TODAY.
REALLY? I CAN'T WAIT.
SHE GETS MORE AND MORE INTO IT EVERY YEAR.
THIS WAS LAST YEAR'S CHRISTMAS CAKE.
OH, WOW.
WAS IT GOOD?
IT WAS OKAY.
YOU CERTAINLY TOOK A LOT OF PICTURES OF IT.

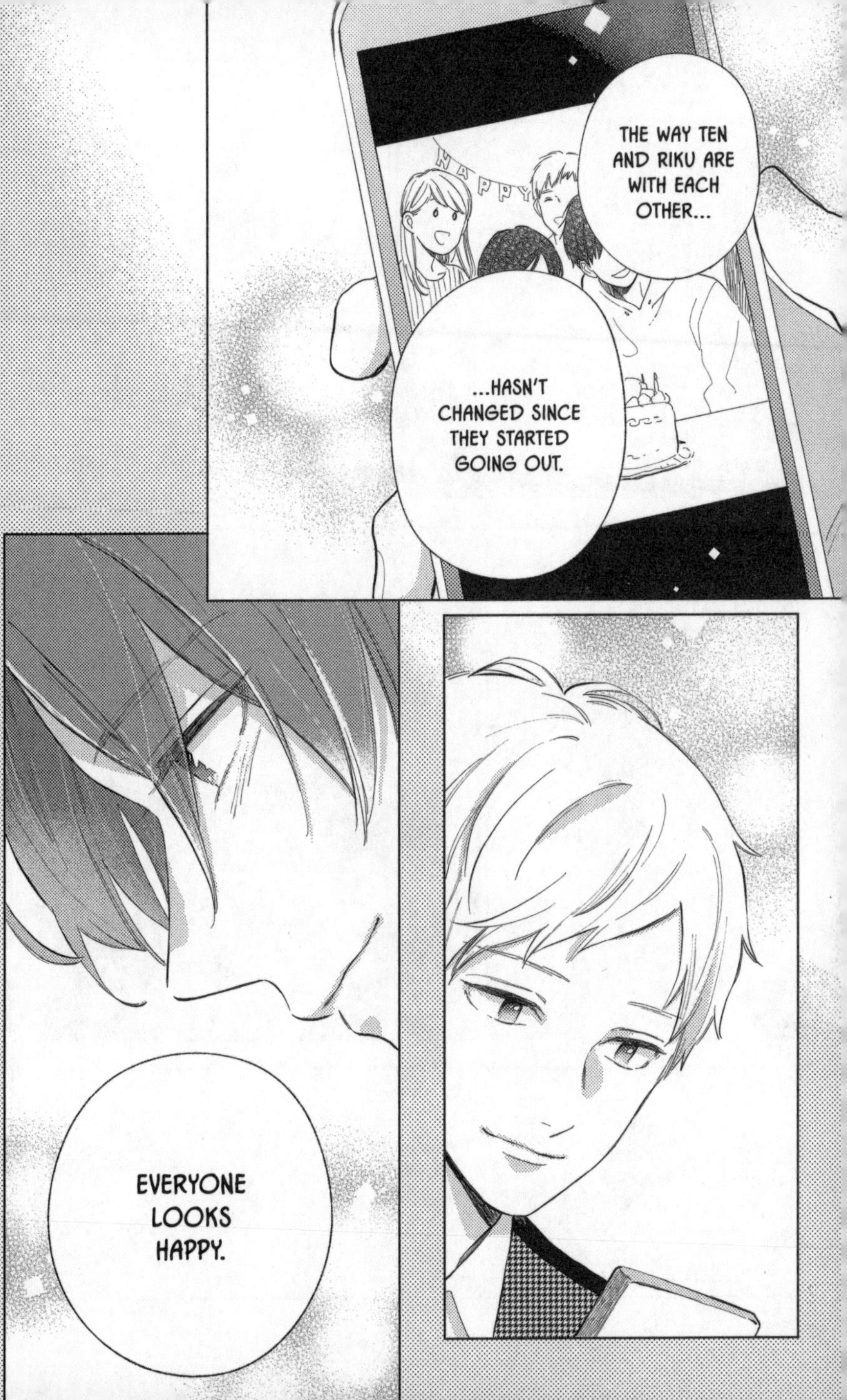
THE WAY TEN AND RIKU ARE WITH EACH OTHER...
...HASN'T CHANGED SINCE THEY STARTED GOING OUT.
EVERYONE LOOKS HAPPY.

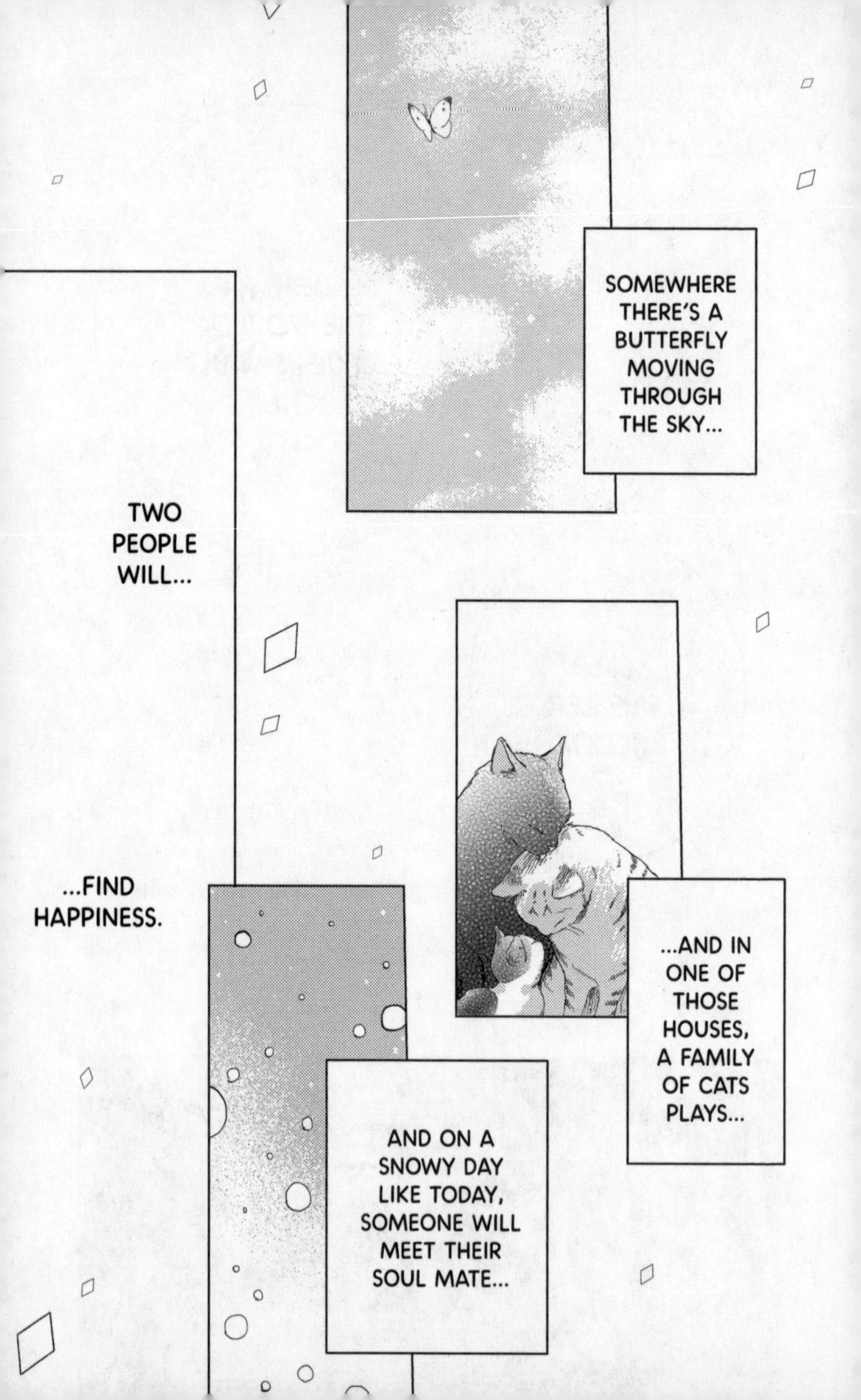
SOMEWHERE THERE'S A BUTTERFLY MOVING THROUGH THE SKY...
...AND IN ONE OF THOSE HOUSES, A FAMILY OF CATS PLAYS...
AND ON A SNOWY DAY LIKE TODAY, SOMEONE WILL MEET THEIR SOUL MATE...
TWO PEOPLE WILL...
...FIND HAPPINESS.

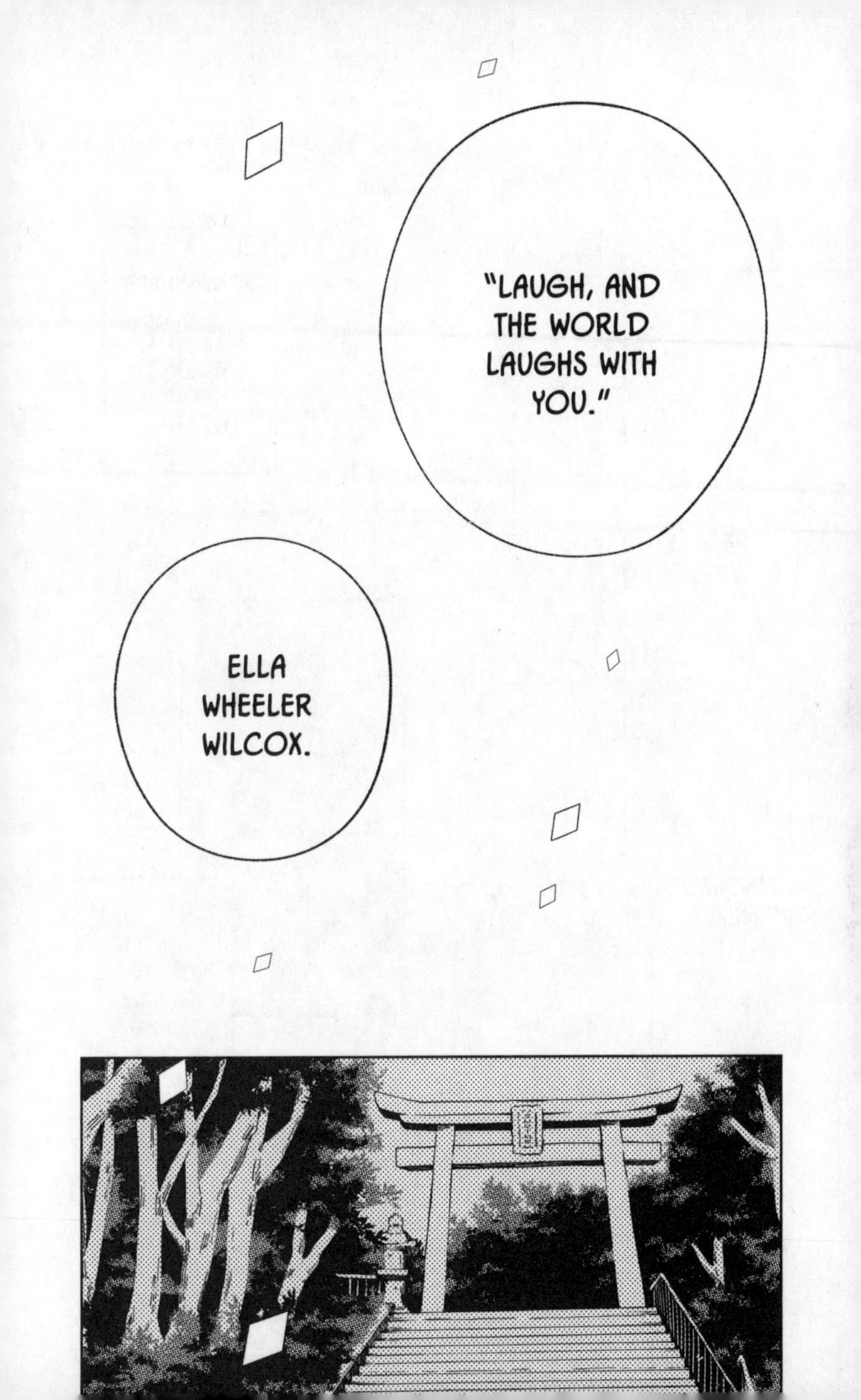
"LAUGH, AND THE WORLD LAUGHS WITH YOU."
ELLA WHEELER WILCOX.

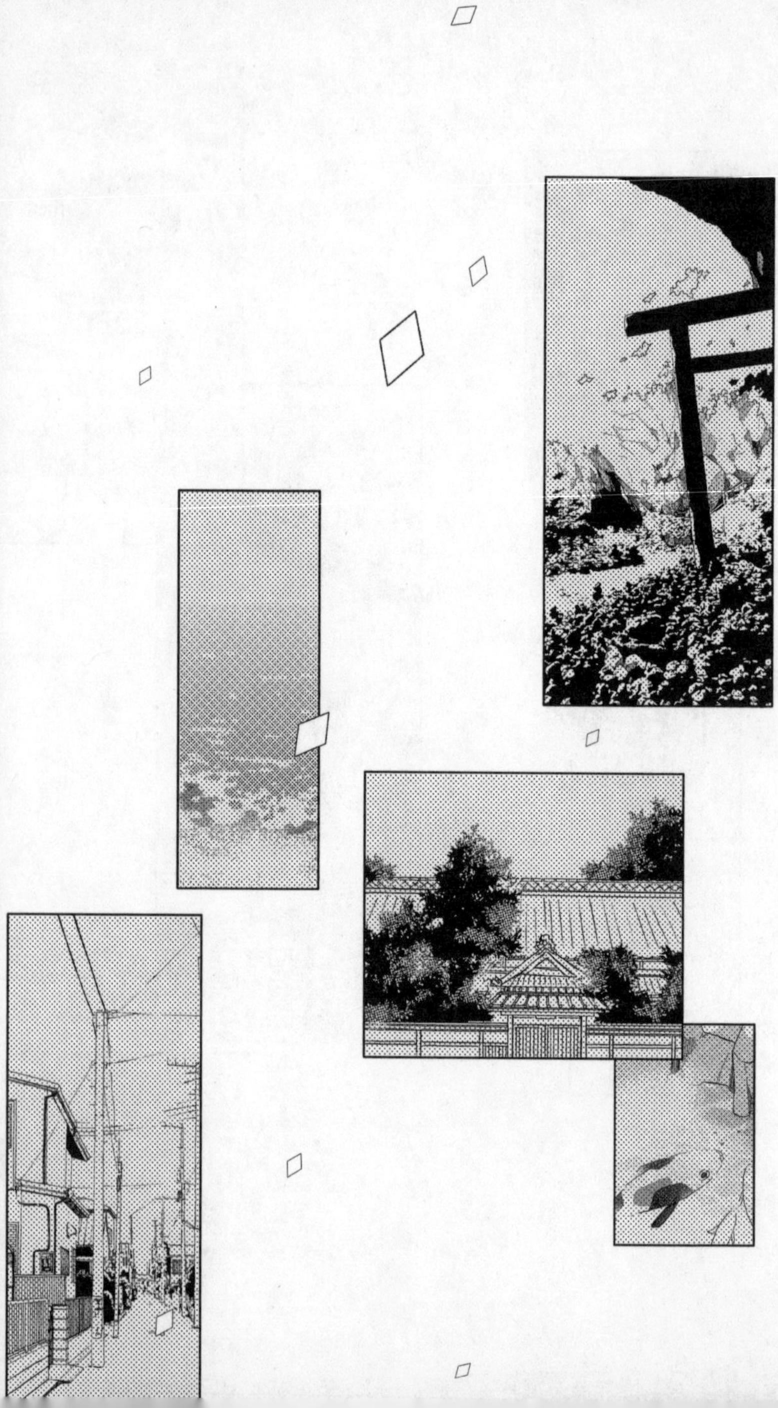

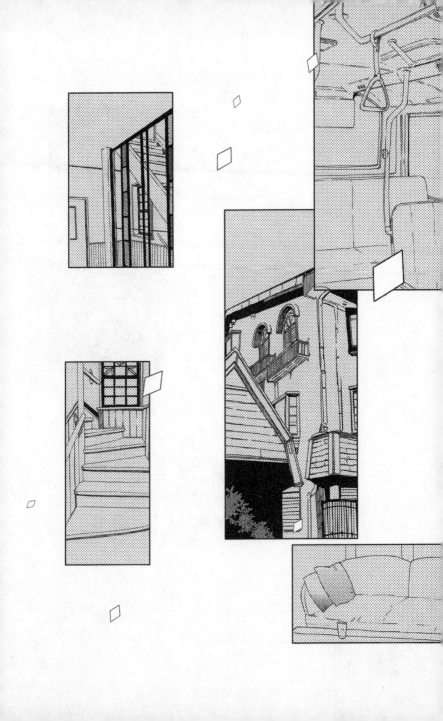

KAWAGUCHI
DENTISTRY

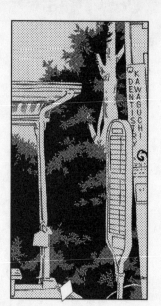

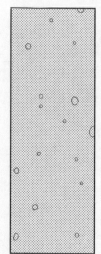

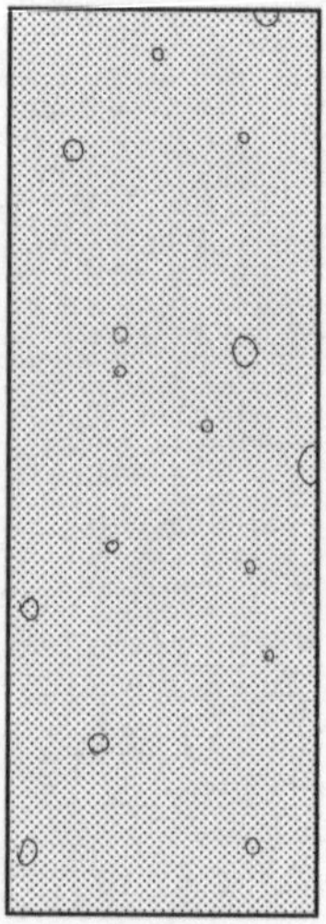

Shortcake Cake/End

Bonus Story 1

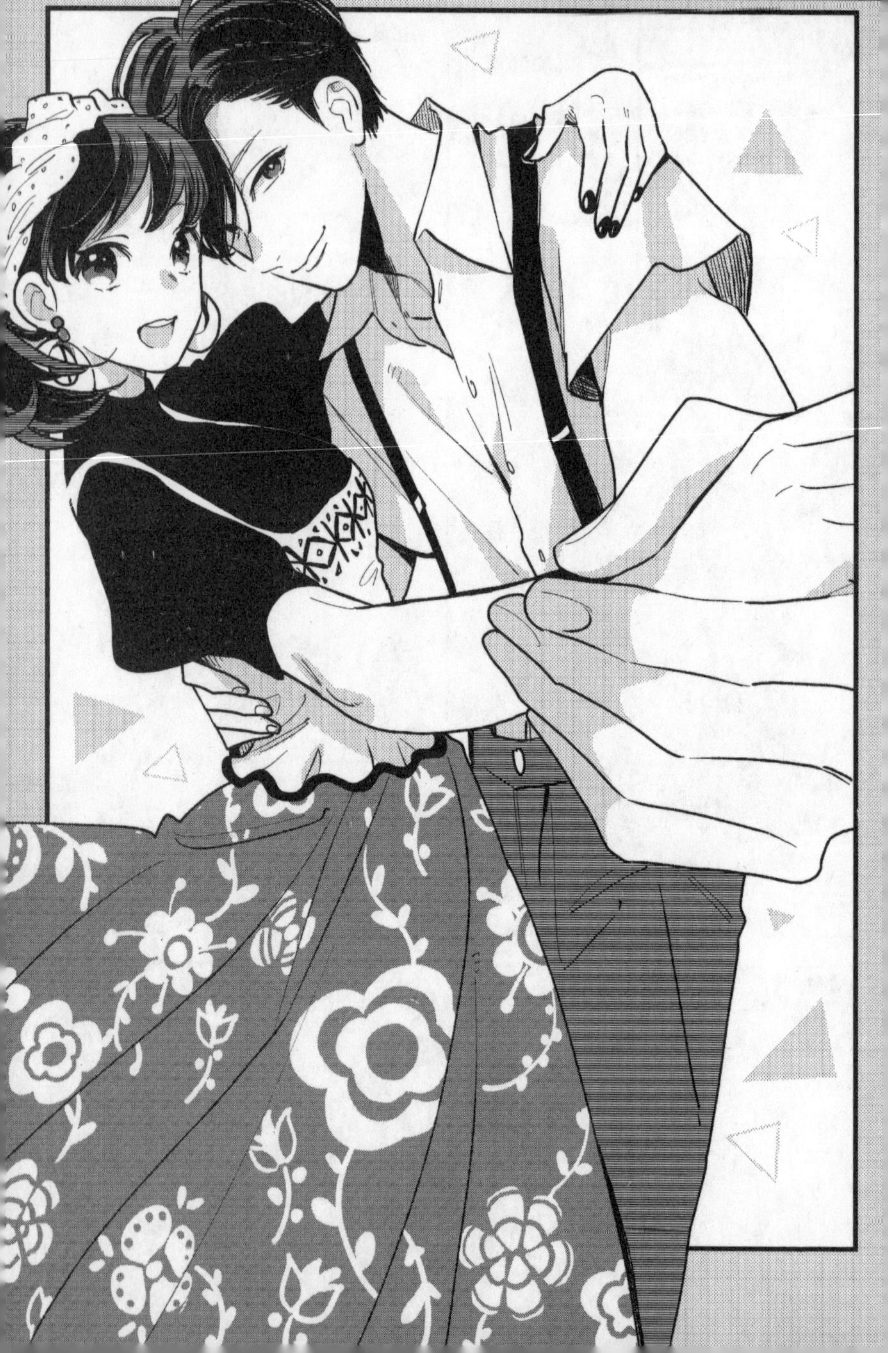

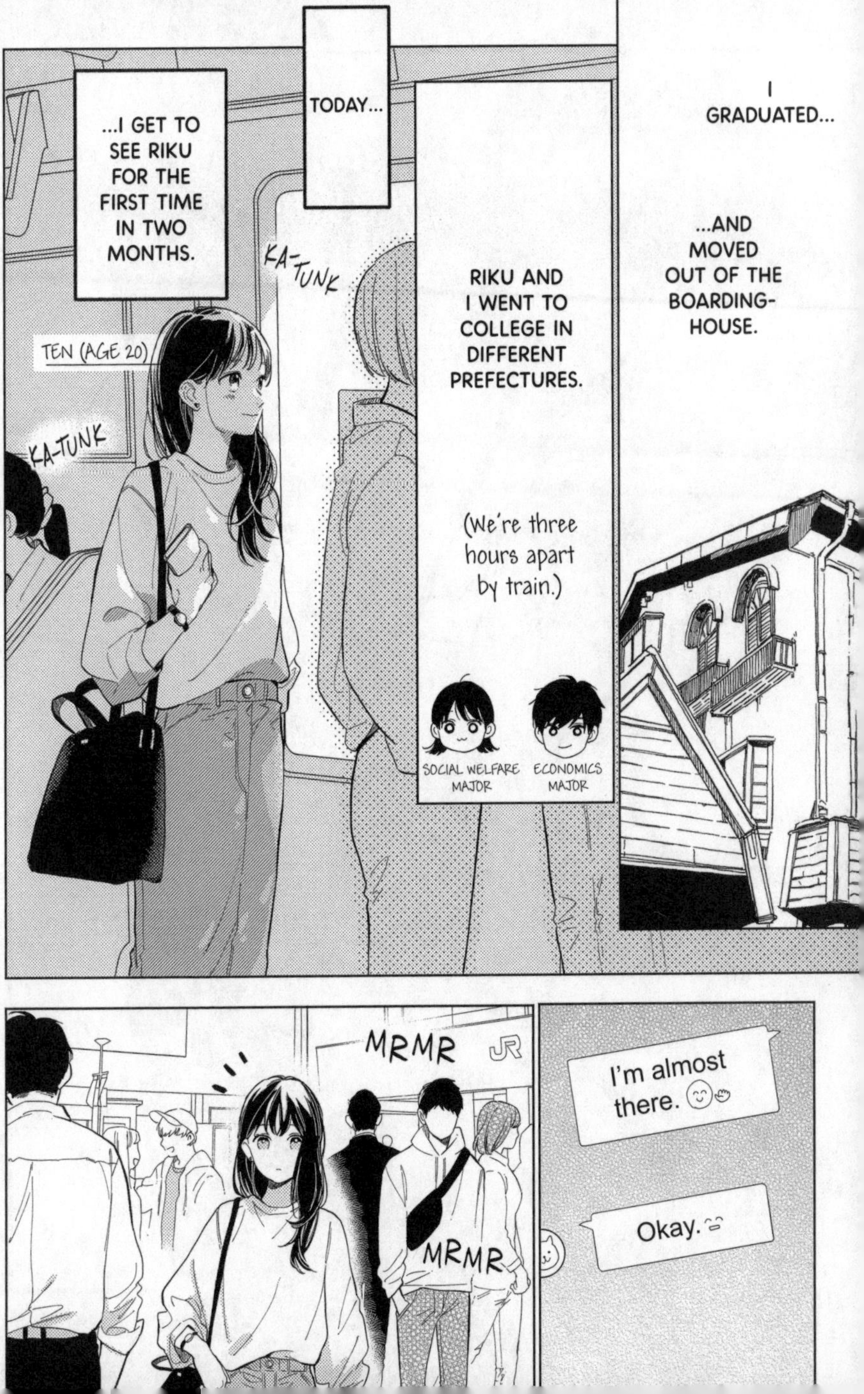
I GRADUATED...
...AND MOVED OUT OF THE BOARDING-HOUSE.
RIKU AND I WENT TO COLLEGE IN DIFFERENT PREFECTURES.
(We're three hours apart by train.)
SOCIAL WELFARE MAJOR
ECONOMICS MAJOR
TODAY...
...I GET TO SEE RIKU FOR THE FIRST TIME IN TWO MONTHS.
KA-TUNK
TEN (AGE 20)
KA-TUNK
I'm almost there.
Okay.
MRMR
JR
MRMR

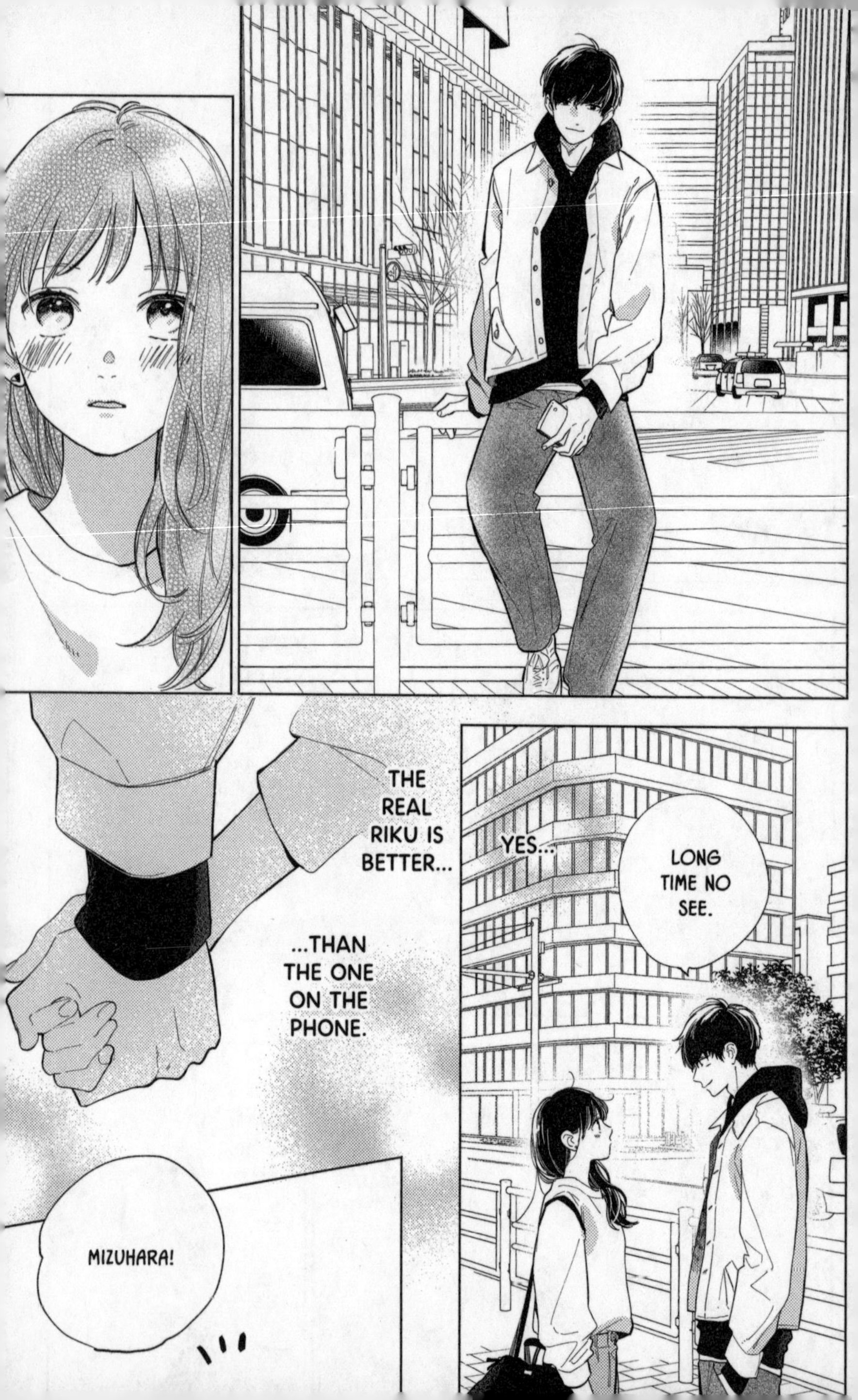
LONG TIME NO SEE.
YES...
THE REAL RIKU IS BETTER...
...THAN THE ONE ON THE PHONE.
MIZUHARA!

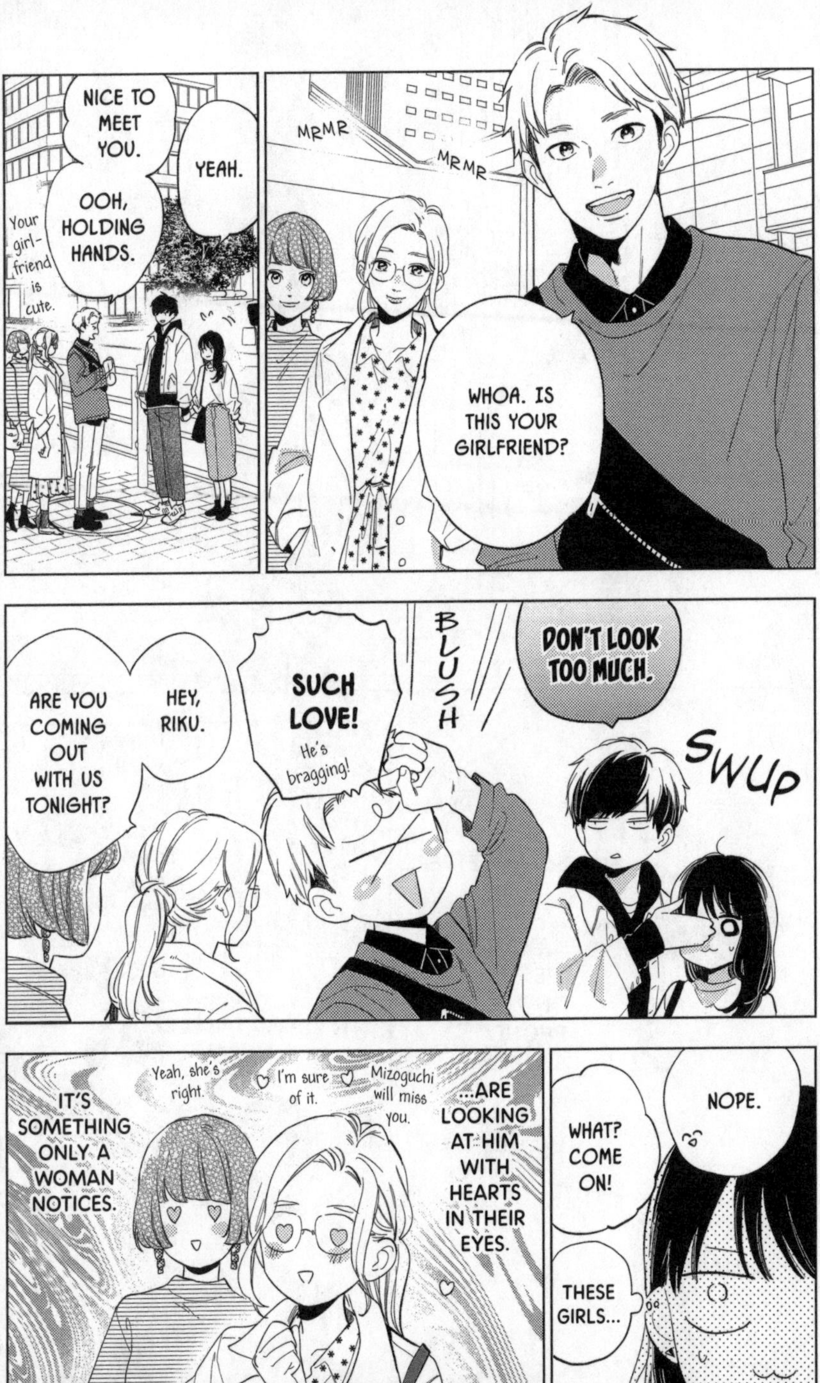
MRMR
MRMR
WHOA. IS THIS YOUR GIRLFRIEND?
YEAH.
NICE TO MEET YOU.
OOH, HOLDING HANDS.
Your girlfriend is cute.
DON'T LOOK TOO MUCH.
SWUP
BLUSH
SUCH LOVE!
He's bragging!
HEY, RIKU.
ARE YOU COMING OUT WITH US TONIGHT?
NOPE.
WHAT? COME ON!
THESE GIRLS...
...ARE LOOKING AT HIM WITH HEARTS IN THEIR EYES.
Mizoguchi will miss you.
I'm sure of it.
Yeah, she's right.
IT'S SOMETHING ONLY A WOMAN NOTICES.

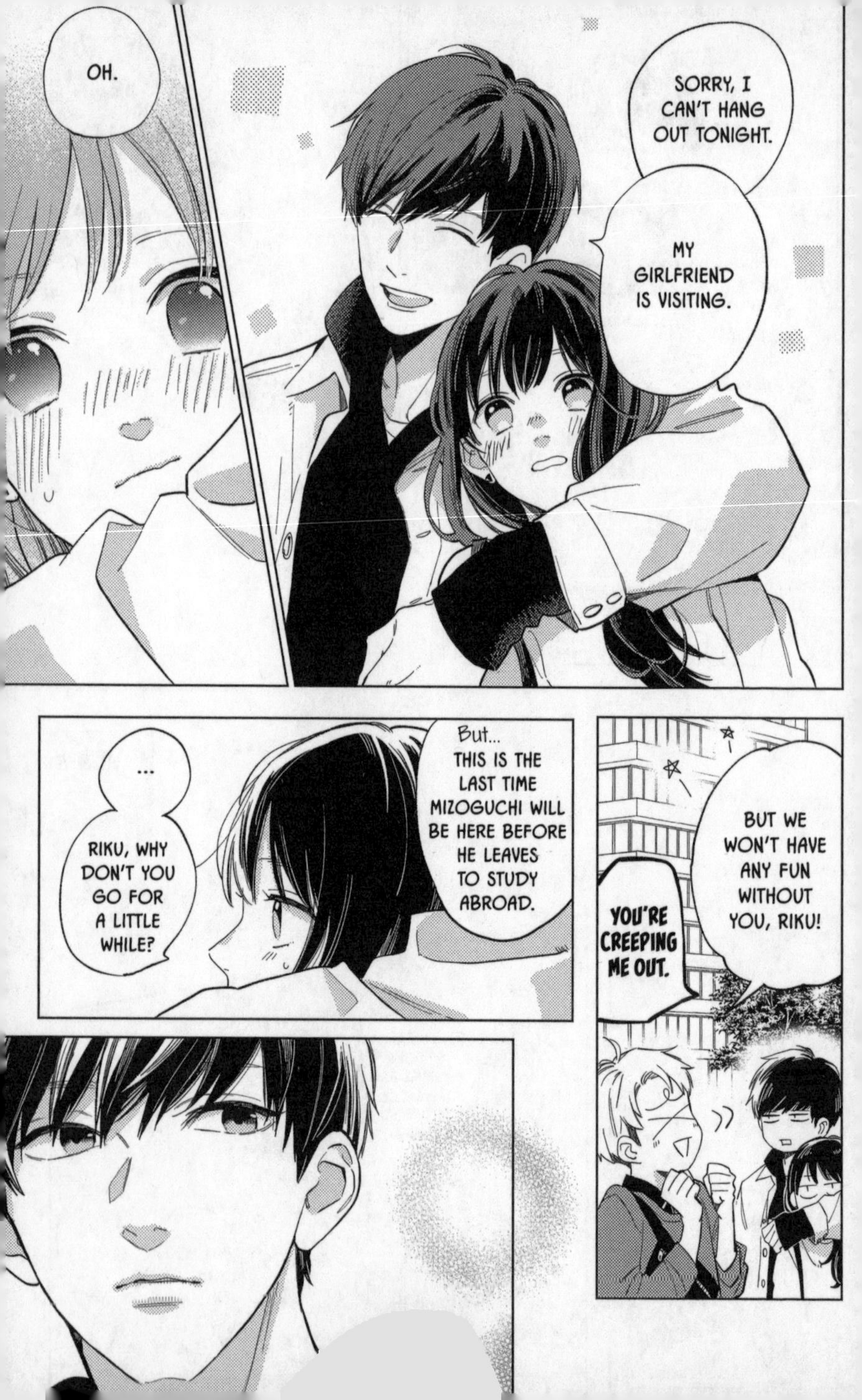
SORRY, I CAN'T HANG OUT TONIGHT.
MY GIRLFRIEND IS VISITING.
OH.
BUT WE WON'T HAVE ANY FUN WITHOUT YOU, RIKU!
YOU'RE CREEPING ME OUT.
But... THIS IS THE LAST TIME MIZOGUCHI WILL BE HERE BEFORE HE LEAVES TO STUDY ABROAD.
...
RIKU, WHY DON'T YOU GO FOR A LITTLE WHILE?

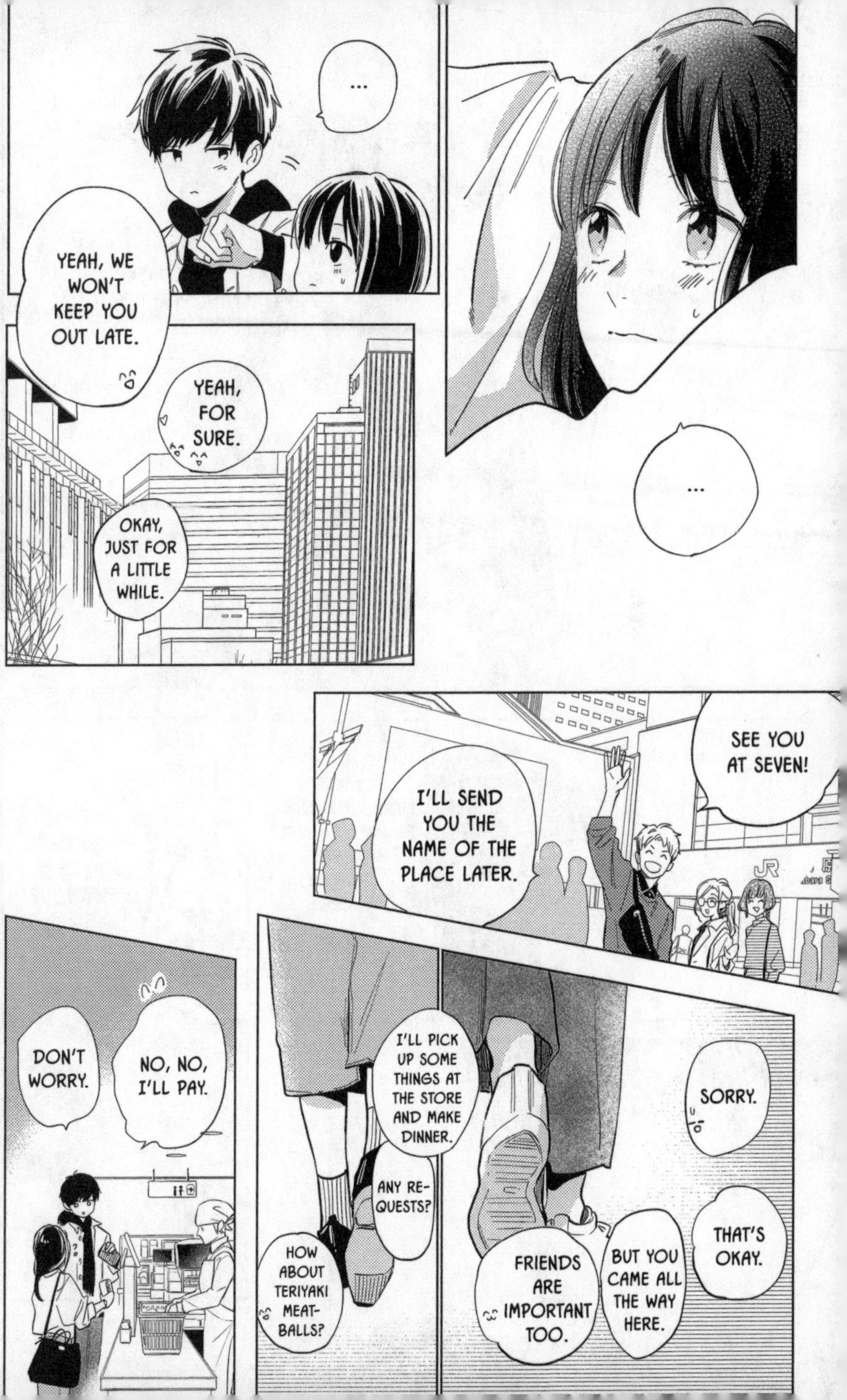
...
...
YEAH, WE WON'T KEEP YOU OUT LATE.
YEAH, FOR SURE.
OKAY, JUST FOR A LITTLE WHILE.
SEE YOU AT SEVEN!
I'LL SEND YOU THE NAME OF THE PLACE LATER.
SORRY.
THAT'S OKAY.
BUT YOU CAME ALL THE WAY HERE.
FRIENDS ARE IMPORTANT TOO.
I'LL PICK UP SOME THINGS AT THE STORE AND MAKE DINNER.
ANY REQUESTS?
HOW ABOUT TERIYAKI MEAT-BALLS?
NO, NO, I'LL PAY.
DON'T WORRY.

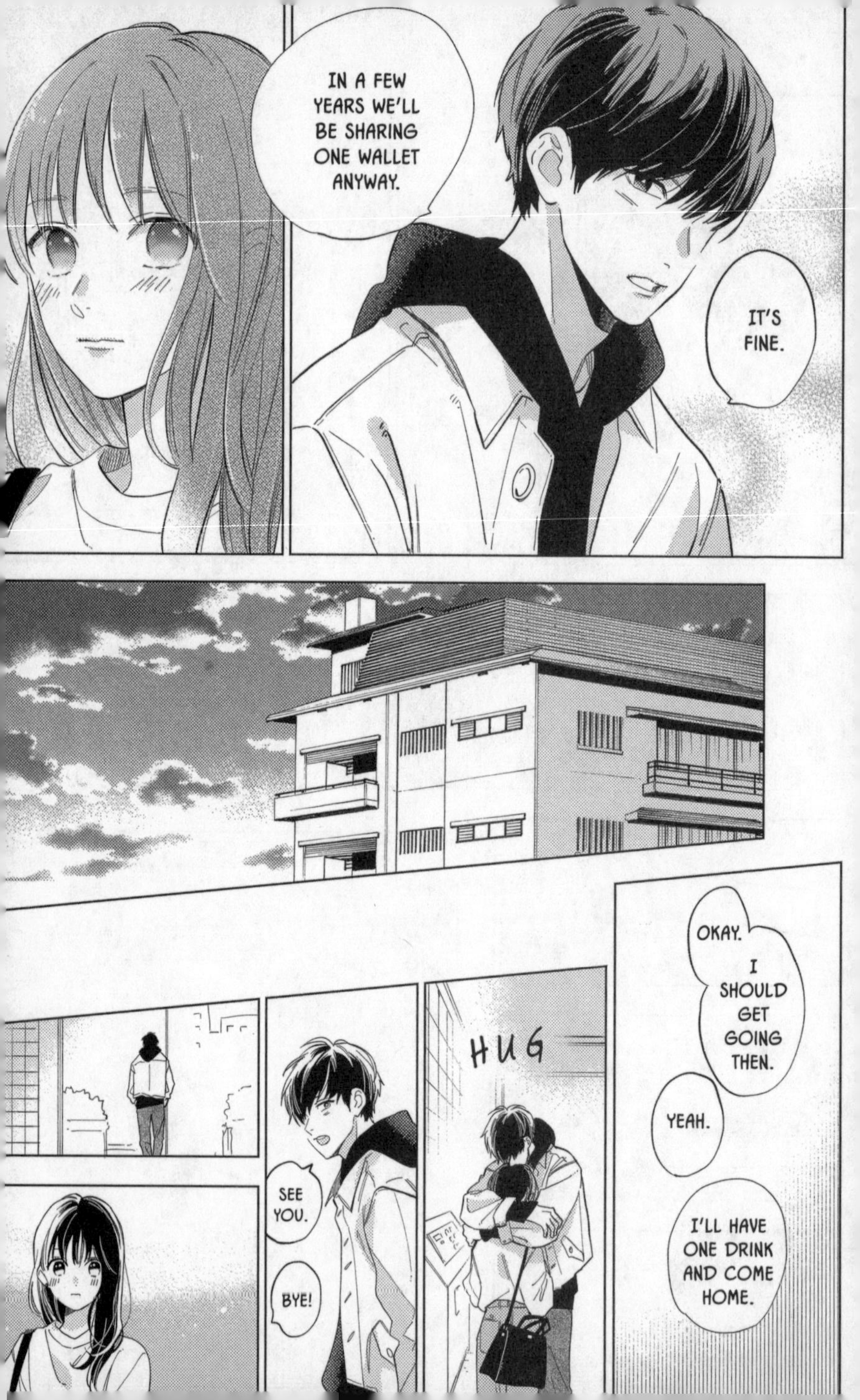
IT'S FINE.
IN A FEW YEARS WE'LL BE SHARING ONE WALLET ANYWAY.
OKAY. I SHOULD GET GOING THEN.
YEAH.
I'LL HAVE ONE DRINK AND COME HOME.
HUG
SEE YOU.
BYE!

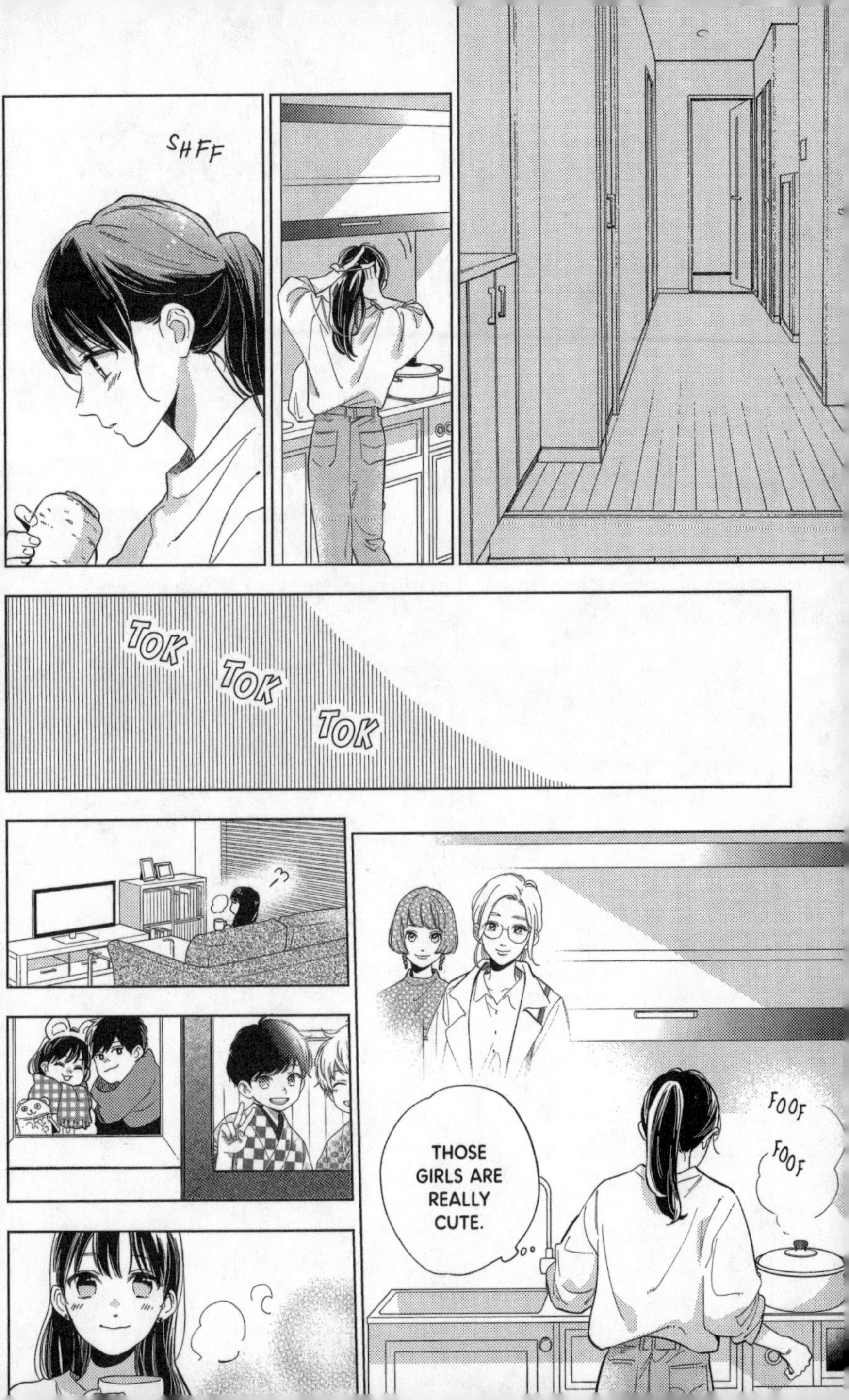
SHFF
TOK
TOK
TOK
FOOF
FOOF
THOSE GIRLS ARE REALLY CUTE.

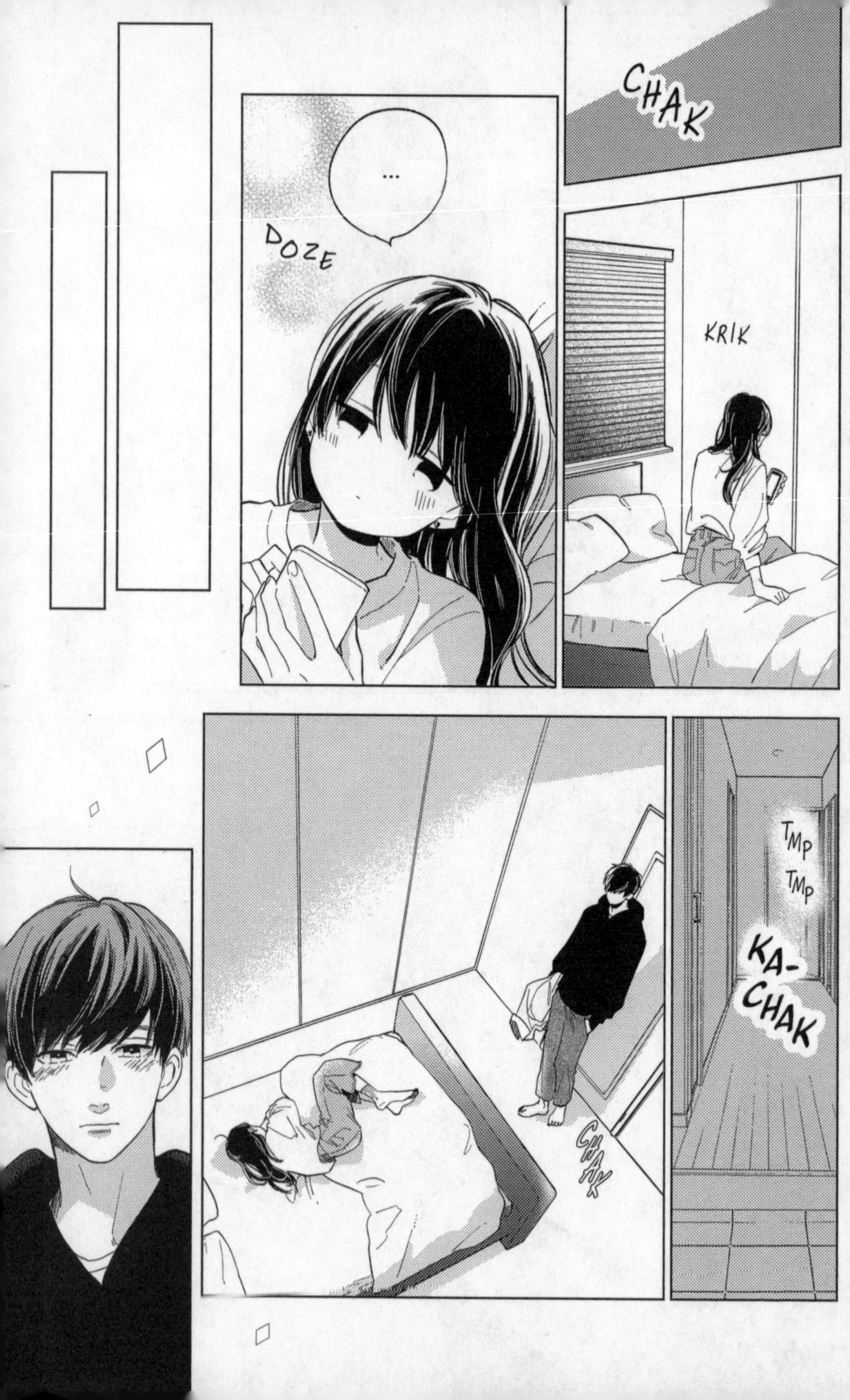
CHAK
KRIK
...
DOZE
TMP
TMP
KA-
CHAK
CHAK

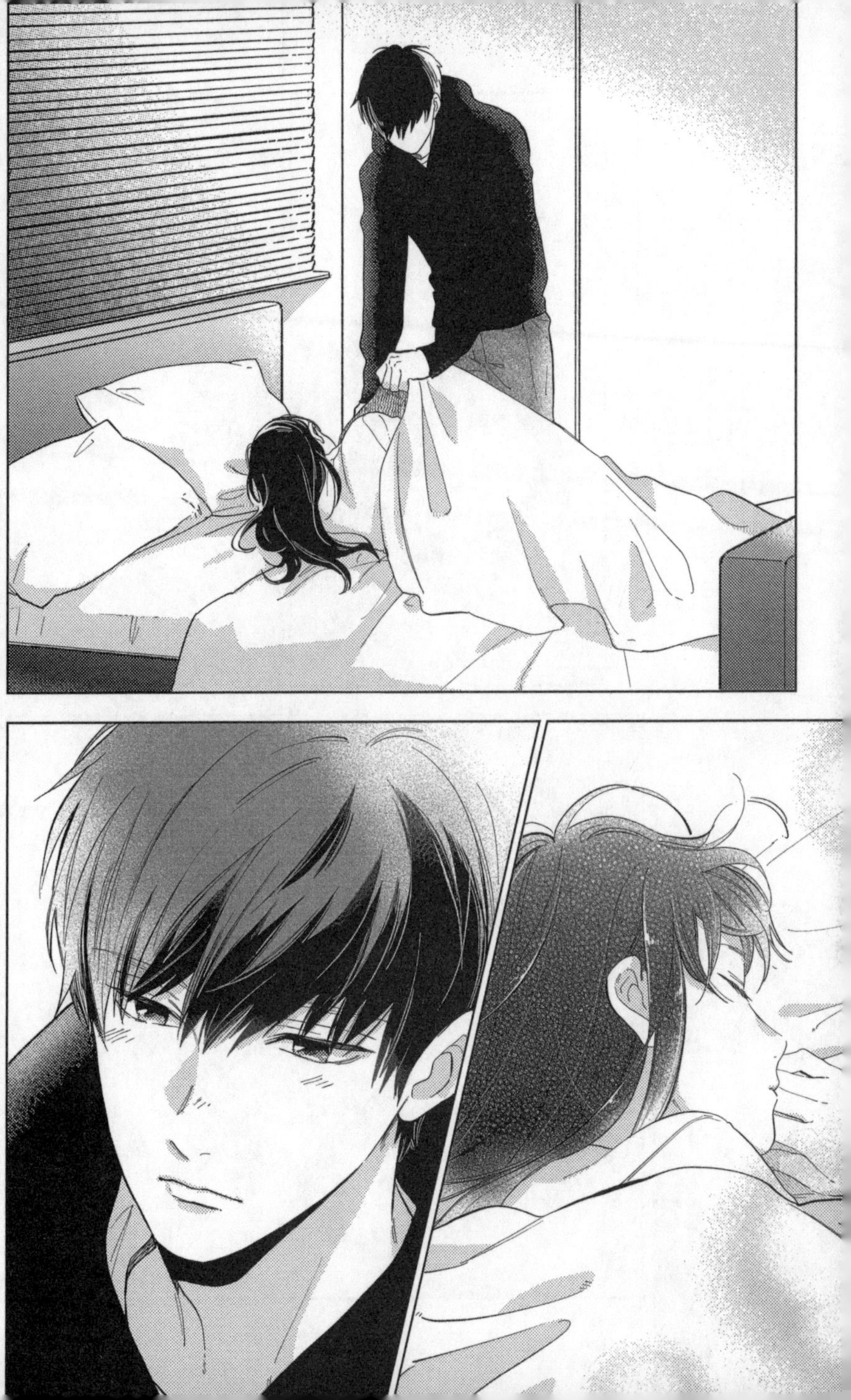

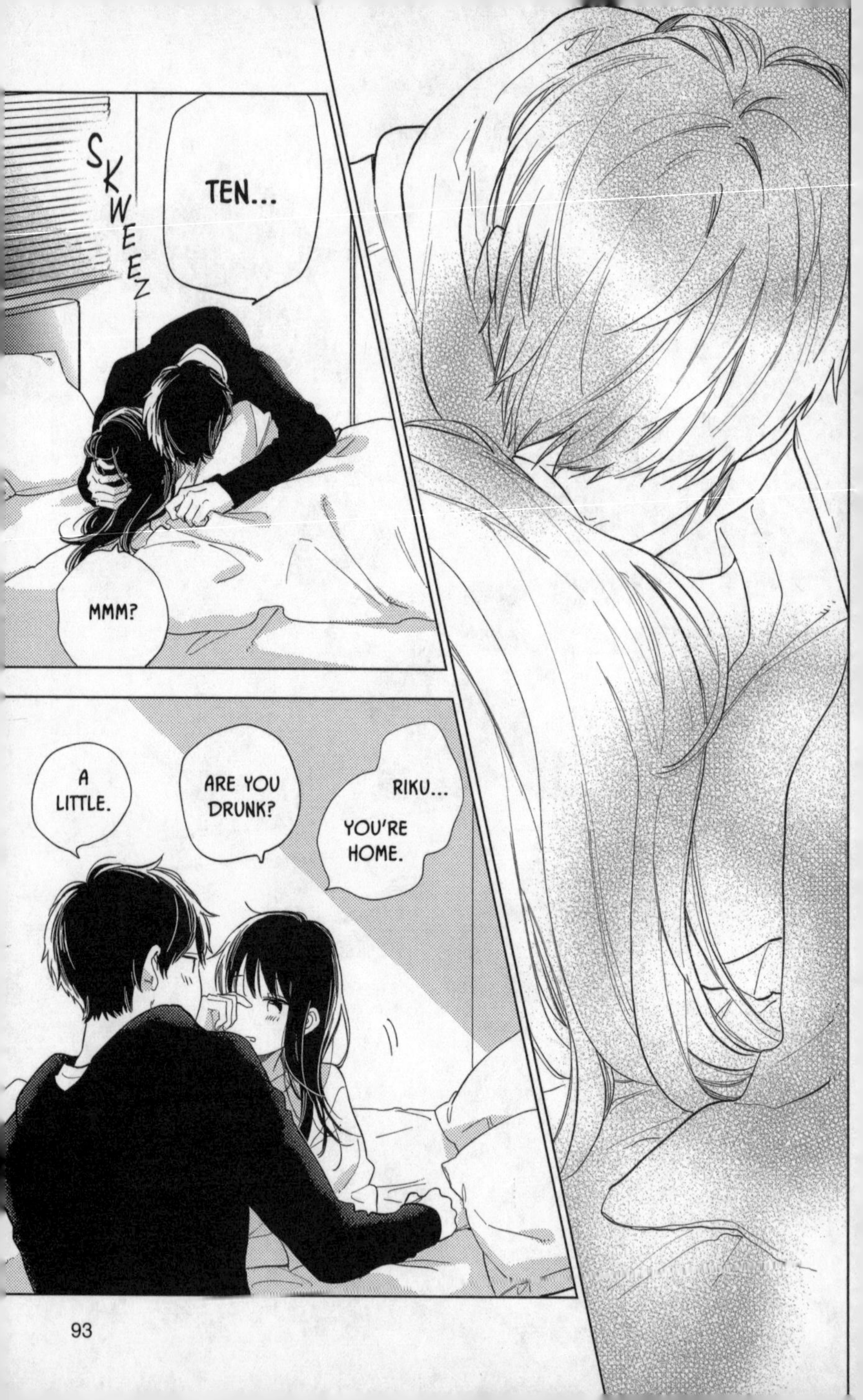
TEN...
SKWEEZ
MMM?
RIKU...
YOU'RE HOME.
ARE YOU DRUNK?
A LITTLE.

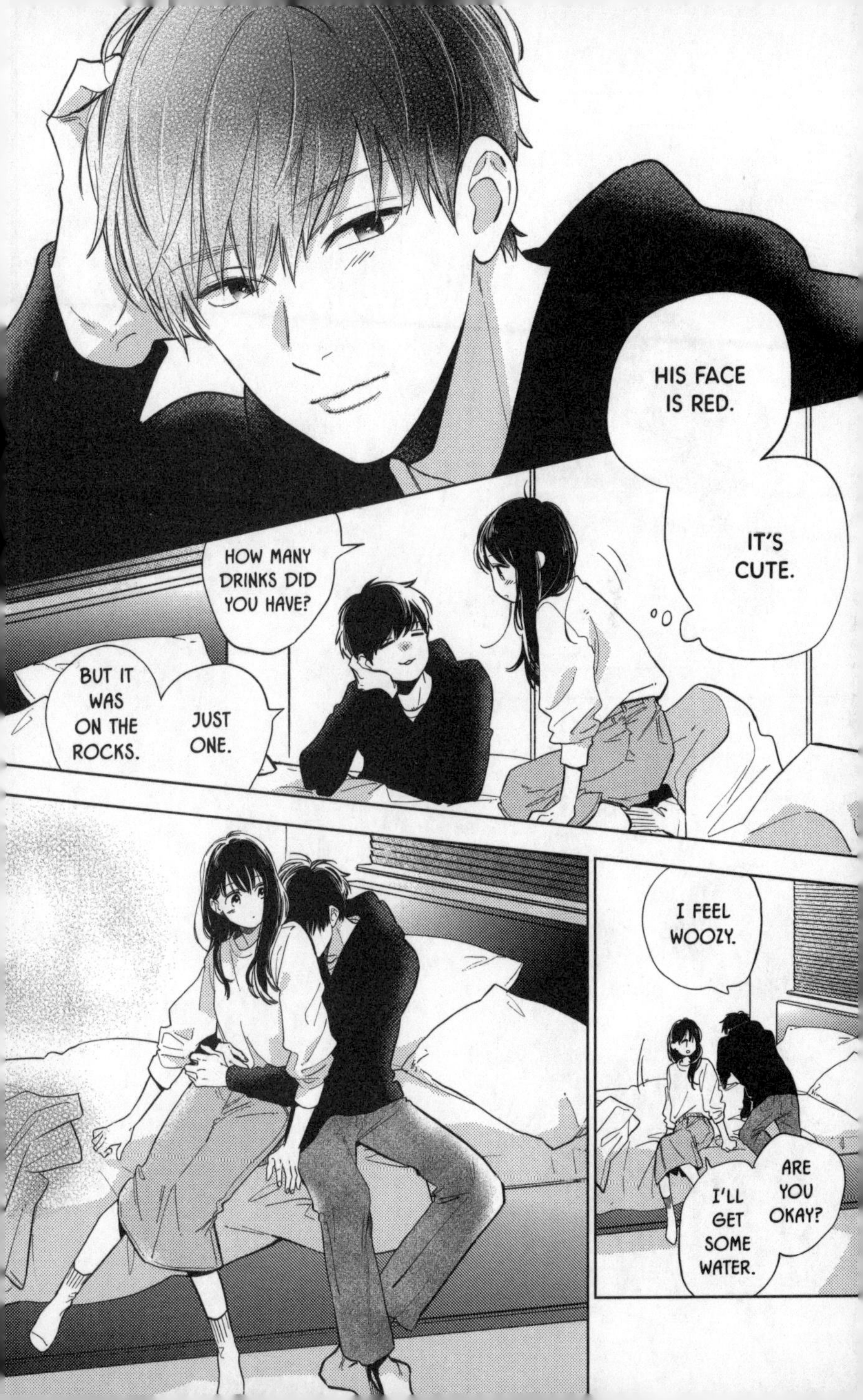
HIS FACE IS RED.
IT'S CUTE.
HOW MANY DRINKS DID YOU HAVE?
JUST ONE.
BUT IT WAS ON THE ROCKS.
I FEEL WOOZY.
ARE YOU OKAY?
I'LL GET SOME WATER.

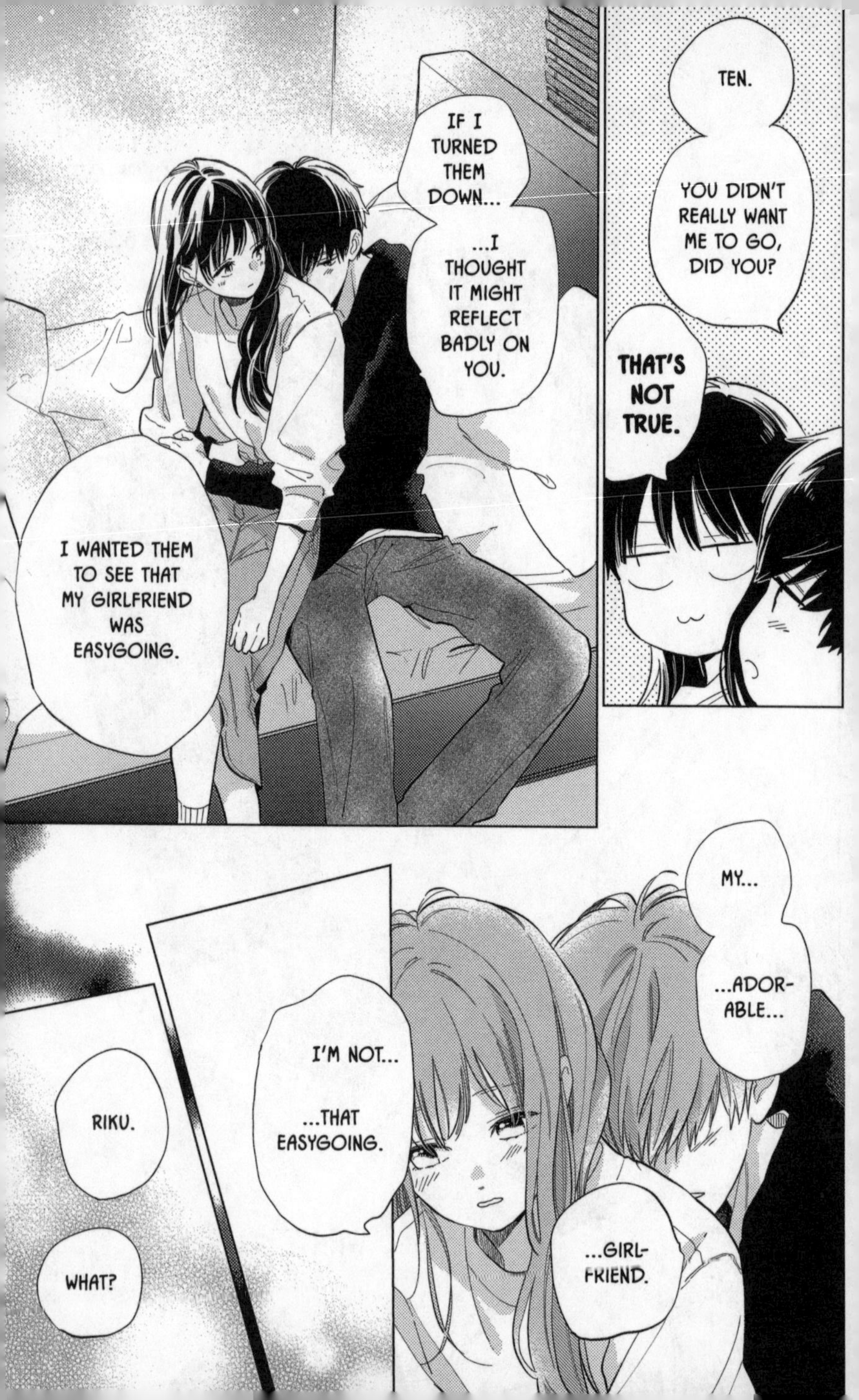
TEN.
YOU DIDN'T REALLY WANT ME TO GO, DID YOU?
THAT'S NOT TRUE.
IF I TURNED THEM DOWN...
...I THOUGHT IT MIGHT REFLECT BADLY ON YOU.
I WANTED THEM TO SEE THAT MY GIRLFRIEND WAS EASYGOING.
MY...
...ADORABLE...
...GIRLFRIEND.
I'M NOT...
...THAT EASYGOING.
RIKU.
WHAT?

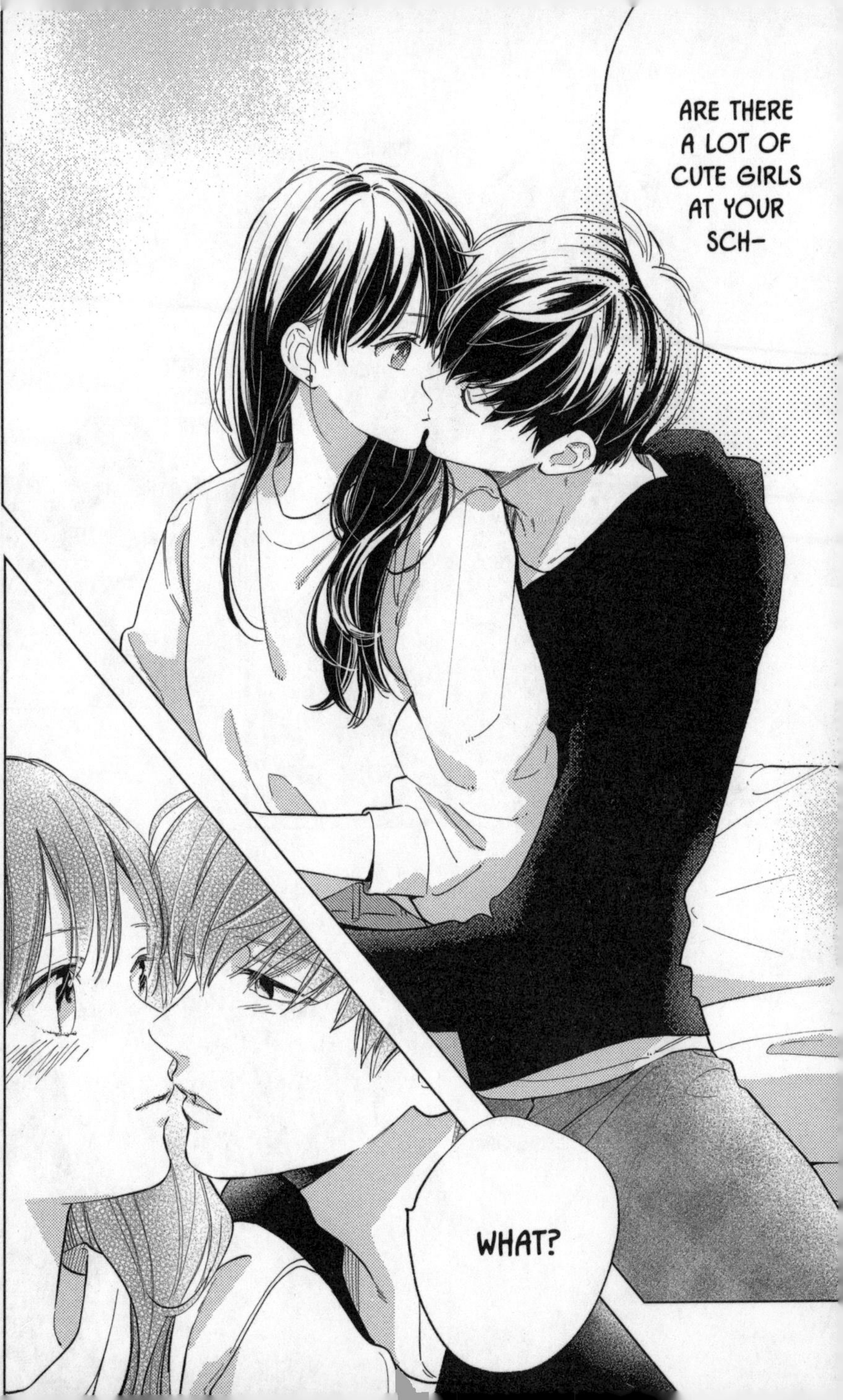
ARE THERE A LOT OF CUTE GIRLS AT YOUR SCH-
WHAT?

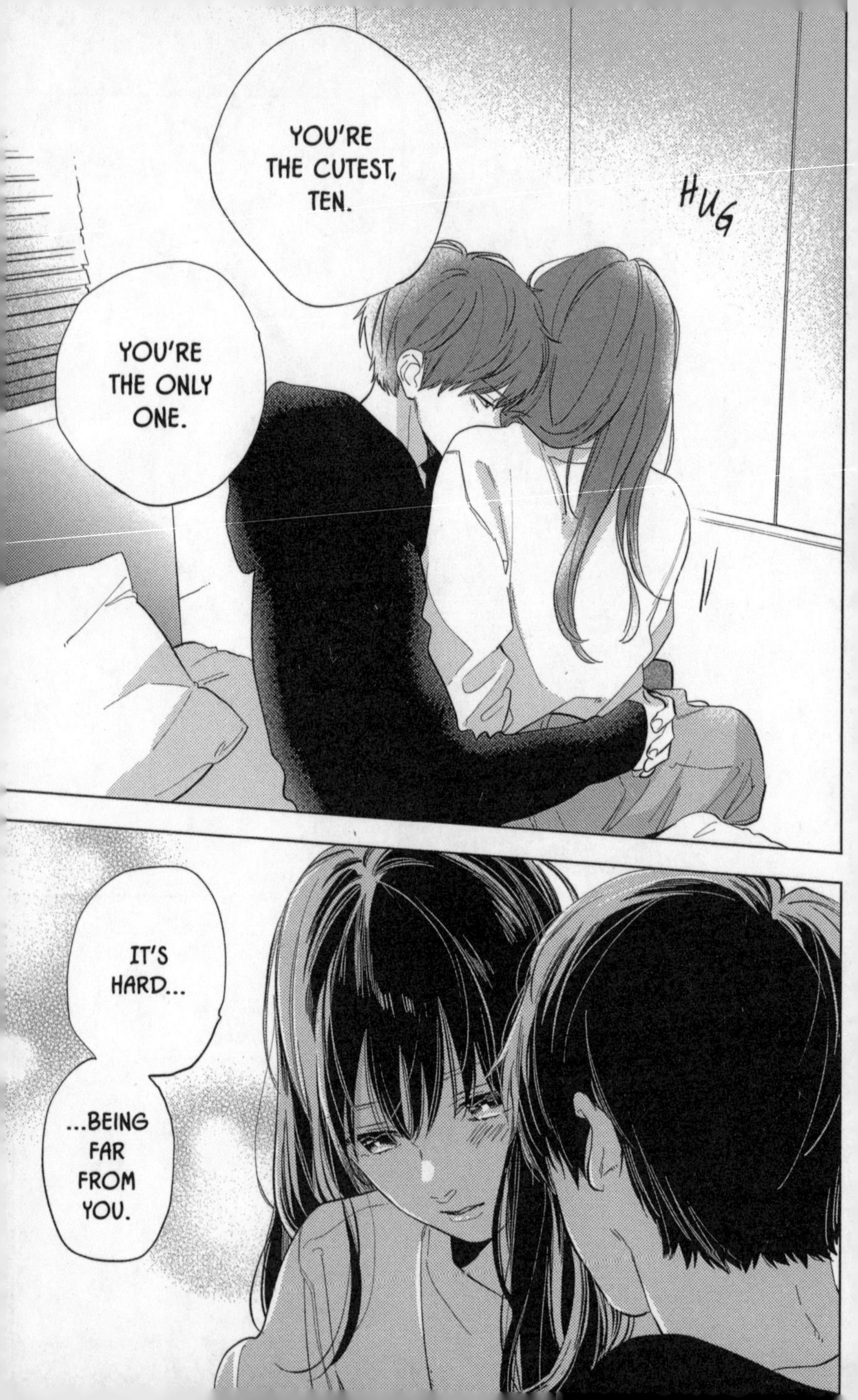
HUG
YOU'RE THE CUTEST, TEN.
YOU'RE THE ONLY ONE.
IT'S HARD...
...BEING FAR FROM YOU.

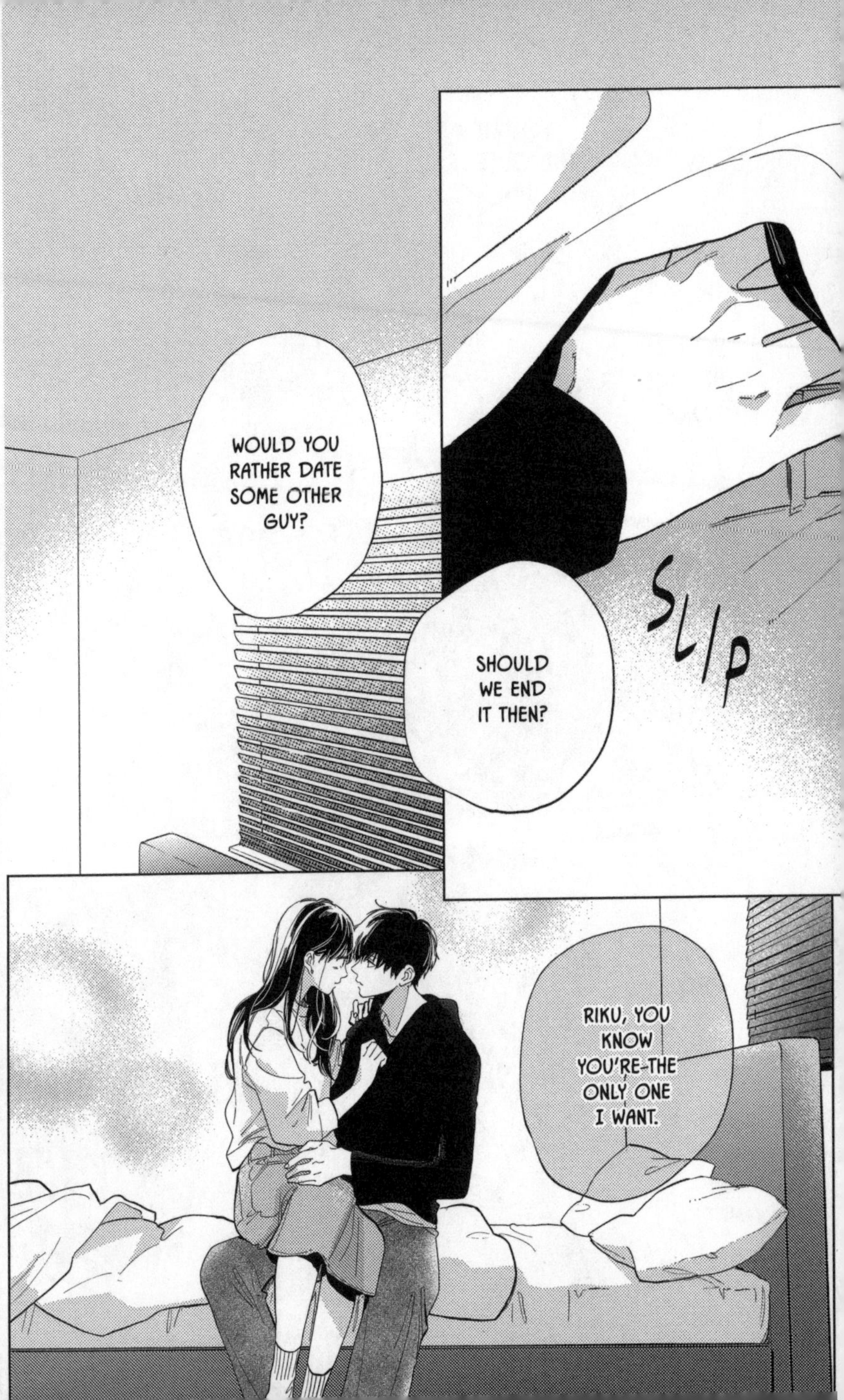
SLIP
SHOULD WE END IT THEN?
WOULD YOU RATHER DATE SOME OTHER GUY?
RIKU, YOU KNOW YOU'RE THE ONLY ONE I WANT.

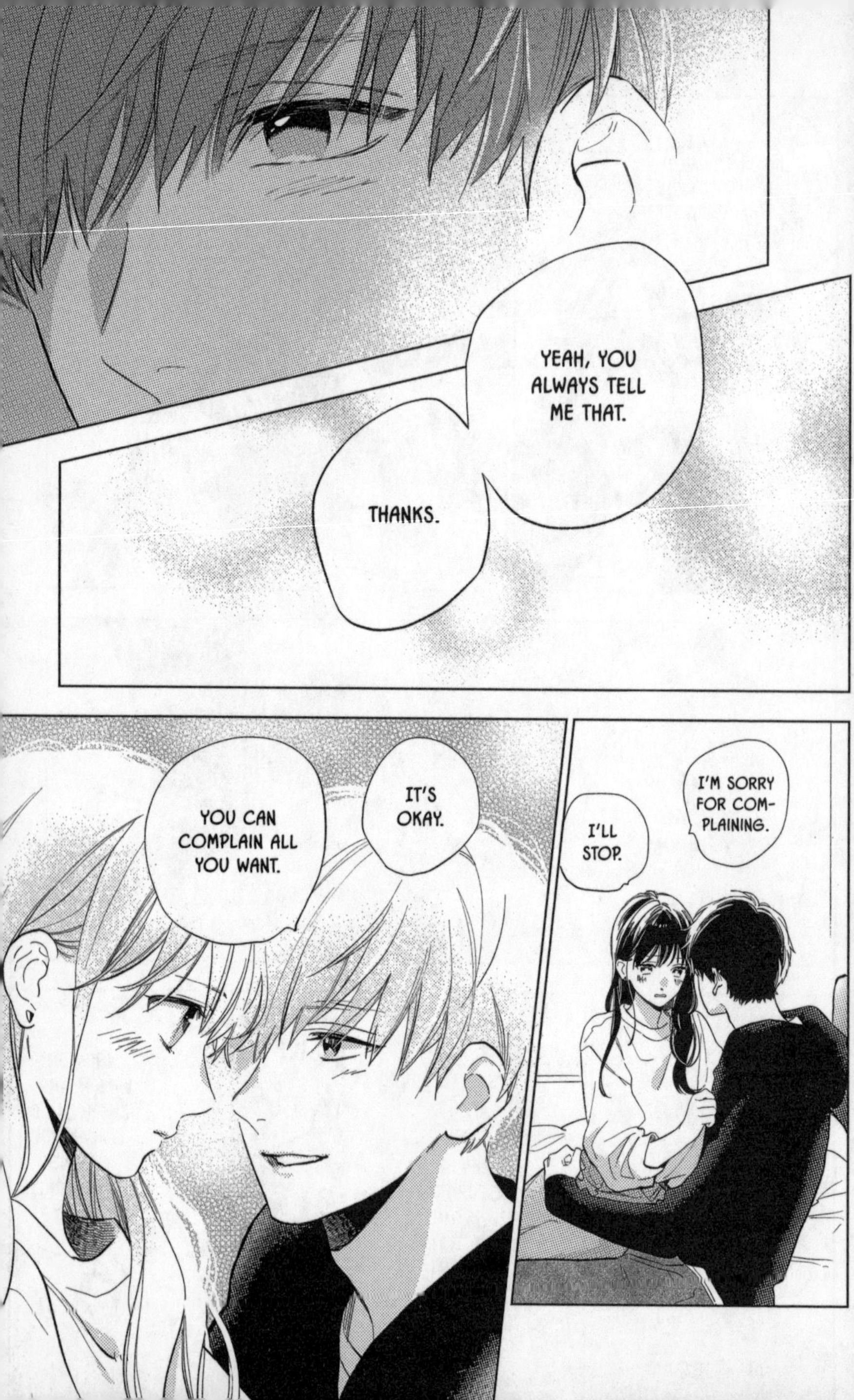
YEAH, YOU ALWAYS TELL ME THAT.
THANKS.
I'M SORRY FOR COM-PLAINING.
I'LL STOP.
IT'S OKAY.
YOU CAN COMPLAIN ALL YOU WANT.

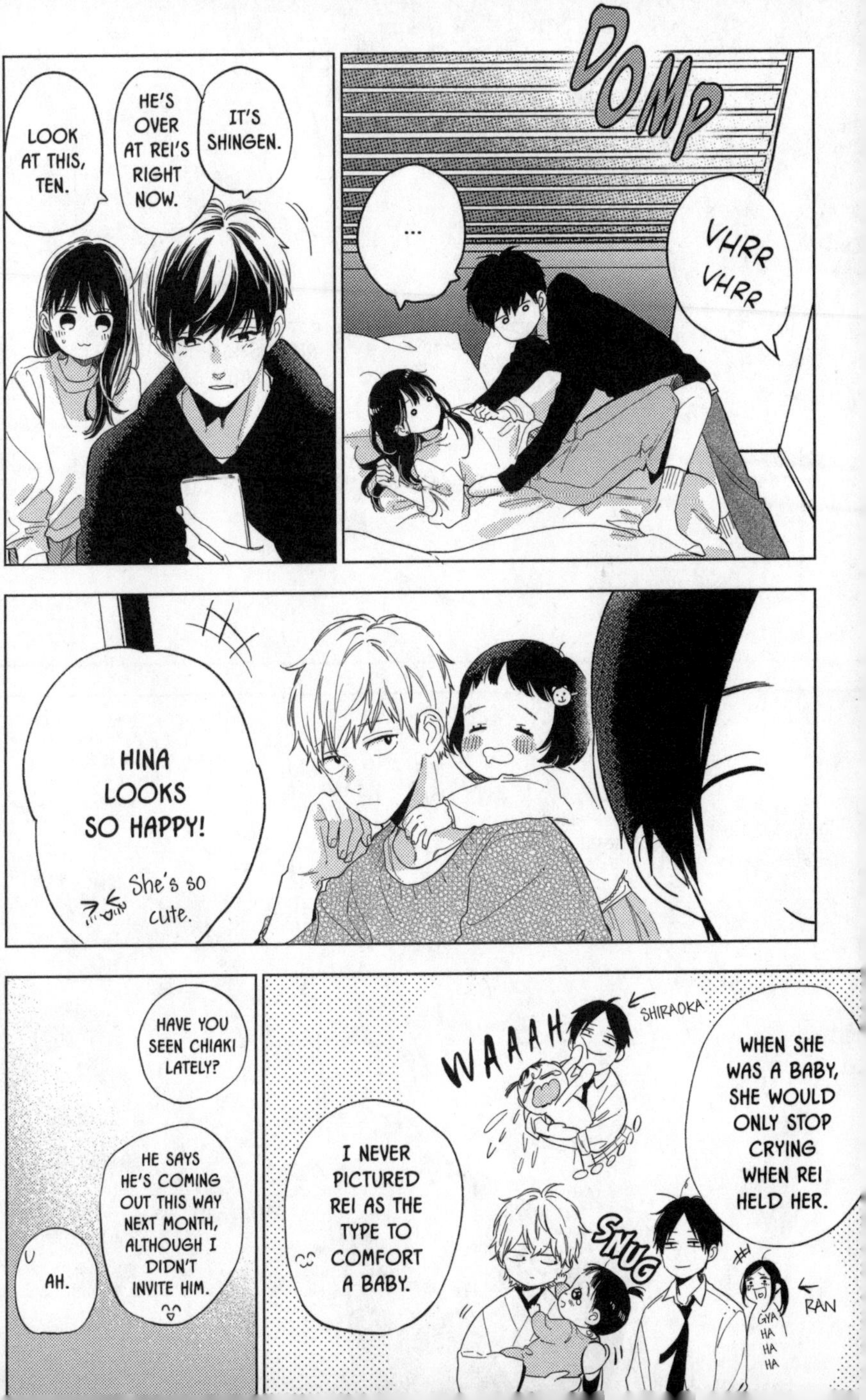
DOMP
...
VHRR VHRR
IT'S SHINGEN.
HE'S OVER AT REI'S RIGHT NOW.
LOOK AT THIS, TEN.
HINA LOOKS SO HAPPY!
She's so cute.
WHEN SHE WAS A BABY, SHE WOULD ONLY STOP CRYING WHEN REI HELD HER.
SHIRAOKA
WAAAH
I NEVER PICTURED REI AS THE TYPE TO COMFORT A BABY.
SNUG
RAN
GYA HA HA HA
HAVE YOU SEEN CHIAKI LATELY?
HE SAYS HE'S COMING OUT THIS WAY NEXT MONTH, ALTHOUGH I DIDN'T INVITE HIM.
AH.

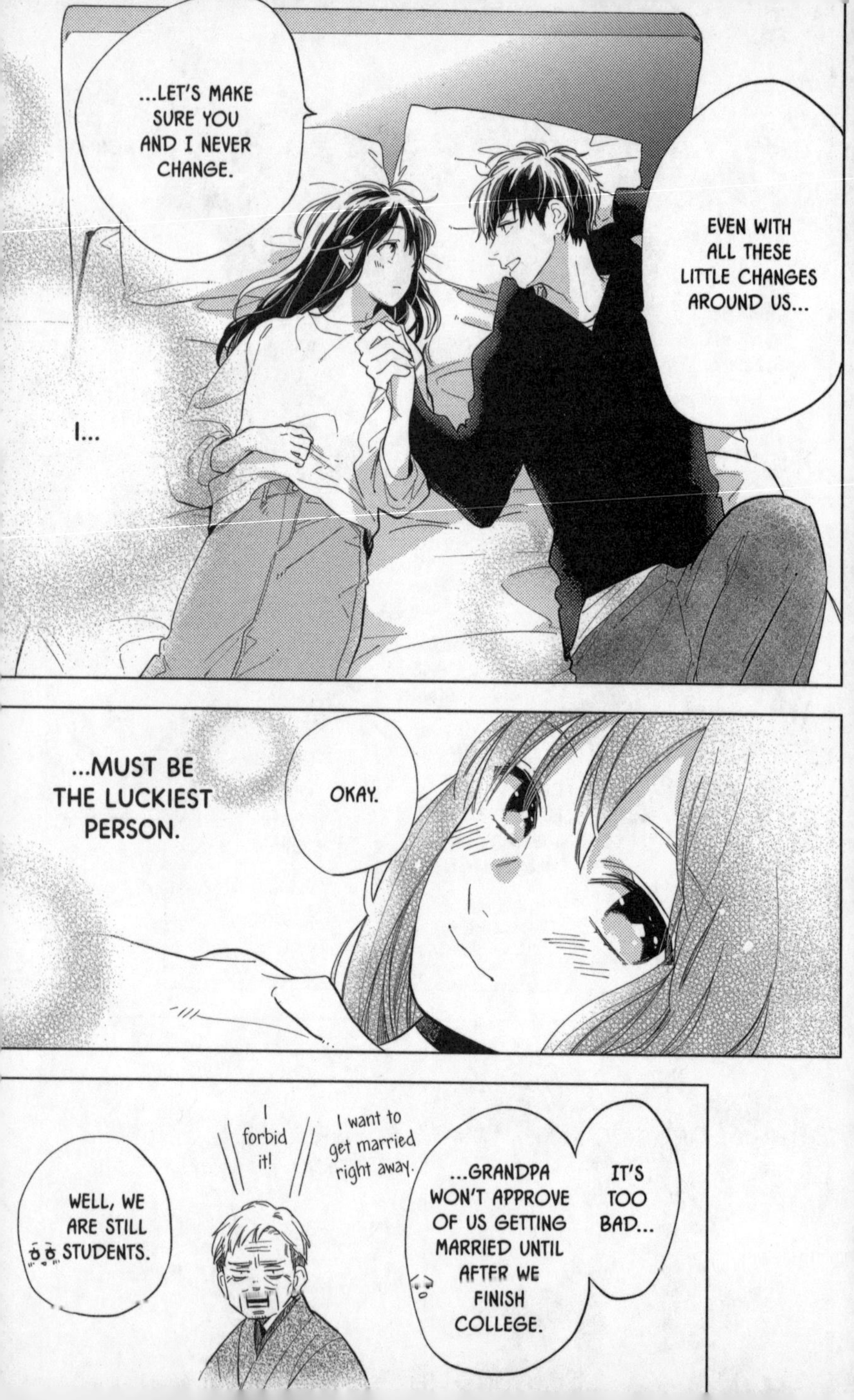
EVEN WITH ALL THESE LITTLE CHANGES AROUND US...
...LET'S MAKE SURE YOU AND I NEVER CHANGE.
I...
OKAY.
...MUST BE THE LUCKIEST PERSON.
IT'S TOO BAD...
...GRANDPA WON'T APPROVE OF US GETTING MARRIED UNTIL AFTFR WE FINISH COLLEGE.
I want to get married right away.
I forbid it!
WELL, WE ARE STILL STUDENTS.

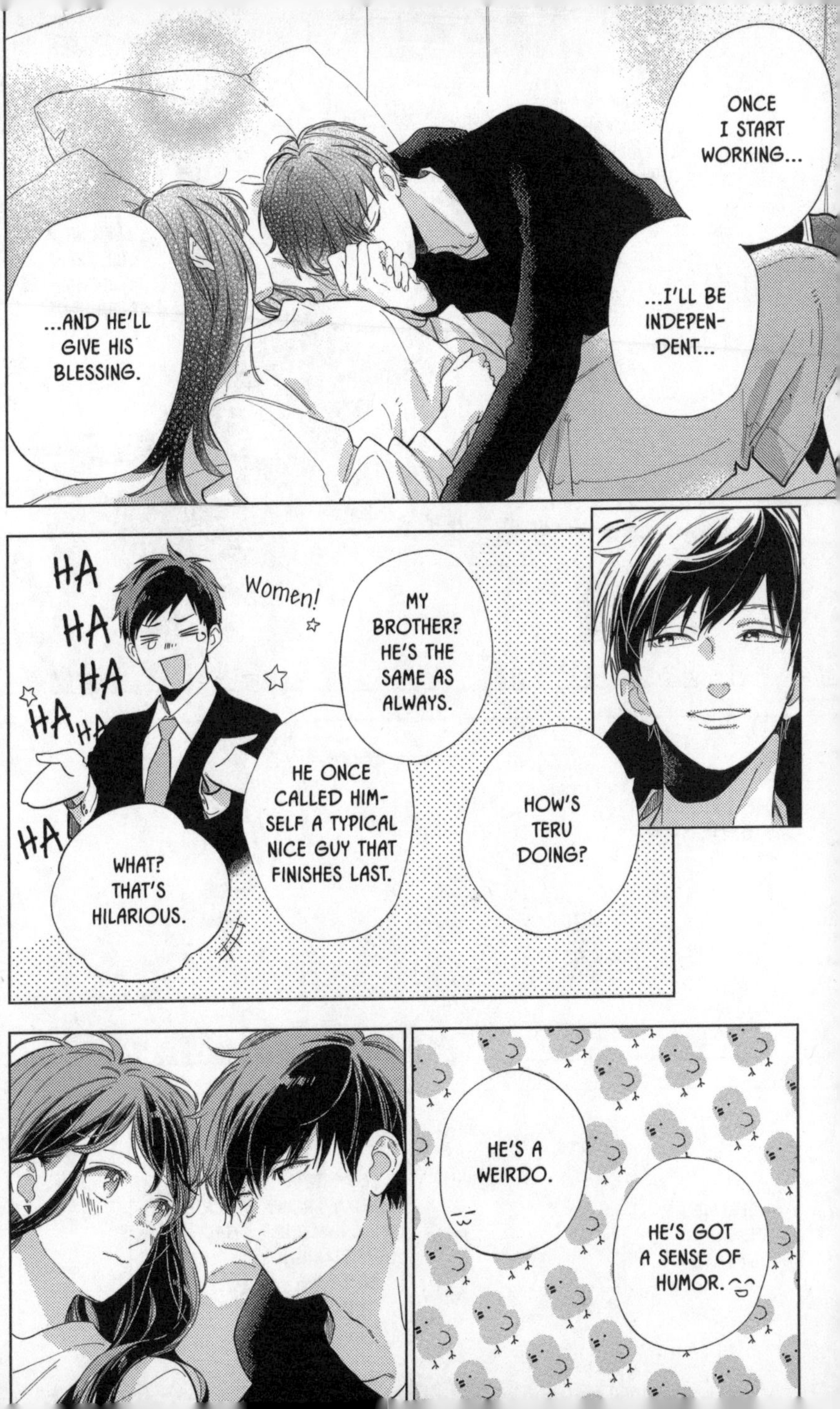
ONCE I START WORKING...
...I'LL BE INDEPEN-DENT...
...AND HE'LL GIVE HIS BLESSING.
HOW'S TERU DOING?
MY BROTHER? HE'S THE SAME AS ALWAYS.
Women!
HE ONCE CALLED HIM-SELF A TYPICAL NICE GUY THAT FINISHES LAST.
HA HA HA HA HA HA
WHAT? THAT'S HILARIOUS.
HE'S A WEIRDO.
HE'S GOT A SENSE OF HUMOR.

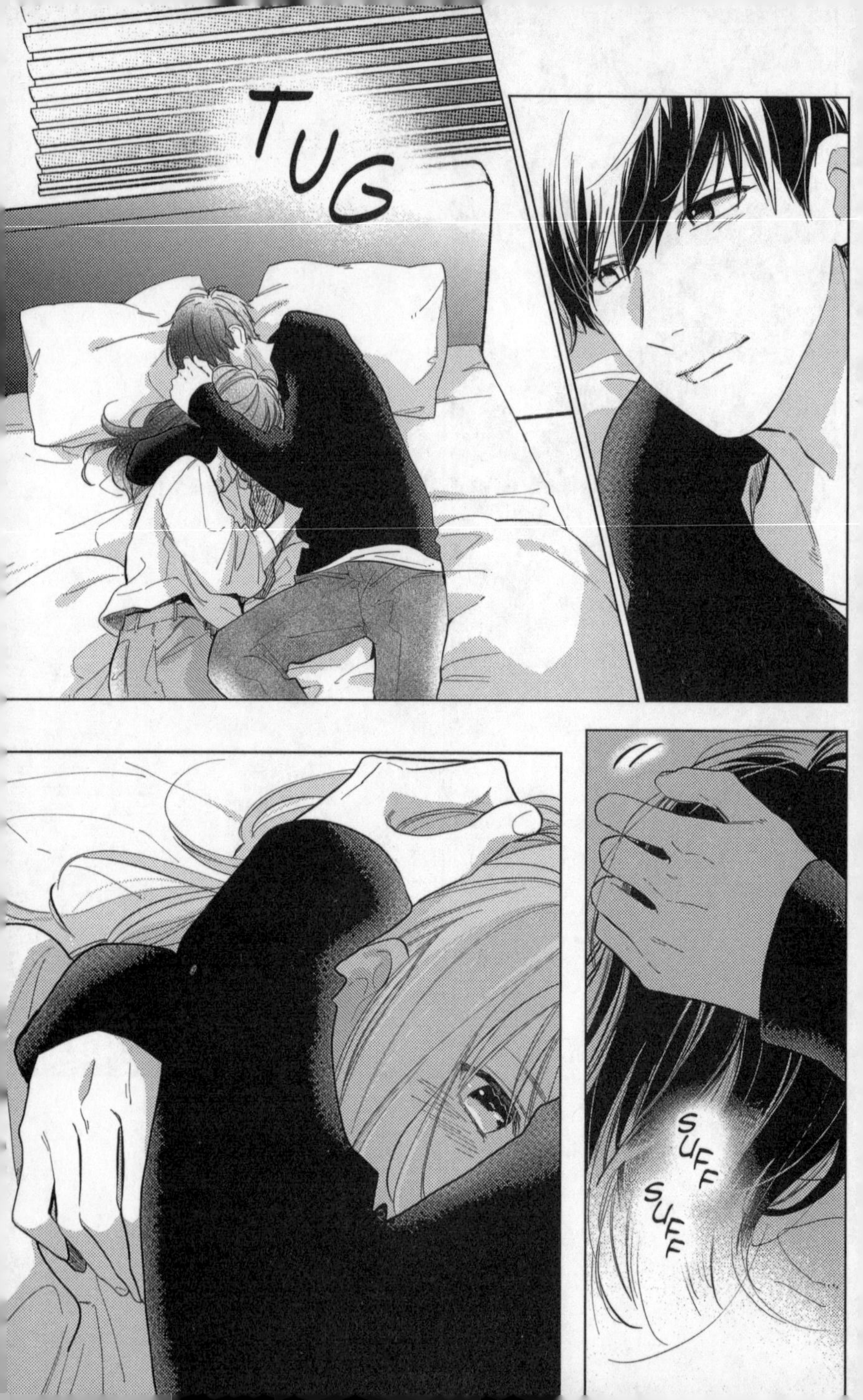
TUG
SUFF SUFF

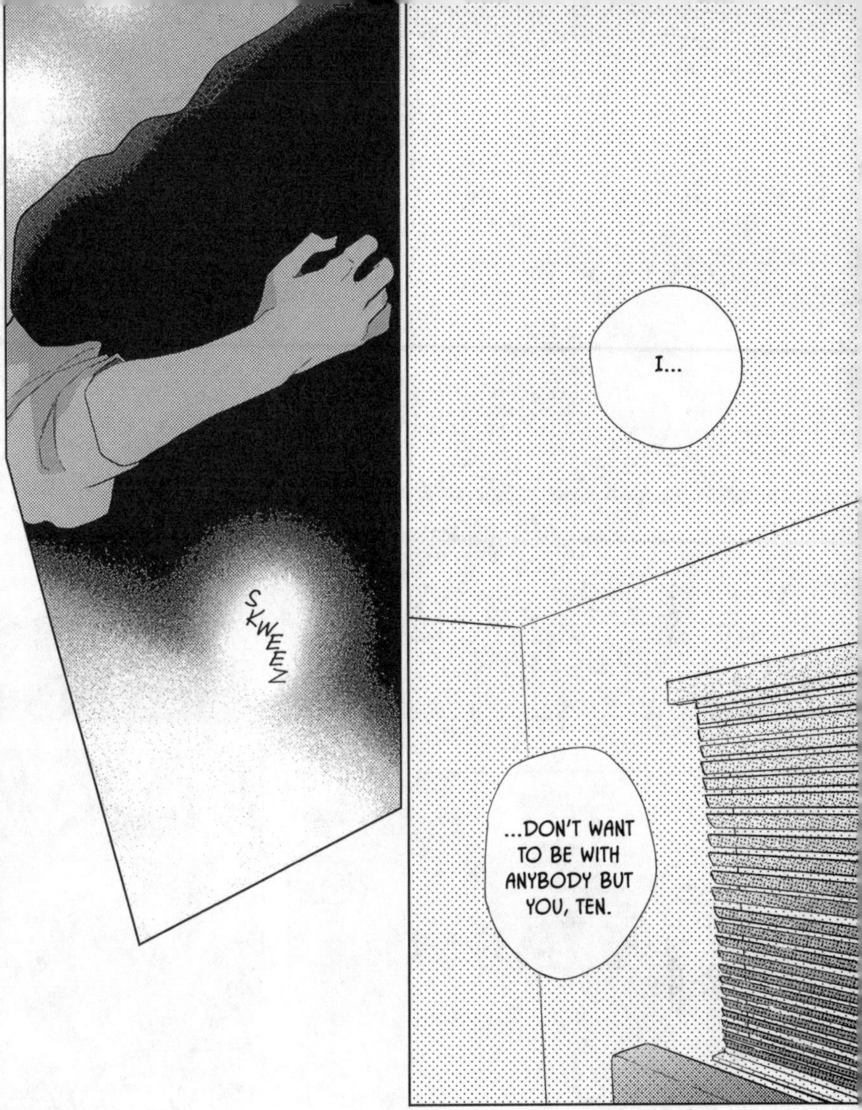
I...
...DON'T WANT TO BE WITH ANYBODY BUT YOU, TEN.
SKWEEZ

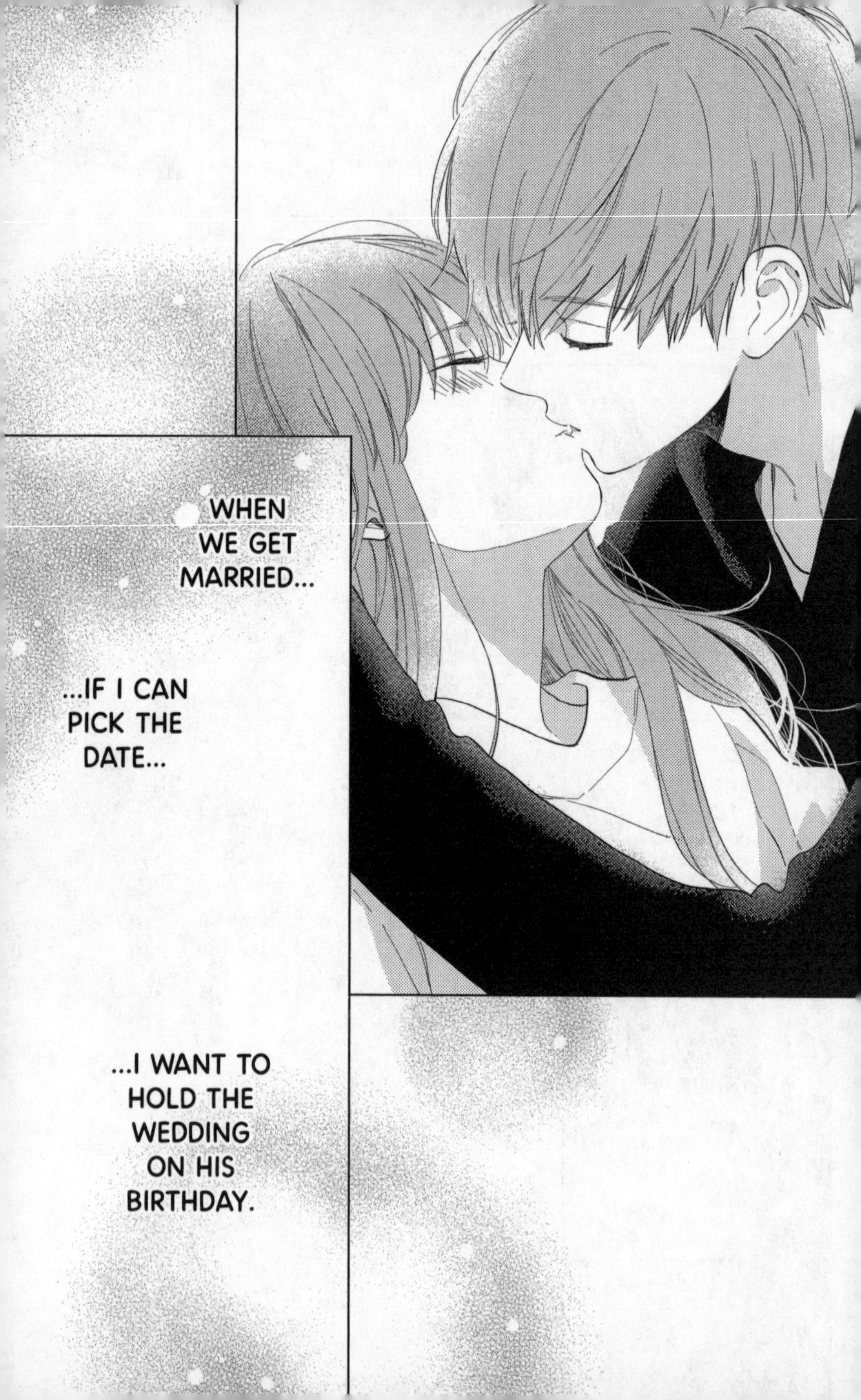
WHEN WE GET MARRIED...
...IF I CAN PICK THE DATE...
...I WANT TO HOLD THE WEDDING ON HIS BIRTHDAY.

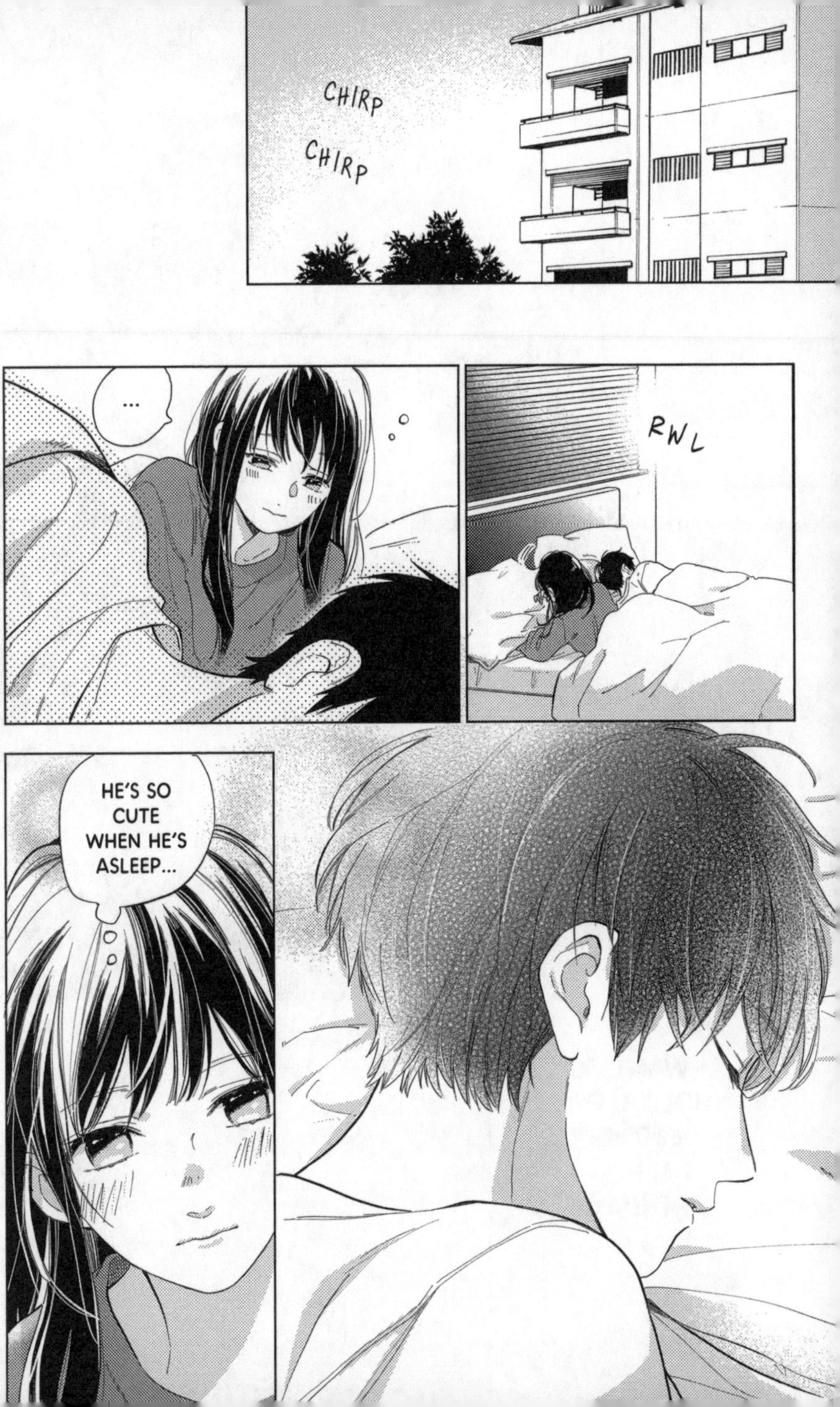
CHIRP
CHIRP
RWL
...
HE'S SO CUTE WHEN HE'S ASLEEP...

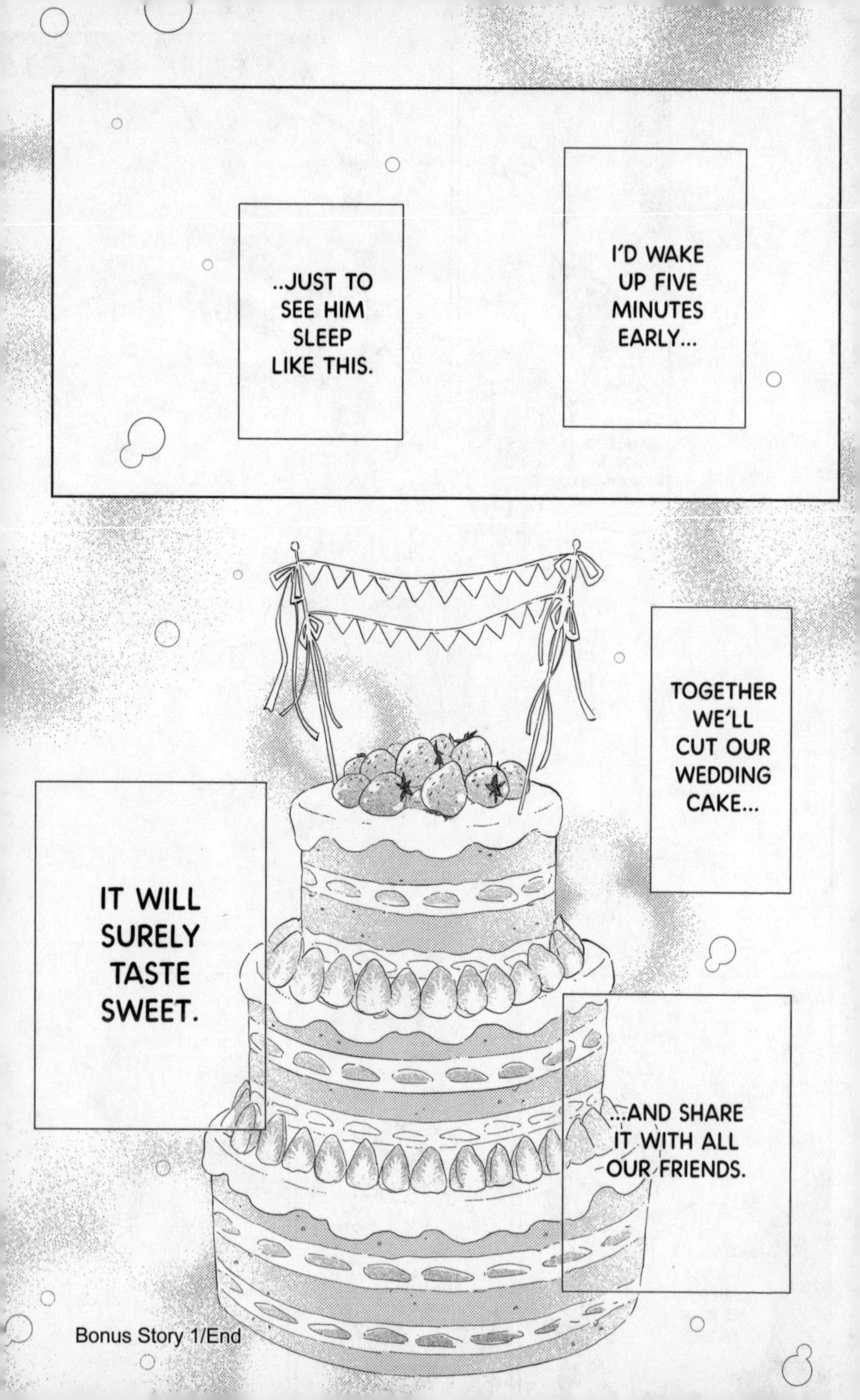
I'D WAKE UP FIVE MINUTES EARLY...
..JUST TO SEE HIM SLEEP LIKE THIS.
TOGETHER WE'LL CUT OUR WEDDING CAKE...
...AND SHARE IT WITH ALL OUR FRIENDS.
IT WILL SURELY TASTE SWEET.

Bonus Story 1/End

Bonus Story 2

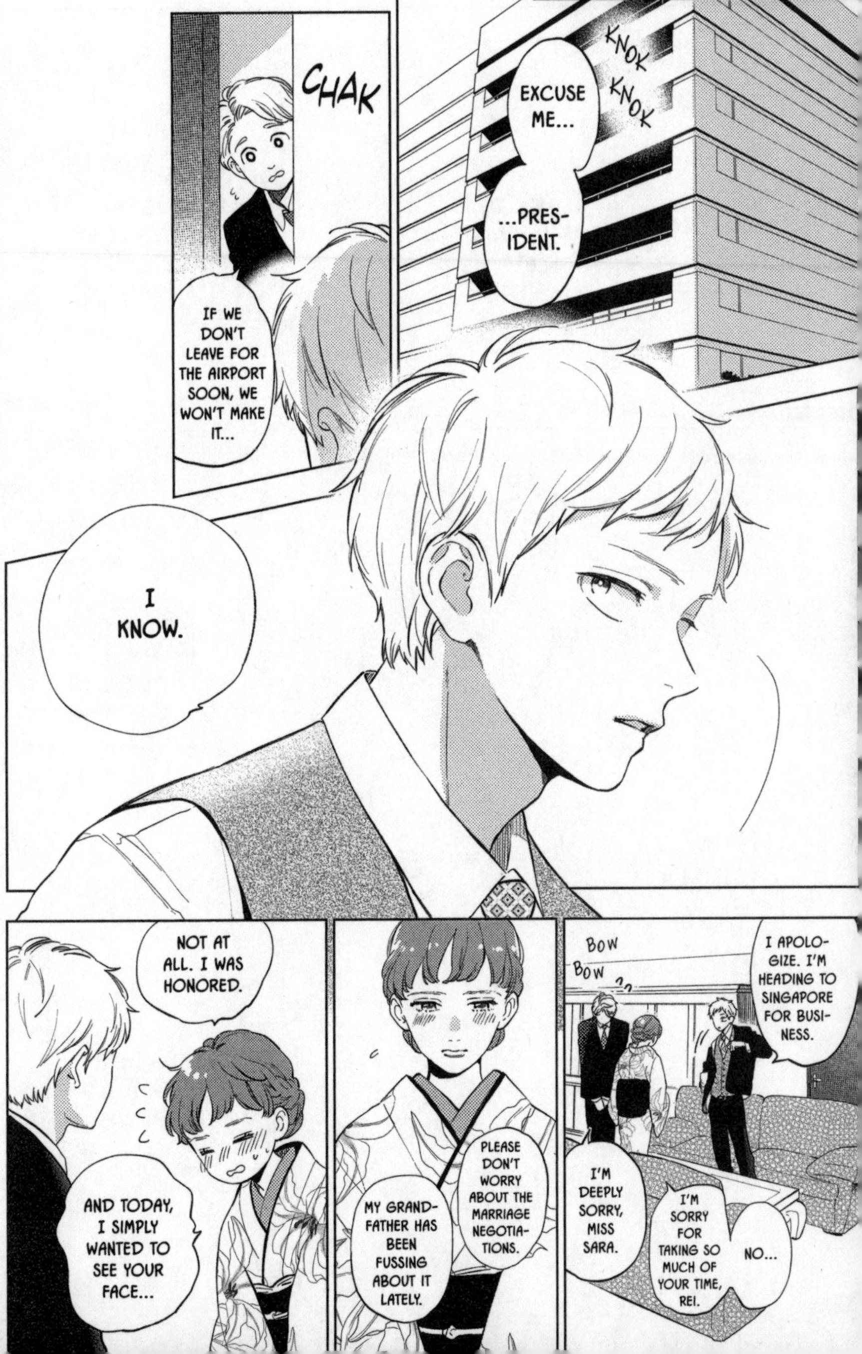
KNOK KNOK
EXCUSE ME...
...PRESIDENT.
CHAK
IF WE DON'T LEAVE FOR THE AIRPORT SOON, WE WON'T MAKE IT...
I KNOW.
I APOLOGIZE. I'M HEADING TO SINGAPORE FOR BUSINESS.
BOW BOW
I'M DEEPLY SORRY, MISS SARA.
I'M SORRY FOR TAKING SO MUCH OF YOUR TIME, REI.
NO...
PLEASE DON'T WORRY ABOUT THE MARRIAGE NEGOTIATIONS.
MY GRANDFATHER HAS BEEN FUSSING ABOUT IT LATELY.
NOT AT ALL. I WAS HONORED.
AND TODAY, I SIMPLY WANTED TO SEE YOUR FACE...

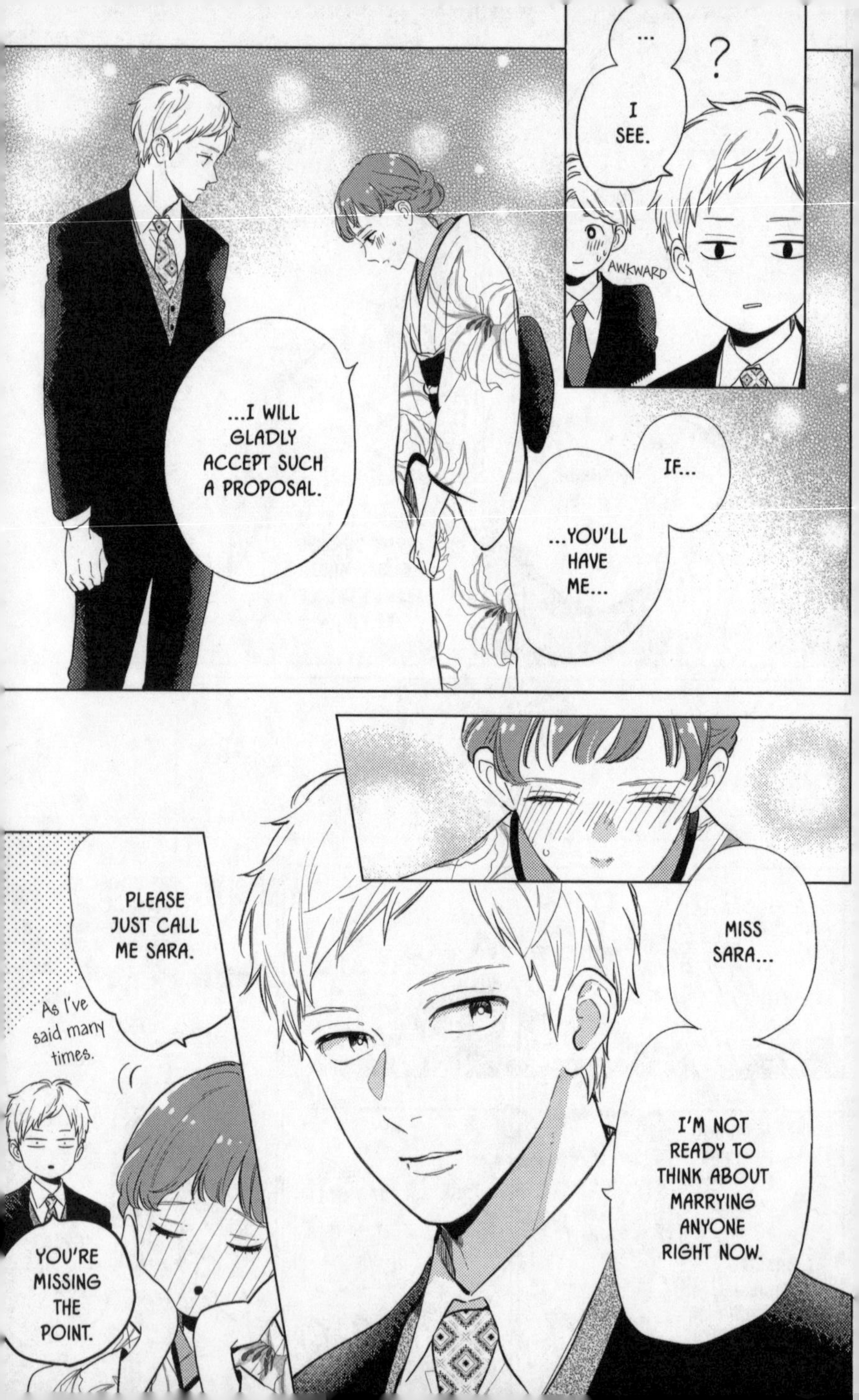
...
I SEE.
?
AWKWARD
IF...
...YOU'LL HAVE ME...
...I WILL GLADLY ACCEPT SUCH A PROPOSAL.
MISS SARA...
I'M NOT READY TO THINK ABOUT MARRYING ANYONE RIGHT NOW.
PLEASE JUST CALL ME SARA.
As I've said many times.
YOU'RE MISSING THE POINT.

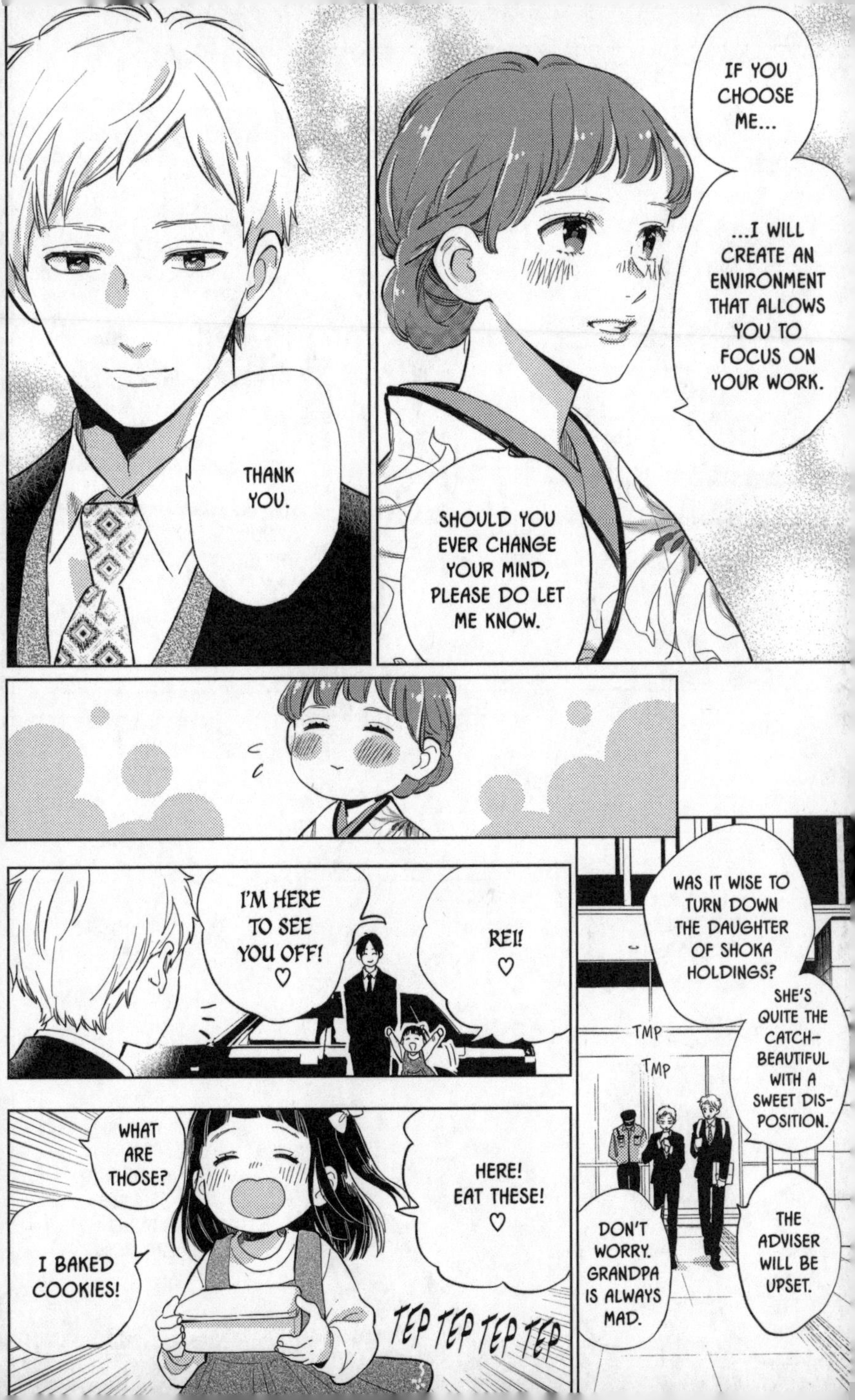
IF YOU CHOOSE ME...
...I WILL CREATE AN ENVIRONMENT THAT ALLOWS YOU TO FOCUS ON YOUR WORK.
SHOULD YOU EVER CHANGE YOUR MIND, PLEASE DO LET ME KNOW.
THANK YOU.
WAS IT WISE TO TURN DOWN THE DAUGHTER OF SHOKA HOLDINGS?
SHE'S QUITE THE CATCH—BEAUTIFUL WITH A SWEET DISPOSITION.
TMP
TMP
THE ADVISER WILL BE UPSET.
DON'T WORRY. GRANDPA IS ALWAYS MAD.
REI! ♡
I'M HERE TO SEE YOU OFF! ♡
HERE! EAT THESE! ♡
WHAT ARE THOSE?
I BAKED COOKIES!
TEP TEP TEP TEP

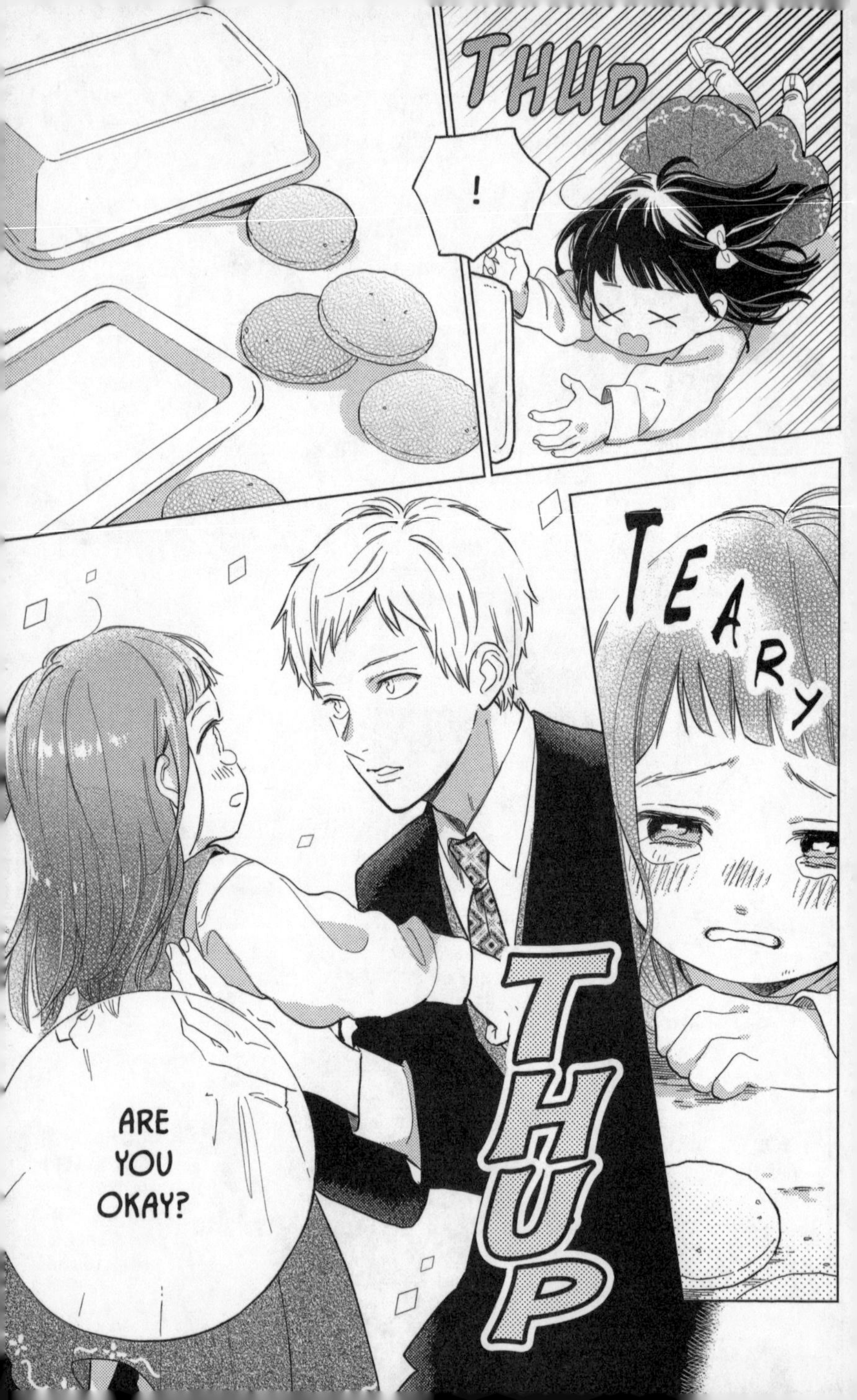
THUD
!
TEARY
THUP
ARE YOU OKAY?

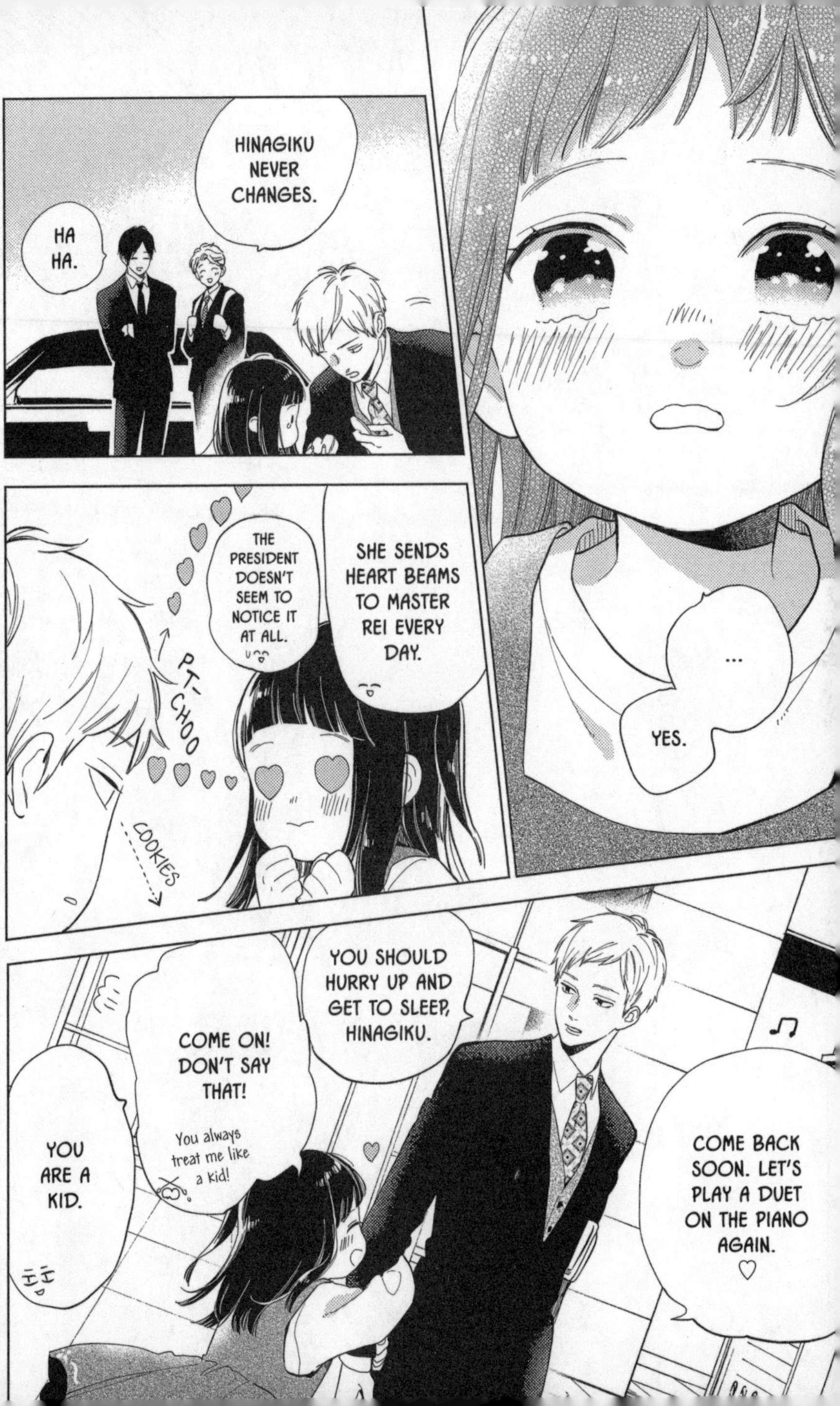
...
YES.
HINAGIKU NEVER CHANGES.
HA HA.
SHE SENDS HEART BEAMS TO MASTER REI EVERY DAY.
THE PRESIDENT DOESN'T SEEM TO NOTICE IT AT ALL.
PT-CHOO
COOKIES
COME BACK SOON. LET'S PLAY A DUET ON THE PIANO AGAIN. ♡
YOU SHOULD HURRY UP AND GET TO SLEEP, HINAGIKU.
COME ON! DON'T SAY THAT!
You always treat me like a kid!
YOU ARE A KID.

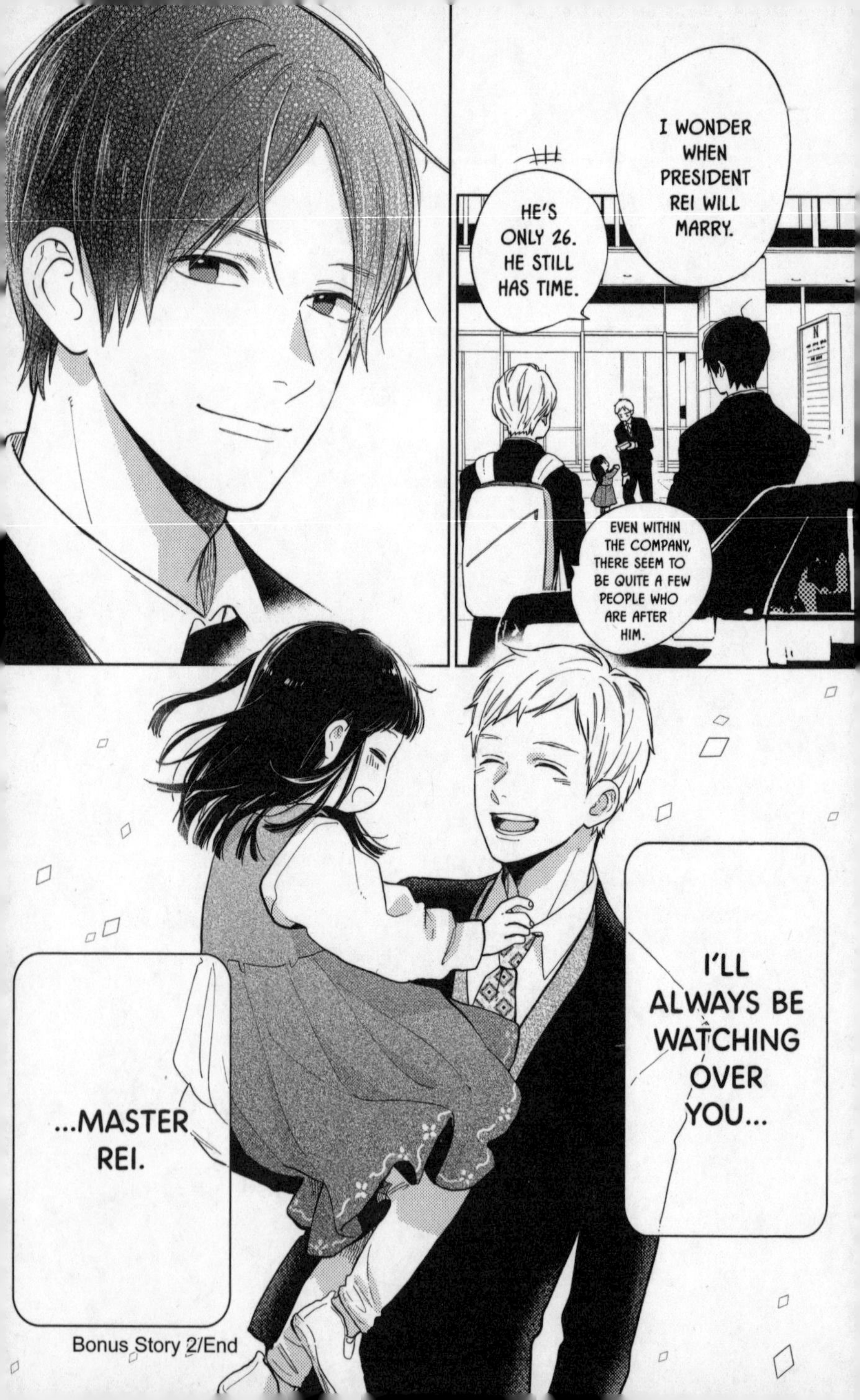
I WONDER WHEN PRESIDENT REI WILL MARRY.
HE'S ONLY 26. HE STILL HAS TIME.
EVEN WITHIN THE COMPANY, THERE SEEM TO BE QUITE A FEW PEOPLE WHO ARE AFTER HIM.
I'LL ALWAYS BE WATCHING OVER YOU...
...MASTER REI.
Bonus Story 2/End

Hello. Volume 12 is the final volume of this series. We hope you'll read through this latter half as well.

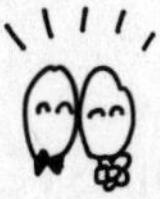

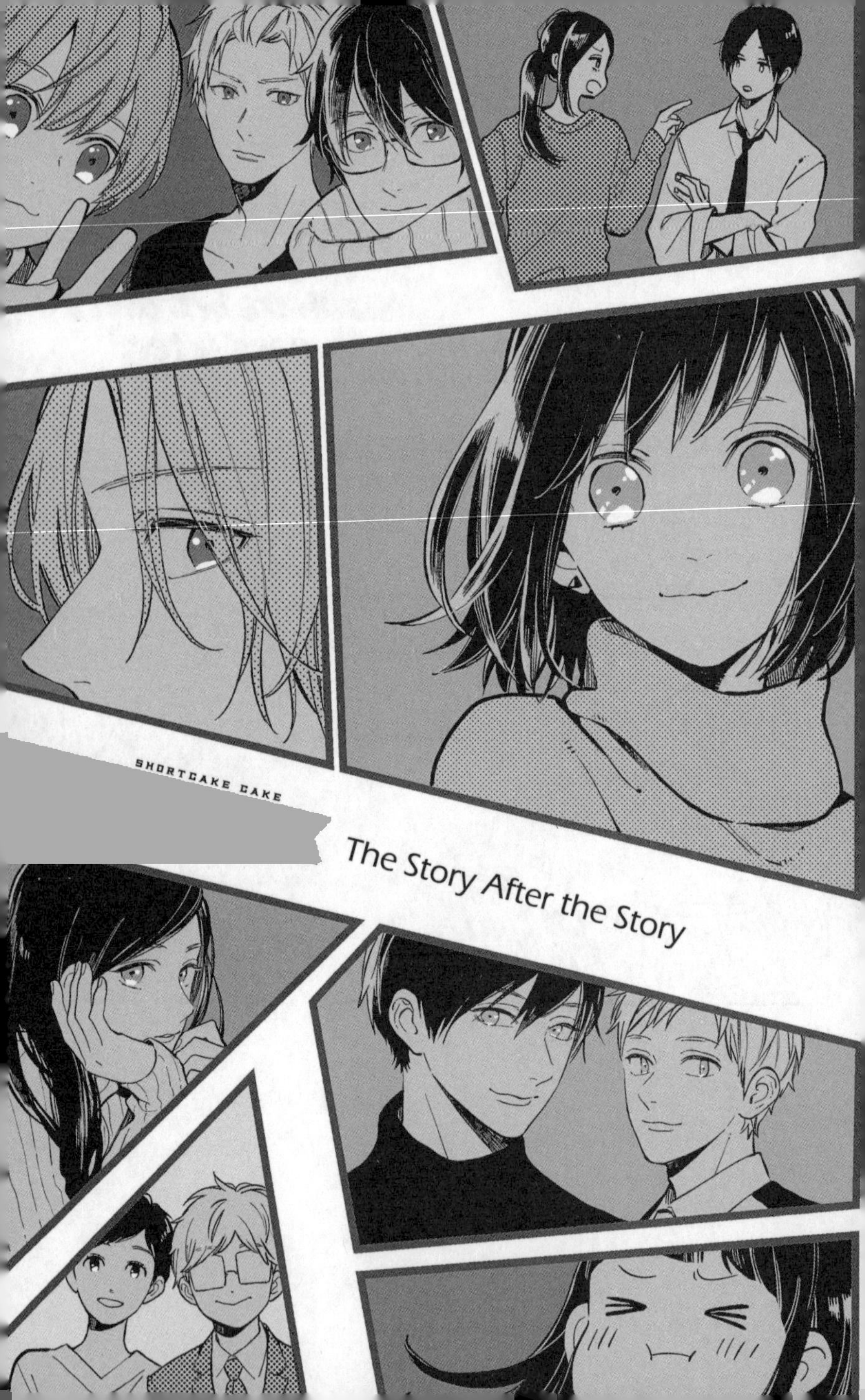
SHORTCAKE CAKE
The Story After the Story

Mizuhara brothers years later

THEY OCCASIONALLY PLAY VIDEO GAMES TOGETHER.

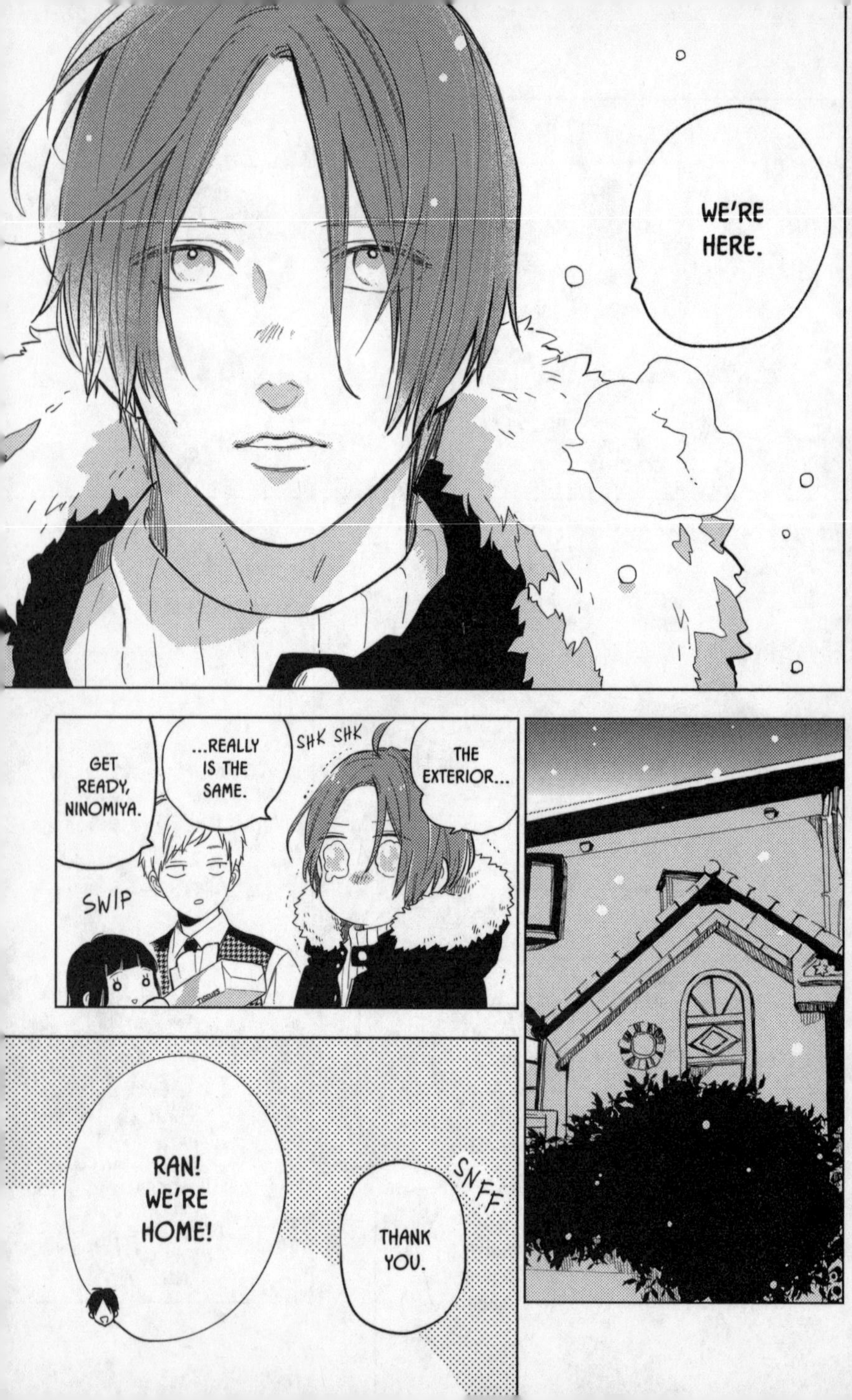
WE'RE HERE.
THE EXTERIOR...
SHK SHK
...REALLY IS THE SAME.
GET READY, NINOMIYA.
SWIP
SNFF
THANK YOU.
RAN! WE'RE HOME!

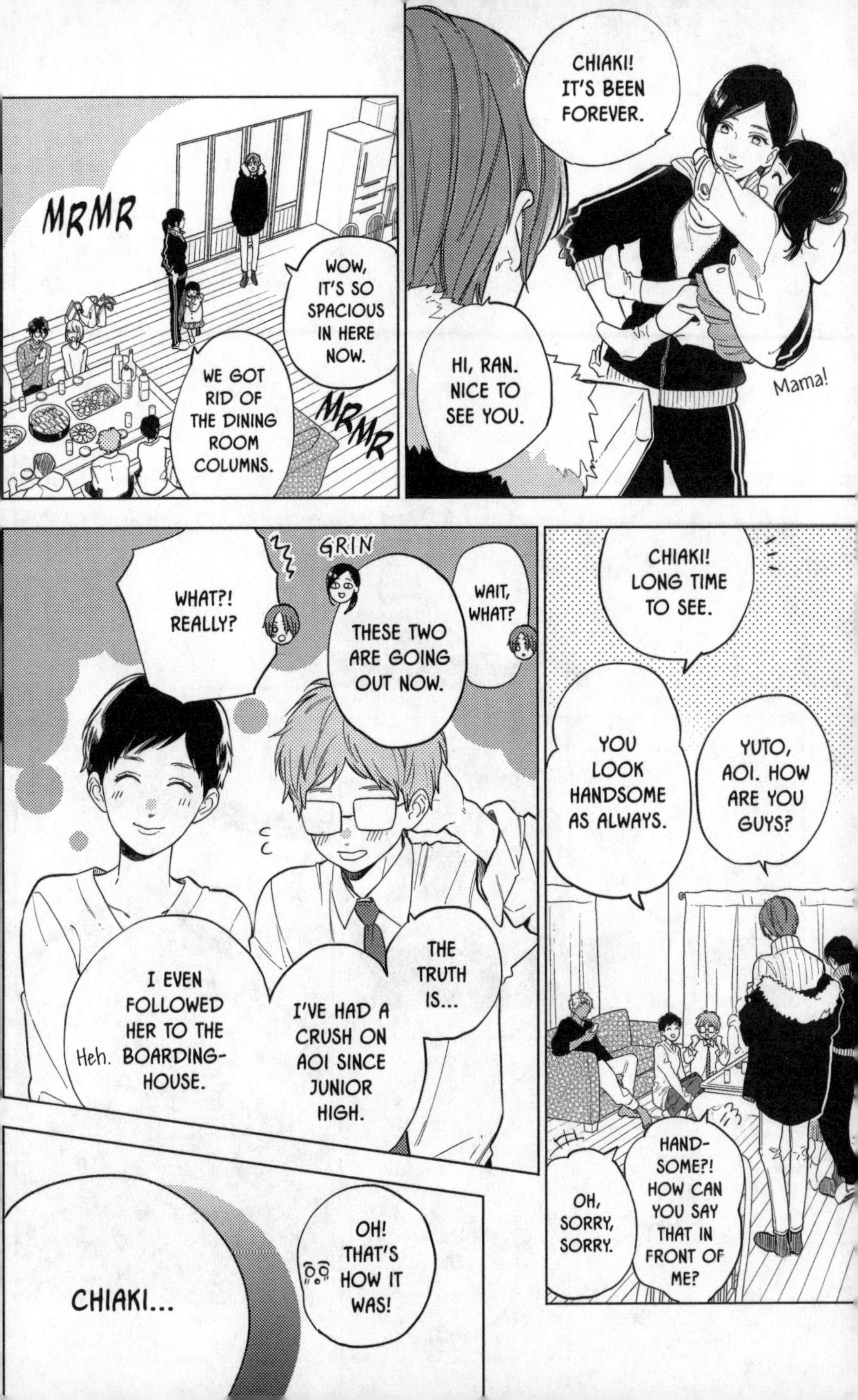
CHIAKI! IT'S BEEN FOREVER.
HI, RAN. NICE TO SEE YOU.
Mama!
MRMR
WOW, IT'S SO SPACIOUS IN HERE NOW.
WE GOT RID OF THE DINING ROOM COLUMNS.
MRMR
CHIAKI! LONG TIME TO SEE.
YUTO, AOI. HOW ARE YOU GUYS?
YOU LOOK HANDSOME AS ALWAYS.
HAND-SOME?! HOW CAN YOU SAY THAT IN FRONT OF ME?
OH, SORRY, SORRY.
GRIN
WAIT, WHAT?
THESE TWO ARE GOING OUT NOW.
WHAT?! REALLY?
THE TRUTH IS...
I'VE HAD A CRUSH ON AOI SINCE JUNIOR HIGH.
I EVEN FOLLOWED HER TO THE BOARDING-HOUSE.
Heh.
OH! THAT'S HOW IT WAS!
CHIAKI...

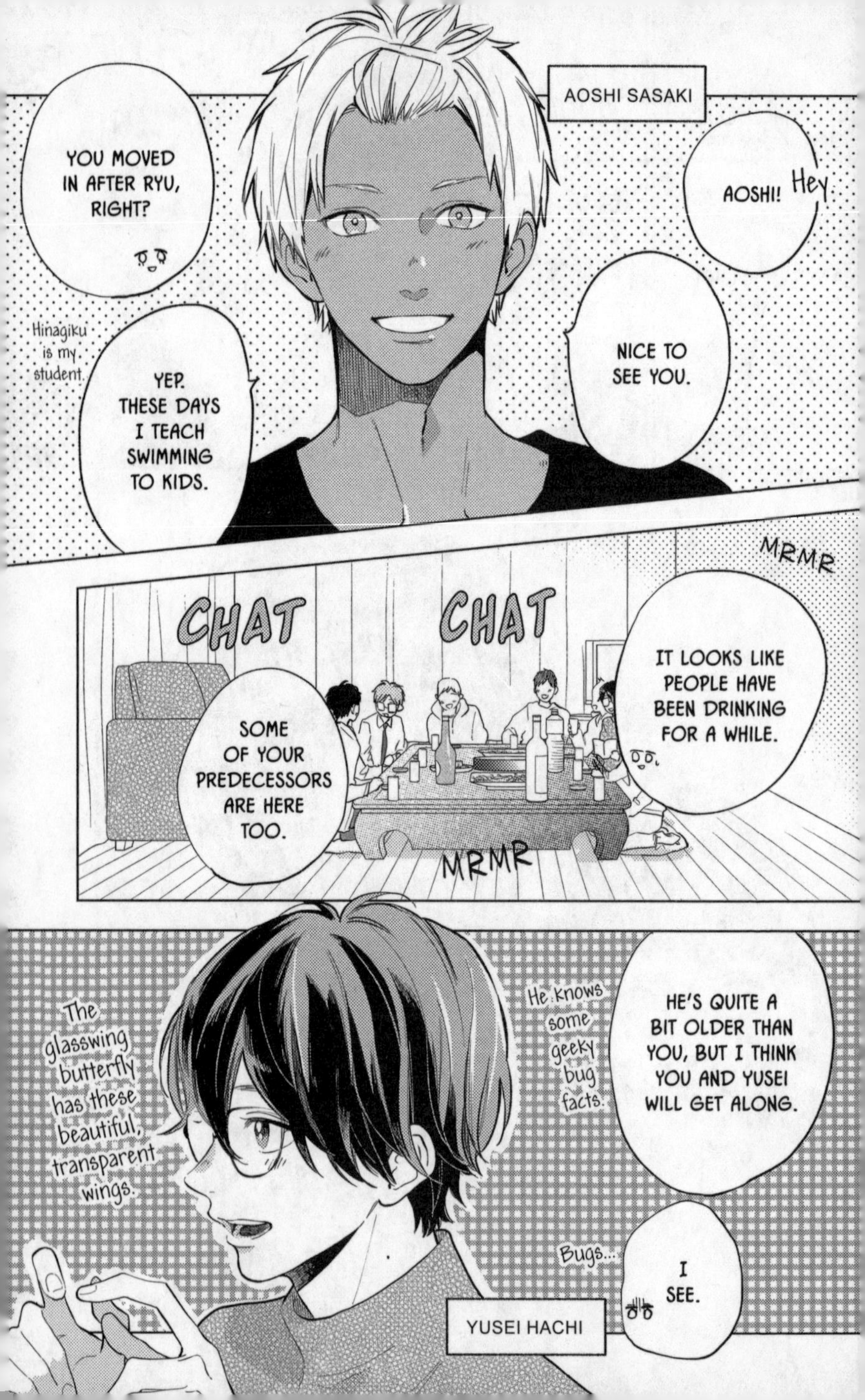
Hey
AOSHI!
AOSHI SASAKI
NICE TO SEE YOU.
YOU MOVED IN AFTER RYU, RIGHT?
YEP. THESE DAYS I TEACH SWIMMING TO KIDS.
Hinagiku is my student.
MRMR
IT LOOKS LIKE PEOPLE HAVE BEEN DRINKING FOR A WHILE.
CHAT CHAT
SOME OF YOUR PREDECESSORS ARE HERE TOO.
MRMR
HE'S QUITE A BIT OLDER THAN YOU, BUT I THINK YOU AND YUSEI WILL GET ALONG.
I SEE.
Bugs...
He knows some geeky bug facts.
YUSEI HACHI
The glasswing butterfly has these beautiful, transparent wings.

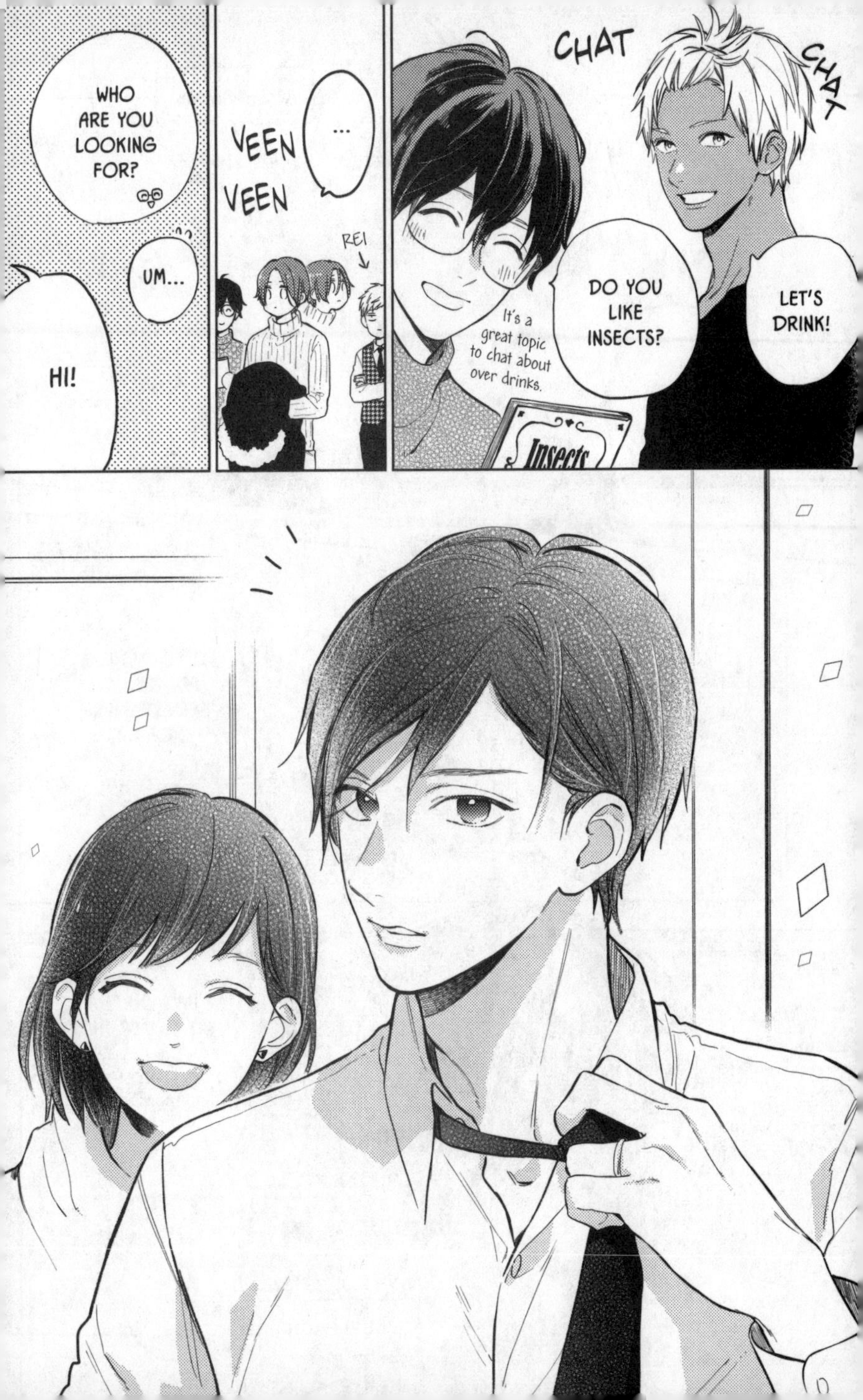
CHAT
CHAT
LET'S DRINK!
DO YOU LIKE INSECTS?
It's a great topic to chat about over drinks.
Insects
...
VEEN VEEN
REI
WHO ARE YOU LOOKING FOR?
UM...
HI!

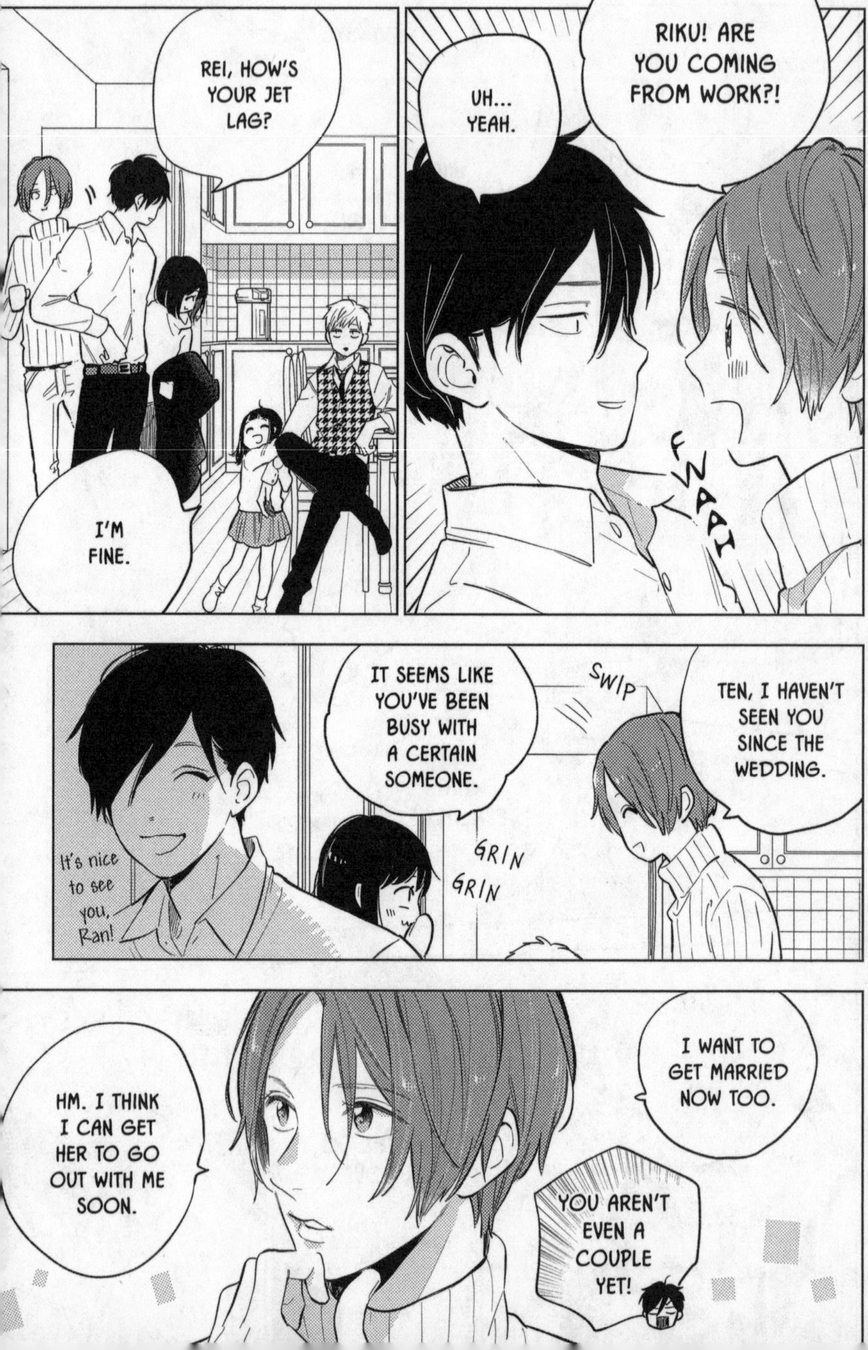
RIKU! ARE YOU COMING FROM WORK?!
UH... YEAH.
FWAAI
REI, HOW'S YOUR JET LAG?
I'M FINE.
TEN, I HAVEN'T SEEN YOU SINCE THE WEDDING.
SWIP
IT SEEMS LIKE YOU'VE BEEN BUSY WITH A CERTAIN SOMEONE.
GRIN GRIN
It's nice to see you, Ran!
I WANT TO GET MARRIED NOW TOO.
YOU AREN'T EVEN A COUPLE YET!
HM. I THINK I CAN GET HER TO GO OUT WITH ME SOON.

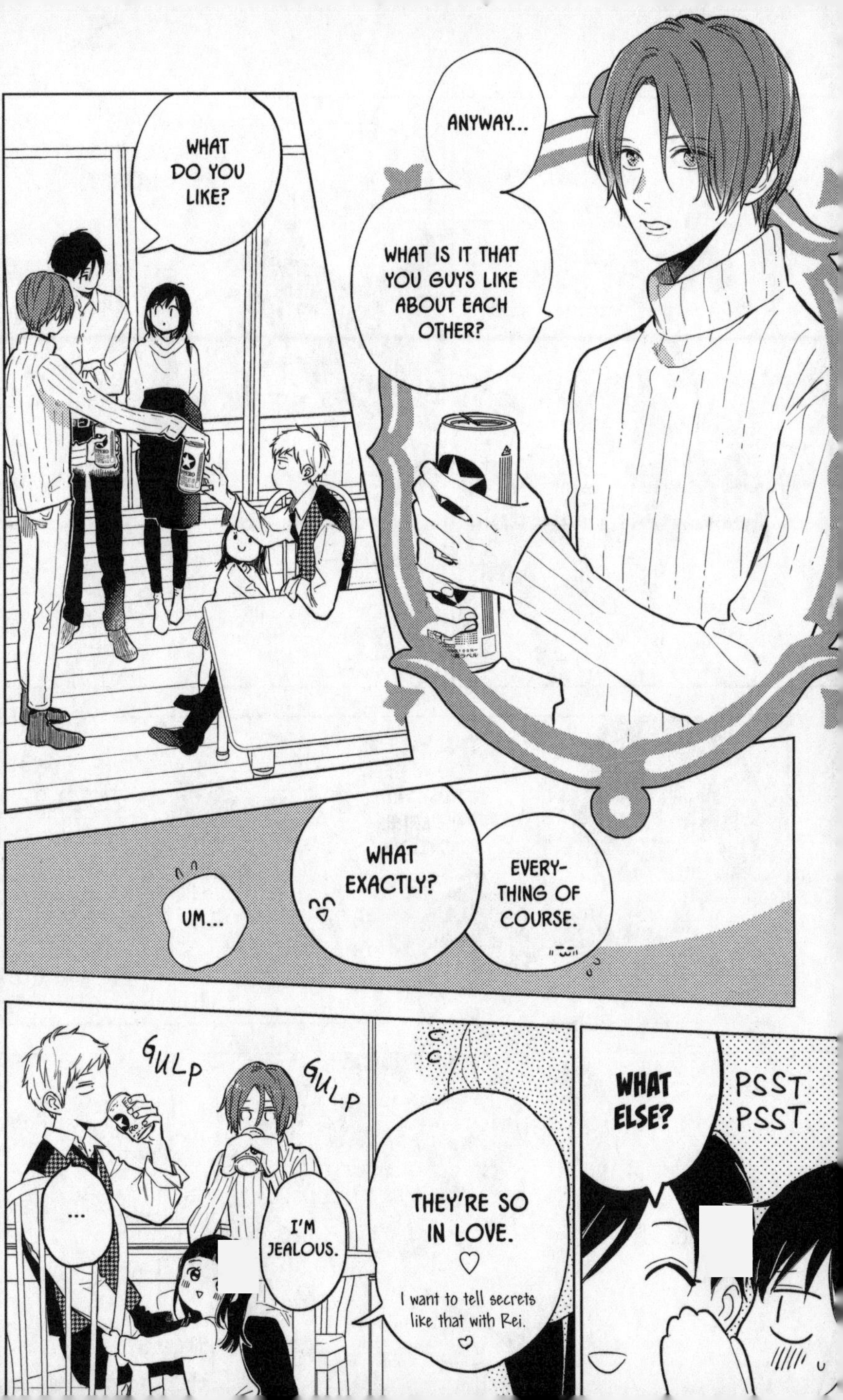

ANYWAY...
WHAT IS IT THAT YOU GUYS LIKE ABOUT EACH OTHER?
WHAT DO YOU LIKE?
EVERY-THING OF COURSE.
WHAT EXACTLY?
UM...
PSST PSST
WHAT ELSE?
THEY'RE SO IN LOVE. ♡
I want to tell secrets like that with Rei. ♡
GULP
GULP
I'M JEALOUS.
...

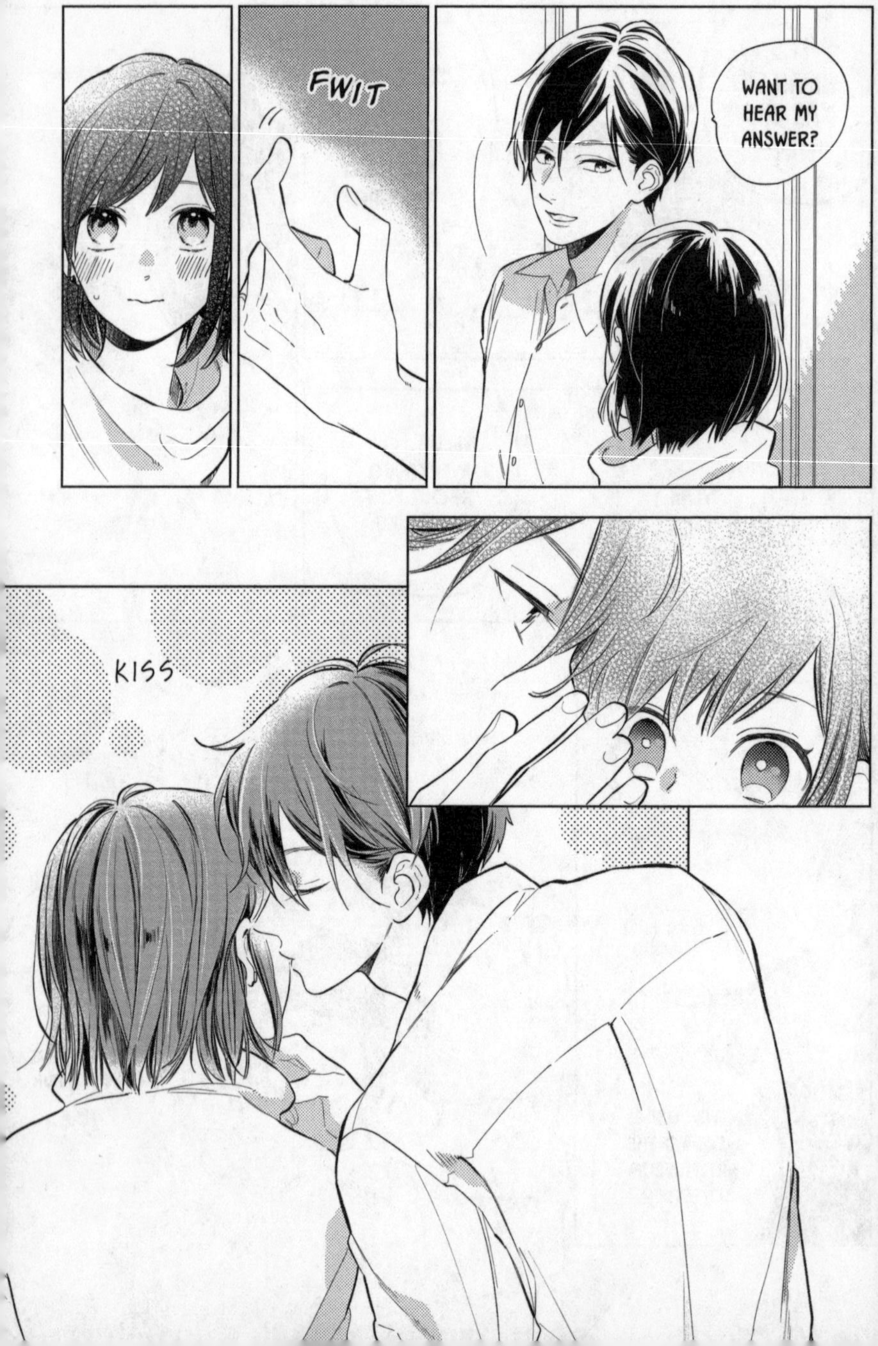
WANT TO HEAR MY ANSWER?
FWIT
KISS

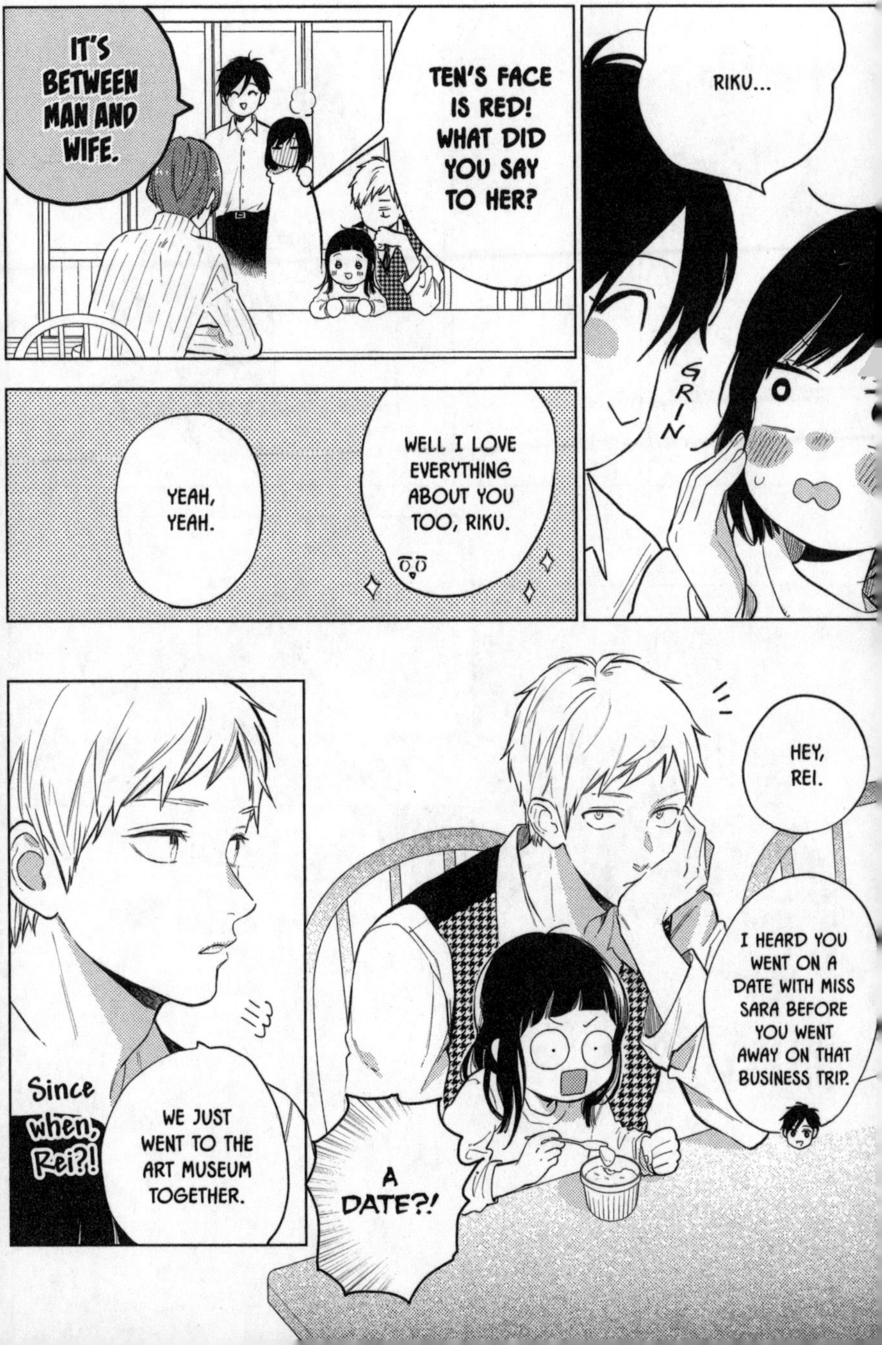
RIKU...
GRIN
TEN'S FACE IS RED! WHAT DID YOU SAY TO HER?
IT'S BETWEEN MAN AND WIFE.
WELL I LOVE EVERYTHING ABOUT YOU TOO, RIKU.
YEAH, YEAH.
HEY, REI.
I HEARD YOU WENT ON A DATE WITH MISS SARA BEFORE YOU WENT AWAY ON THAT BUSINESS TRIP.
A DATE?!
WE JUST WENT TO THE ART MUSEUM TOGETHER.
Since when, Rei?!

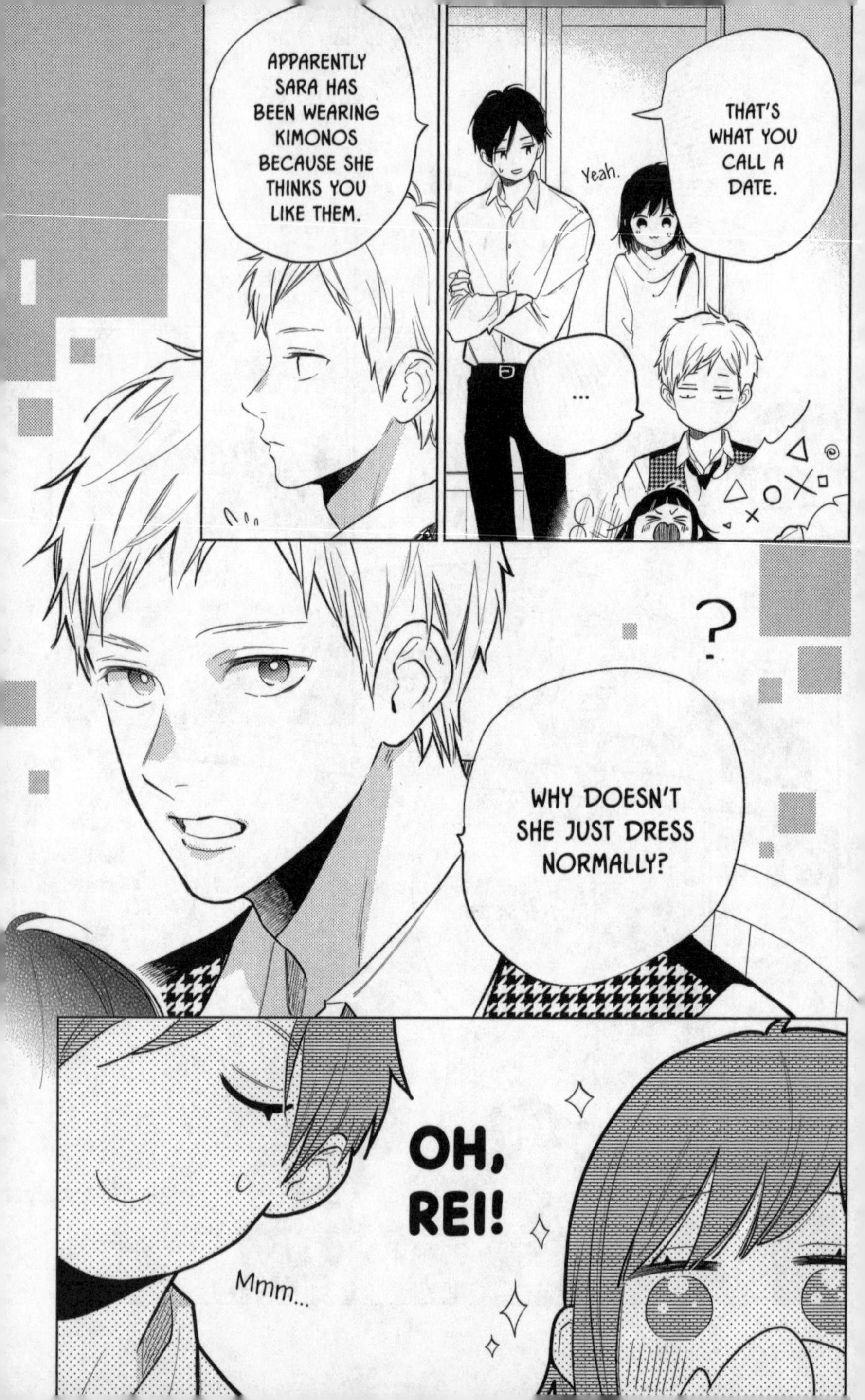
THAT'S WHAT YOU CALL A DATE.
Yeah.
...
APPARENTLY SARA HAS BEEN WEARING KIMONOS BECAUSE SHE THINKS YOU LIKE THEM.
?
WHY DOESN'T SHE JUST DRESS NORMALLY?
OH, REI!
Mmm...

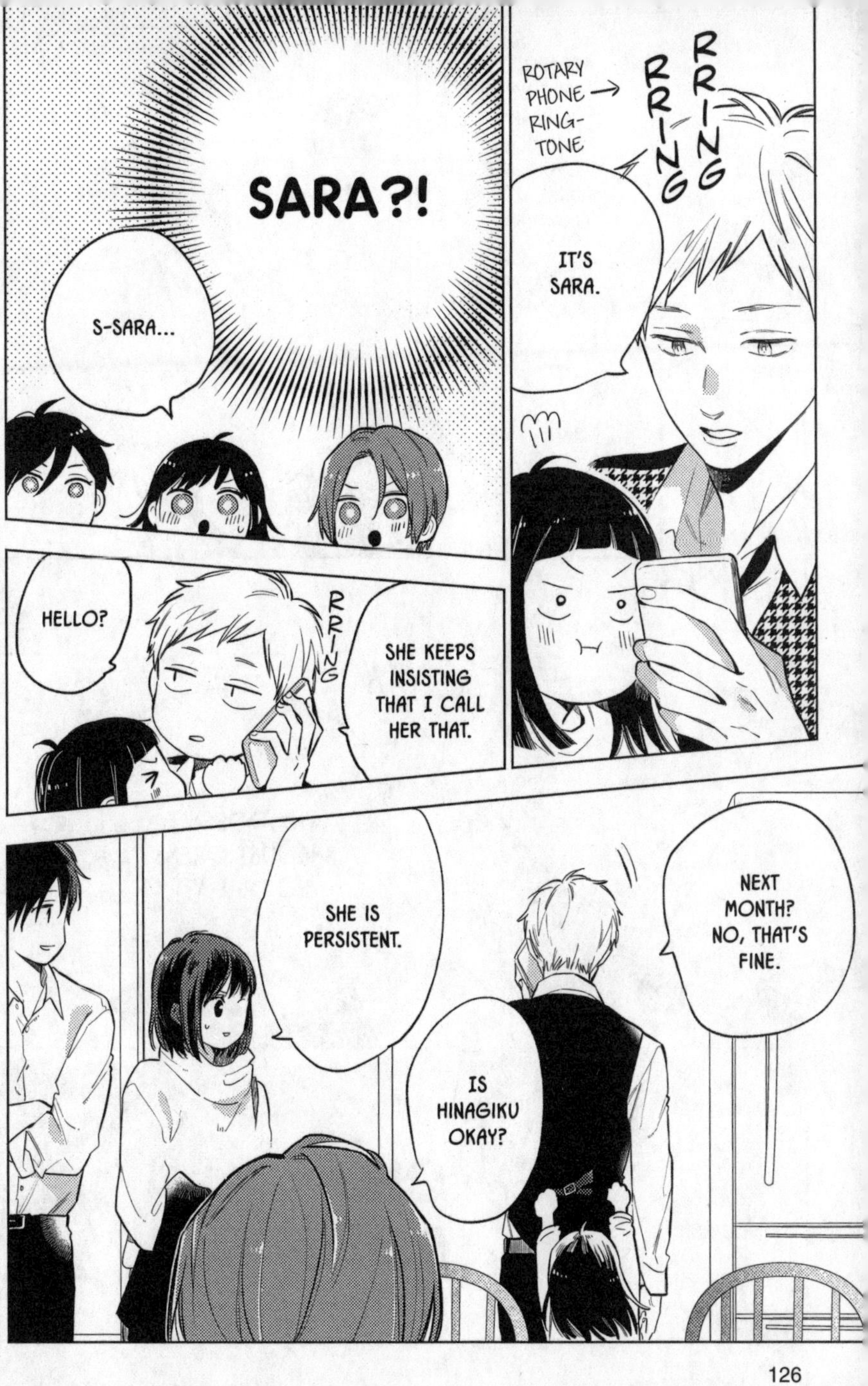
ROTARY PHONE RINGTONE
RRING RRING
IT'S SARA.
SARA?!
S-SARA...
RRING
SHE KEEPS INSISTING THAT I CALL HER THAT.
HELLO?
NEXT MONTH? NO, THAT'S FINE.
SHE IS PERSISTENT.
IS HINAGIKU OKAY?

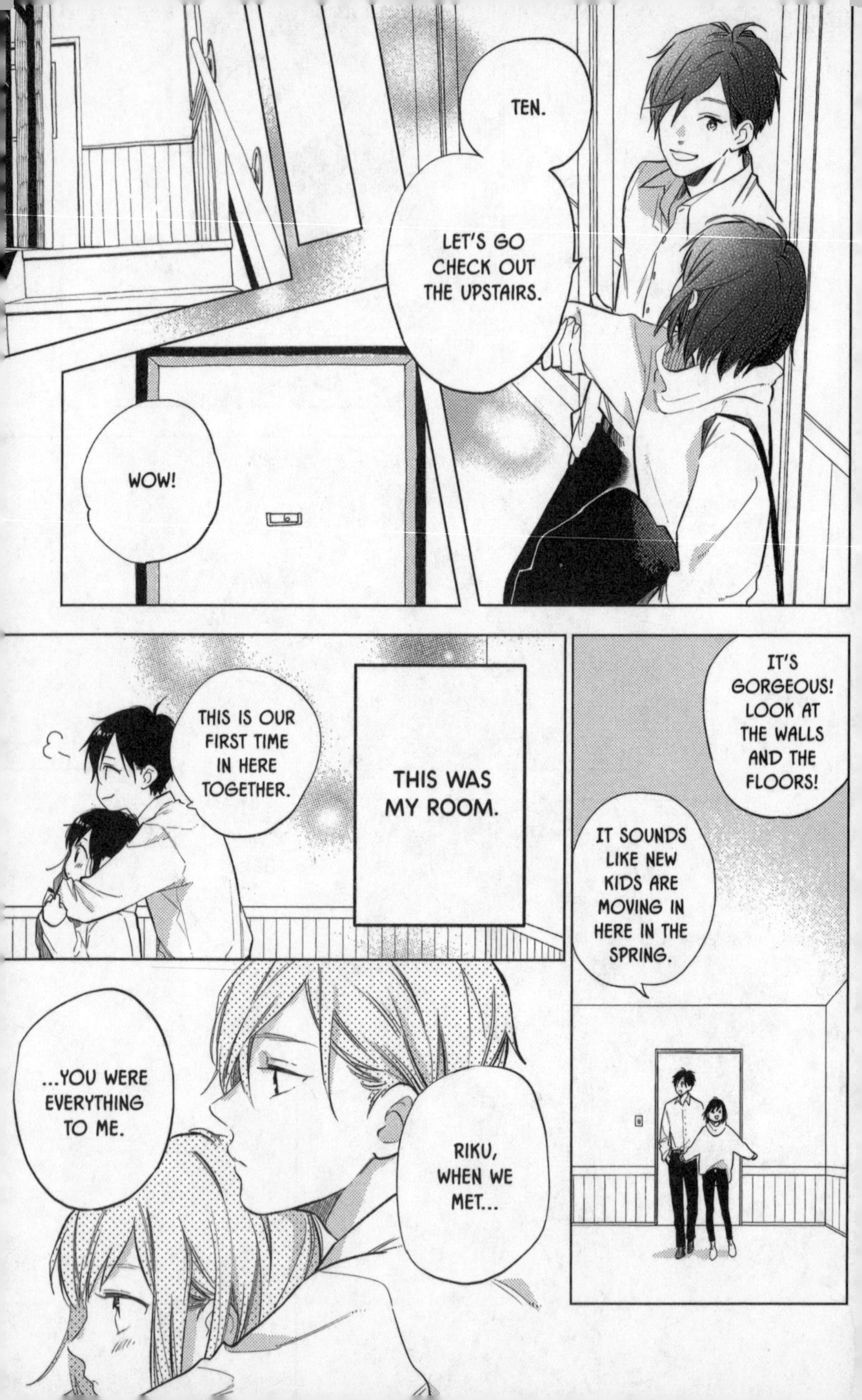
TEN.
LET'S GO CHECK OUT THE UPSTAIRS.
WOW!
IT'S GORGEOUS! LOOK AT THE WALLS AND THE FLOORS!
IT SOUNDS LIKE NEW KIDS ARE MOVING IN HERE IN THE SPRING.
THIS WAS MY ROOM.
THIS IS OUR FIRST TIME IN HERE TOGETHER.
RIKU, WHEN WE MET...
...YOU WERE EVERYTHING TO ME.

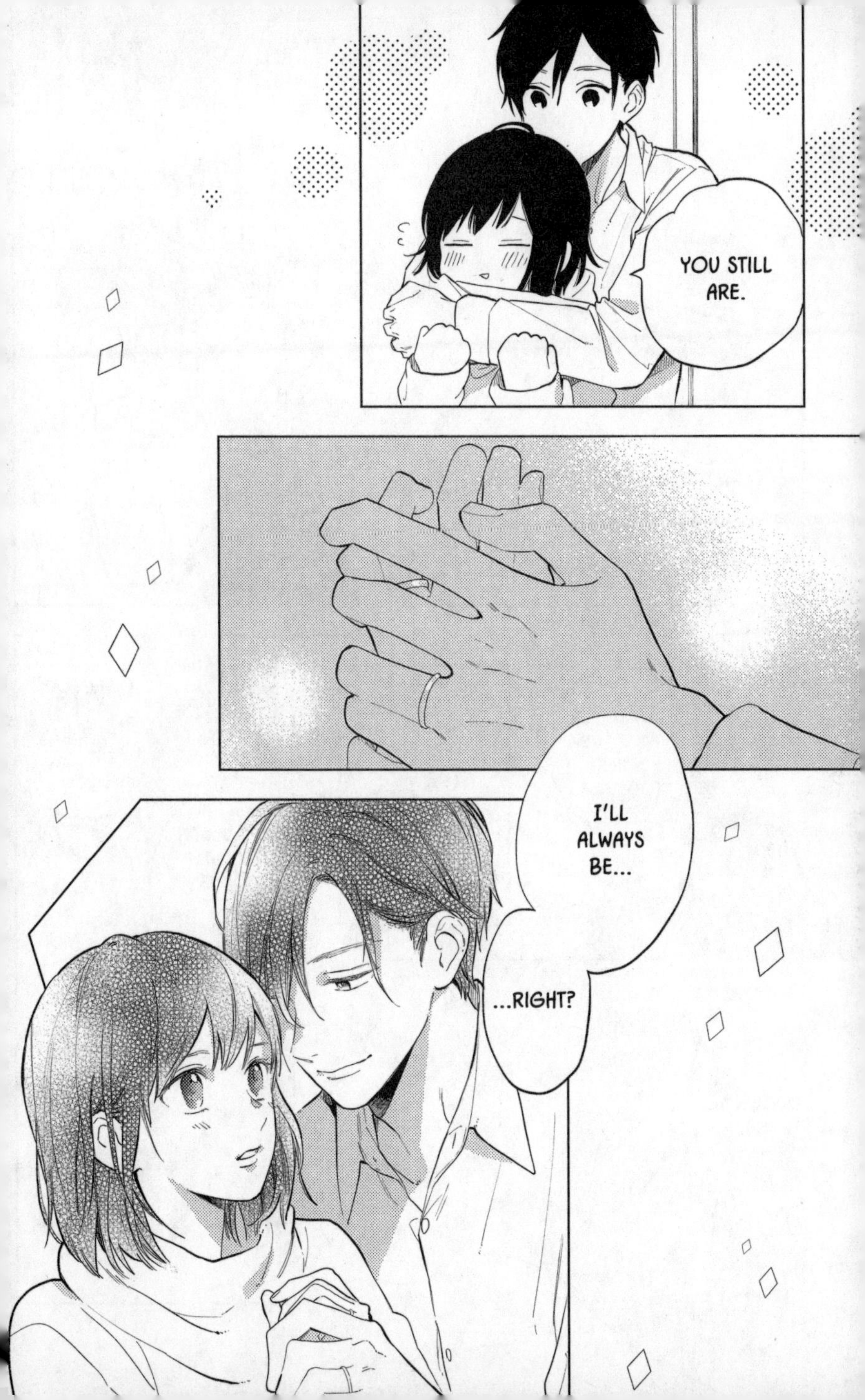
YOU STILL ARE.
I'LL ALWAYS BE...
...RIGHT?

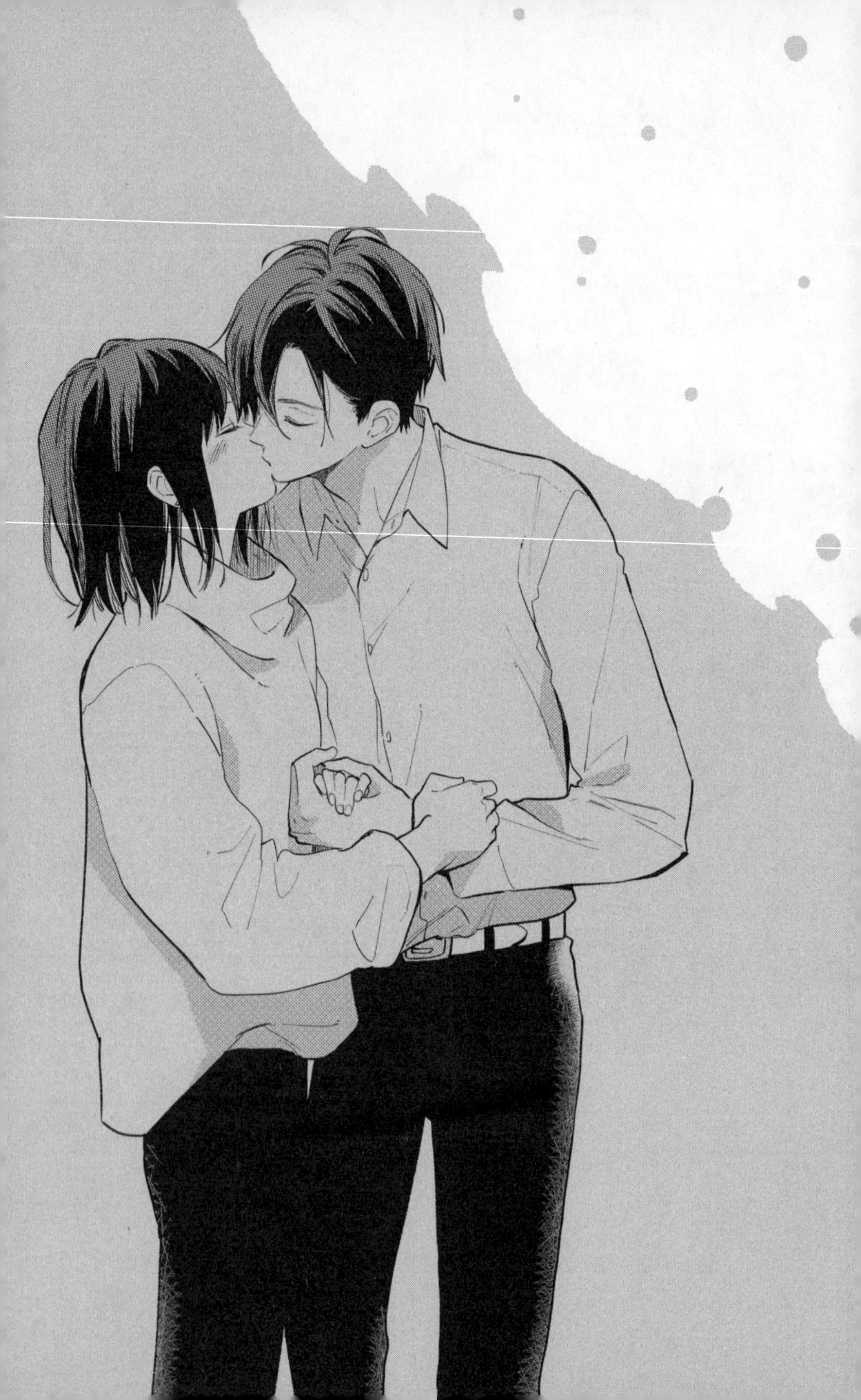

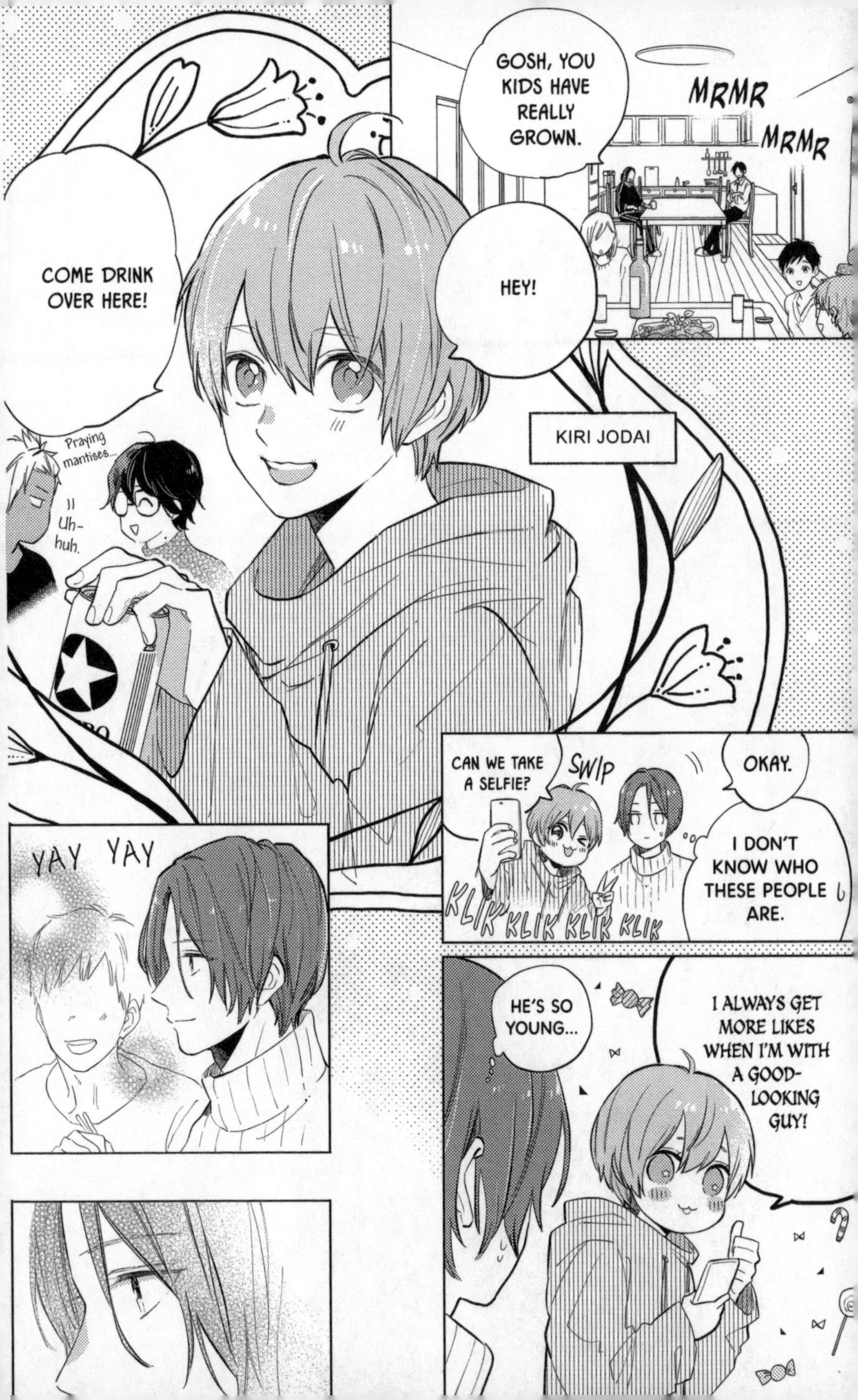
GOSH, YOU KIDS HAVE REALLY GROWN.
MRMR
MRMR
HEY!
COME DRINK OVER HERE!
KIRI JODAI
Praying mantises...
Uh-huh.
CAN WE TAKE A SELFIE?
SWIP
OKAY.
I DON'T KNOW WHO THESE PEOPLE ARE.
KLIK KLIK KLIK KLIK
YAY YAY
I ALWAYS GET MORE LIKES WHEN I'M WITH A GOOD-LOOKING GUY!
HE'S SO YOUNG...

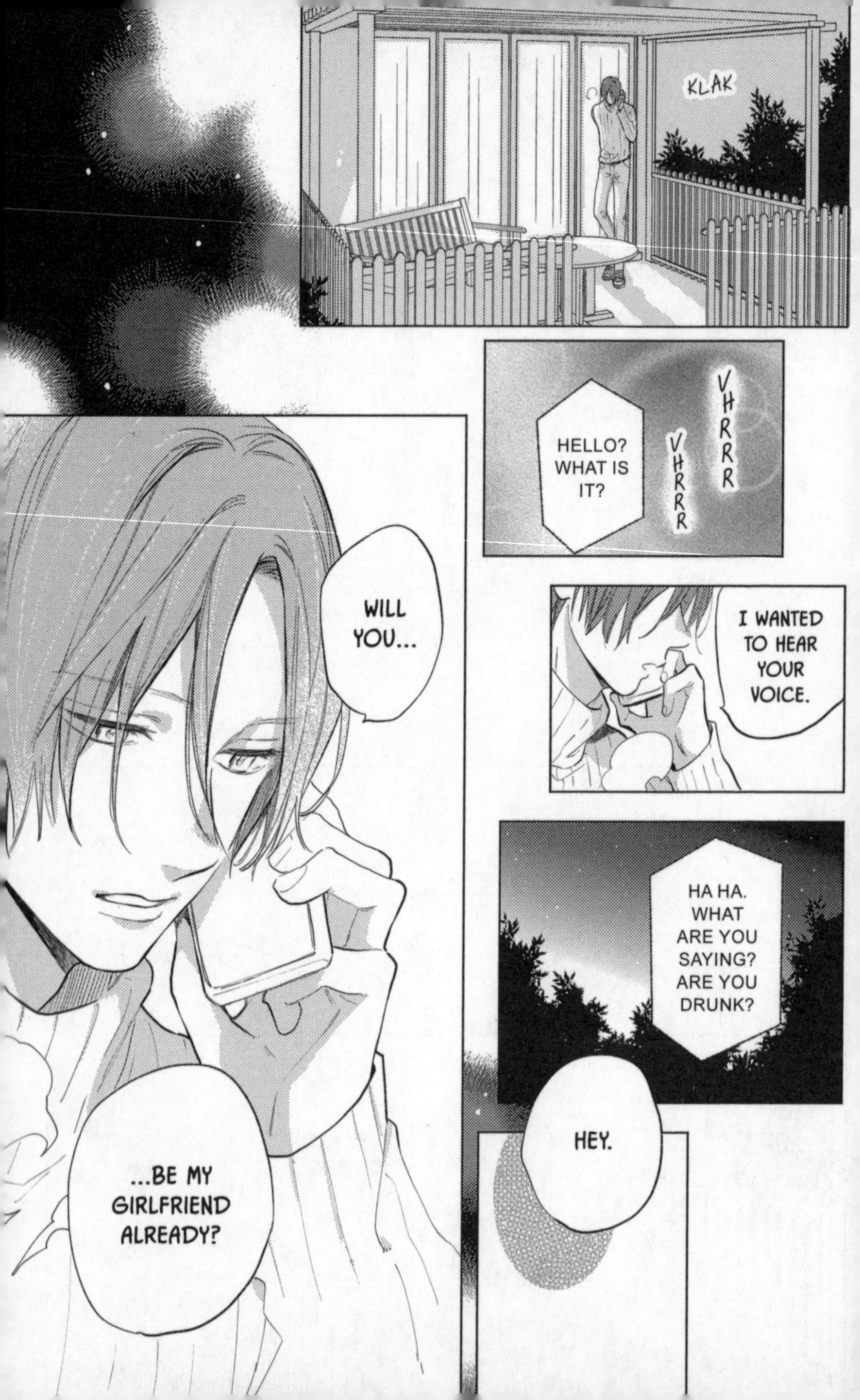
KLAK
VHRRR
VHRRR
HELLO? WHAT IS IT?
I WANTED TO HEAR YOUR VOICE.
HA HA. WHAT ARE YOU SAYING? ARE YOU DRUNK?
HEY.
WILL YOU...
...BE MY GIRLFRIEND ALREADY?

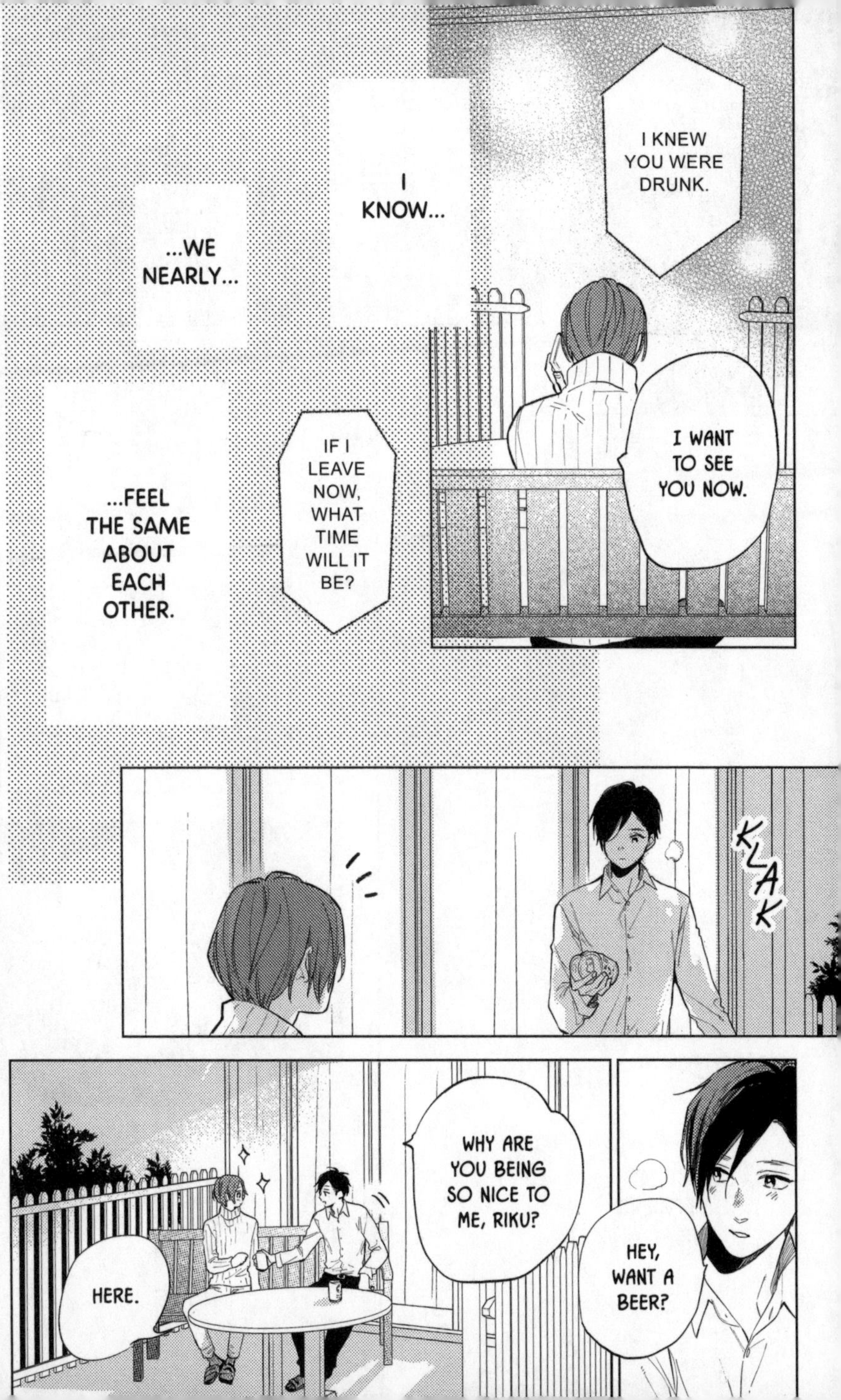
I KNEW YOU WERE DRUNK.
I WANT TO SEE YOU NOW.
I KNOW...
...WE NEARLY...
IF I LEAVE NOW, WHAT TIME WILL IT BE?
...FEEL THE SAME ABOUT EACH OTHER.
KLAK
HEY, WANT A BEER?
WHY ARE YOU BEING SO NICE TO ME, RIKU?
HERE.

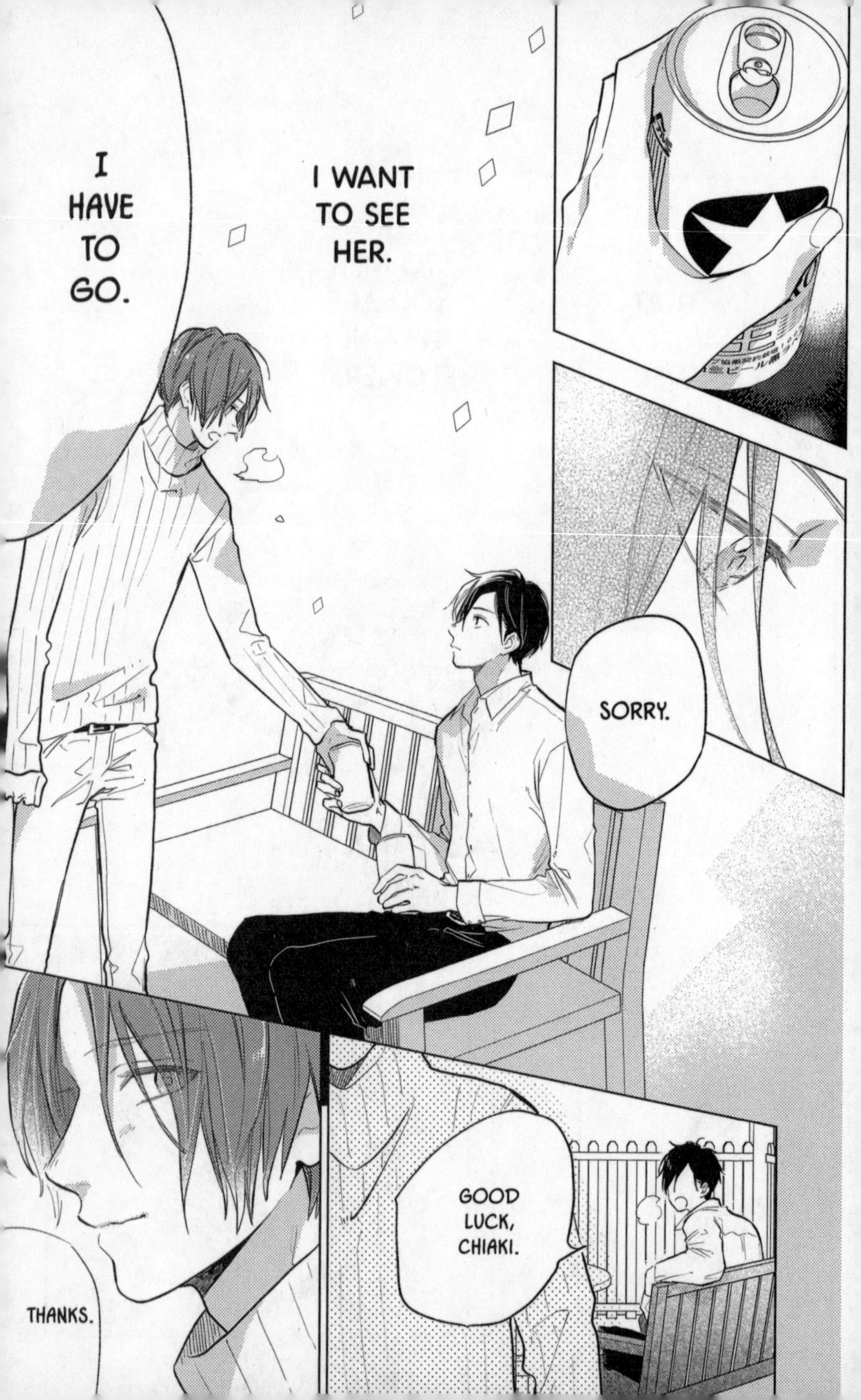
SORRY.
I WANT TO SEE HER.
I HAVE TO GO.
GOOD LUCK, CHIAKI.
THANKS.

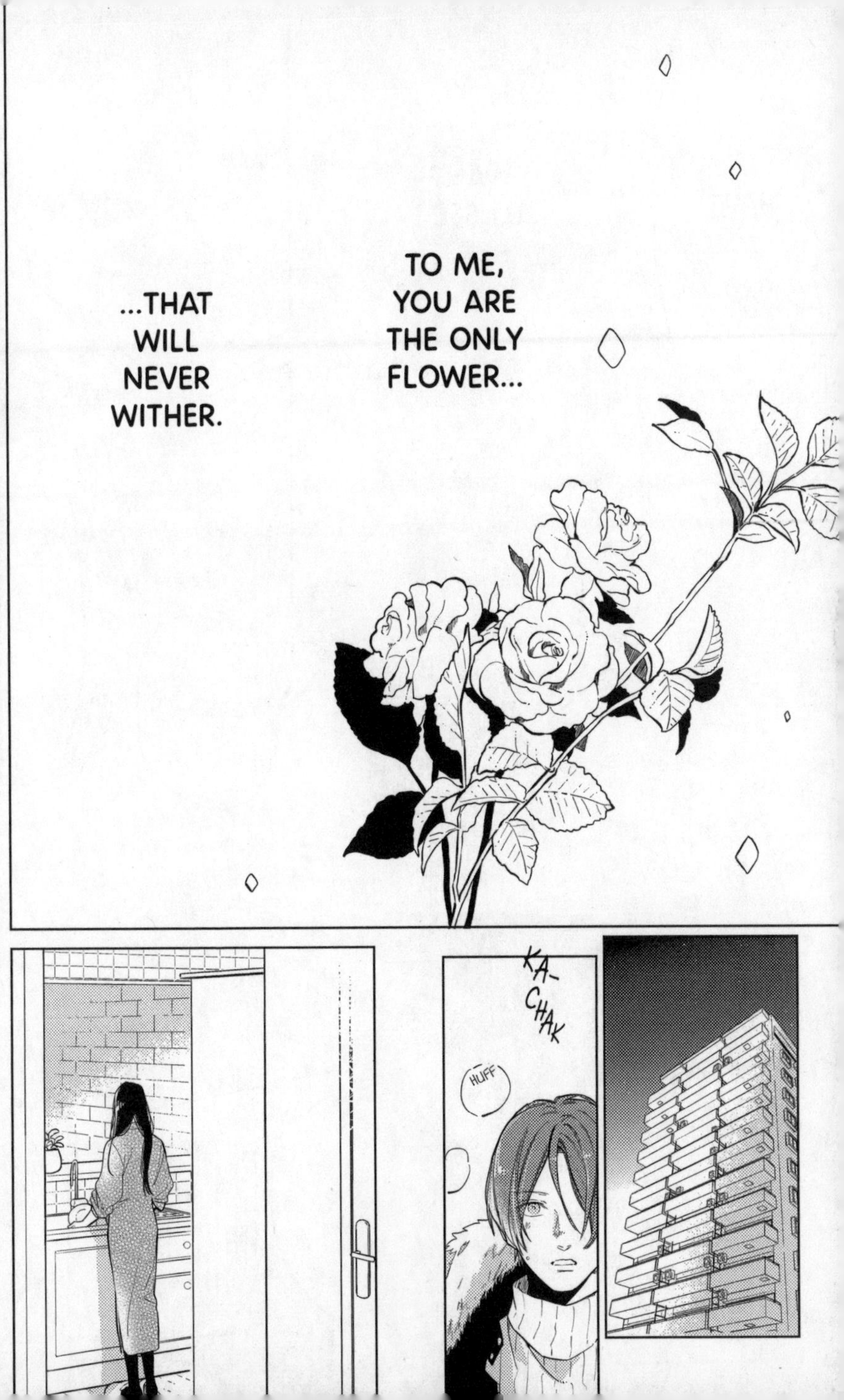
TO ME, YOU ARE THE ONLY FLOWER...
...THAT WILL NEVER WITHER.
KA-CHAK
HUFF

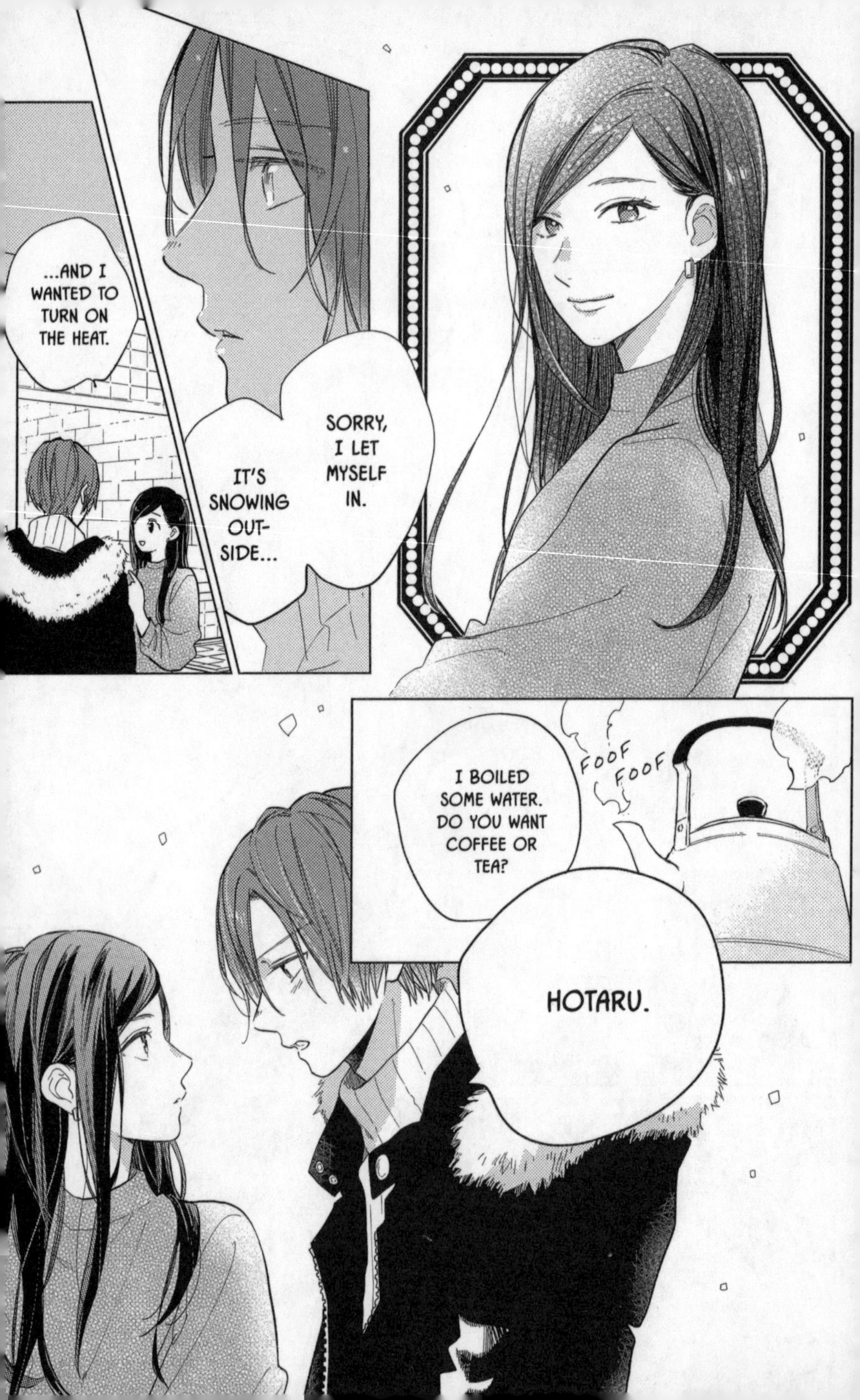
SORRY, I LET MYSELF IN.
IT'S SNOWING OUTSIDE...
...AND I WANTED TO TURN ON THE HEAT.
FOOF FOOF
I BOILED SOME WATER. DO YOU WANT COFFEE OR TEA?
HOTARU.

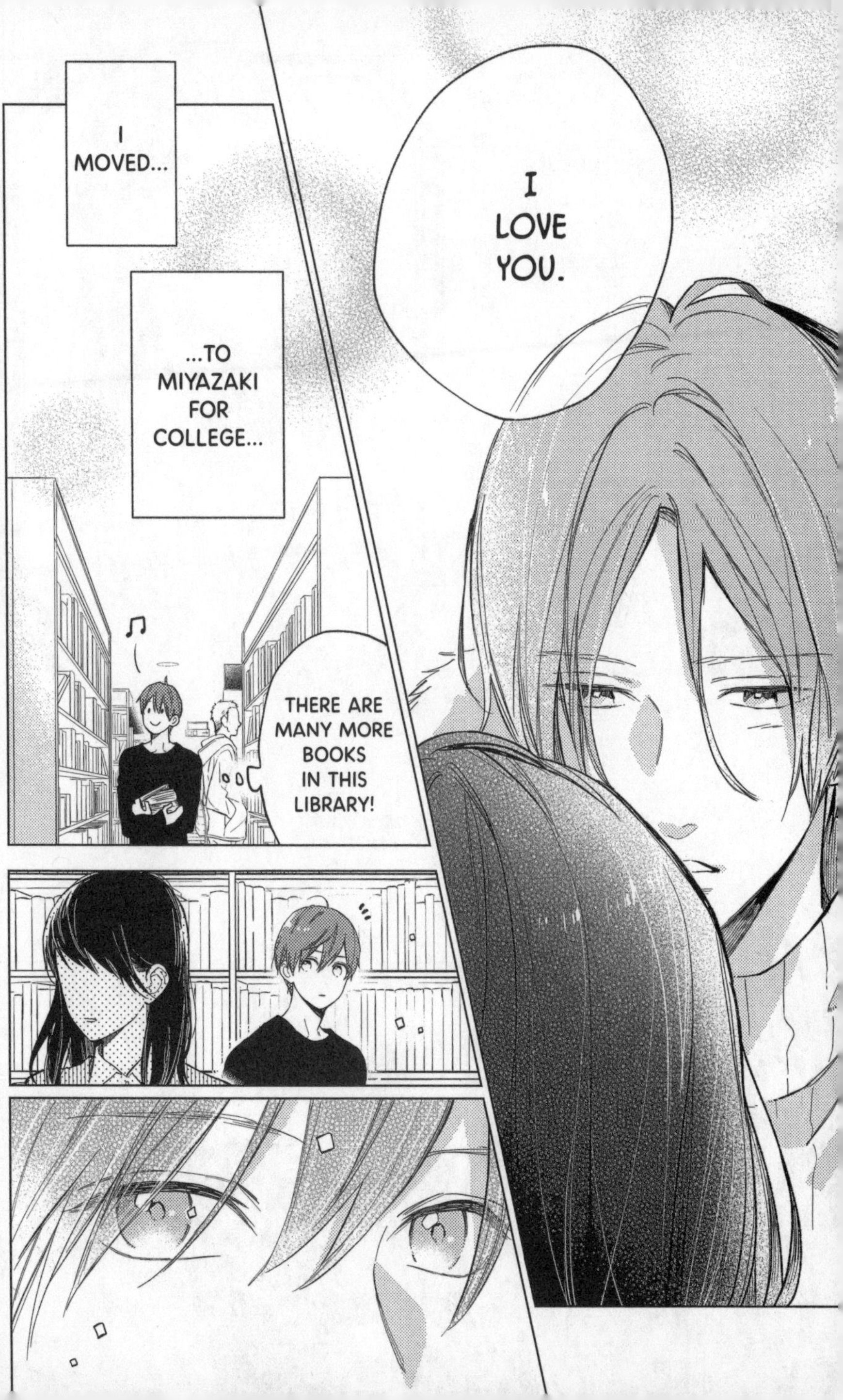
I LOVE YOU.
I MOVED...
...TO MIYAZAKI FOR COLLEGE...
THERE ARE MANY MORE BOOKS IN THIS LIBRARY!

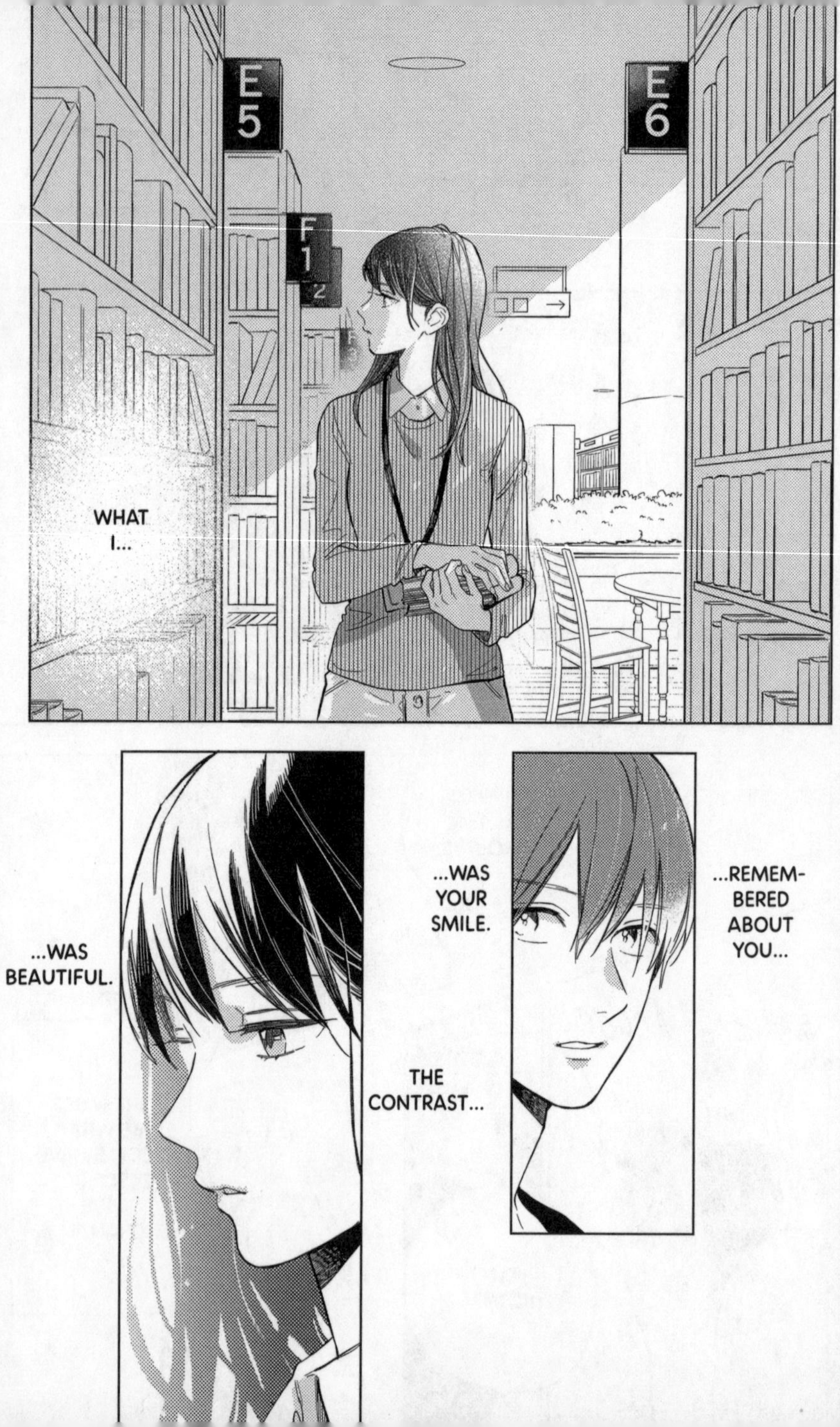
WHAT I...
...REMEM-BERED ABOUT YOU...
...WAS YOUR SMILE.
THE CONTRAST...
...WAS BEAUTIFUL.

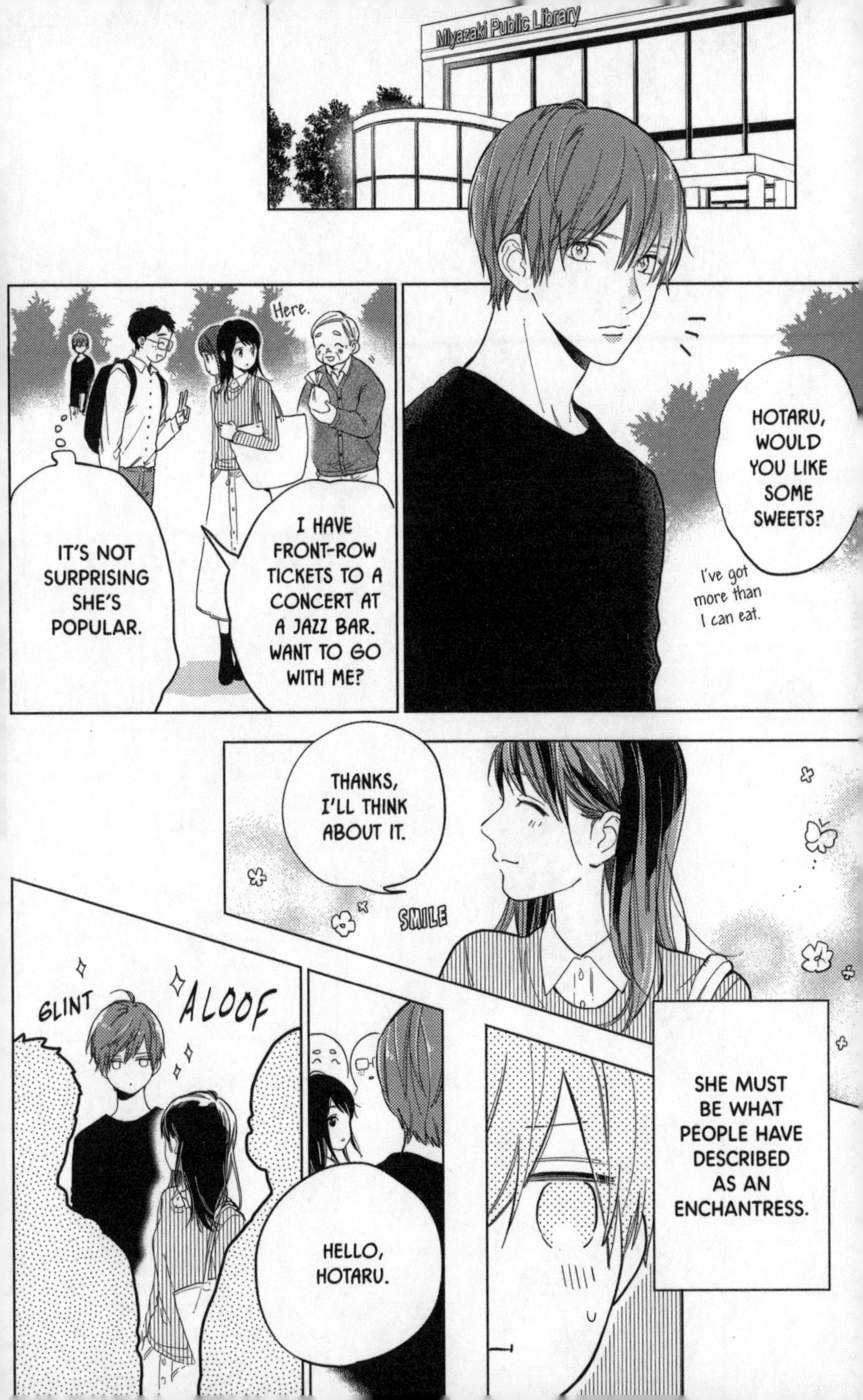
Miyazaki Public Library
HOTARU, WOULD YOU LIKE SOME SWEETS?
I've got more than I can eat.
Here.
I HAVE FRONT-ROW TICKETS TO A CONCERT AT A JAZZ BAR. WANT TO GO WITH ME?
IT'S NOT SURPRISING SHE'S POPULAR.
THANKS, I'LL THINK ABOUT IT.
SMILE
SHE MUST BE WHAT PEOPLE HAVE DESCRIBED AS AN ENCHANTRESS.
HELLO, HOTARU.
ALOOF
GLINT

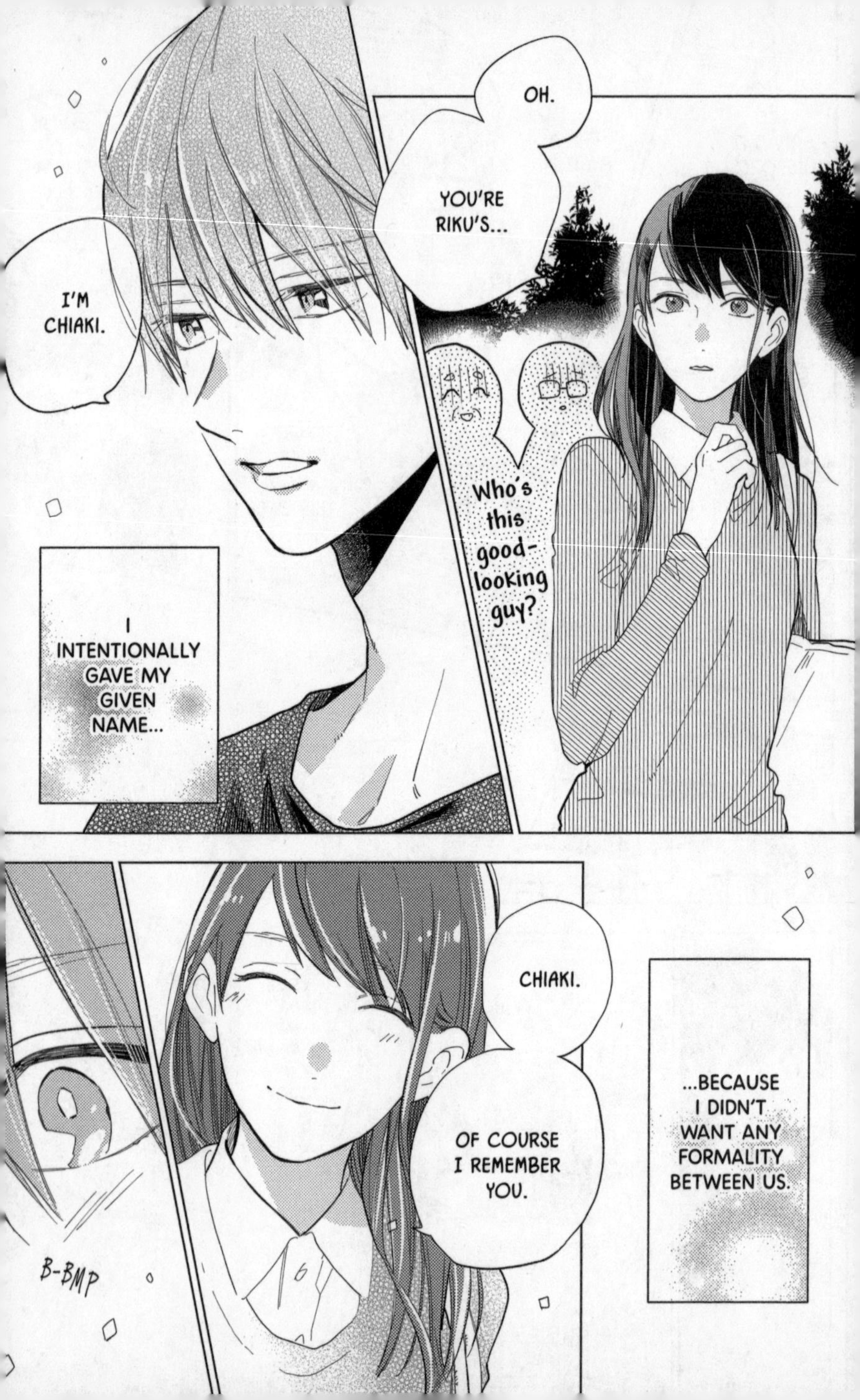
OH.
YOU'RE RIKU'S...
Who's this good-looking guy?
I'M CHIAKI.
I INTENTIONALLY GAVE MY GIVEN NAME...
...BECAUSE I DIDN'T WANT ANY FORMALITY BETWEEN US.
CHIAKI.
OF COURSE I REMEMBER YOU.
B-BMP

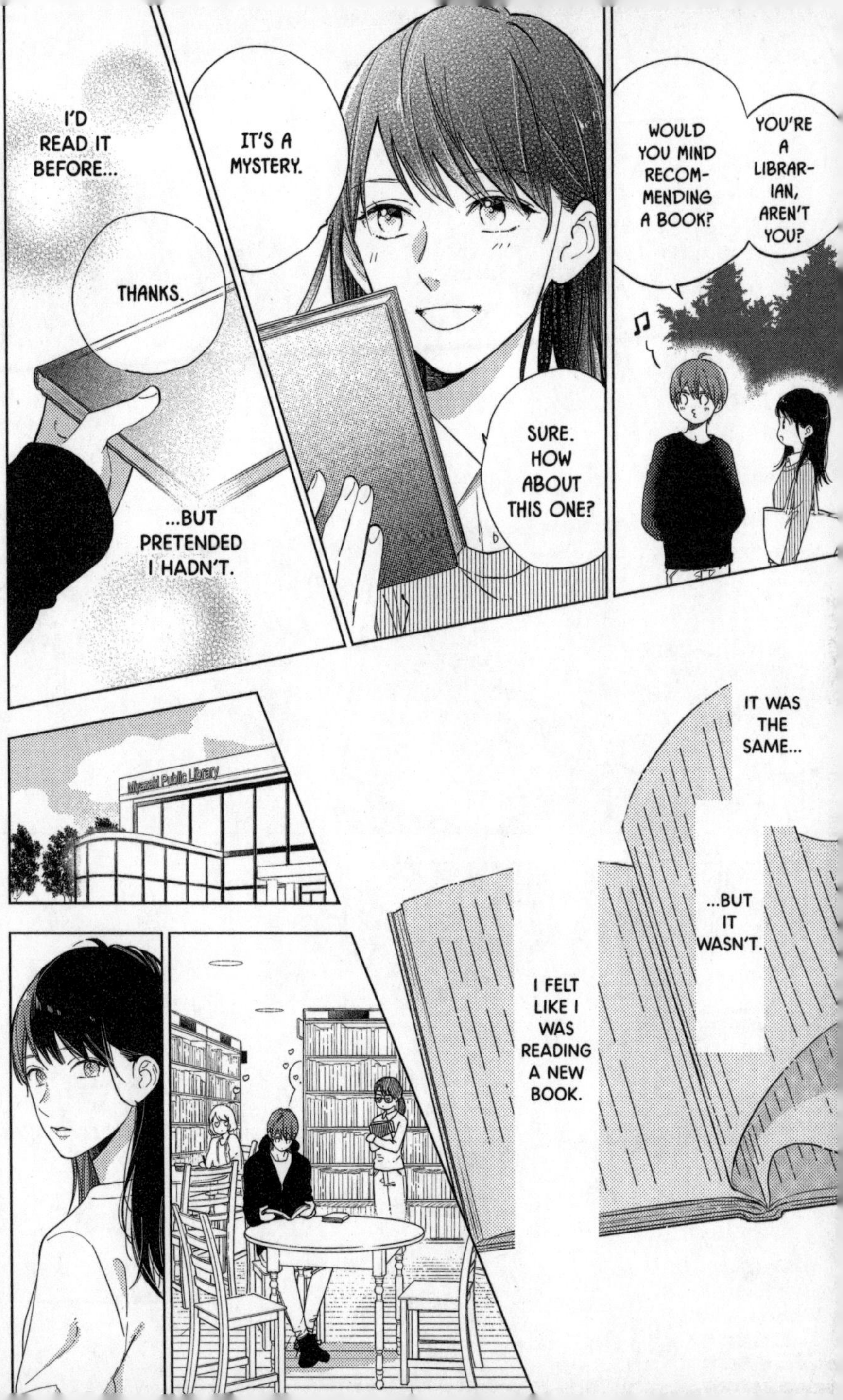
YOU'RE A LIBRARIAN, AREN'T YOU?
WOULD YOU MIND RECOMMENDING A BOOK?
SURE. HOW ABOUT THIS ONE?
IT'S A MYSTERY.
THANKS.
I'D READ IT BEFORE...
...BUT PRETENDED I HADN'T.
IT WAS THE SAME...
...BUT IT WASN'T.
I FELT LIKE I WAS READING A NEW BOOK.
Miyazaki Public Library

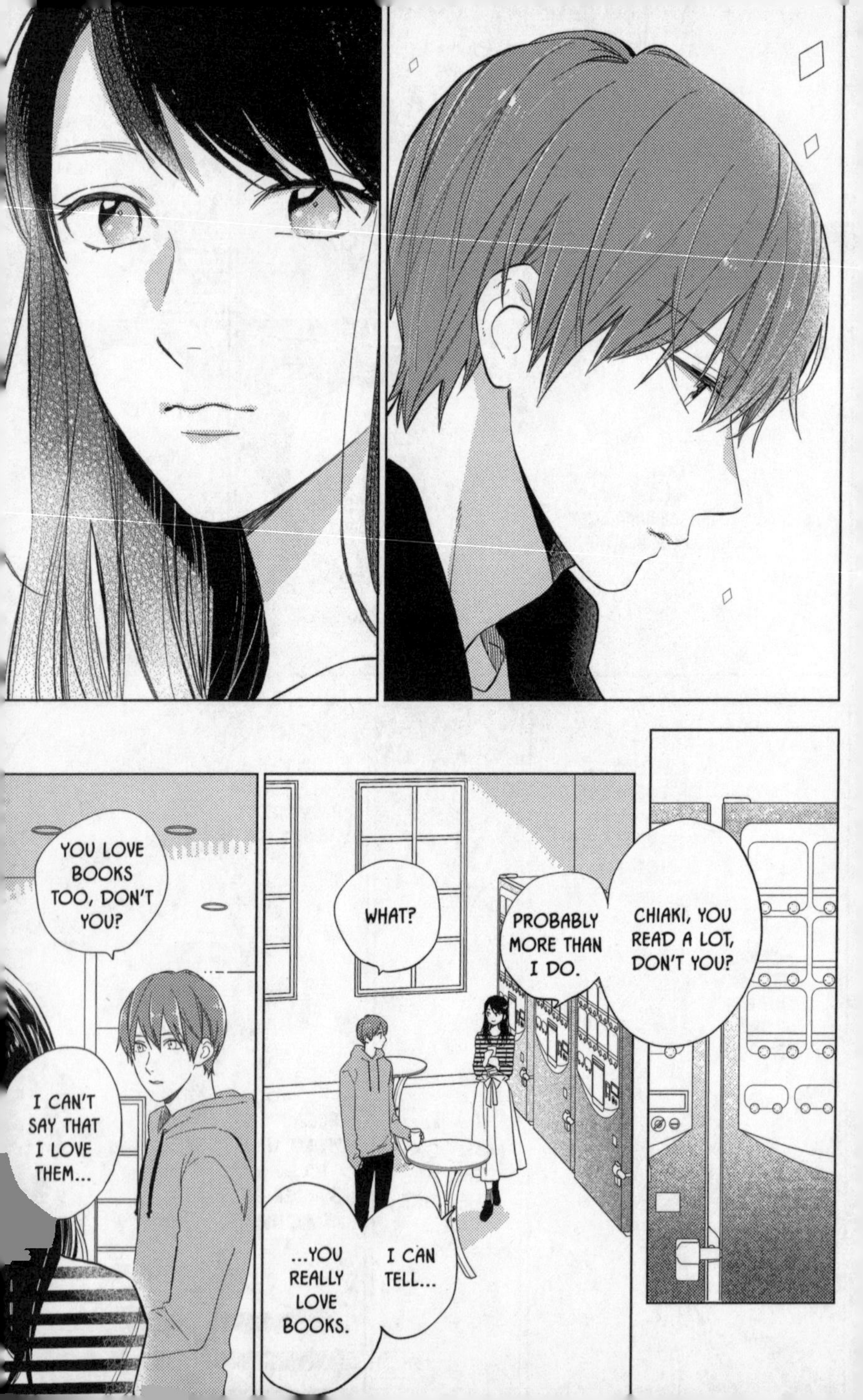
CHIAKI, YOU READ A LOT, DON'T YOU?
PROBABLY MORE THAN I DO.
WHAT?
I CAN TELL...
...YOU REALLY LOVE BOOKS.
YOU LOVE BOOKS TOO, DON'T YOU?
I CAN'T SAY THAT I LOVE THEM...

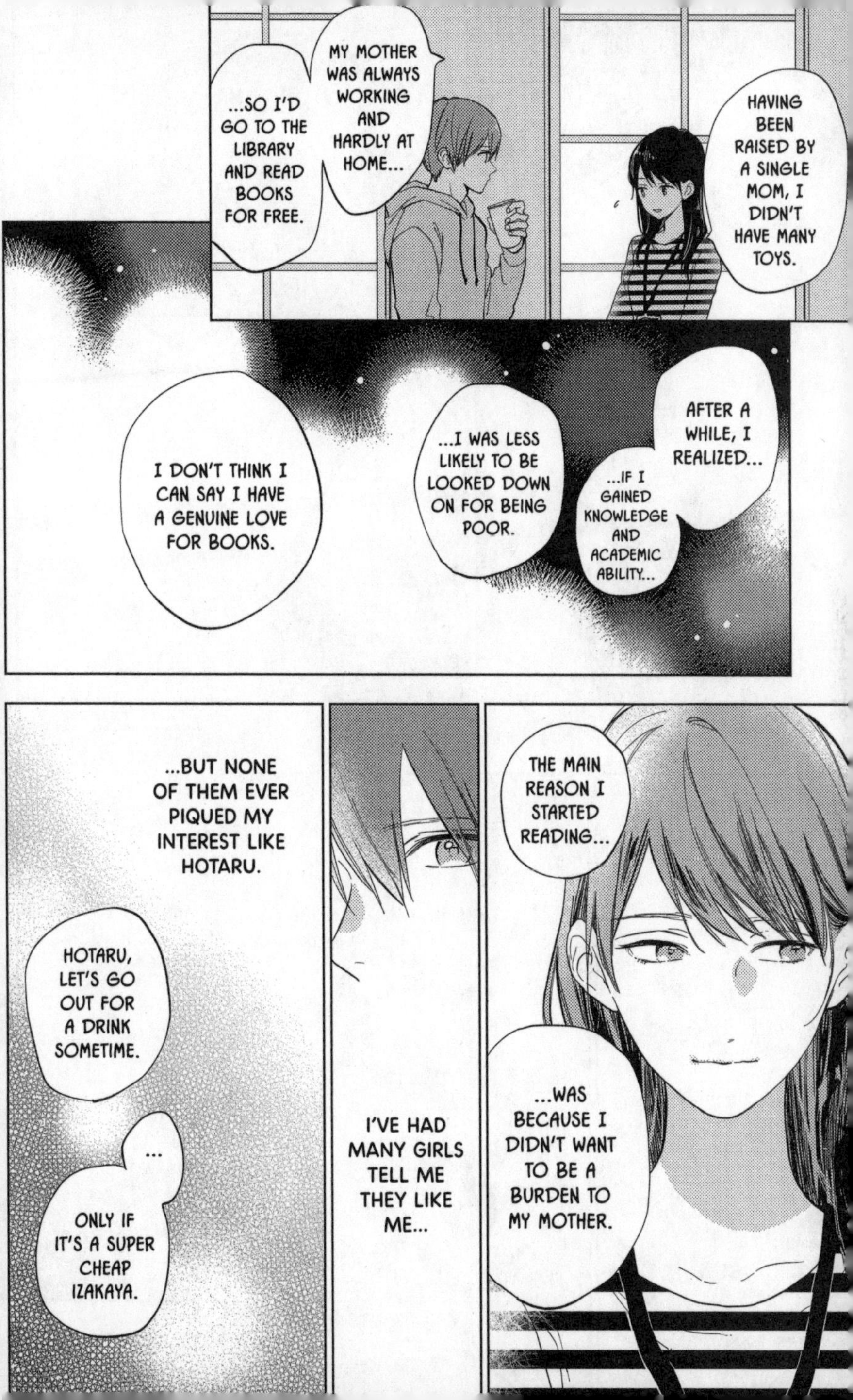
HAVING BEEN RAISED BY A SINGLE MOM, I DIDN'T HAVE MANY TOYS.
MY MOTHER WAS ALWAYS WORKING AND HARDLY AT HOME...
...SO I'D GO TO THE LIBRARY AND READ BOOKS FOR FREE.
AFTER A WHILE, I REALIZED...
...IF I GAINED KNOWLEDGE AND ACADEMIC ABILITY...
...I WAS LESS LIKELY TO BE LOOKED DOWN ON FOR BEING POOR.
I DON'T THINK I CAN SAY I HAVE A GENUINE LOVE FOR BOOKS.
THE MAIN REASON I STARTED READING...
...WAS BECAUSE I DIDN'T WANT TO BE A BURDEN TO MY MOTHER.
I'VE HAD MANY GIRLS TELL ME THEY LIKE ME...
...BUT NONE OF THEM EVER PIQUED MY INTEREST LIKE HOTARU.
HOTARU, LET'S GO OUT FOR A DRINK SOMETIME.
...
ONLY IF IT'S A SUPER CHEAP IZAKAYA.

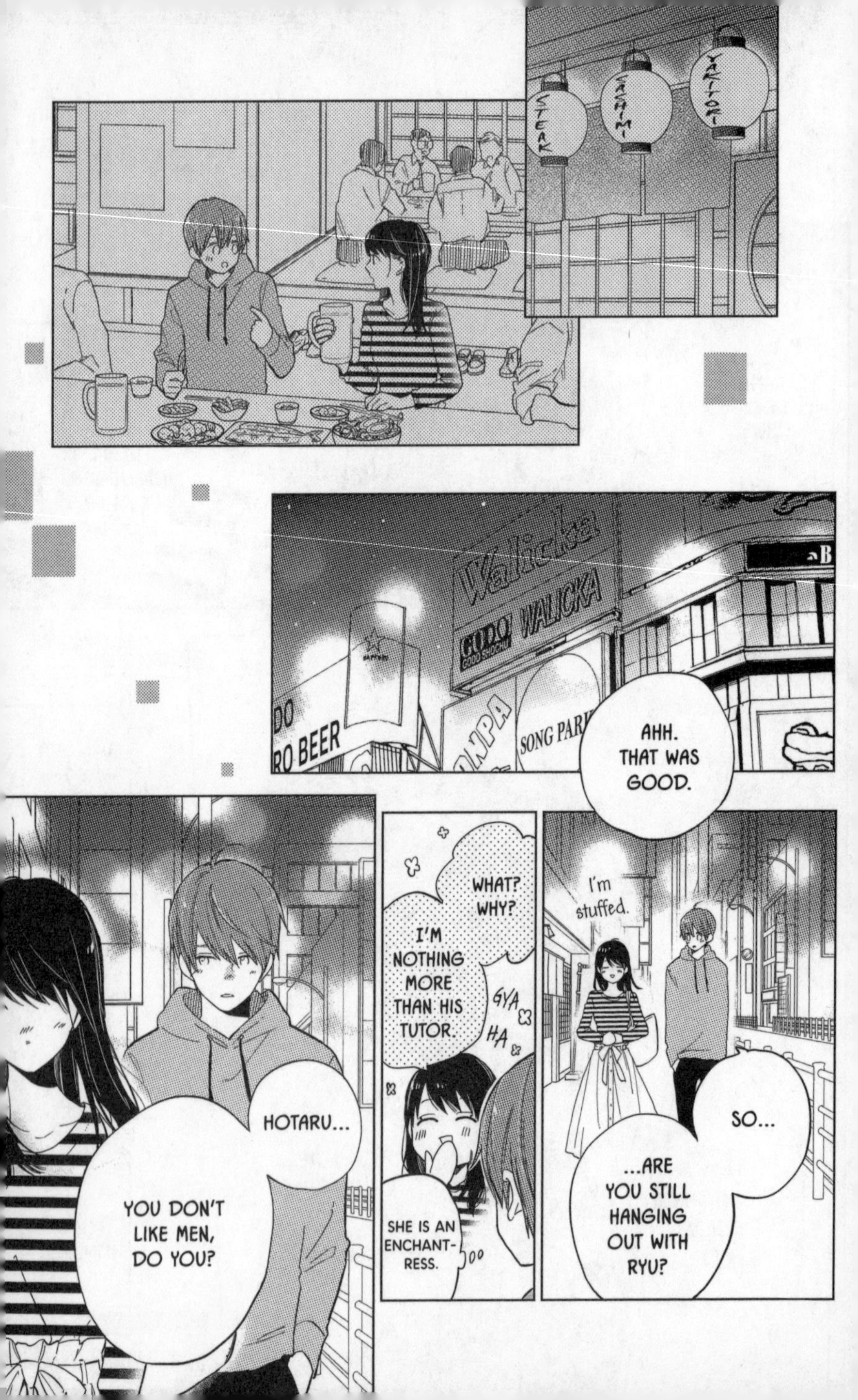
YAKITORI
SASHIMI
STEAK
Walicka
GODO GOOD SHOCHU
WALICKA
SONG PARK
DO
RO BEER
AHH. THAT WAS GOOD.
I'm stuffed.
SO...
...ARE YOU STILL HANGING OUT WITH RYU?
WHAT? WHY?
I'M NOTHING MORE THAN HIS TUTOR.
GYA HA
SHE IS AN ENCHANTRESS.
HOTARU...
YOU DON'T LIKE MEN, DO YOU?

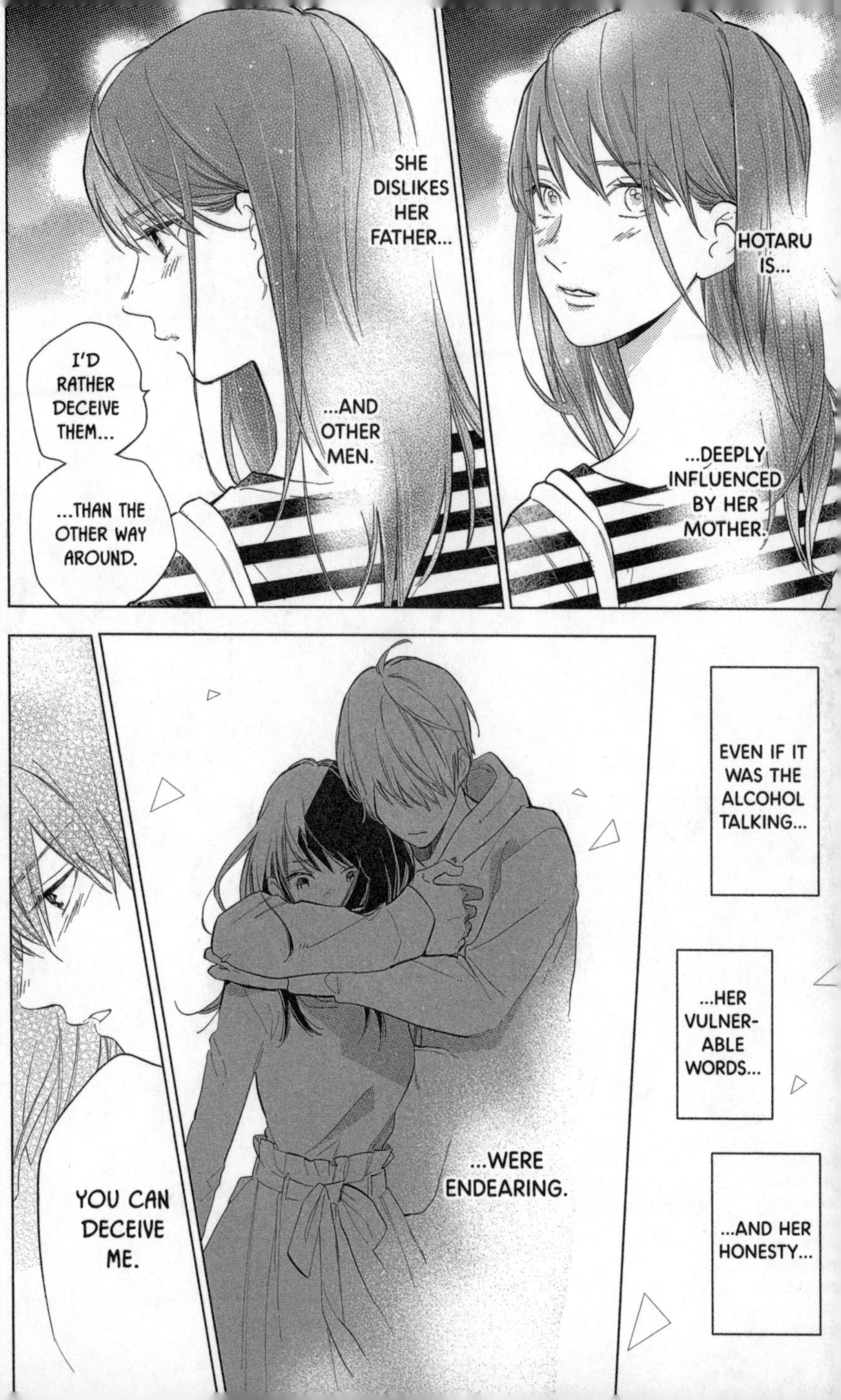
HOTARU IS...
...DEEPLY INFLUENCED BY HER MOTHER.
SHE DISLIKES HER FATHER...
...AND OTHER MEN.
I'D RATHER DECEIVE THEM...
...THAN THE OTHER WAY AROUND.
EVEN IF IT WAS THE ALCOHOL TALKING...
...HER VULNER-ABLE WORDS...
...AND HER HONESTY...
...WERE ENDEARING.
YOU CAN DECEIVE ME.

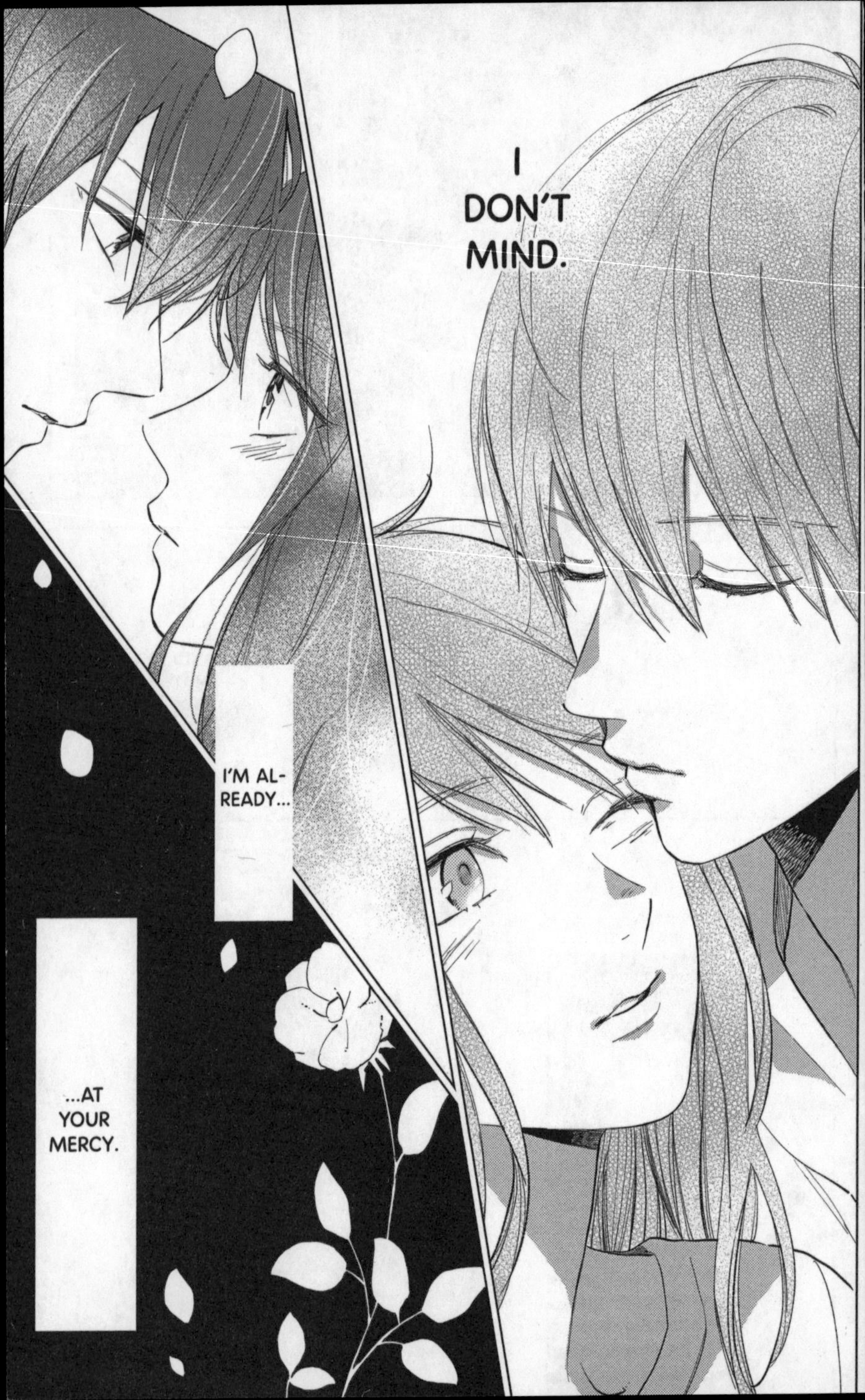
I DON'T MIND.
I'M AL-READY...
...AT YOUR MERCY.

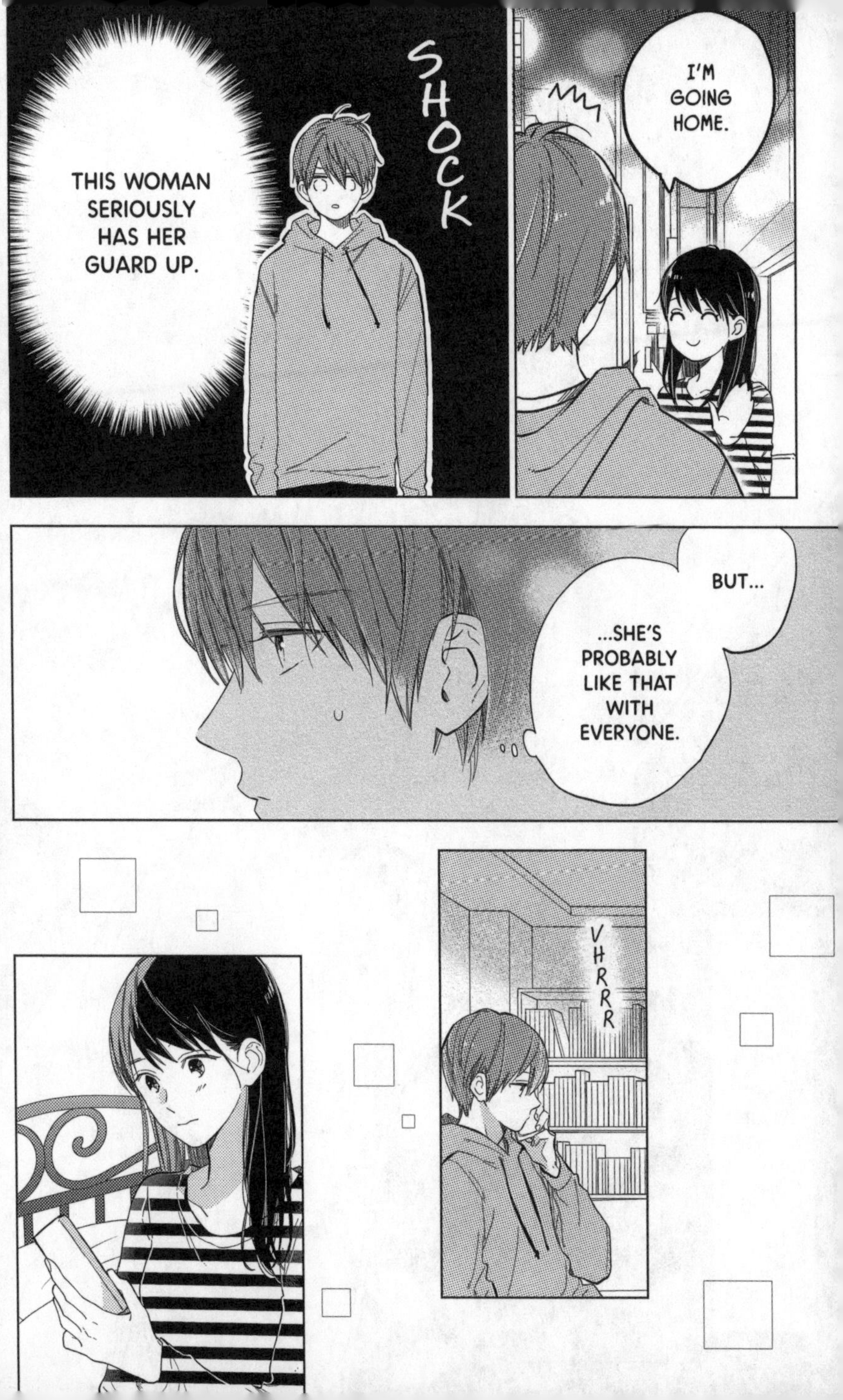
I'M GOING HOME.
SHOCK
THIS WOMAN SERIOUSLY HAS HER GUARD UP.
BUT...
...SHE'S PROBABLY LIKE THAT WITH EVERYONE.
VHRRR

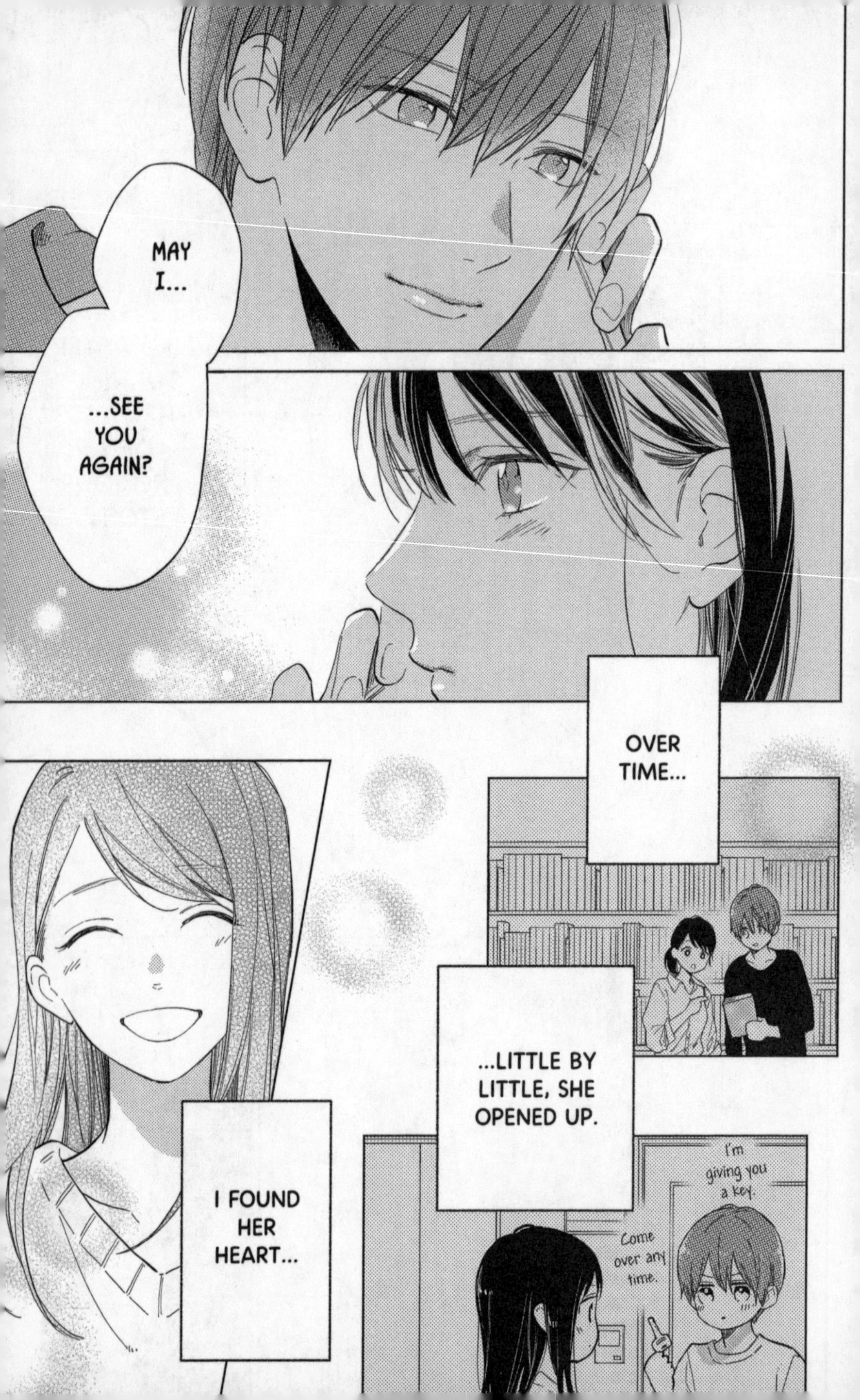
MAY I...
...SEE YOU AGAIN?
OVER TIME...
...LITTLE BY LITTLE, SHE OPENED UP.
I'm giving you a key.
Come over any time.
I FOUND HER HEART...

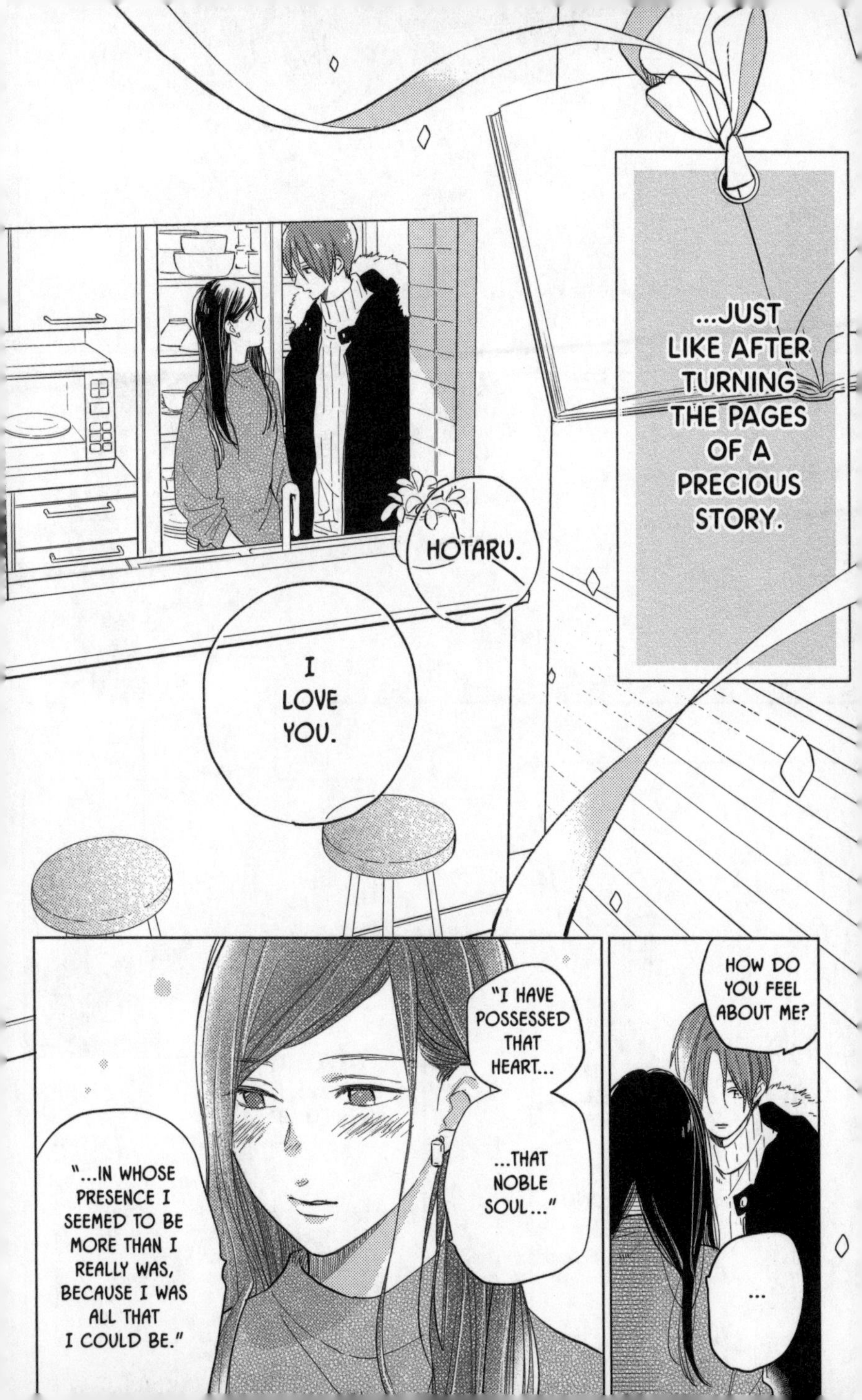
...JUST LIKE AFTER TURNING THE PAGES OF A PRECIOUS STORY.
HOTARU.
I LOVE YOU.
HOW DO YOU FEEL ABOUT ME?
...
"I HAVE POSSESSED THAT HEART...
...THAT NOBLE SOUL..."
"...IN WHOSE PRESENCE I SEEMED TO BE MORE THAN I REALLY WAS, BECAUSE I WAS ALL THAT I COULD BE."

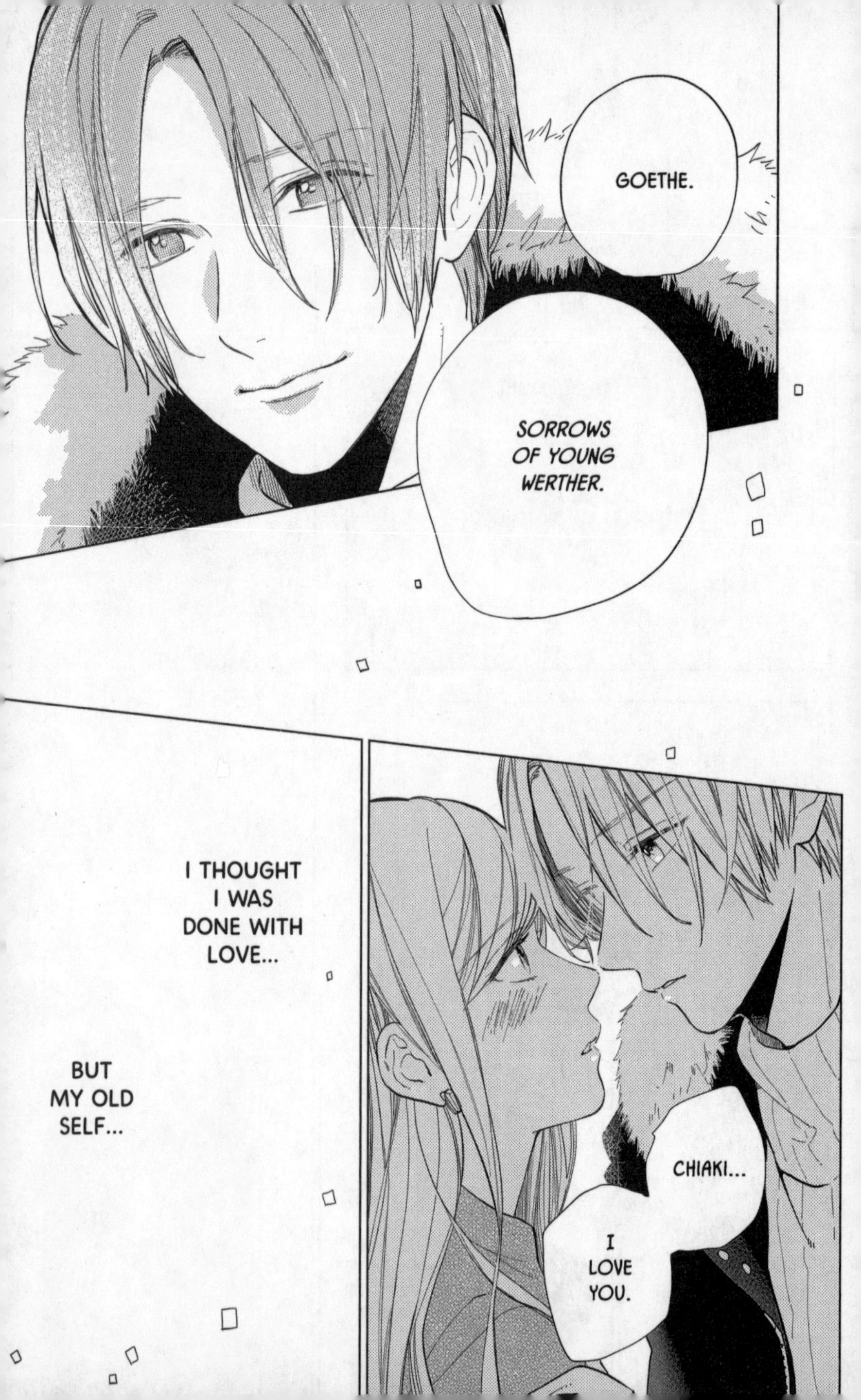
GOETHE.
SORROWS OF YOUNG WERTHER.
CHIAKI...
I LOVE YOU.
I THOUGHT I WAS DONE WITH LOVE...
BUT MY OLD SELF...

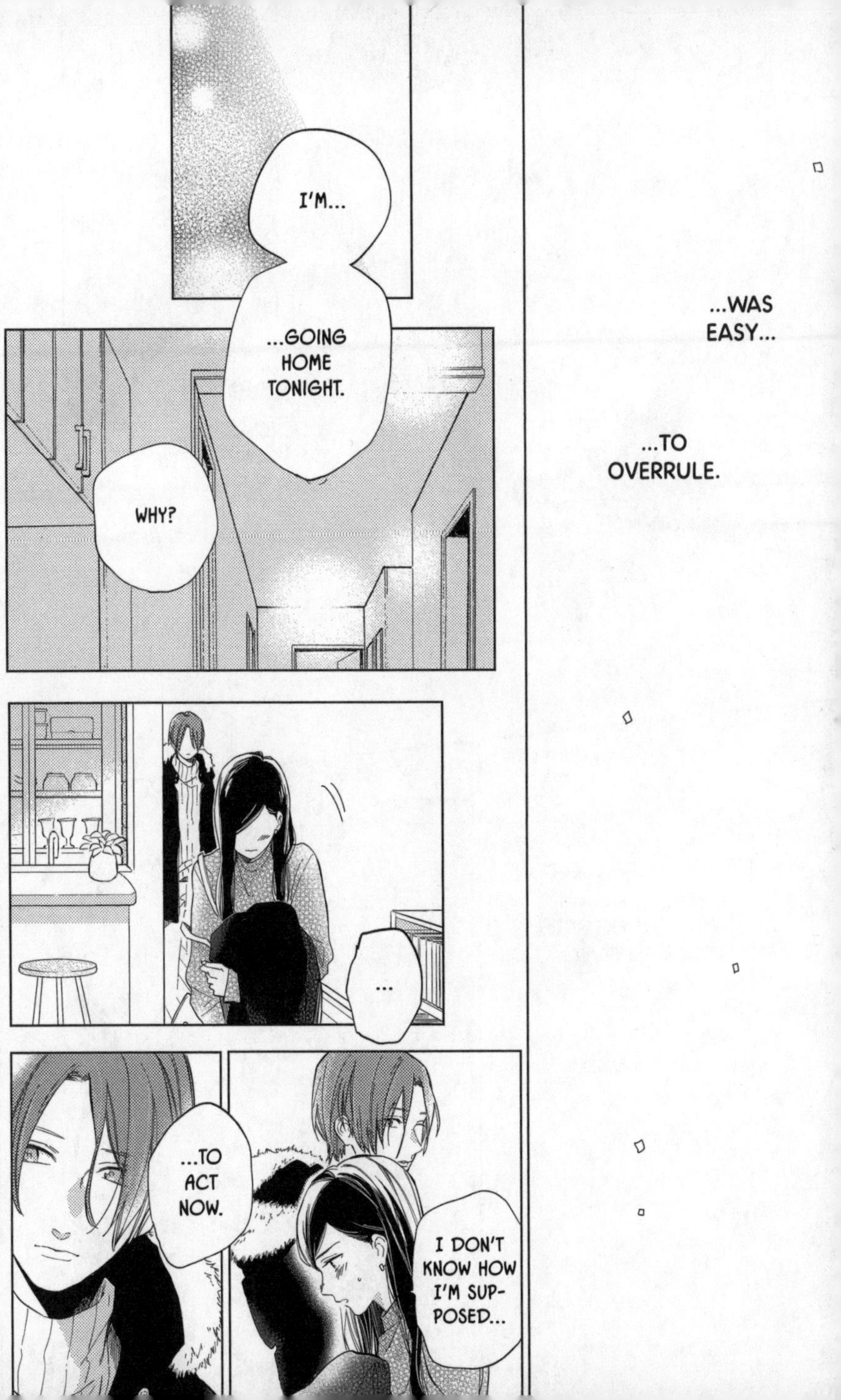
...WAS EASY...
...TO OVERRULE.
I'M...
...GOING HOME TONIGHT.
WHY?
...
I DON'T KNOW HOW I'M SUPPOSED...
...TO ACT NOW.

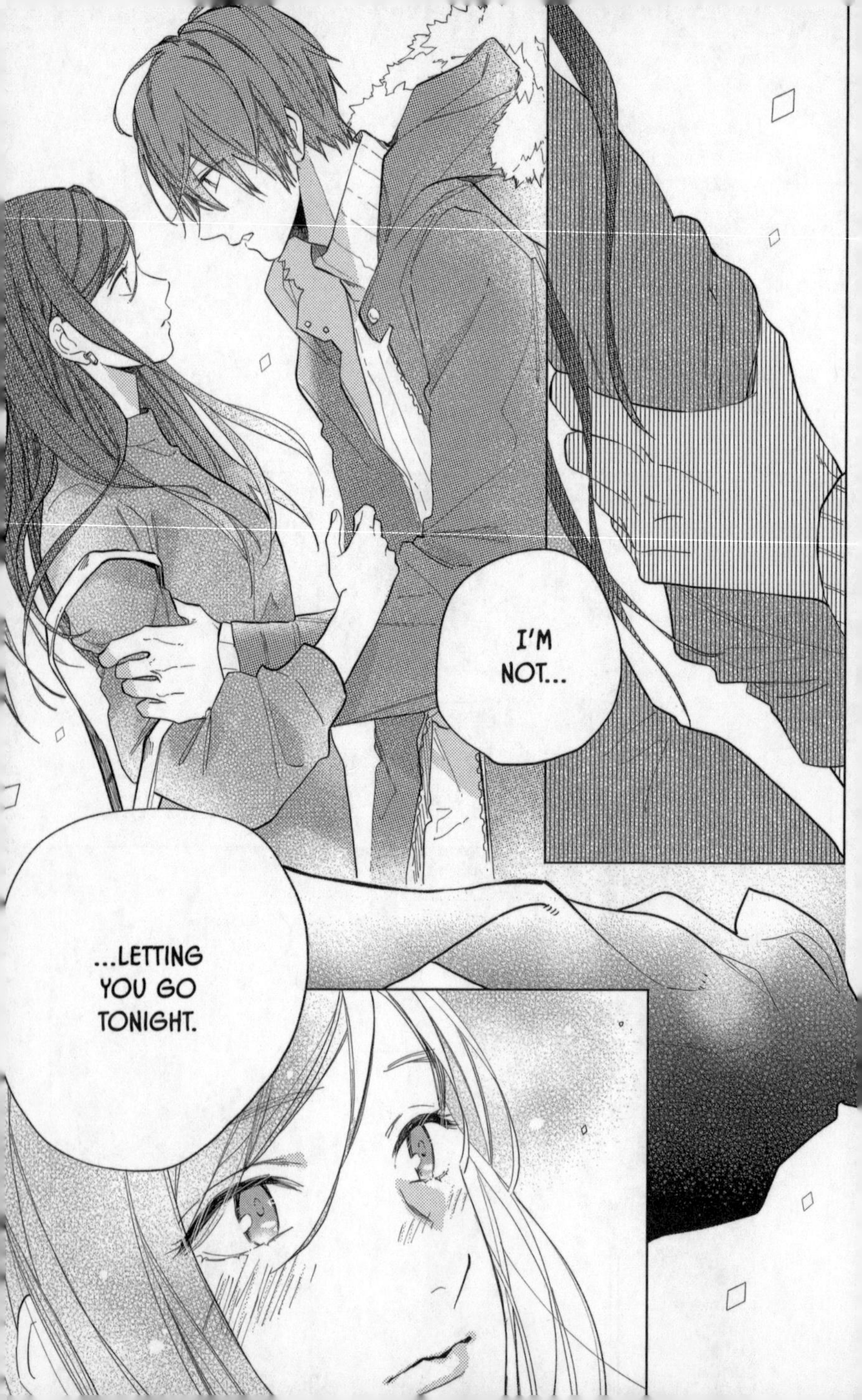
I'M NOT...
...LETTING YOU GO TONIGHT.

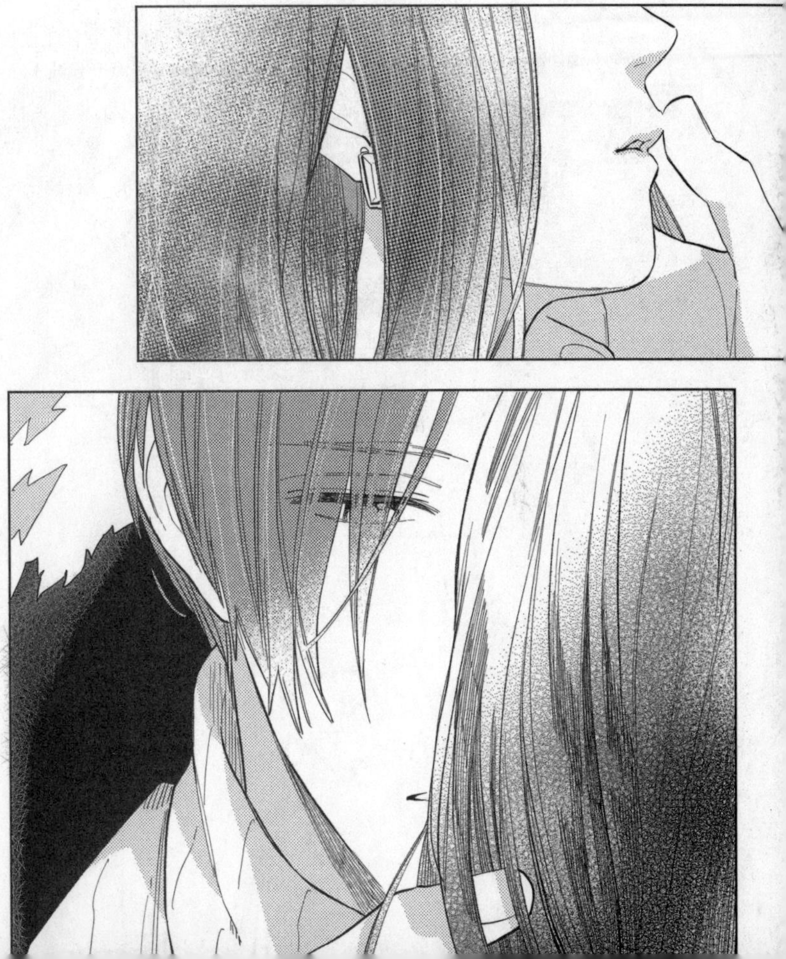

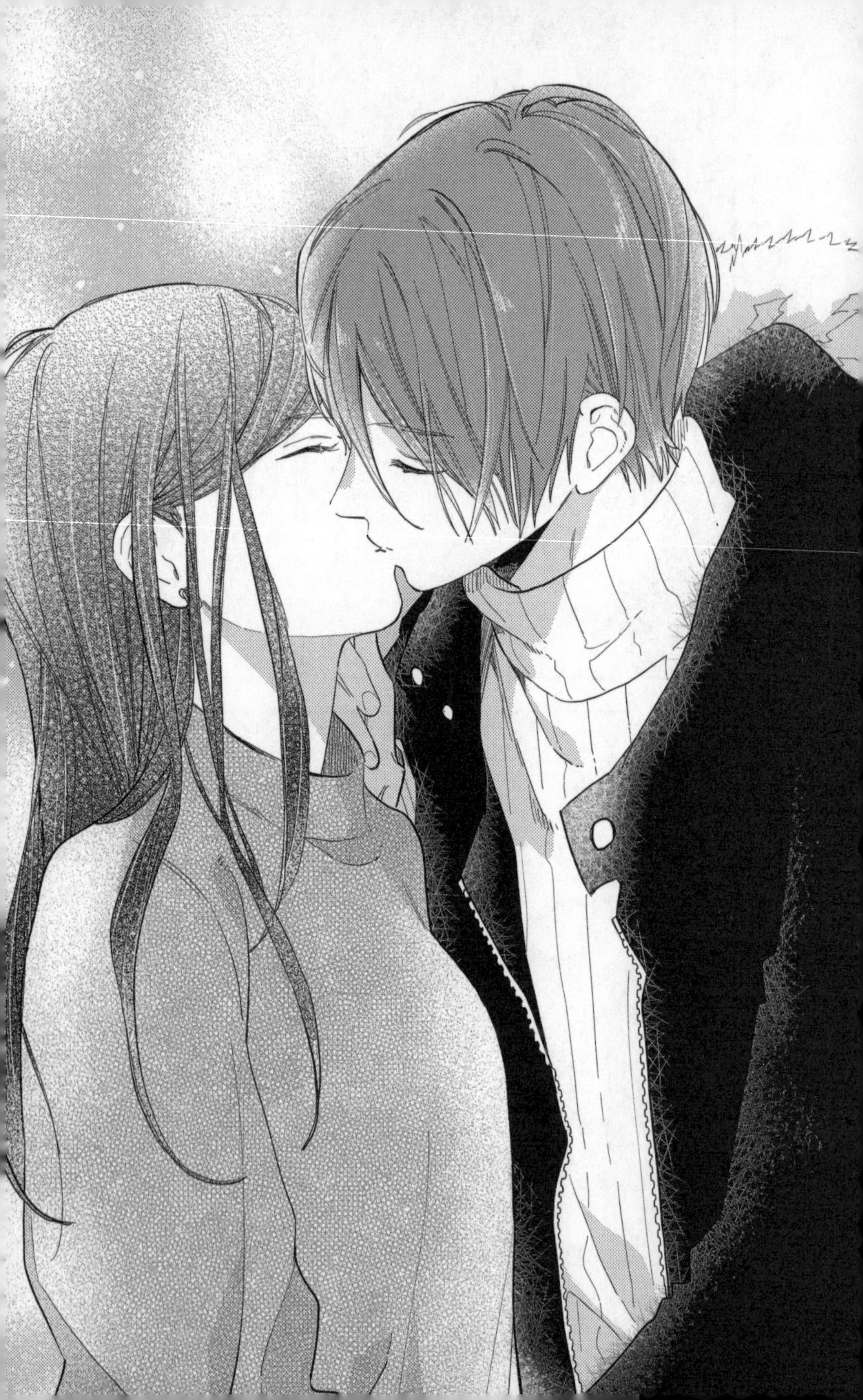

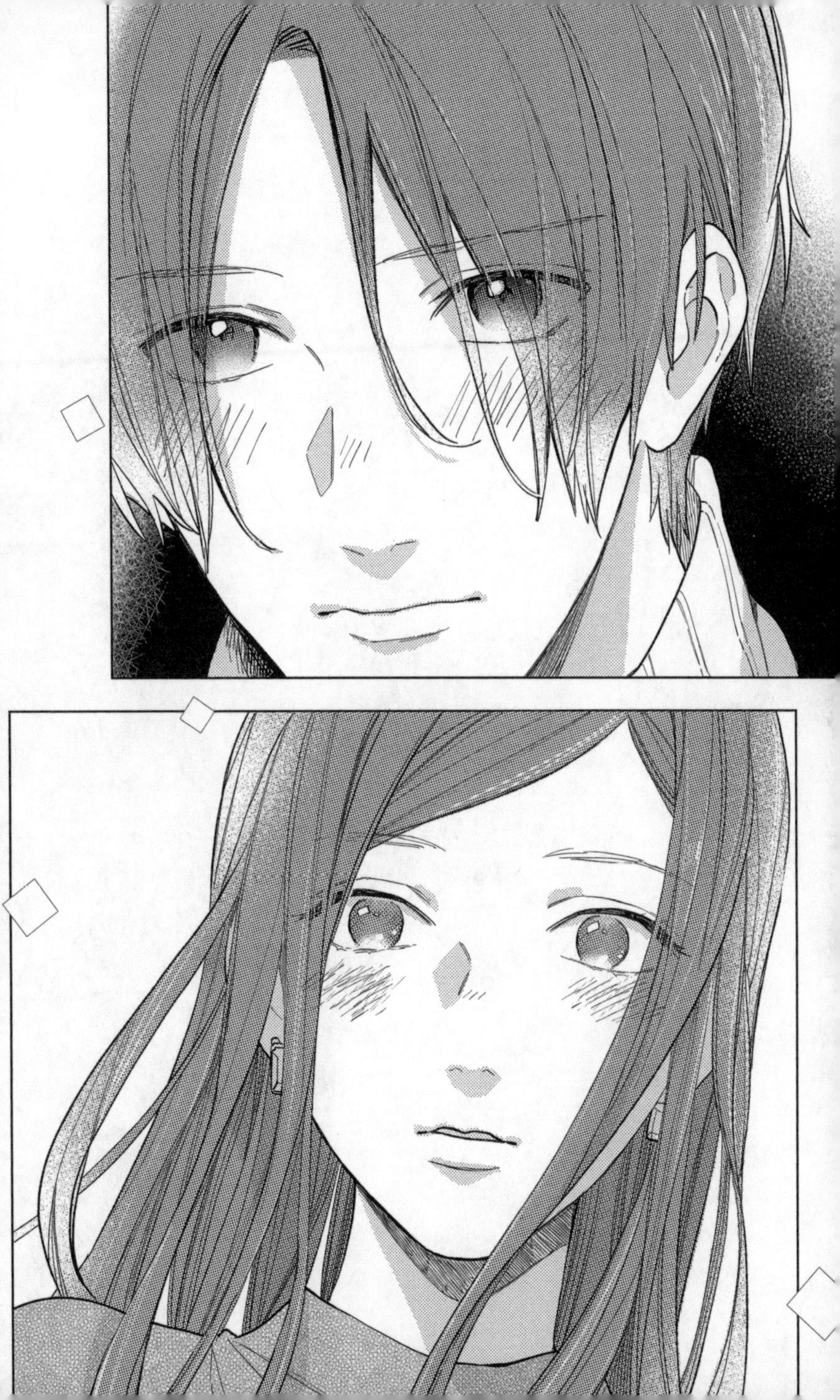

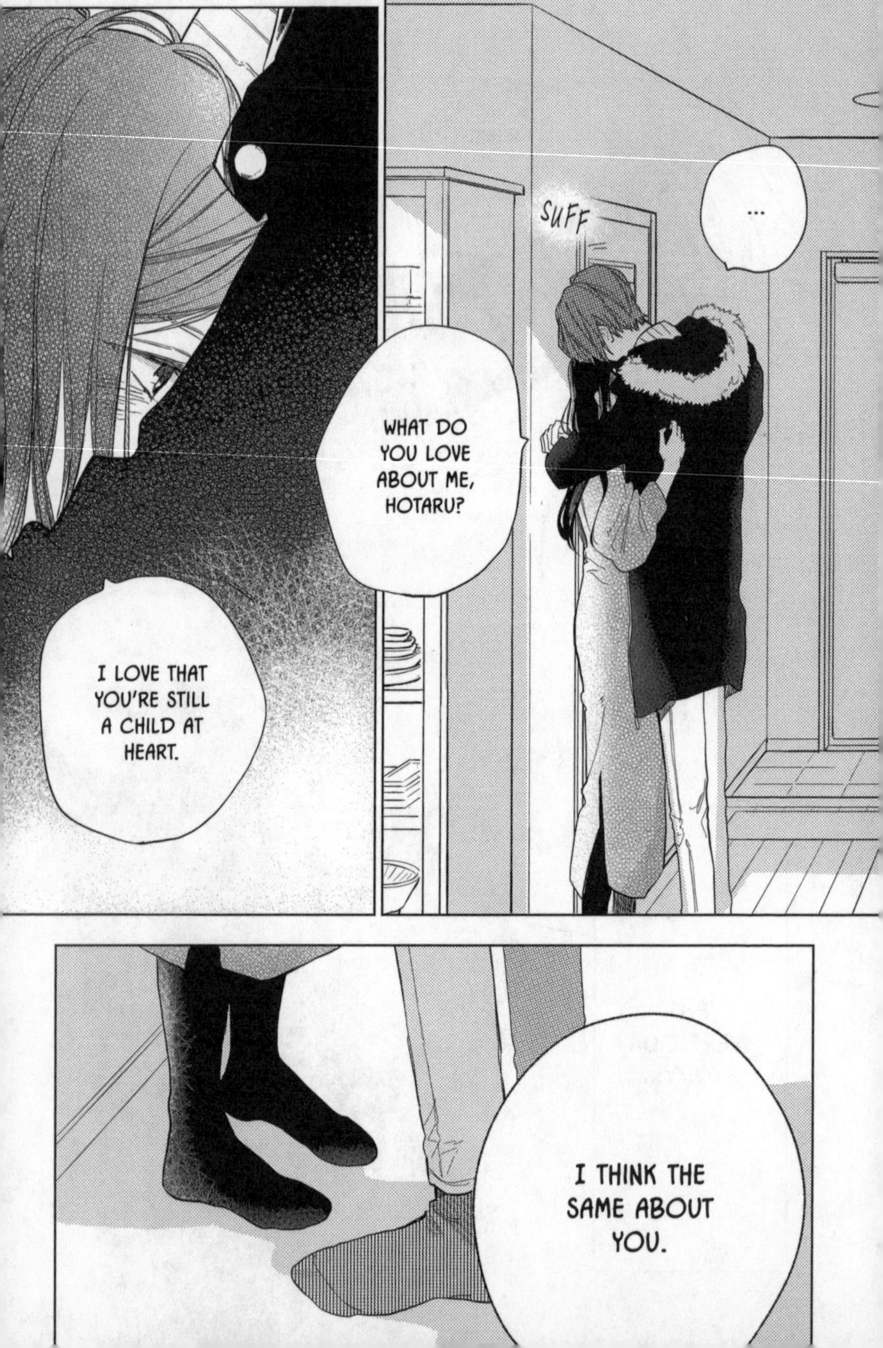
...
SUFF
WHAT DO YOU LOVE ABOUT ME, HOTARU?
I LOVE THAT YOU'RE STILL A CHILD AT HEART.
I THINK THE SAME ABOUT YOU.

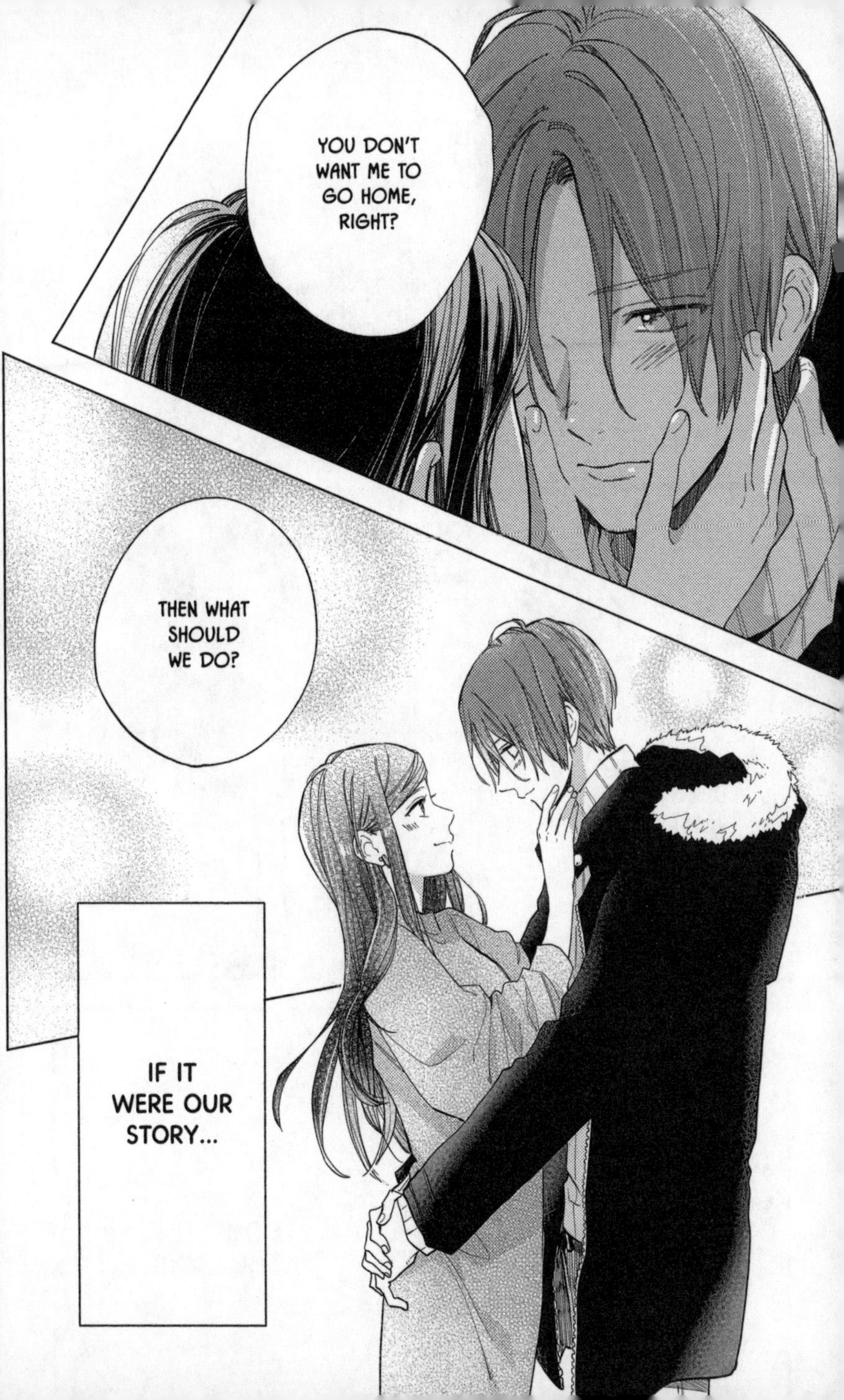
YOU DON'T WANT ME TO GO HOME, RIGHT?
THEN WHAT SHOULD WE DO?
IF IT WERE OUR STORY...

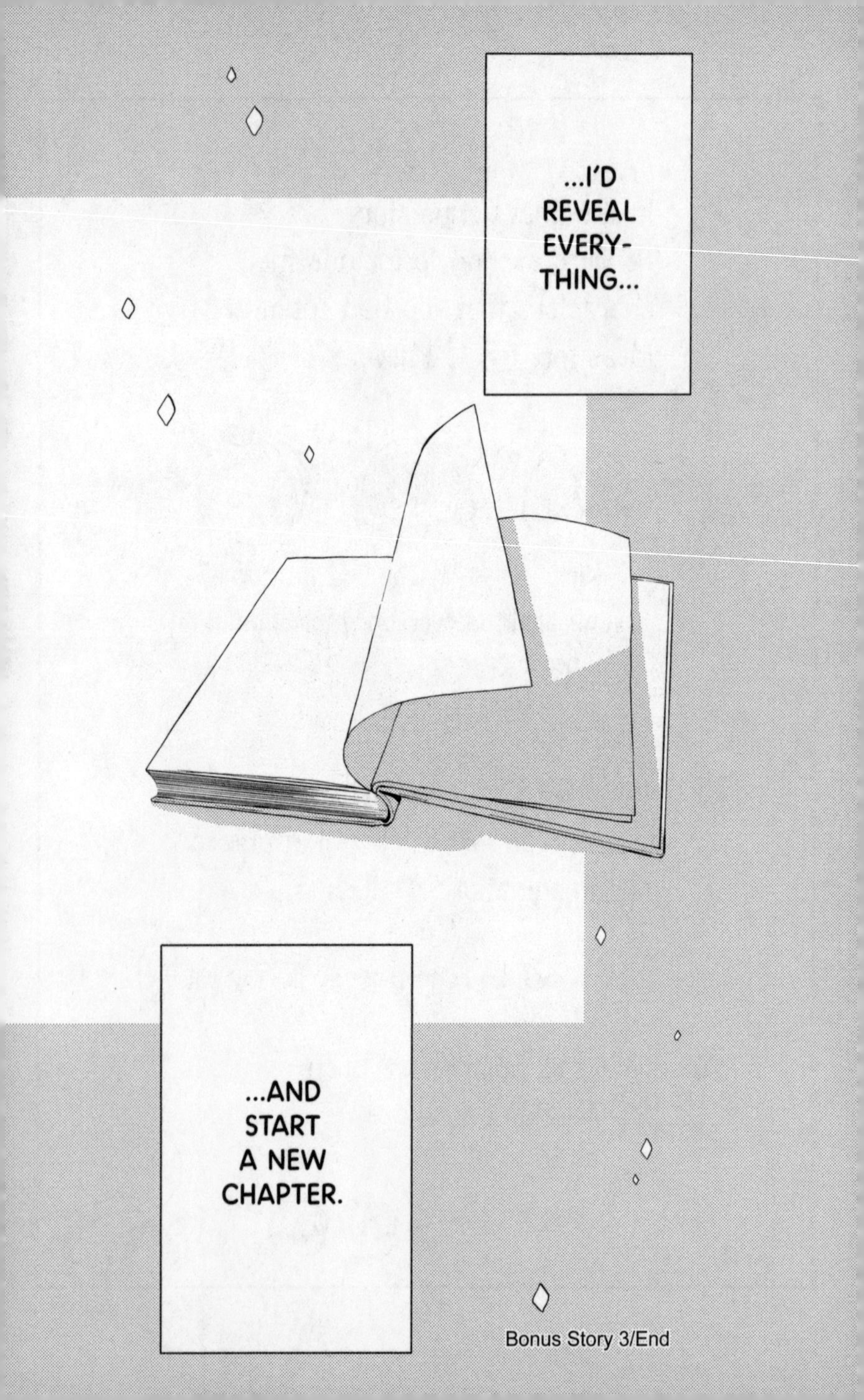
...I'D REVEAL EVERY-THING...
...AND START A NEW CHAPTER.
Bonus Story 3/End

In the final bonus story, we were excited to include the characters that you had submitted ideas for. ≡3 Phew.

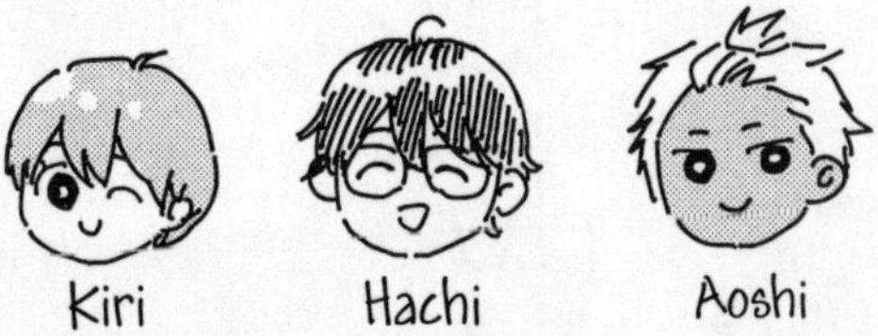
Kiri
Hachi
Aoshi

Thanks again to everybody for submitting your ideas. ♡

We decided to leave Rei's relationship up in the air. We'll leave that one to your imagination.

I know who I think he should be with... HEH HEH HEH

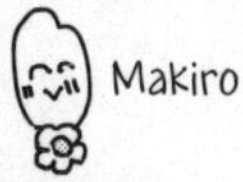
Makiro

Riku and Chiaki have been best friends ever since.

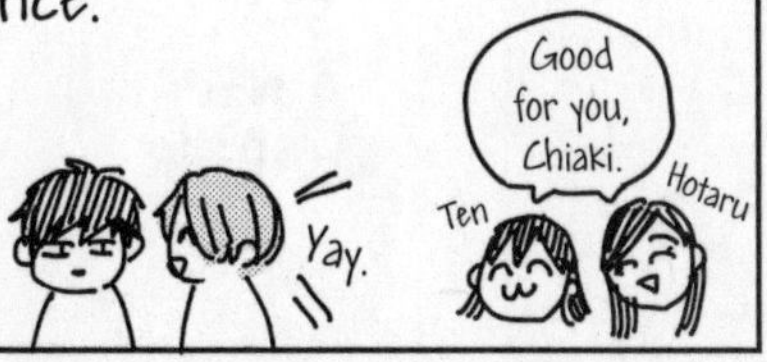
Hotaru
Good for you, Chiaki.
Ten
Yay.

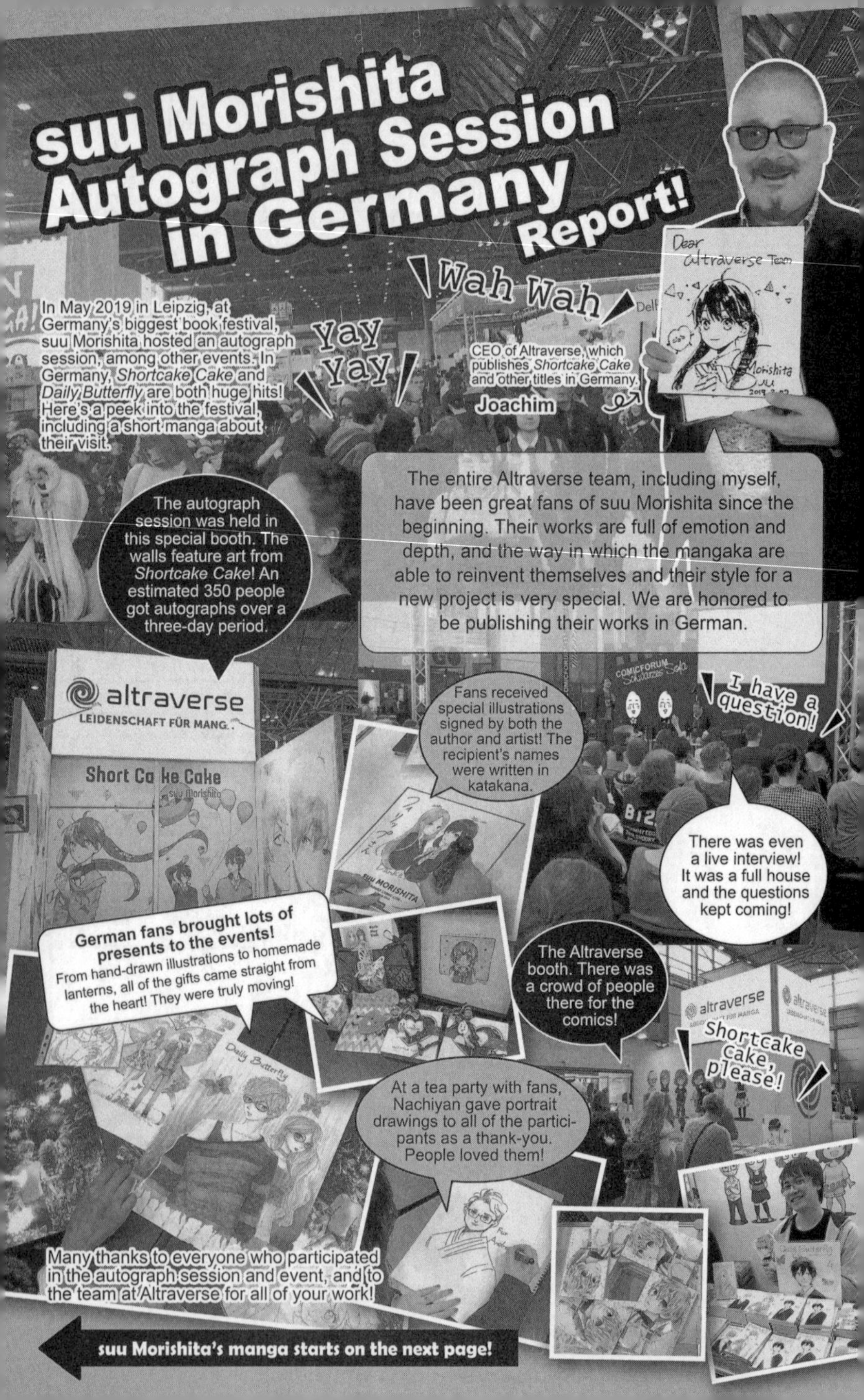
suu Morishita Autograph Session in Germany Report!
In May 2019 in Leipzig, at Germany's biggest book festival, suu Morishita hosted an autograph session, among other events. In Germany, *Shortcake Cake* and *Daily Butterfly* are both huge hits! Here's a peek into the festival, including a short manga about their visit.
Wah Wah
Yay Yay
CEO of Altraverse, which publishes *Shortcake Cake* and other titles in Germany.
Joachim
Dear altraverse Team
Morishita suu
The entire Altraverse team, including myself, have been great fans of suu Morishita since the beginning. Their works are full of emotion and depth, and the way in which the mangaka are able to reinvent themselves and their style for a new project is very special. We are honored to be publishing their works in German.
The autograph session was held in this special booth. The walls feature art from *Shortcake Cake*! An estimated 350 people got autographs over a three-day period.
altraverse
LEIDENSCHAFT FÜR MANGA
Short Cake Cake
suu Morishita
Fans received special illustrations signed by both the author and artist! The recipient's names were written in katakana.
SUU MORISHITA
COMICFORUM
I have a question!
There was even a live interview! It was a full house and the questions kept coming!
German fans brought lots of presents to the events!
From hand-drawn illustrations to homemade lanterns, all of the gifts came straight from the heart! They were truly moving!
The Altraverse booth. There was a crowd of people there for the comics!
altraverse
Shortcake Cake, please!
Daily Butterfly
At a tea party with fans, Nachiyan gave portrait drawings to all of the participants as a thank-you. People loved them!
Many thanks to everyone who participated in the autograph session and event, and to the team at Altraverse for all of your work!
suu Morishita's manga starts on the next page!

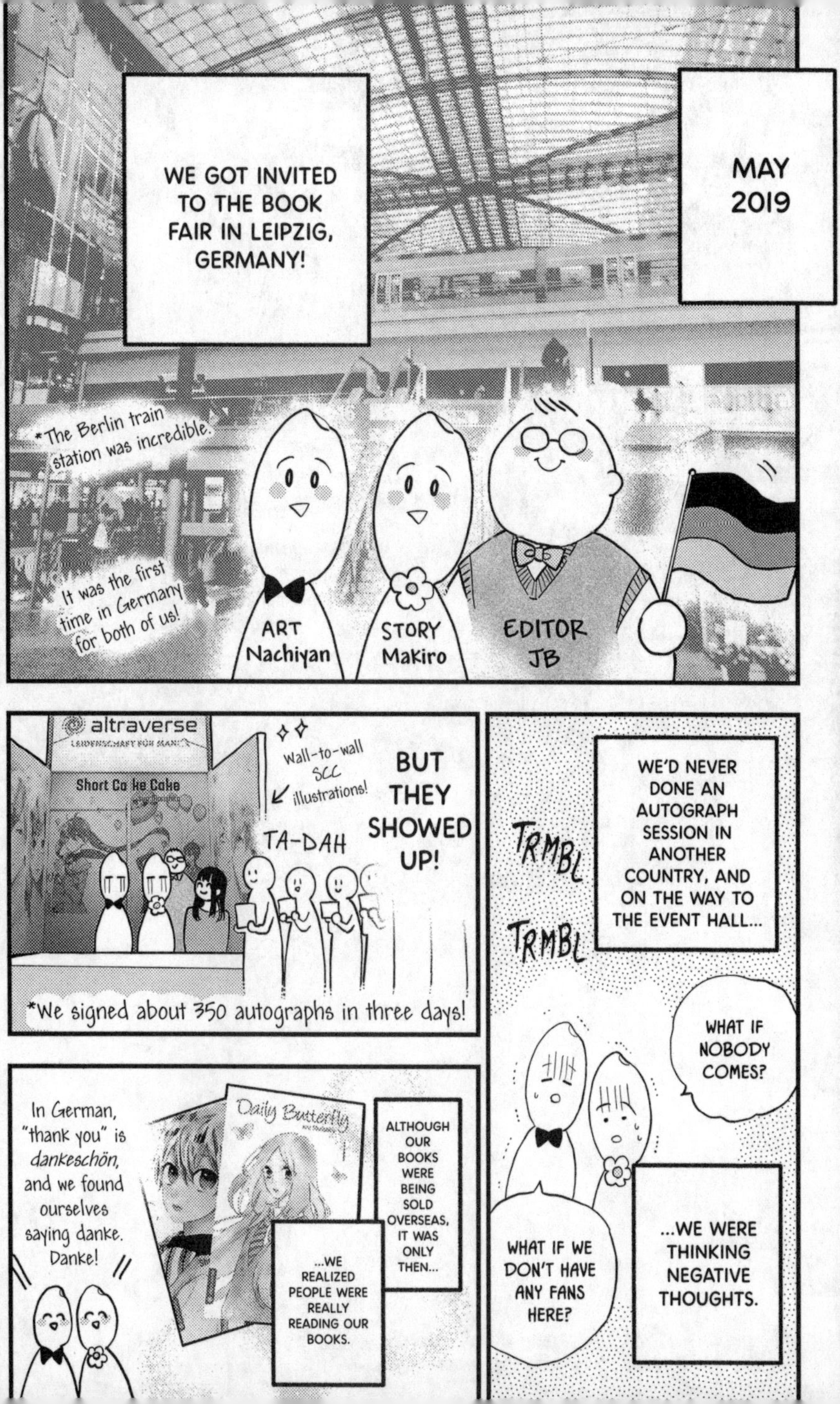
MAY 2019
WE GOT INVITED TO THE BOOK FAIR IN LEIPZIG, GERMANY!
EDITOR JB
STORY Makiro
ART Nachiyan
*The Berlin train station was incredible.
It was the first time in Germany for both of us!
WE'D NEVER DONE AN AUTOGRAPH SESSION IN ANOTHER COUNTRY, AND ON THE WAY TO THE EVENT HALL...
TRMBL
TRMBL
WHAT IF NOBODY COMES?
WHAT IF WE DON'T HAVE ANY FANS HERE?
...WE WERE THINKING NEGATIVE THOUGHTS.
BUT THEY SHOWED UP!
Wall-to-wall SCC illustrations!
altraverse
Short Cake Cake
TA-DAH
*We signed about 350 autographs in three days!
ALTHOUGH OUR BOOKS WERE BEING SOLD OVERSEAS, IT WAS ONLY THEN...
...WE REALIZED PEOPLE WERE REALLY READING OUR BOOKS.
Daily Butterfly
In German, "thank you" is dankeschön, and we found ourselves saying danke. Danke!

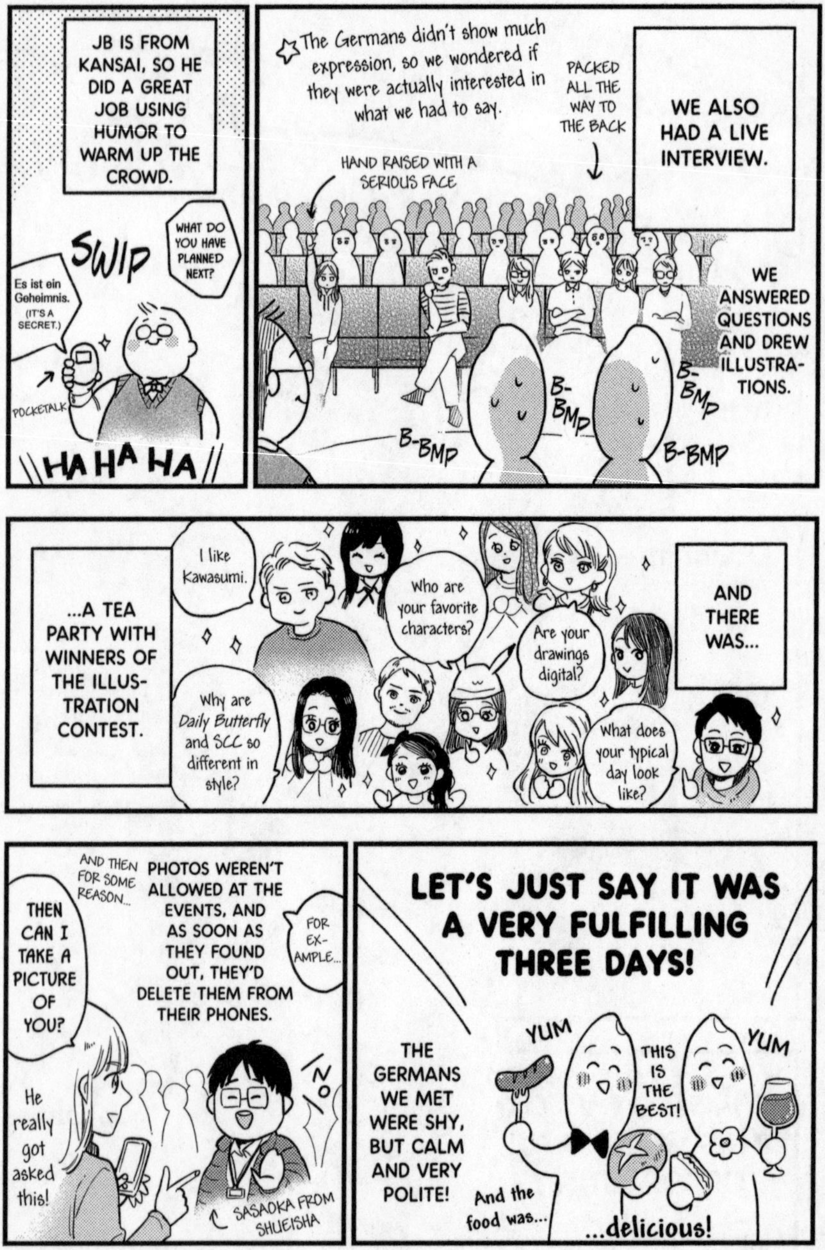
WE ALSO HAD A LIVE INTERVIEW.
PACKED ALL THE WAY TO THE BACK
The Germans didn't show much expression, so we wondered if they were actually interested in what we had to say.
HAND RAISED WITH A SERIOUS FACE
WE ANSWERED QUESTIONS AND DREW ILLUSTRATIONS.
B-BMP
B-BMP
B-BMP
B-BMP
JB IS FROM KANSAI, SO HE DID A GREAT JOB USING HUMOR TO WARM UP THE CROWD.
WHAT DO YOU HAVE PLANNED NEXT?
SWIP
Es ist ein Geheimnis. (IT'S A SECRET.)
POCKETALK
HA HA HA
AND THERE WAS...
Are your drawings digital?
Who are your favorite characters?
I like Kawasumi.
What does your typical day look like?
Why are Daily Butterfly and SCC so different in style?
...A TEA PARTY WITH WINNERS OF THE ILLUSTRATION CONTEST.
LET'S JUST SAY IT WAS A VERY FULFILLING THREE DAYS!
YUM
THIS IS THE BEST!
YUM
THE GERMANS WE MET WERE SHY, BUT CALM AND VERY POLITE!
And the food was...
...delicious!
PHOTOS WEREN'T ALLOWED AT THE EVENTS, AND AS SOON AS THEY FOUND OUT, THEY'D DELETE THEM FROM THEIR PHONES.
AND THEN FOR SOME REASON...
FOR EXAMPLE...
THEN CAN I TAKE A PICTURE OF YOU?
NO
He really got asked this!
SASAOKA FROM SHUEISHA

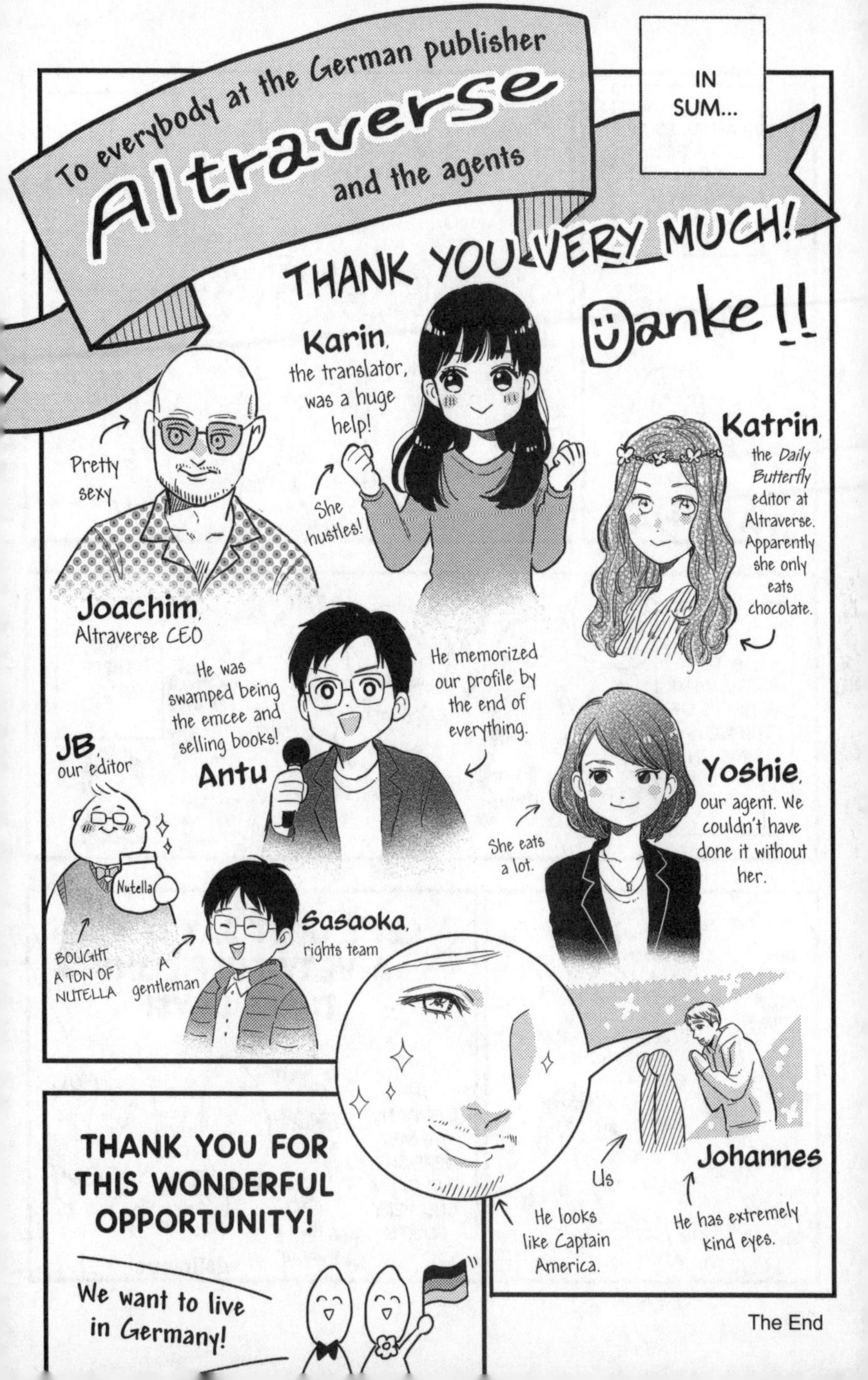
IN SUM...
To everybody at the German publisher
Altraverse
and the agents
THANK YOU VERY MUCH!
Danke!!
Katrin, the Daily Butterfly editor at Altraverse. Apparently she only eats chocolate.
Karin, the translator, was a huge help!
She hustles!
Pretty sexy
Joachim, Altraverse CEO
He memorized our profile by the end of everything.
He was swamped being the emcee and selling books!
Antu
Yoshie, our agent. We couldn't have done it without her.
She eats a lot.
JB, our editor
Nutella
Sasaoka, rights team
A gentleman
BOUGHT A TON OF NUTELLA
Johannes
Us
He has extremely kind eyes.
He looks like Captain America.
THANK YOU FOR THIS WONDERFUL OPPORTUNITY!
We want to live in Germany!

The End

Hello.

Since this is the last volume, I think it's appropriate to look back to the time before this manga came to be. (J, our editor, made this scrapbookesque.)

Right around when we were working on volume 7 of our previous series, *Hibi Chocho*, I started thinking about making the next series about a boardinghouse, with the title *Shortcake Cake*. (I had the character Atohira mention shortcake at the cultural festival.)

The boardinghouse idea came from my (Makiro's) experience in high school. There were kids at our school who were from another island and living in a boardinghouse, and I once snuck into the house just like Ten. I remember thinking it was neat that kids from different schools were living under one roof.

I wondered what would happen in a love triangle where the two rivals were close friends. Riku and Chiaki's relationship was born from there.

I thought it would be a shame if one of the rivals got the girl and the other faded away, so I thought I would build in a bigger challenge for the three to overcome.

The name "Ten" came from the idea that she would shine a light on the male protagonist's dark side. And I was happy that readers noticed that together, Ten and Terasu (Ten's brother) made up the name "Amaterasu."

Riku rarely showed his true self, and because of it he was a challenging character to portray. In contrast, even at the draft stage, Shiraoka and Rei were easy. Apparently Chiaki was difficult from an artistic perspective.

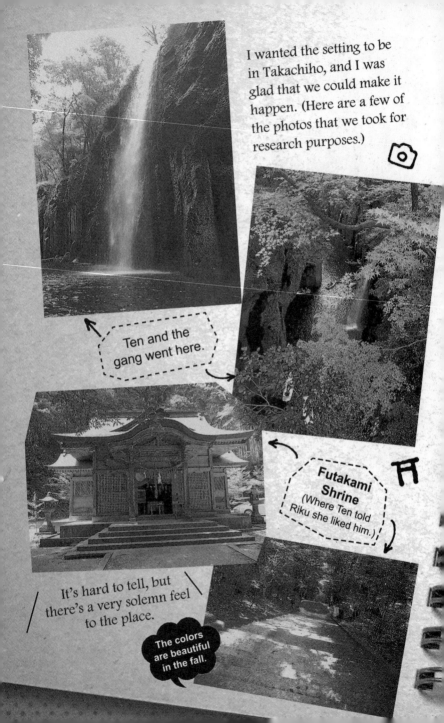

I wanted the setting to be in Takachiho, and I was glad that we could make it happen. (Here are a few of the photos that we took for research purposes.)

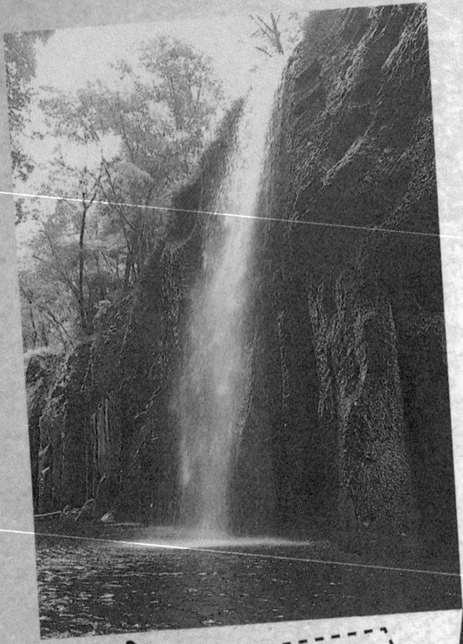

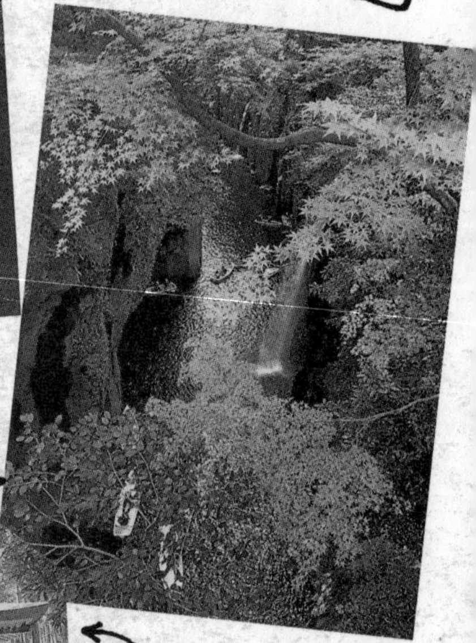

Ten and the gang went here.

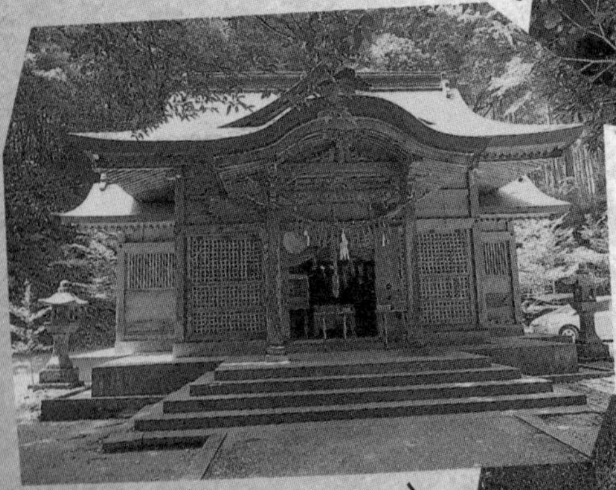

Futakami Shrine
(Where Ten told Riku she liked him.)

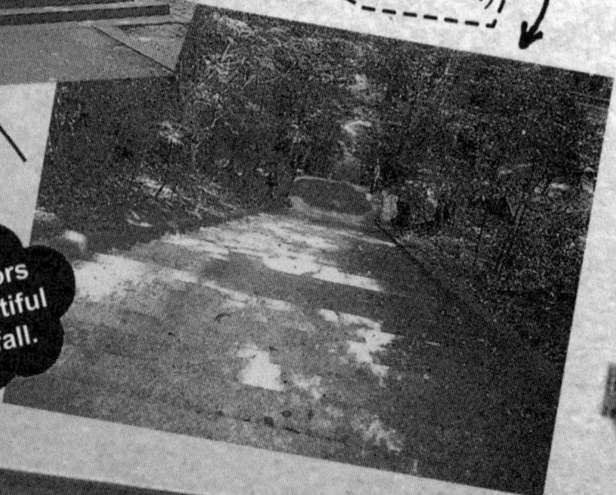

It's hard to tell, but there's a very solemn feel to the place.

The colors are beautiful in the fall.

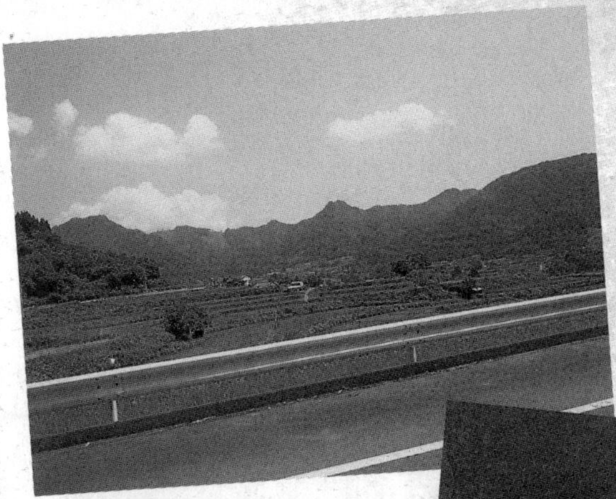

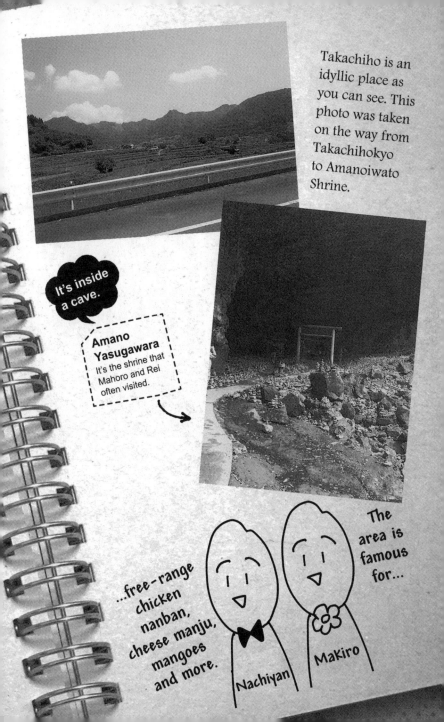

Takachiho is an idyllic place as you can see. This photo was taken on the way from Takachihokyo to Amanoiwato Shrine.

It's inside a cave.

Amano Yasugawara
It's the shrine that Mahoro and Rei often visited.

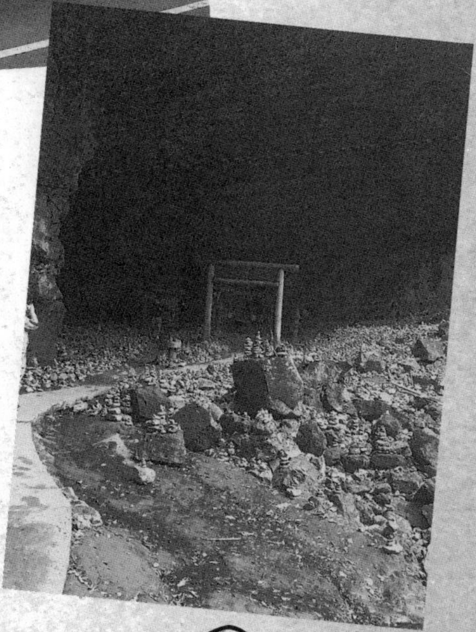

The area is famous for...

...free-range chicken nanban, cheese manju, mangoes and more.

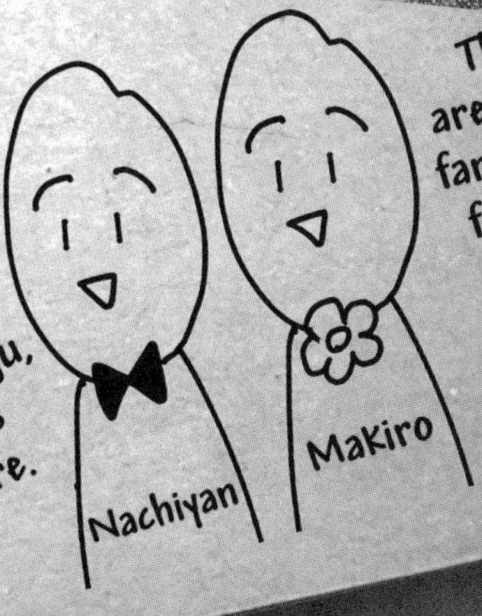
Nachiyan
Makiro

Thank you for your questions!

Q&A Corner

ART
STORY

Nachiyan Makiro

We'll answer the questions you sent in!

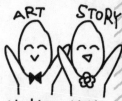

Q. What do you do to relax?

Submitted by Y. from Osaka

A. I stare at my miniatures collection. (Nachiyan)

I play with my kids or go shopping. (Makiro)

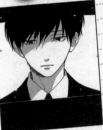

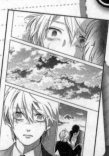

Q. In the beginning, Ten was compared to a boulder—where did this idea come from?

Submitted by Y. from Osaka

A. The setting for *Shortcake Cake* is Takachiho, and in Takachiho there is a legend about the goddess Amaterasu. She caused the world to go dark when she hid herself in Amanoiwato, and after that the Yaoyorozu no Kami held a meeting at Amano Yasugawara. We took the idea of boulder to mean firm and unwavering.

Q. What's your favorite scene?

Submitted by N. from Chiba

A. The scene at the cemetery in volume 8

I like this one because I think that I was able to draw it to Makiro's expectations. Also, I really like Ten's monologue from the beginning of chapter 61. Please see if you can find it. (*^^*) (Nachiyan)

A. Rei's scene in volume 11

I like the pauses, Rei's expressions and that there are just a lot of emotions concentrated in one place. (Makiro)

Q. Do Riku and his mom see each other anymore?

Submitted by N. from Chiba

A. Hotaru and Riku see each other once in a while. It's not that Ayame and Riku never see each other, but it's rare for them. (It's partly Riku's own will, but mostly out of courtesy to Rei.)

Q. At the end of volume 9, I was surprised to see you say you were drawing digitally. When did you start doing so?

Submitted by N. from Tochigi

A. We started using digital tools when we began *Shortcake Cake*, but we didn't fully switch over until around volume 7.

Q. How did you end up making manga together? Submitted by S. from Gifu

A. We started out as friends in high school. Right around when we each got married, Nachiyan read *Bakuman*, and after talking about making a comic together we submitted our work. We debuted about half a year after that.

Q. In volume 1, Riku's bangs are very long. When did he cut them?

Submitted by T. in Nigata

A. Unlike Chiaki, Riku changes his hairstyle frequently.

Q. I like the characters' clothing. Where do you get your inspiration?

Submitted by Y. in Gifu

A. We look at trending styles on WEAR and peek into thrift stores. We also like looking at clothing catalogs for different brands.

A F T E R W O R D

I had plans for the last page of the final chapter locked in pretty early, but when it came to drafting out the final chapter, I decided I wanted to give the final scene to Chiaki, which is why things ended up the way they did.

I put what I liked best about each character into the story.

Thank you, Nachiyan, for your beautiful drawings and layouts. And thank you to J, who became our editor around volume 7 and always favored Rei.

I hope to make more manga with you again.

I sense that it will be hard to continue making one manga after another, but I also feel that with this story I started to finally understand and appreciate what it means to create manga.

Although the story itself is over, I'd like to reread it periodically.

Thank you for reading through to the end.

—Makiro

Thank you for reading through to the end.

While we were in serialization, there were many things that did not go as planned, and it felt rather difficult.

Now, I feel grateful to our readers. I feel we were finally able to bring the story together in the way we really wanted to.

I'm truly grateful to our editor, J. Thank you very much!

I hope that this book will sit on many readers' bookshelves for a very long time.

Thank you.

—Nachiyan

I deeply relate to Rei for his lack of skill in spite of being the older brother. When I met with the creators, I constantly had Rei on my mind. I imagine many readers saw themselves in the characters as they moved through the story. I hope this story becomes a deeply memorable one for you.

—Editor J

{ Special Thanks }
Editor J
Designer Kawatani (Kawatani Design)
The Margaret Editorial Department
Assistant Nao Hamaguchi
Background Assistants Saya Aoi and Mako
The many people who helped along the way
And to all our readers ✢

SHORTCAKE CAKE
Title Page Collection
Chapter 61

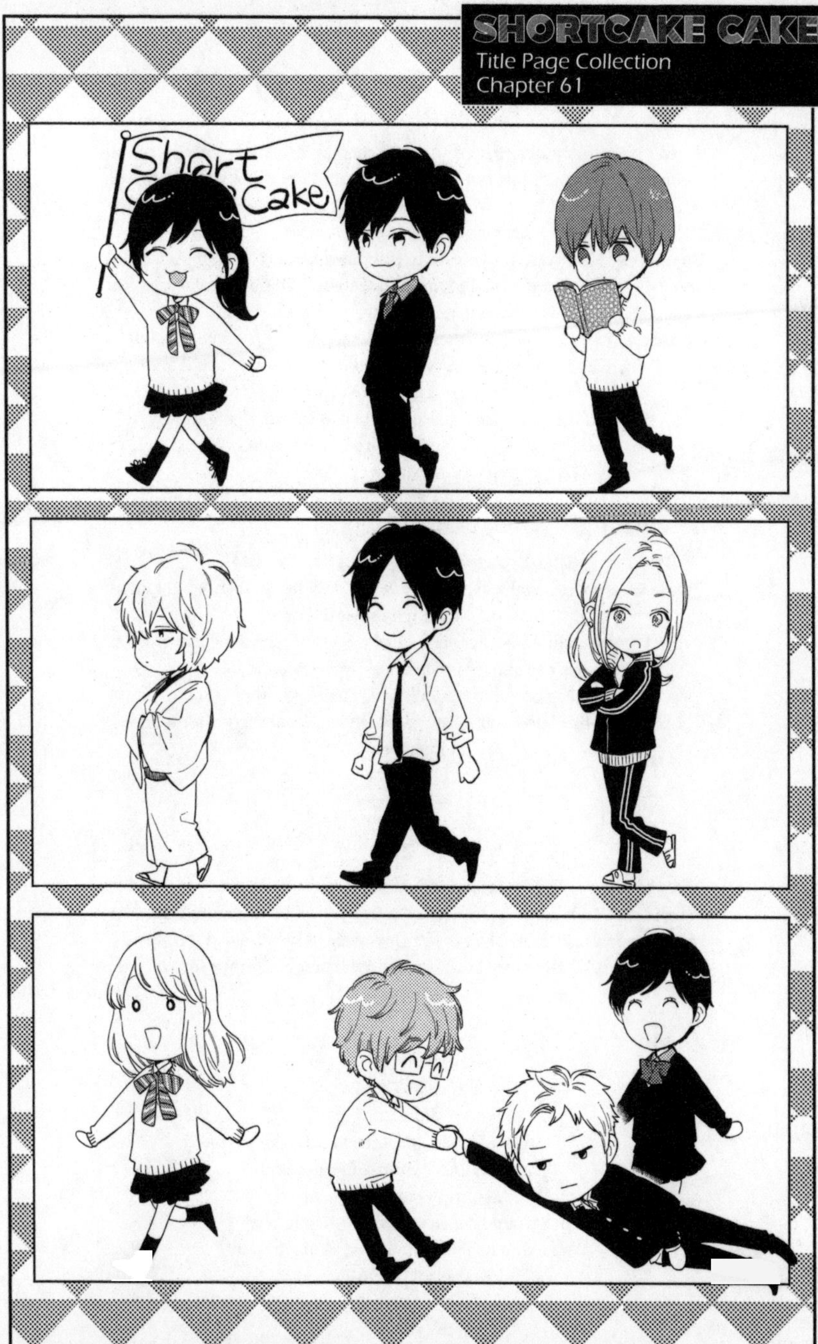
Short
Cake

SHORTCAKE CAKE
Title Page Collection
Issue 7 Magazine Cover

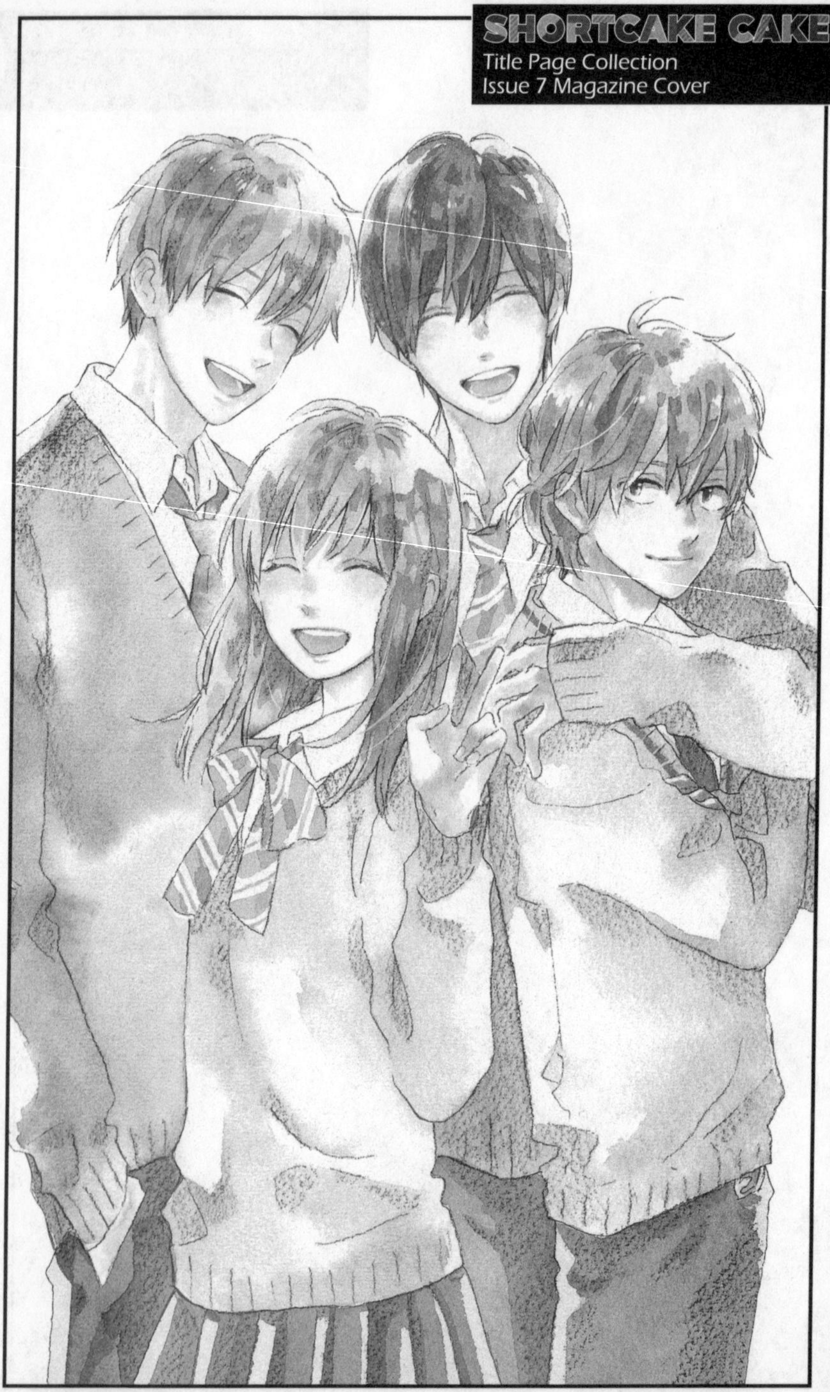

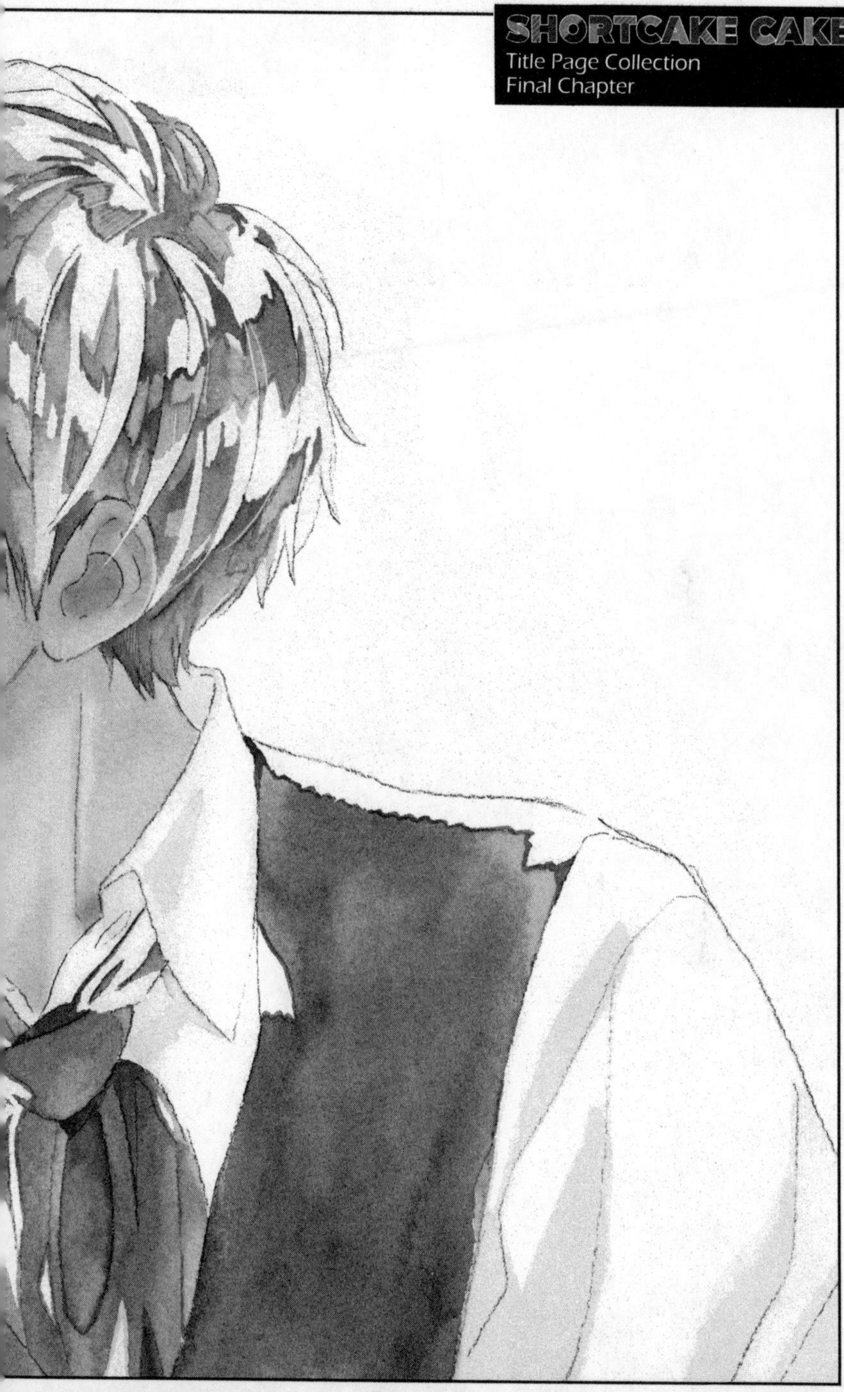
SHORTCAKE CAKE
Title Page Collection
Final Chapter

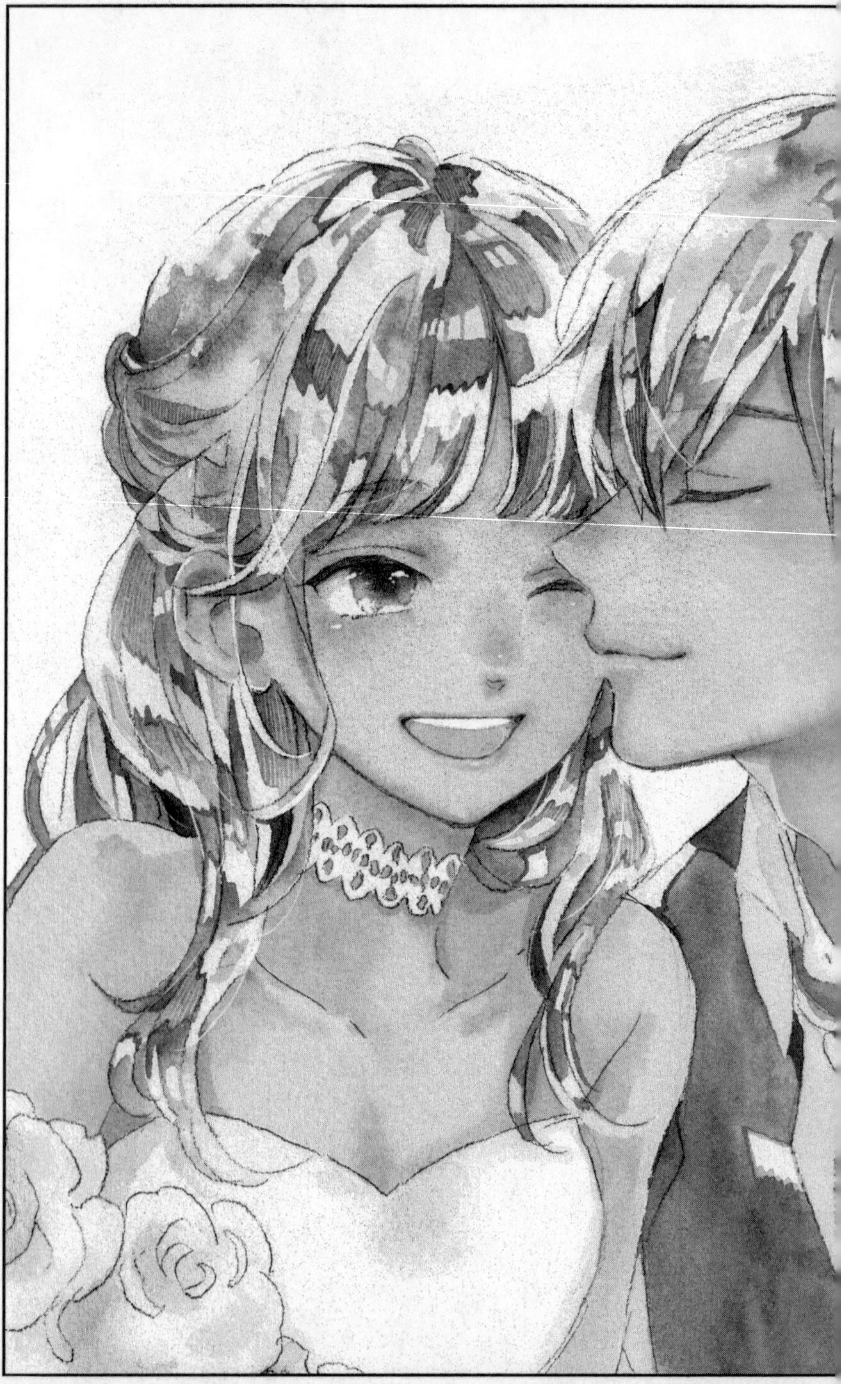

It would make us happy if someone out there was thinking that now they've finished the final volume, they want to pick up volume 1 and read the series all over again.

—suu Morishita

suu Morishita is a creator duo. The story is by Makiro, and the art is by Nachiyan. In 2010 they debuted with the one-shot "Anote Konote." Their works include *Hibi Chouchou* and *Shortcake Cake*.

SHORTCAKE CAKE

VOLUME 12
SHOJO BEAT EDITION

STORY + ART BY **suu Morishita**

TRANSLATION **Emi Louie-Nishikawa**
TOUCH-UP ART + LETTERING **Inori Fukuda Trant**
DESIGN **Joy Zhang**
EDITOR **Nancy Thistlethwaite**

SHORTCAKE CAKE © 2015 by Suu Morishita
All rights reserved.
First published in Japan in 2015 by SHUEISHA Inc., Tokyo.
English translation rights arranged by SHUEISHA Inc.

Printed in the U.S.A.

Published by VIZ Media, LLC
P.O. Box 77010
San Francisco, CA 94107

10 9 8 7 6 5 4 3 2 1
First printing, May 2021

viz.com   shojobeat.com

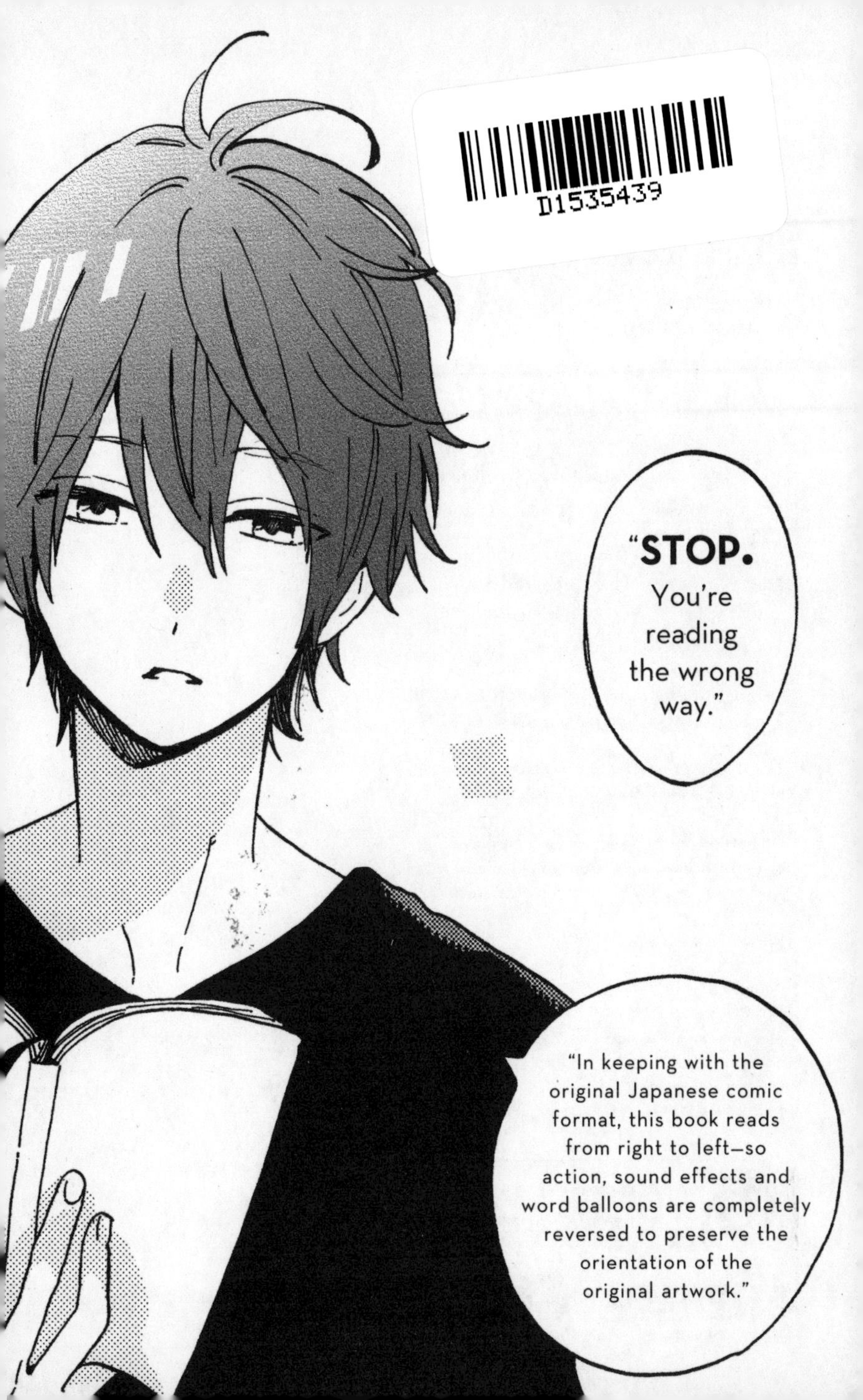
"STOP. You're reading the wrong way."
"In keeping with the original Japanese comic format, this book reads from right to left—so action, sound effects and word balloons are completely reversed to preserve the orientation of the original artwork."